Texts in Computer Science

Editors
David Gries
Fred B. Schneider

For further volumes:
http://www.springer.com/series/3191

Steven Homer • Alan L. Selman

Computability and Complexity Theory

Second Edition

 Springer

Steven Homer
Computer Science Department
Boston University
Boston Massachusetts
USA
homer@bu.edu

Alan L. Selman
Department of Computer Science
and Engineering
University at Buffalo
The State University of New York
Buffalo New York
USA
selman@buffalo.edu

Series Editors
David Gries
Department of Computer Science
Upson Hall
Cornell University
Ithaca, NY 14853-7501, USA

Fred B. Schneider
Department of Computer Science
Upson Hall
Cornell University
Ithaca, NY 14853-7501, USA

ISSN 1868-0941   e-ISSN 1868-095X
ISBN 978-1-4899-8971-0   ISBN 978-1-4614-0682-2 (eBook)
DOI 10.1007/978-1-4614-0682-2
Springer New York Dordrecht Heidelberg London

Printed on acid-free paper

Springer is part of Springer Science+Business Media (www.springer.com)

*We dedicate this book to our wives,
Michelle and Sharon*

Preface to the First Edition 2001

The theory of computing provides computer science with concepts, models, and formalisms for reasoning about both the resources needed to carry out computations and the efficiency of the computations that use these resources. It provides tools to measure the difficulty of combinatorial problems both absolutely and in comparison with other problems. Courses in this subject help students gain analytic skills and enable them to recognize the limits of computation. For these reasons, a course in the theory of computing is usually required in the graduate computer science curriculum.

The harder question to address is which topics such a course should cover. We believe that students should learn the fundamental models of computation, the limitations of computation, and the distinctions between feasible and intractable. In particular, the phenomena of NP-completeness and NP-hardness have pervaded much of science and transformed computer science. One option is to survey a large number of theoretical subjects, typically focusing on automata and formal languages. However, these subjects are less important to theoretical computer science, and to computer science as a whole, now than in the past. Many students have taken such a course as part of their undergraduate education. We chose not to take that route because computability and complexity theory are the subjects that we feel deeply about and that we believe are important for students to learn. Furthermore, a graduate course should be scholarly. It is better to treat important topics thoroughly than to survey the field.

This textbook is intended for use in an introductory graduate course in theoretical computer science. It contains material that should be core knowledge in the theory of computation for all graduate students in computer science. It is self-contained and is best suited for a one-semester course. Most of the text can be covered in one semester by moving expeditiously through the core material of Chaps. 1 through 5 and then covering parts of Chap. 6. We will give more details about this below.

As a graduate course, students should have some prerequisite preparation. The ideal preparation would be the kind of course that we mentioned above: an undergraduate course that introduced topics such as automata theory, formal languages, computability theory, or complexity theory. We stress, however, that there is nothing in such a course that a student needs to know before studying this text. Our personal experience suggests that we cannot presume that all of our students have taken such an undergraduate course. For those students who have not, we advise that they need at least some prior exposure that will have developed mathematical skills. Prior courses in mathematical logic, algebra (at the level of groups, rings, or fields), or number theory, for example, would all serve this purpose.

Despite the diverse backgrounds of our students, we have found that graduate students are capable of learning sophisticated material when it is explained clearly and precisely. That has been our goal in writing this book.

This book also is suitable for advanced undergraduate students who have satisfied the prerequisites. It is an appropriate first course in complexity theory for students who will continue to study and work in this subject area.

The text begins with a preliminary chapter that gives a brief description of several topics in mathematics. We included this in order to keep the book self-contained and to ensure that all students have a common notation. Some of these sections simply enable students to understand some of the important examples that arise later. For example, we include a section on number theory and algebra that includes all that is necessary for students to understand that primality belongs to NP.

The text starts properly with classical computability theory. We build complexity theory on top of that. Doing so has the pedagogical advantage that students learn a qualitative subject before advancing to a quantitative one. Also, the concepts build from one to the other. For example, although we give a complete proof that the satisfiability problem is NP-complete, it is easy for students to understand that the bounded halting problem is NP-complete, because they already know that the classical halting problem is c.e.-complete.

We use the terms *partial computable* and *computably enumerable (c.e.)* instead of the traditional terminology, *partial recursive* and *recursively enumerable (r.e.)*, respectively. We do so simply to eliminate confusion. Students of computer science know of "recursion" as a programming paradigm. We do not prove here that Turing-computable partial functions are equivalent to partial recursive functions, so by not using that notation, we avoid the matter altogether. Although the notation we are using has been commonplace in the computability theory and mathematical logic community for several years, instructors might want to advise their students that the older terminology seems commonplace within the theoretical computer science community. Computable functions are defined on the set of words over a finite alphabet, which we identify with the set of natural numbers in a straightforward manner. We use the term *effective*, in the nontechnical, intuitive sense, to denote computational processes on other data types. For example, we will say that a set of Turing machines is "effectively enumerable" if its set of indices is computably enumerable.

Chapter 4 concludes with a short list of topics that students should know from the chapters on computability theory before proceeding to study complexity theory. We advise instructors who wish to minimize coverage of computability theory to refer to this list. Typically, we do not cover the second section on the recursion theorem (Sect. 3.10) in a one-semester course. Although we do not recommend it, it is possible to begin the study of complexity theory after learning the first five sections of Chap. 4 and at least part of Sect. 3.9 on oracle Turing machines, Turing reductions, and the arithmetical hierarchy.

In Chap. 5, we treat general properties of complexity classes and relationships between complexity classes. These include important older results such as the space and time hierarchy theorems, as well as the more recent result of Immerman and Szelepcsényi that space-bounded classes are closed under complements. Instructors might be anxious to get to NP-complete problems (Chap. 6) and NP-hard problems (Chap. 7), but students need to learn the basic results of complexity theory and it is instructive for them to understand the relationships between P, NP, and other deterministic and nondeterministic, low-level complexity classes. Students should learn that nondeterminism is not well understood in general, that P =? NP is not an isolated question, and that other classes have complete problems as well (which we take up in Chap. 7). Nevertheless, Chap. 5 is a long chapter. Many of the results in this chapter are proved by complicated Turing-machine simulations and counting arguments, which give students great insight, but can be time-consuming to cover. For this reason, instructors might be advised to survey some of this material if the alternative would mean not having sufficient time for the later chapters.

Homework exercises are an important part of this book. They are embedded in the text where they naturally arise, and students should not proceed without working on them. Many are simple exercises, whereas others are challenging. Often we leave important but easy-to-prove propositions as exercises. We provide additional problems at the end of chapters, which extend and apply the material covered there.

Once again, our intent has been to write a text that is suitable for all graduate students, that provides the right background for those who will continue to study complexity theory, and that can be taught in one semester. There are several important topics in complexity theory that cannot be treated properly in a one-semester course. Currently we are writing a second part to this text, which will be suitable for an optional second semester course, covering nonuniform complexity (Boolean circuits), parallelism, probabilistic classes, and interactive protocols.

Preface to the Second Edition 2011

At long last we have written this second part, and here it is. We corrected a myriad of typos, a few technical glitches, and some pedagogical issues in the first part.

Chapter 8, the first of the new chapters, is on nonuniformity. Here we study Boolean circuits, advice classes, define P/poly, and establish the important result of Karp–Lipton. Then we define and show basic properties of Schöning's low and high hierarchies. We need this for results that will come later in Chap. 10. Specifically, in that chapter we prove that the Graph Nonisomorphism Problem (GNI) is in the operator class $BP \cdot NP$ and that the Graph Isomorphism Problem (GI) is in the low hierarchy. Then it follows immediately that GI cannot be NP-complete unless the polynomial hierarchy collapses. Of course, primarily this chapter studies properties of the fundamental probabilistic complexity classes.

We study the alternating Turing machine and uniform circuit classes, especially NC, in Chap. 9. In the next chapter, we introduce counting classes and prove the famous results of Valiant and Vazirani and of Toda. The text ends with a thorough treatment of the proof that IP is identical to PSPACE, including worked-out examples. We include a section on Arthur-Merlin games and point out that $BP \cdot NP = AM$, thereby establishing some of the results that classify this class.

We have found that the full text can be taught in one academic year. We hope that the expanded list of topics gives instructors flexibility in choosing topics to cover.

Thanks to everyone who sent us comments and corrections, and a special thanks to our students who demonstrated solvability of critical homework exercises.

Boston and Buffalo

Steven Homer
Alan Selman

Contents

Chapter 1
Preliminaries

We begin with a limited number of mathematical notions that a student should know before beginning with this text. This chapter is short because we assume some earlier study of data structures and discrete mathematics.

1.1 Words and Languages

In the next chapter we will become familiar with models of computing. The basic data type of our computers will be "symbols," for our computers manipulate symbols. The notion of symbol is undefined, but we define several more concepts in terms of symbols.

A finite set $\Sigma = \{a_1, \ldots, a_k\}$ of symbols is called a finite *alphabet*. A *word* is a finite sequence of symbols. The *length* of a word w, denoted $|w|$, is the number of symbols composing it. The *empty* word is the unique word of length 0 and is denoted as λ. Note that λ is *not* a symbol in the alphabet. The empty word is not a set, so do not confuse the empty word λ with the empty set $\emptyset$.

Σ^* denotes the set of all words over the alphabet Σ. A *language* is a set of words. That is, L is a language if and only if $L \subseteq \Sigma^*$. A *prefix* of a word is a substring that begins the word.

Example 1.1. Let $w = abcce$. The prefixes of w are

$$\lambda, a, ab, abc, abcc, abcce.$$

Define *suffixes* similarly.

The *concatenation* of two words x and y is the word xy. For any word w, $\lambda w = w\lambda = w$. If $x = uvw$, then v is a subword of x. If u and w are not both λ, then v is a proper subword.

S. Homer and A.L. Selman, *Computability and Complexity Theory*,
Texts in Computer Science, DOI 10.1007/978-1-4614-0682-2_1,
© Springer Science+Business Media, LLC 2011

Some operations on languages:

union $L_1 \cup L_2$
intersection $L_1 \cap L_2$
complement $\overline{L} = \Sigma^* - L$
concatenation $L_1 L_2 = \{xy \mid x \in L_1 \text{ and } y \in L_2\}$.

The *powers* of a language L are defined as follows:

$$L^0 = \{\lambda\},$$

$$L^1 = L,$$

$$L^{n+1} = L^n L, \text{ for } n \geq 1.$$

The *Kleene closure* of a language L is the language

$$L^* = \bigcup_{i=0}^{\infty} L^i.$$

Note that $\lambda \in L^*$, for all L. Applying this definition to $L = \Sigma$, we get, as we said above, that Σ^* is the set of all words. Note that $\emptyset^* = \{\lambda\}$.

Define $L^+ = \bigcup_{i=1}^{\infty} L^i$. Then, $\lambda \in L^+ \Leftrightarrow \lambda \in L$.

Theorem 1.1. *For any language S, $S^{**} = S^*$.*

Homework 1.1 *Prove Theorem 1.1.*

The *lexicographic* ordering of Σ^* is defined by $w < w'$ if $|w| < |w'|$ or if $|w| = |w'|$ and w comes before w' in ordinary dictionary ordering.

If A is a language and n is a positive integer, $A^{=n} = A \cap \Sigma^n$ denotes the set of words of length n that belongs to A.

1.2 *K*-adic Representation

Let N denote the set of all natural numbers, i.e., $N = \{0, 1, 2, 3, \ldots\}$. We need to represent the natural numbers as words over a finite alphabet. Normally we do this using binary or decimal notation, but k-adic notation, which we introduce here, has the advantage of providing a one-to-one and onto correspondence between Σ^* and N.

Let Σ be a finite alphabet with k symbols. Call the symbols $1, \ldots, k$. Every word over Σ will denote a unique natural number.

Let $x = \sigma_n \cdots \sigma_1 \sigma_0$ be a word in Σ^*. Define

$$N_k(\lambda) = 0,$$

$$N_k(x) = N_k(\sigma_n \cdots \sigma_1 \sigma_0)$$

$$= \sigma_n * k^n + \cdots + \sigma_1 * k^1 + \sigma_0.$$

$N_k(x)$ is the number that the word x represents.

Example 1.2. Let $\Sigma = \{1,2,3\}$. The string 233 denotes the integer

$$N_3(233) = 2 * 3^2 + 3 * 3^1 + 3 * 3^0 = 18 + 9 + 3 = 30.$$

Also,

$$N_k(\lambda) = 0,$$

$$N_k(xa) = k * N_k(x) + a$$

is a recursive definition of N_k.

To see that N_k maps Σ^* onto the natural numbers, we need to show that every natural number has a k-adic representation. Given m, we want a word $s_n \ldots s_1 s_0$ such that $m = s_n * k^n + \cdots + s_1 * k^1 + s_0$. Note that $m = [s_n * k^{n-1} + \cdots + s_1] * k + s_0$. Let $a_0 = s_n * k^{n-1} + \cdots + s_1$. Then, $a_0 k = \max\{ak \mid ak < m\}$. Use this equation to find a_0. Then, $s_0 = m - a_0 k$. Iterate the process with a_0 until all values are known.

1.3   Partial Functions

Suppose that P is a program whose input values are natural numbers. It is possible that P does not halt on all possible input values. Suppose that P is designed to compute exactly one output value, again a natural number, for each input value on which it eventually halts. Then P computes a *partial function* on the natural numbers. This is the fundamental data type that is studied in computability theory.

The partial function differs somewhat from the function of ordinary mathematics. If f is a partial function defined on N, then for some values of $x \in N$, $f(x)$ is well defined; i.e., there is a value $y \in N$ such that $y = f(x)$. For other values of $x \in N$, $f(x)$ is undefined; i.e., $f(x)$ does not exist. When $f(x)$ is defined, we say $f(x)$ *converges* and we write $f(x) \downarrow$. When $f(x)$ is undefined, we say $f(x)$ *diverges* and we write $f(x) \uparrow$.

Given a partial function f, we want to know whether, given values x, does $f(x)$ converge and if so, what is the value of $f(x)$? Can the values of f be computed (by a computer program), and if so can f be efficiently computed?

We will also be concerned with subsets of the natural numbers and with relations defined on the natural numbers.

Given a set A (i.e., $A \subseteq N$), we want to know, for values x, whether $x \in A$. Is there an algorithm that for all x, will determine whether $x \in A$? For relations, the question is essentially the same. Given a k-ary relation R and values $x_1, \ldots, x_k$, is $R(x_1, \ldots, x_k)$ true? Is there a computer program that for all input tuples will decide the question? If so, is there an efficient solution?

This discussion assumed that the underlying data type is the set of natural numbers, N. As we just learned, it is equivalent to taking the underlying data type to be Σ^*, where Σ is a finite alphabet. We will pun freely between these two points of view.

1.4 Graphs

A *graph* is a pair $G = (V, E)$ consisting of a finite, nonempty set V of vertices and a set E of *edges*. An *edge* is an unordered pair of distinct vertices. (For $v \in V$, (v, v) cannot be an edge because the vertices are not distinct.) If (u, v) is an edge, then u and v are vertices; we say that u and v are *adjacent*. A graph is *complete* if every pair of distinct vertices is connected by an edge.

A *subgraph* of $G = (V, E)$ is a graph $G' = (V', E')$ such that

1. $V' \subseteq V$, and
2. E' consists of edges (v, w) in E such that both v and w are in V'.

If E' consists of all edges (v, w) in E such that both v and w are in V', then G' is called an *induced subgraph* of G.

In most contexts (v, w) denotes an ordered pair, but when discussing graphs, we abuse notation by using (v, w) to denote edges, which are unordered pairs.

A *path* is a sequence of vertices connected by edges. The length of a path is the number of edges on the path. (A single vertex is a path of length 0.) A *simple path* is a path that does not repeat any vertex or edge, except possibly the first and last vertices. A *cycle* is a simple path of length at least 1 that starts and ends in the same vertex. Observe that the length of a cycle must be at least 3 because v and u, v, u are not cycles. A *Hamiltonian circuit* is a cycle that contains every vertex in the graph.

Example 1.3. The sequence $1, 2, 4, 3, 5, 1$ is a Hamiltonian circuit of the graph in Fig. 1.1.

A graph is *connected* if every two vertices has a path between them. The number of edges at a vertex is the *degree* of the vertex.

A *directed graph* (*digraph*) consists of a set of *vertices* and a set of *arcs*. An arc is an ordered pair. Figure 1.2 gives an example.

A *path* in a digraph is a sequence of vertices $v_1, \ldots, v_n$ such that for every i, $1 \leq i < n$, there is an arc from v_i to v_{i+1}. A digraph is *strongly connected* if there is a path from any vertex to any other vertex.

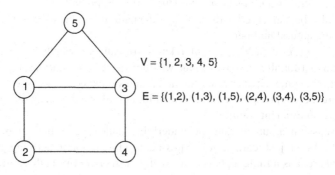

$V = \{1, 2, 3, 4, 5\}$

$E = \{(1,2), (1,3), (1,5), (2,4), (3,4), (3,5)\}$

Fig. 1.1 A graph $G = (V, E)$

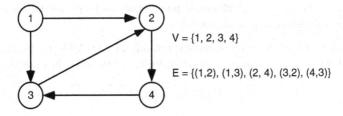

$V = \{1, 2, 3, 4\}$

$E = \{(1,2), (1,3), (2, 4), (3,2), (4,3)\}$

Fig. 1.2 A digraph $G = (V,E)$

An (undirected) *tree* is a connected graph with no cycles.

For a directed graph we define a cycle just as for an undirected graph. Note that there can be cycles of length 2 in directed graphs. For directed graphs we define a tree as follows:

1. There is exactly one vertex, called the root, that no arcs enter;
2. Every other vertex is entered by exactly one arc; and
3. There is a path from the root to every vertex.

If (u,v) is an arc in a tree, then u is a *parent* of v, and v is a *child* of u. If there is a path from u to v, then u is an *ancestor* of v, and v is a *descendant* of u. A vertex with no children is called a *leaf*. A *vertex u* together with all its descendants is a *subtree*, and u is the root of that subtree.

The *depth* of a vertex u in a tree is the length of the path from the root to u. The *height* of u is the length of a longest path from u to a leaf. The *height of the tree* is the height of the root. Finally, when the children of each vertex are ordered, we call this an *ordered tree*. A *binary tree* is a tree such that each child of a vertex is either a *left* child or a *right* child, and no vertex has more than one left child or right child.

1.5 Propositional Logic

Propositional logic provides a mathematical formalism that is useful for representing and manipulating statements of fact that are either true or false.

Let $U = \{u_1, u_2, u_3, \ldots\}$ be a set of Boolean variables (i.e., ranging over $\{0,1\}$, where we identify 0 with False and 1 with True). We associate the binary Boolean connectives $\wedge$ and $\vee$, and the unary connective $\neg$, with AND, inclusive-OR, and NOT, respectively. However, their exact semantic meaning will be given shortly. For now, they are purely syntactic.

The class of *propositional formulas* is defined inductively as follows:

1. Every propositional variable is a propositional formula;
2. If A and B are propositional formulas, then the expressions $(A \wedge B)$, $(A \vee B)$, and $(\neg A)$ are propositional formulas.

When convenient, we will eliminate parentheses in propositional formulas in accordance with the usual precedence rules.

Definition 1.1. Let F be a propositional formula and let $\text{VAR}(F)$ be the set of variables that occur in F. An *assignment* (or *truth-assignment*) t is a function

$$t : \text{VAR}(F) \to \{0, 1\}.$$

An assignment induces a truth-value to the formula F by induction, as follows:

1.
$$t((A \wedge B)) = \begin{cases} 1 & \text{if } t(A) = t(B) = 1; \\ 0 & \text{otherwise.} \end{cases}$$

2.
$$t((A \vee B)) = \begin{cases} 0 & \text{if } t(A) = t(B) = 0; \\ 1 & \text{otherwise.} \end{cases}$$

3.
$$t((\neg A)) = \begin{cases} 1 & \text{if } t(A) = 0; \\ 0 & \text{otherwise.} \end{cases}$$

Using these rules, given any formula F and an assignment t to $\text{VAR}(F)$, we can evaluate $t(F)$ to determine whether the assignment makes the formula True or False. Also, these rules ascribe meaning to the connectives. It is common to present the truth-values of a formula F under all possible assignments as a finite table, called a *truth-table*.

If $u \in U$ is a Boolean variable, it is common to write $\bar{u}$ in place of $(\neg u)$. Variables u and negated variables $\bar{u}$ are called *literals*.

Example 1.4. The propositional formula $(u_1 \vee \overline{u_2}) \wedge (\overline{u_1} \vee u_2)$ has the following truth-table:

u_1	u_2	$(u_1 \vee \overline{u_2}) \wedge (\overline{u_1} \vee u_2)$
1	1	1
1	0	0
0	1	0
0	0	1

Definition 1.2. An assignment t *satisfies* a formula F if $t(F) = 1$. A formula F is *satisfiable* if there exists an assignment to its variables that satisfies it.

We will learn in Chap. 6 that the satisfiable formulas play an exceedingly important role in the study of complexity theory.

Definition 1.3. A formula is *valid* (or is a *tautology*) if every assignment to its variables satisfies it.

Proposition 1.1. *A formula F is a tautology if and only if $(\neg F)$ is not satisfiable.*

Homework 1.2 *Prove Proposition 1.1.*

Definition 1.4. Two formulas F and G are *equivalent* if for every assignment t to $\text{VAR}(F) \cup \text{VAR}(G)$, $t(F) = t(G)$.

Next we define two special syntactic "normal" forms of propositional formulas. We will show that every formula is equivalent to one in each of these forms.

A formula is a *conjunction* if it is of the form $(A_1 \wedge A_2 \wedge \cdots A_n)$, where each A_i is a formula, and we often abbreviate this using the notation $\bigwedge_{1 \leq i \leq n} A_i$. Similarly, a *disjunction* is a formula of the form $(A_1 \vee A_2 \vee \cdots A_n)$, which we can write as $\bigvee_{1 \leq i \leq n} A_i$.

A *clause* is a disjunction of literals. (For example, $u_1 \vee \overline{u_3} \vee u_8$ is a clause.) Observe that a clause is satisfied by an assignment if and only if the assignment makes at least one of its literals true.

Definition 1.5. A propositional formula G is in *conjunctive normal form* if it is a conjunction of clauses.

Example 1.5. $(u_1 \vee \overline{u_2}) \wedge (\overline{u_1} \vee u_2)$ is in conjunctive normal form, the assignment $t(u_1) = t(u_2) = 1$ satisfies the formula, but it is not a tautology.

Example 1.6. $(u_1 \wedge \overline{u_1})$ is in conjunctive normal form and has no satisfying assignment.

Homework 1.3 *Show that every formula is equivalent to one in conjunctive normal form. (You will need to use elementary laws of propositional logic such as DeMorgan's laws, which state that $\neg(A \wedge B)$ is equivalent to $(\neg A \vee \neg B)$ and that $\neg(A \vee B)$ is equivalent to $(\neg A \wedge \neg B)$.)*

Since a formula in conjunctive normal form is a conjunction of clauses, it is a conjunction of a disjunction of literals. Analogously, we define a formula to be in *disjunctive normal form* if it is a disjunction of a conjunction of literals.

Example 1.7. $(u_1 \wedge \overline{u_2}) \vee (\overline{u_1} \wedge u_2)$ is in disjunctive normal form.

Using the technique of Homework 1.3, every propositional formula is equivalent to one in disjunctive normal form.

1.5.1 Boolean Functions

A *Boolean function* is a function $f : \{0,1\}^n \to \{0,1\}$, where $n \geq 1$. A truth-table is just a tabular presentation of a Boolean function, so every propositional formula defines a Boolean function by its truth-table.

Conversely, let $f : \{0,1\}^n \to \{0,1\}$ be a Boolean function. Then, we can represent f by the following formula F_f in disjunctive normal form whose truth-table is f. For each n-tuple $(a_1, \ldots, a_n) \in \{0,1\}^n$ such that $f(a_1, \ldots, a_n) = 1$, write the conjunction of literals $(l_1 \wedge \cdots \wedge l_n)$, where $l_i = u_i$ if $a_i = 1$ and $l_i = \overline{u_i}$ if $a_i = 0$ (where $1 \leq i \leq n$, and $u_1, \ldots, u_n$ are Boolean variables). Then, define F_f to be the disjunction of each such conjunction of literals.

1.6 Cardinality

The *cardinality* of a set is a measure of its size. Two sets A and B have the *same cardinality* if there is a bijection $h : A \to B$. In this case we write $\mathrm{card}(A) = \mathrm{card}(B)$. If there exists a one-to-one function h from A to B, then $\mathrm{card}(A) \leq \mathrm{card}(B)$. For finite sets $A = \{a_1, \ldots, a_k\}$, $k \geq 1$, $\mathrm{card}(A) = k$. A set A is *countable* if $\mathrm{card}(A) = \mathrm{card}(N)$ or A is finite. A set A is *countably infinite* if $\mathrm{card}(A) = \mathrm{card}(N)$.

A set is *enumerable* if it is the empty set or there is a function $f : N \to_{\text{onto}} A$. In this case A can be written as a sequence: Writing a_i for $f(i)$, we have

$$A = range(f) = \{a_0, a_1, a_2, \ldots\} = \{a_i \mid i \geq 0\}.$$

To call a set enumerable is to say that its elements can be counted. Observe that an enumeration need not be one-to-one. Since $a_i = a_j$, for $i \neq j$, is possible, it is possible that some elements of A are counted more than once.

Theorem 1.2. *A set is enumerable if and only if it is countable.*

Homework 1.4 *Prove Theorem 1.2.*

The cardinality of N is denoted $\aleph_0$.

Theorem 1.3. *A set A is countable if and only if* $\mathrm{card}(A) \leq \aleph_0$.

That is, $\aleph_0$ is the smallest nonfinite cardinality. (Of course, at the moment we have no reason to expect that there is any other nonfinite cardinality.)

Proof. Suppose $\mathrm{card}(A) \leq \aleph_0$. Then there is a one-to-one function f from A to N. Suppose $f[A]$ has a largest element k. Then A is a finite set. Suppose $f[A]$ does not have a largest member. Let a_0 be the unique member of A such that $f(a_0)$ is the smallest member of $f[A]$. Let a_{n+1} be the unique member of A such that $f(a_{n+1})$ is the smallest member of $f[A] - \{f(a_0), \ldots, f(a_n)\}$. It follows that A is enumerable.

The reverse direction is straightforward. $\square$

Homework 1.5 *If* $\mathrm{card}(A) \leq \mathrm{card}(B)$ *and* $\mathrm{card}(B) \leq \mathrm{card}(C)$, *then* $\mathrm{card}(A) \leq \mathrm{card}(C)$.

Homework 1.6 *(This is a hard problem, known as the Cantor–Bernstein Theorem.) If* $\mathrm{card}(A) \leq \mathrm{card}(B)$ *and* $\mathrm{card}(B) \leq \mathrm{card}(A)$, *then* $\mathrm{card}(A) = \mathrm{card}(B)$.

Example 1.8. $\{< x,y > \mid x,y \in N\}$ is countable. An enumeration is

$$< 0,0 >, < 0,1 >, < 1,0 >, < 0,2 >, \ldots.$$

Example 1.9. The set of rational numbers is countable.

Example 1.10. The set of programs in any programming language is countably infinite. For each language there is a finite alphabet Σ such that each program is in Σ^*. Because programs may be arbitrarily long, there are infinitely many of them. There are $\aleph_0$ many programs.

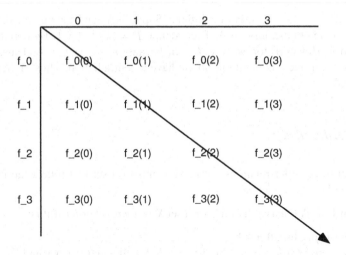

Fig. 1.3 The diagonalization technique

The proof of the following theorem employs the technique of *diagonalization*. Diagonalization was invented by the mathematician George Cantor (1845–1918), who created the theory of sets that we now take for granted. This is an important technique in theoretical computer science, so it would be wise to master this easy application first.

Theorem 1.4. *The set of all functions from N to N is not countable.*

Proof. Let $A = \{f \mid f : N \rightarrow N\}$. Suppose A is countable. Then there is an enumeration $f_0, f_1, \ldots$ of A. (Think of all the values of each f_i laid out on an infinite matrix: The idea is to define a function that cannot be on this matrix because it differs from all of the values on the diagonal. This is illustrated in Fig. 1.3.) Define a function g by $g(x) = f_x(x) + 1$, for all $x \in N$. Then, g is a function on N, but observe that g cannot be in the enumeration of all functions. That is, if $g \in A$, then for some natural number k, $g = f_k$. But g cannot equal f_k because $g(k) \neq f_k(k)$. Thus, we have contradicted the assumption that the set of all functions can be enumerated. Thus, A is not countable. □

Consider your favorite programming language. As there are countably many programs but there are uncountably many functions defined on N, there are functions that your favorite programming language cannot compute. All reasonable general-purpose programming systems compute the exact same set of functions, so it follows that there are functions defined on N that are not computable by any program in any programming system.

For any set A, $\mathscr{P}(A) = \{S \mid S \subseteq A\}$ denotes the power set of A.

Theorem 1.5. $\mathscr{P}(N)$ *has cardinality greater than* $\aleph_0$.

Proof. Let $A = \mathscr{P}(N)$. Clearly, A is infinite. Suppose A can be enumerated, and let $S_0, S_1, \ldots$ be an enumeration of A. Then, define $T = \{k \mid k \notin S_k\}$. By definition, T belongs to A. However, for every k, $T \neq S_k$ because $k \in T \Leftrightarrow k \notin S_k$. Thus, T is a set that is not in the enumeration. So we have a contradiction. Thus, A cannot be enumerated.   □

1.6.1   Ordered Sets

It is useful to consider relations on the elements of a set that reflect the intuitive notion of ordering these elements.

Definition 1.6. A binary relation ρ on a set X is a *partial order* if it is:

1. *Reflexive* ($a \rho a$, for all $a \in X$),
2. *Antisymmetric* ($a \rho b$ and $b \rho a$ implies $a = b$, for all a and b in X), and
3. *Transitive* ($a \rho b$ and $b \rho c$ implies $a \rho c$, for all a, b, and c in X).

A partial order is a *linear order* on X if, in addition, for all a and b in X, $a \rho b$ or $b \rho a$. A *partially ordered set* (*linearly ordered set*) is a pair $\langle X, \rho \rangle$, where ρ is a partial order (linear order, respectively) on X. Let Z denote the set of integers.

Example 1.11. 1. $\langle Z, \leq \rangle$ and $\langle Z, \geq \rangle$ are linearly ordered sets, where $\leq$ and $\geq$ denote the customary well-known orderings on Z.
2. For any set A, $\langle \mathscr{P}(A), \subseteq \rangle$ is a partially ordered set.
3. $\langle Z, \{(a,b) \mid a, b \in Z$ and a is an integral multiple of $b\} \rangle$ is a partially ordered set.
4. Let $\mathscr{C}$ be any collection of sets; then

$$\langle \{card(X) \mid X \in \mathscr{C}\}, \leq \rangle$$

is a linear order.

1.7   Elementary Algebra

Here we present some useful algebra and number theory. In the next several pages we will barely scratch the surface of these exceedingly rich subjects. This material is not needed for the main body of the course, but is useful for understanding several examples in later chapters.

1.7.1   Rings and Fields

Definition 1.7. A *ring* is a system $\langle R, +, \cdot, 0 \rangle$ that satisfies the following axioms, where R is a nonempty set, 0 is an element of R, and $+$ and $\cdot$ are operations on R. For arbitrary members a, b, and c of R:

(A1) $a+b=b+a$ (commutative law of addition);
(A2) $(a+b)+c=a+(b+c)$ (associative law of addition);
(A3) $a+0=a$ (zero element);
(A4)   for every $a \in R$, there exists $x \in R$ such that $a+x=0$ (existence of additive inverses);
(A5) $(ab)c=a(bc)$[1] (associative law of multiplication);
(A6) $a(b+c)=ab+ac$;
(A7) $(b+c)a=ba+bc$ (distributive laws).

A ring is *commutative* if in addition it satisfies the following axiom:

(A8) $ab=ba$ (commutative law of multiplication).

A ring is *ring with unity* if there is an element 1 belonging to R such that

(A9) $1a=a1=a$.

Definition 1.8. A *field* is a commutative ring with unity $\langle R, +, \cdot, 0, 1 \rangle$ such that

(A10)   for every $a \neq 0$, $a \in R$, there exists $x \in R$ such that $ax=1$ (existence of multiplicative inverses).

Note that 0 and 1 do not denote numbers – they are elements of R that obey the appropriate axioms.

Remember that Z denotes the set of integers and let Q denote the set of all rational numbers. Then, using ordinary integer addition and multiplication and integers 0 and 1, Z forms a ring but not a field. The rational numbers Q, with its ordinary operations, forms a field.

Theorem 1.6. *Each nonzero element in a field has a unique multiplicative inverse.*

Proof. Suppose that s and t are two multiplicative inverses of a. Then

$$s = s1 = s(at) = (sa)t = (as)t = 1t = t.$$

$\square$

The unique multiplicative inverse of an element a in a field is denoted a^{-1}.

Definition 1.9. Let m be an integer greater than 1 and let a and b be integers. Then a is *congruent to b modulo m* if m divides $a-b$.

We indicate that m divides $a-b$ by writing $m|a-b$, and we write $a \equiv b$ (mod m) to denote that a is congruent to b modulo m. Let $\mathrm{rm}(a,m)$ denote the remainder when dividing a by m (eg., $\mathrm{rm}(5,2)=1$).

Theorem 1.7. *The following are elementary facts about congruence modulo m.*

1. $a \equiv b$ (mod m) *if and only if* $\mathrm{rm}(a,m) = \mathrm{rm}(b,m)$.

---

[1] As is customary, we write ab instead of writing $a \cdot b$.

2.

$$a \equiv b \ (\text{mod } m) \Rightarrow \text{ for all integers } x,$$

$$a + x \equiv b + x \ (\text{mod } m),$$

$$ax \equiv bx \ (\text{mod } m), \text{ and}$$

$$-a \equiv -b \ (\text{mod } m).$$

3. *Congruence modulo m is an equivalence relation.*

Homework 1.7 *Prove Theorem 1.7.*

Given $m > 1$, the equivalence class containing the integer a is the set

$$[a] = \{x \mid x \equiv a \ (\text{mod } m)\}.$$

We call $[a]$ an *equivalence class modulo m*. Let Z_m denote the set of equivalence classes modulo m, and let $r = \text{rm}(a, m)$, so for some integer q, $a = qm + r$ and $0 \leq r < m$. Then, $a - r = qm$, so $a \equiv r \ (\text{mod } m)$ and hence $[a] = [r]$. That is, every integer is congruent modulo m to one of the m integers $0, 1, \ldots, m - 1$. Finally, no two of these are congruent modulo m. Thus, there are exactly m equivalence classes modulo m, and they are the sets $[0], [1], \ldots, [m - 1]$. We have learned that $Z_m = \{[0], [1], \ldots, [m - 1]\}$.

Now we will show that Z_m forms a useful number system. We define operations on Z_m as follows: $[a] + [b] = [a + b]$ and $[a][b] = [ab]$. The definition is well founded, i.e., independent of choice of representative member of each equivalence class, because

$$\text{rm}(a + b, m) \equiv \text{rm}(a, m) + \text{rm}(b, m) \ (\text{mod } m)$$

and

$$\text{rm}(ab, m) \equiv \text{rm}(a, m) \cdot \text{rm}(b, m) \ (\text{mod } m).$$

We state the following theorem.

Theorem 1.8. *For each positive integer m, $\langle Z_m, +, \cdot, [0], [1] \rangle$ is a ring with unity.*

Homework 1.8 *Prove the theorem by verifying each of the properties A1 to A8.*

Definition 1.10. A commutative ring with unity $\langle R, +, \cdot, 0, 1 \rangle$ is an *integral domain* if for all $a, b \in R$,

(A11) $ab = 0$ implies $a = 0$ or $b = 0$ (absence of nontrivial zero divisors).

The integers with their usual operations form an integral domain.

Theorem 1.9. *Every field is an integral domain.*

Proof. Suppose that $ab = 0$. We show that if $a \neq 0$, then $b = 0$, so suppose that $a \neq 0$. Then the following holds:

$$b = 1b = \left(a^{-1}a\right)b = a^{-1}(ab) = a^{-1}0 = 0.$$

This completes the proof.   □

Our goal is to show that if p is a prime number, then Z_p is a field. First, though, let us observe that if m is not a prime number, then Z_m is not even an integral domain: Namely, there exist positive integers a and b, $0 < a < b < m$, such that $m = ab$. Hence, in Z_m, $[a][b] = 0$; yet $[a] \neq 0$ and $[b] \neq 0$.

To show that Z_p is a field when p is prime, we need to show that the equation

$$ax \equiv 1 \ (\text{mod } p)$$

is solvable[2] for each integer $a \in \{1, \ldots, p-1\}$. For this purpose, we introduce the following notation.

Definition 1.11. For nonzero integers $a, b \in Z$, define

$$(a, b) = \{ax + by \mid x, y \in Z\}$$

to be the set of all *linear combinations* of a and b, and define

$$(a) = \{ax \mid x \in Z\}.$$

Definition 1.12. For nonzero integers $a, b \in Z$, the positive integer d is a *greatest common divisor* of a and b if

(i) d is a divisor of a and b, and
(ii) every divisor of both a and b is a divisor of d.

We write $d = \gcd(a, b)$.

Lemma 1.1. $(a, b) = (d)$, *where* $d = \gcd(a, b)$.

Proof. Since a and b are nonzero integers, there is a positive integer in (a, b). Let d be the least positive integer in (a, b). Clearly, $(d) \subseteq (a, b)$.

We show $(a, b) \subseteq (d)$: Suppose $c \in (a, b)$. Then, there exist integers q and r such that $c = qd + r$, with $0 \leq r < d$. Since c and d are in (a, b), it follows that $r = c - qd$ is in (a, b) also. However, since $0 \leq r < d$ and d is the least positive integer in (a, b), it must be the case that $r = 0$. Hence, $c = qd$, which belongs to (d). Thus, $(d) = (a, b)$.

All that remains is to show that $d = \gcd(a, b)$. Since a and b belong to (d), d is a common divisor of (a) and (b). If c is any other common divisor of (a) and (b), then c divides every number of the form $ax + by$. Thus, $c \mid d$, which proves that $d = \gcd(a, b)$. $\square$

Definition 1.13. Two integers a and b are *relatively prime* if $\gcd(a, b) = 1$.

Theorem 1.10. *If p is a prime number, then $\langle Z_p, +, \cdot, [0], [1] \rangle$ is a field.*

---

[2]That is, we show for each integer $a \in \{1, \ldots, p-1\}$ that there exists an integer x such that $ax \equiv 1$ (mod p).

Proof. Let $[a]$ be a nonzero member of Z_p. Then, $[a] \neq [0]$, so $a \not\equiv 0 \pmod{p}$. That is, p does not divide a. Thus, since p is prime, a and p are relatively prime. Now, let us apply Lemma 1.1: There exist integers x and y such that $1 = ax + py$. We can rewrite this as $1 - ax = py$ to see that $ax \equiv 1 \pmod{p}$. Hence, $[a][x] = [1]$, which is what we wanted to prove.   □

Lemma 1.1 proves that the greatest common divisor of two integers always exists, but does not give a method of finding it. Next we present the *Euclidean Algorithm*, which computes $\gcd(x,y)$ for integers x and y. Later in the course we will analyze this algorithm to show that it is efficient.

If $d = \gcd(x,y)$, then d is the greatest common divisor of $-x$ and y, of x and $-y$, and of $-x$ and $-y$, as well. Thus, in the following algorithm we assume that x and y are positive integers.

> EUCLIDEAN ALGORITHM
> input positive integers x and y in binary notation;
> **repeat**
> $\quad$ $x := \text{rm}(x,y)$;
> $\quad$ exchange x and y
> **until** $y = 0$;
> output x.

Let us understand the algorithm and see that it is correct. Let $r_1 = \text{rm}(x,y)$, so for some quotient q_1, $x = q_1 y + r_1$. Since $r_1 = x - q_1 y$, every number that divides x and y also divides r_1. Thus, d divides r_1, where $d = \gcd(x,y)$. Now we will show that $\gcd(x,y) = \gcd(y,r_1)$. We know already that d is a common divisor of y and r_1. If there were a common divisor $d_1 > d$ that divides y and r_1, then this value d_1 would also divide x. Thus, d would not be the greatest common divisor of x and y.

The Euclidean Algorithm reduces the problem of finding $\gcd(x,y)$ to that of finding $\gcd(y,r_1)$, where $r_1 < y$. Since the remainder is always nonnegative and keeps getting smaller, it must eventually be zero. Suppose this occurs after n iterations. Then we have the following system of equations:

$$x = q_1 y + r_1, 0 < r_1 < y,$$

$$y = q_2 r_1 + r_2, 0 < r_2 < r_1,$$

$$r_1 = q_3 r_2 + r_3, 0 < r_3 < r_2,$$

$$r_2 = q_4 r_3 + r_4, 0 < r_4 < r_3,$$

$$\vdots$$

$$r_{n-2} = q_n r_{n-1}.$$

Finally,

$$d = \gcd(x,y) = \gcd(y,r_1) = \gcd(r_1,r_2) = \cdots = \gcd(r_{n-2},r_{n-1}) = r_{n-1},$$

and r_{n-1} is the final value of x, which completes the argument that the Euclidean Algorithm computes $d = \gcd(x, y)$.

1.7.2 Groups

Definition 1.14. A *group* is a system $\langle G, \cdot, 1 \rangle$ that satisfies the following axioms, where G is a nonempty set, 1 is an element of G, and $\cdot$ is an operation on G:

(A5) $(ab)c = a(bc)$
(A9) $1a = a1 = a$; and
(A12) for every $a \in G$ there exists $x \in G$ such that $ax = 1$.

A group is *commutative* if in addition it satisfies axiom (A8), the commutative law of multiplication.

The set of integers Z forms a commutative group $\langle Z, +, 0 \rangle$ known as the *additive group of the integers*; for every positive integer m, $\langle Z_m, +, [0] \rangle$ is a commutative group. It follows from Theorem 1.10 that if p is a prime number, then $\langle Z_p - \{[0]\}, \cdot, [1] \rangle$ is a commutative group. More generally, for every field $\langle F, +, \cdot, 0, 1, \rangle$, the nonzero elements of F form a commutative group $\langle F - \{0\}, \cdot, 1 \rangle$ known as the *multiplicative group of the field*.

Definition 1.15. The *order* of a group $\langle G, \cdot, 1 \rangle$, written $o(G)$, is the number of elements in G if G is finite, and is infinite otherwise.

The *order* of an element a in G, $o(a)$, is the least positive m such that $a^m = 1$. If no such integer exists, then $o(a)$ is infinite.

The order of the additive group of the integers is infinite. The order of the additive group $\langle Z_m, +, [0] \rangle$ is m, while, for p a prime, the order of the multiplicative group of the nonzero elements of Z_p is $p - 1$.

Definition 1.16. Let H be a nonempty subset of G. H is a *subgroup* of G (or more precisely $\langle H, \cdot, 1 \rangle$ is a *subgroup* of $\langle G, \cdot, 1 \rangle$) if H contains the identity element 1 and $\langle H, \cdot, 1 \rangle$ is a group.

Let $\langle G, \cdot, 1 \rangle$ be a group and $a \in G$. Then the set $H = \{a^i \mid i \in Z\}$ is a subgroup of G. We claim that H contains $o(a)$ many elements. Of course, if H is infinite, then $o(a)$ is infinite. Suppose that H is finite, and let $o(a) = m$. Let $a^k \in H$. Then for some integer q and $0 \le r < m$, $a^k = a^{qm+r} = (a^m)^q a^r = 1a^r = a^r$. Thus, $H = \{1, a, \dots, a^{m-1}\}$, so H contains at most $o(a)$ elements. If $o(H) < o(a)$, then for some i and j, $0 \le i < j < o(a)$, $a^i = a^j$. Hence, $a^{j-i} = 1$. However, $j - i < o(a)$, which is a contradiction. Thus, $o(H) = o(a)$.

Definition 1.17. If G contains an element a such that $G = \{a^i \mid i \in Z\}$, then G is a *cyclic* group and a is a *generator*.

For any group $\langle G, \cdot, 1 \rangle$ and $a \in G$, $H = \{a^i \mid i \in Z\}$ is a cyclic subgroup of G and a is a generator of the subgroup.

1.7.2.1 Cosets

Now we come to a remarkable point: Every subgroup H of a group G partitions G into disjoint cosets.

Definition 1.18. Given a subgroup H of a group G and element $a \in G$, define $aH = \{ah \mid h \in H\}$. The set aH is called a *coset* of H.

The following lemma lists the basic properties of cosets.

Lemma 1.2. *Let a and b be members of a group G and let H be a subgroup of G.*

1. *$aH \cap bH \neq \emptyset$ implies $aH = bH$.*
2. *For finite subgroups H, aH contains $o(H)$ many elements.*

Proof. Suppose that aH and bH have an element $c = ah' = bh''$ ($h', h'' \in H$) in common. Let $h \in H$. Then, $bh = bh''h''^{-1}h = a(h'h''^{-1}h)$, which belongs to aH. Thus, $aH \subseteq bH$. Similarly, bH contains every element of aH, and so $aH = bH$.

To see that aH has $o(H)$ many elements, we note that the mapping $h \mapsto ah$ (from H to aH) is one-to-one: Each element $x = ah$, $h \in H$, in the coset aH is the image of the unique element $h = a^{-1}x$.   □

The element $a = a1 \in aH$. Thus, every element of G belongs to some coset, and because distinct cosets are disjoint, every element of G belongs to a unique coset. The cosets of H partition G. Thus, the proof of the next theorem follows immediately.

Theorem 1.11 (Lagrange). *Let H be a subgroup of a finite group G. Then, $o(H) \mid o(G)$.*

Lagrange's theorem has several important corollaries.

Corollary 1.1. *If G is a finite group and $a \in G$, then $a^{o(G)} = 1$.*

Proof. For some nonzero integer n, $o(G) = n \cdot o(a)$, so

$$a^{o(G)} = a^{n \cdot o(a)} = (a^{o(a)})^n = 1^n = 1.$$ □

Corollary 1.2. *Every group of order p, where p is prime, is a cyclic group.*

As a consequence, for each prime p, the additive group $\langle Z_p, +, [0] \rangle$ is a cyclic group.

We apply Corollary 1.1 to the multiplicative group $\langle Z_p - \{[0]\}, \cdot, [1] \rangle$ to obtain the following corollary.

Corollary 1.3 (Fermat). *If a is an integer, p is prime, and p does not divide a, then $a^{p-1} \equiv 1 \pmod{p}$.*

1.7.3 Number Theory

Our goal is to show that the multiplicative group of the nonzero elements of a finite field is a cyclic group. We know from Corollary 1.3 that for each prime number p and integer a, $1 \leq a \leq p-1$, $a^{p-1} \equiv 1 \pmod{p}$. However, we do not yet know whether there is a generator g, $1 \leq g \leq p-1$, such that $p-1$ is the *least* power m such that $g^m \equiv 1 \pmod{p}$. This is the result that will conclude this section. We begin with the following result, known as the *Chinese Remainder Theorem*.

Theorem 1.12 (Chinese Remainder Theorem). *Let $m_1, \ldots, m_k$ be pairwise relatively prime positive integers; that is, for all i and j, $1 \leq i, j \leq k$, $i \neq j$, $\gcd(m_i, m_j) = 1$. Let $a_1, \ldots, a_k$ be arbitrary integers. Then there is an integer x that satisfies the following system of simultaneous congruences:*

$$x \equiv a_1 \pmod{m_1}$$

$$x \equiv a_2 \pmod{m_2}$$

$$\vdots$$

$$x \equiv a_k \pmod{m_k}.$$

Furthermore, there is a unique solution in the sense that any two solutions are congruent to one another modulo the value $M = m_1 m_2 \cdots m_k$.

Proof. For every i, $1 \leq i \leq k$, define $M_i = M/m_i$. Then, clearly, $\gcd(m_i, M_i) = 1$. By Lemma 1.1, there exist c_i and d_i such that $c_i M_i + d_i m_i = 1$, so $c_i M_i \equiv 1 \pmod{m_i}$. Take $x = \sum_i a_i c_i M_i$. For any i, consider the ith term of the sum: For each $j \neq i$, $m_i | M_j$. Thus, every term in the sum other than the ith term is divisible by m_i. Hence, $x \equiv a_i c_i M_i \equiv a_i \pmod{m_i}$, which is what we needed to prove.

Now we prove uniqueness modulo M. Suppose that x and y are two different solutions to the system of congruences. Then, for each i, $x - y \equiv 0 \pmod{m_i}$. It follows that $x - y \equiv 0 \pmod{M}$, and this completes the proof. $\square$

The Euler *phi-function* $\phi(m)$ is defined to be the number of integers less than m that are relatively prime to m. If p is a prime, then $\phi(p) = p - 1$.

Theorem 1.13. *If m and n are relatively prime positive integers, then $\phi(mn) = \phi(m)\phi(n)$.*

Proof. We compute $\phi(mn)$. For each $1 \leq i < mn$, let r_1 be the remainder of dividing i by m and let r_2 be the remainder of dividing i by n. Then $0 \leq r_1 < m$, $0 \leq r_2 < n$, $i \equiv r_1 \pmod{m}$, and $i \equiv r_2 \pmod{n}$. Furthermore, for each such r_1 and r_2, by the

Chinese Remainder Theorem, there is exactly one value i, $1 \leq i < mn$, such that $i \equiv r_1 \pmod{m}$ and $i \equiv r_2 \pmod{n}$. Consider this one-to-one correspondence between integers $1 \leq i < mn$ and pairs of integers (r_1, r_2), $0 \leq r_1 < m$, $0 \leq r_2 < n$, such that $i \equiv r_1 \pmod{m}$ and $i \equiv r_2 \pmod{n}$: Note that i is relatively prime to mn if and only if i is relatively prime to m and i is relatively prime to n. This occurs if and only if r_1 is relatively prime to m and r_2 is relatively prime to n. The number of such i is $\phi(mn)$, while the number of such pairs (r_1, r_2) is $\phi(m)\phi(n)$. Thus, $\phi(mn) = \phi(m)\phi(n)$. ☐

Let the prime numbers in increasing order be

$$p_1 = 2, p_2 = 3, p_3 = 5, \ldots.$$

Every positive integer a has a unique factorization as a product of powers of primes of the form

$$a = p_0^{a_o} p_1^{a_1} \cdots p_i^{a_i},$$

where $a_i = 0$ for all but at most finitely many i.

Let us compute $\phi(p^a)$ for a prime power p^a. The numbers less than p^a that are *not* relatively prime to p^a are exactly those that are divisible by p. If $n \geq p^{a-1}$, then $n \cdot p \geq p^{a-1} \cdot p = p^a$. So, the numbers less than p^a that have p as a divisor are $p, 2 \cdot p, \ldots, (p^{a-1} - 1) \cdot p$. Hence, there are $(p^{a-1} - 1)$ integers less than p^a that are not relatively prime to p^a. It follows that there are

$$\phi(p^a) = (p^a - 1) - (p^{a-1} - 1) = (p^a - p^{a-1})$$

positive integers less than p^a that are relatively prime to p^a.

We define a function f on the positive integers by $f(n) = \sum_{d|n} \phi(d)$. We need to prove for all positive integers n, that $f(n) = n$.

Lemma 1.3. $f(p^a) = p^a$, *for any prime power p^a.*

Proof. The divisors of p^a are p^j for $0 \leq j \leq a$, so

$$f(p^a) = \sum_{j=0}^{a} \phi(p^j) = 1 + \sum_{j=1}^{a} (p^j - p^{j-1}) = p^a.$$

☐

Lemma 1.4. *If m and n are relatively prime positive integers, then $f(mn) = f(m)f(n)$.*

Proof. Every divisor d of mn can be written uniquely as a product $d = d_1 d_2$, where d_1 is a divisor of m and d_2 is a divisor of n. Conversely, for every divisor d_1 of m and d_2 of n, $d = d_1 d_2$ is a divisor of mn. Note that d_1 and d_2 are relatively prime. Thus, by Theorem 1.13, $\phi(d) = \phi(d_1)\phi(d_2)$. It follows that

$$f(mn) = \sum_{d|mn} \phi(d)$$

$$= \sum_{d_1|m} \sum_{d_2|n} \phi(d_1)\phi(d_2)$$

$$= \sum_{d_1|m} \phi(d_1) \sum_{d_2|n} \phi(d_2)$$

$$= f(m)f(n).$$

$\square$

Theorem 1.14. *For every positive integer n, $\sum_{d|n} \phi(d) = n$.*

Proof. The integer n is a product of relatively prime terms of the form p^a, so the proof follows immediately from Lemmas 1.3 and 1.4. $\square$

1.7.3.1 Polynomials

Let $\langle F, +, \cdot, 0, 1 \rangle$ be a field and let x be a symbol. The expression

$$\sum_0^k a_k x^k,$$

where the *coefficients* a_i, $i \leq k$, belong to F, is a *polynomial*. The degree of a polynomial is the largest number k such that the coefficient $a_k \neq 0$; this coefficient is called the *leading* coefficient. One adds or multiplies polynomials according to the rules of high school algebra. With these operations the set of all polynomials over F forms a *polynomial ring* $F[x]$. We say that g *divides* f, where $f, g \in F[x]$, if there is a polynomial $h \in F[x]$ such that $f = gh$. An element $a \in F$ is a *root* of a polynomial $f(x) \in F[x]$ if $f(a) = 0$.

Homework 1.9 *Verify that $F[x]$ is a ring.*

Theorem 1.15. *If $f(x), g(x) \in F[x]$, $g(x)$ is a polynomial of degree n, the leading coefficient of $g(x)$ is 1, and $f(x)$ is of degree $m \geq n$, then there exist unique polynomials $q(x)$ and $r(x)$ in $F[x]$ such that $f(x) = q(x)g(x) + r(x)$, and $r(x) = 0$ or the degree of $r(x)$ is less than the degree of $g(x)$.*

The proof proceeds by applying the *division algorithm*, which we now sketch: Suppose that $f(x) = \sum_0^m a_m x^m$. We can make the leading coefficient a_m vanish by subtracting from f a multiple of g, namely, $a_m x^{m-n} g(x)$. After this subtraction, if the degree is still not less than n, then we can again remove the leading coefficient by subtracting another multiple of $g(x)$. Continuing this way, we eventually have $f(x) - q(x)g(x) = r(x)$, where the degree of $r(x)$ is of lower degree than $g(x)$ or equal to zero.

Lemma 1.5. *If a is a root of $f(x) \in F[x]$, then $f(x)$ is divisible by $x - a$.*

Proof. Applying the division algorithm, we get $f(x) = q(x)(x-a) + r$, where $r \in F$ is a constant. Substitute a for the x to see that $0 = f(a) = q(a) \cdot 0 + r = r$. Thus, $f(x) = q(x)(x-r)$. □

Theorem 1.16. *If $a_1, \ldots, a_k$ are different roots of $f(x)$, then $f(x)$ is divisible by the product $(x - a_1)(x - a_2) \cdots (x - a_k)$.*

The proof is by mathematical induction in which Lemma 1.5 provides the base case $k = 1$.

Corollary 1.4. *A polynomial in $F[x]$ of degree n that is distinct from zero has at most n roots in F.*

This concludes our tutorial on polynomials. We turn now to show that the multiplicative group of the nonzero elements of a finite field is cyclic.

Let $\langle F, +, \cdot, 0, 1 \rangle$ be a finite field with q elements. Then the multiplicative subgroup of nonzero elements of F has order $q - 1$. Our goal is to show that this group has a generator g of order $q - 1$. By Lagrange's theorem, Theorem 1.11, we know that the order of every nonzero element a in F is a divisor of $q - 1$. Our first step is to show that for every positive integer $d|(q-1)$, there are either 0 or $\phi(d)$ nonzero elements in F of order d.

Lemma 1.6. *For every $d|(q-1)$, there are either 0 or $\phi(d)$ nonzero elements in F of order d.*

Proof. Let $d|(q-1)$, and suppose that some element a has order d. We will show that there must be $\phi(d)$ elements of order d. By definition, each of the elements $a, a^2, \ldots, a^d = 1$ is distinct. Each of these powers of a is a root of the polynomial $x^d - 1$. Thus, by Corollary 1.4, since every element of order d is a root of this polynomial, every element of order d must be among the powers of a. Next we will show that a^j, $1 \leq j < d$, has order d if and only if $\gcd(j, d) = 1$. From this, it follows immediately that there are $\phi(d)$ elements of order d.

Let $\gcd(j, d) = 1$, where $1 \leq j < d$, and suppose that a^j has order $c < d$. Then $(a^c)^j = (a^j)^c = 1$ and $(a^c)^d = (a^d)^c = 1$. By Lemma 1.1, since j and d are relatively prime, there are integers u and v such that $1 = uj + vd$. Clearly, one of these integers must be positive and the other negative. Assume that $u > 0$ and $v \leq 0$. Then $(a^c)^{uj} = 1$ and $(a^c)^{-vd} = 1$, so dividing on both sides, we get $a^c = (a^c)^{uj+vd} = 1$. However, since $c < d$, this contradicts the fact that $o(a) = d$. Thus, our supposition that $o(a^j) < d$ is false; a^j has order d.

Conversely, suppose that $\gcd(j, d) = d' > 1$. Then d/d' and j/d' are integers, so $(a^j)^{d/d'} = (a^d)^{j/d'} = 1$. Thus, $o(a^j) \leq d/d' < d$.

This completes the proof. □

Theorem 1.17. *The multiplicative group of the nonzero elements of a finite field is cyclic. If the finite field has q elements, then there exist $\phi(q-1)$ generators.*

Proof. Let $\langle F, +, \cdot, 0, 1 \rangle$ be a finite field with q elements. We need to show that the multiplicative group $\langle F - \{0\}, +, \cdot, 1 \rangle$ has a generator, an element a of order $q - 1$. Every element a has some order d such that $d | (q - 1)$, and by Lemma 1.6, for every such d, there are either 0 or $\phi(d)$ nonzero elements in F of order d. By Theorem 1.14, $\sum_{d | (q-1)} \phi(d) = q - 1$, which is the number of elements in $F - \{0\}$. Hence, in order for every element to have some order d that is a divisor of $q - 1$, it must be the case for every such d that there are $\phi(d)$ many elements of order d. In particular, there are $\phi(q - 1)$ different elements $g \in F$ of order $q - 1$. Thus, there is a generator, and the multiplicative group of nonzero elements of F is cyclic.   □

Corollary 1.5. *If p is a prime number, then $\langle Z_p - \{[0]\}, \cdot, [1] \rangle$ is a cyclic group.*

For example, the number 2 is a generator of Z_{19}. Namely, the powers of 2 modulo 19 are 2, 4, 8, 16, 13, 7, 14, 9, 18, 17, 15, 11, 3, 6, 12, 5, 10, 1.

Homework 1.10 *What are the other generators for Z_{19}?*

Once considered to be the purest branch of mathematics, devoid of application, number theory is the mathematical basis for the security of electronic commerce, which is fast becoming an annual trillion-dollar industry. Modern cryptography depends on techniques for finding large prime numbers p and generators for Z_p – and on the (still unproven) hypotheses of the computational hardness of factoring integers.

Chapter 2
Introduction to Computability

This subject is primarily concerned with the limitations of computing. As one of the highlights of this study, we will learn several specific problems that computers cannot solve.

A robust theory of computability dates back to the work of Church [Chu36] and Turing [Tur36] and provides models of computation and sophisticated methods that will be useful in our study of complexity theory as well. Although much of that work predated digital computers and was without forethought of modern technology, we know that von Neumann was influenced by Turing's invention of a universal, general-purpose, stored-program computer.

The basic model of computation for our study is the Turing machine, and for complexity theory, is the multitape Turing machine. However, these subjects should not depend too much on the choice of computational model. To this end, we will discuss Church's thesis as well as an expanded version of Church's thesis. Church's thesis states that every computational device can be simulated by a Turing machine. Evidence for this thesis comes from the fact that it has withstood the test of time, and it has been proven for all known reasonable models of sequential computation, including random access machines (RAMs). One of the topics in this chapter is the simulation of RAMs by Turing machines.

We view the study of computability to be an important prelude to the study of complexity theory. First, the models and methods that we learn in these chapters will be important later as well. Second, before concerning ourselves with the question of what problems can be efficiently computed, it is good to appreciate that there is a vast world of problems that we can easily formulate as computational problems but that computers cannot solve.

S. Homer and A.L. Selman, *Computability and Complexity Theory*,
Texts in Computer Science, DOI 10.1007/978-1-4614-0682-2_2,
© Springer Science+Business Media, LLC 2011

2.1   Turing Machines

Even before the invention of modern computers, Alan Turing (1936) described a
theoretical model of a computing machine. Although very simple in structure, the
Turing machine possesses remarkable properties. In particular, a Turing machine is
as powerful as any other computing device.

Computer memory is organized linearly as the cells of an infinite tape. Each cell
of the tape may hold exactly one of a finite number of symbols chosen from a finite
tape alphabet, Γ. Initially, an input word is placed on the otherwise empty tape as a
word w in the input alphabet, Σ. This is shown in Fig. 2.1.

A *finite control* is attached to a head that scans one cell of the tape at a time. What
the control does next, whether it scans a different symbol or prints a new symbol on
the square, depends on its "internal state" as well as the symbol currently being
scanned.

One can think of this as a machine, made of transistors or toothpicks and rubber
bands. It doesn't matter. The combination of whatever the insides look like (the
state) coupled with what symbol is being scanned determines what happens next.

In a move, the machine

1. Prints a new symbol,
2. Shifts its head one cell left or right,
3. Changes state.

The number of states is finite, and at any time only a finite amount of memory
is being used. A machine must have a finite description. A Turing machine has
two designated special states, q_{accept} and q_{reject}. The machine halts (stops operating)
when it enters either of these states. Turing machines may run forever on some
inputs. This is entirely consistent with the experience of most programmers.

We let Q be the finite set of states. We permit symbols to be written on cells of
the tape from a finite alphabet $\Gamma \supseteq \Sigma$.

The next move is determined by a *transition* function

$$\delta : (Q - \{q_{\text{accept}}, q_{\text{reject}}\}) \times \Gamma \to Q \times \Gamma \times \{L, R\}.$$

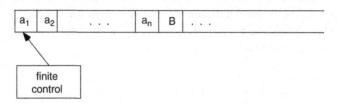

Fig. 2.1 Diagram of a Turing machine

Hence, δ maps a (current state, current symbol scanned) pair into a triple consisting of (the next state, the new symbol to be printed, indication to move the head one cell to the left or right). There is no next move from either q_{accept} or q_{reject}.

Formally, a Turing machine is a system

$$M = \langle Q, \Sigma, \Gamma, \delta, q_0, B, q_{accept}, q_{reject} \rangle,$$

where

Q is the finite set of states,
Γ is the finite tape alphabet,
$B \in \Gamma$, the *blank*,
Σ is the input alphabet, $\Sigma \subseteq \Gamma - \{B\}$,
δ is the transition function,
$q_0 \in Q$ is the *initial state*,
q_{accept} is the accepting state, and
q_{reject} is the rejecting state.

To avoid confusion, we usually take $Q \cap \Gamma = \emptyset$.

If M tries to move left when in the leftmost square, the head stays in the same place and the computation continues. The first instance of the blank symbol B denotes the end of the input word.

Example 2.1. A parity counter. The input is a word w in $\{0,1\}^*$. The Turing machine M is to halt in state q_{accept} if the number of 1's on its tape is odd and to halt in state q_{reject} if the number of 1's is even.

$\Sigma = \{0,1\}$, $\Gamma = \{0,1,B\}$, and $Q = \{q_0, q_1, q_{accept}, q_{reject}\}$ (q_0 for even and q_1 for odd). The transition function δ is often given as a matrix with rows of the form

$$q\ a \mid q'\ b\ D$$

where q is the current state, a is the symbol currently stored in the cell being scanned, q' is the next state, b is the symbol to be written in the cell, and the direction D is either left or right. Hence, we describe the transition function for the parity counter as follows:

$$
\begin{array}{cc|ccc}
q_0 & 0 & q_0 & 0 & R \\
q_0 & 1 & q_1 & 1 & R \\
q_0 & B & q_{reject} & - & - \\
q_1 & 0 & q_1 & 0 & R \\
q_1 & 1 & q_0 & 1 & R \\
q_1 & B & q_{accept} & - & - \\
\end{array}
$$

A Turing machine continues until it reaches the accept or reject state. If it never reaches one of these states, then the computation continues forever.

As a Turing machine computes, changes occur to the state, tape contents, and current head position. A setting of this information is called a configuration.

Formally, we define an *instantaneous description* (ID) or *configuration* of a Turing machine M to be a word $\alpha_1 q \alpha_2$, where $q \in Q$ is the current state and $\alpha_1 \alpha_2$ is the contents of the tape up to the rightmost nonblank or up to the symbol to the left of the head, whichever is rightmost. The tape head is scanning the first symbol of α_2 or B, in case $\alpha_2 = \lambda$.

We define the *next move* relation, denoted by a turnstile, $\vdash_M$. Let

$$X_1 X_2 \ldots X_{i-1} q X_i \ldots X_n$$

be an ID.

1. Suppose $\delta(q, X_i) = (p, Y, L)$. If $i > 1$, then

$$X_1 X_2 \ldots X_{i-1} q X_i \ldots X_n \vdash_M X_1 X_2 \ldots X_{i-2} p X_{i-1} Y X_{i+1} \ldots X_n.$$

If $i = 1$, then

$$q X_1 \ldots X_n \vdash_M p Y X_2 \ldots X_n.$$

2. Suppose $\delta(q, X_i) = (p, Y, R)$. Then

$$X_1 X_2 \ldots X_{i-1} q X_i \ldots X_n \vdash_M X_1 \ldots X_{i-1} Y p X_{i+1} \ldots X_n$$

unless $i - 1 = n$, in which case

$$X_1 \ldots X_n q \vdash_M X_1 \ldots X_n Y p.$$

The relation $\vdash_M^*$ is the reflexive, transitive closure of $\vdash_M$. This means that $C \vdash_M^* D$, where C and D are configurations, if and only if $C = D$ or there is a sequence of configurations $C_1, \ldots, C_k$ such that

$$C = C_1 \vdash C_2 \vdash \cdots \vdash C_k = D.$$

A configuration is *accepting* if the state of the configuration is q_{accept} and is *rejecting* if the state is q_{reject}. Accepting and rejecting configurations are the only *halting* configurations. The Turing machine M *accepts* an input word w if $q_0 w \vdash_M^* I$, where I is an accepting configuration. Similarly, the Turing machine M *rejects* a word w if $q_0 w \vdash_M^* I$, where I is rejecting.

2.2 Turing Machine Concepts

Definition 2.1. Let M be a Turing machine. The language *accepted* by M is

$$L(M) = \{w \in \Sigma^* \mid M \text{ accepts } w\}.$$

A language L, $L \subseteq \Sigma^*$, is *Turing-machine-acceptable* if there is a Turing machine that accepts L.

Note that M might not halt on words w that belong to $\overline{L}$.

Definition 2.2. A language L is *Turing-machine-decidable* if L is accepted by some Turing machine that halts on every input, and a Turing machine that halts on every input and accepts L is called a *decider* for L.

Usually we will write "acceptable" instead of "Turing-machine-acceptable," and write "decidable" instead of "Turing-machine-decidable." Note the distinction between these two definitions. If M accepts L, then, for all words $x \in \Sigma^*$,

$$x \in L \Rightarrow M \text{ eventually enters state } q_{\text{accept}}, \text{ and}$$

$$x \notin L \Rightarrow \text{ either } M \text{ eventually enters state } q_{\text{reject}} \text{ or}$$

$$M \text{ runs forever.}$$

However, if M decides L, then

$$x \in L \Rightarrow M \text{ eventually enters state } q_{\text{accept}}, \text{ and}$$

$$x \notin L \Rightarrow M \text{ eventually enters state } q_{\text{reject}}.$$

Every Turing machine M accepts some language, but a Turing machine might not be a decider for any language at all, simply because it does not halt on all input strings.

Proposition 2.1. *If L is decidable, then $\overline{L}$ is decidable.*

Homework 2.1 *Design Turing machines to decide the following languages[1]:*

1. $\{0^n 1^n 0^n \mid n \geq 1\}$;
2. $\{ww \mid w \in \{0, 1\}^*\}$;
3. $\{ww^R \mid w \in \{0, 1\}^*\}$. *($w^R$ denotes the "reversal" of w, so if $w = a_1 a_2 \cdots a_k$, then $w^R = a_k a_{k-1} \cdots a_1$.)*

Primarily we will be concerned with questions about whether certain languages are either acceptable or decidable, and eventually about whether certain languages have efficient deciders. For this reason, we formulated Turing machines as acceptors of languages. However, it is important to realize that Turing machines can also compute functions. After all, ordinary computing involves both input and output,

---

[1] You should not give the formal descriptions of Turing machines that solve homework problems such as this one. Since Turing-machine programs are unreadable, as is true in general of machine-language programs, it is not desirable to give formal descriptions. Instead, describe in relative detail how the Turing machine moves its head, stores data on its tape, changes states, and so forth. In this manner describe a Turing machine that implements your algorithm for solving the problems.

and output is usually more complex than merely a bit indication of the machine's final state. For this reason, when computing a partial function the final state is no longer relevant. We will continue to assume that a Turing machine that computes a partial function contains the state q_{accept}, but we no longer assume that M contains the state q_{reject}. The state q_{accept} is the only halting state. We arrive at the following definition:

A Turing machine M *computes* the partial function $\phi : (\Sigma^*)^n \to \Sigma^*$ if, when the initial ID is $q_0 w_1 B w_2 B \ldots w_n$, then

1. M eventually enters an accepting configuration if and only if $\phi(w_1, \ldots, w_n) \downarrow$, and
2. If and when M does so, then the accepting configuration is of the form

$$\phi(w_1, \ldots, w_n) q_{\text{accept}}.$$

That is, the tape is is empty except for the value of $\phi(w_1, \ldots, w_n)$, and the Turing machine halts with the head behind this value.

When M executes on an arbitrary input word x, only two possibilities exist: Either M accepts x, in which case $x \in dom(\phi)$ and M outputs the value $\phi(x)$, or M executes forever. Observe that $L(M)$ is the domain of ϕ.

Every Turing machine M and $n \geq 1$ determines the partial function ϕ_M^n of n arguments such that M halts behind $\phi_M^n(w_1, \ldots, w_n)$ if and when M halts after being run on initial ID $q_0 w_1 B w_2 B \ldots w_n$.

A partial function ϕ is *partial computable* if there is some Turing machine that computes it. If $\phi(w_1, \ldots, w_n) \downarrow$ for all $w_1, \ldots, w_n$, then ϕ is *total computable*. Observe that a Turing machine that computes a total computable function accepts and halts on every input. Therefore, if M computes a total computable function, then $L(M) = \Sigma^*$.

It is more traditional to think of the partial computable functions as mappings on the natural numbers. Fixing 2-adic as the representation gives us a unique class of partial computable functions over the natural numbers. Many texts represent the positive integer n by the string 1^{n+1}, but, thinking ahead, from a complexity theoretician's point of view, the more succinct representation is preferable.

2.3 Variations of Turing Machines

Students of computer science should have little difficulty appreciating that Turing machines have as much power as any other computing device. That is, the Turing machine accepts or decides the exact same languages and computes the exact same partial functions as any other computing device. The Turing machine is designed to perform symbol manipulation in a simple, straightforward manner. This is one common view of computing. What might be the differences between a Turing machine and computers we use every day? Both store symbols in storage locations.

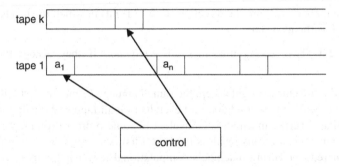

Fig. 2.2 Diagram of a k-tape Turing machine

The latter might store 32 or 64 symbols in one storage location, whereas the Turing machine stores only one symbol in each storage location, but that difference is not essential; rather, it makes the machines that we use more efficient. Both types of machines can change these symbols in one move and change state. The machines that we use have "random access," meaning, for example, that they can be reading the contents of memory location 100 and then, by executing one move, read memory location 1000. The Turing machine can easily simulate that, but must make 900 moves in order to move its head 900 cells to the right. Again, the difference is in efficiency rather than in fundamental computing power.

In part, the rest of this chapter is dedicated to expanding on this brief argument, to provide evidence that the Turing machine is as powerful as any other computer. This hypothesis is known as "Church's thesis." In this section we will introduce two important variations of the Turing-machine model and prove that they are equivalent to Turing machines. The next section discusses Church's thesis in more detail, and then we will examine random access machines more technically than in the previous paragraph.

2.3.1 Multitape Turing Machines

A k-tape Turing machine M, as pictured in Fig. 2.2, has k tapes, each with its own read/write head. When M is in a state q reading the scanned symbol in each tape, M writes over each of these symbols, moves left or right on each tape, and enters a new state.

Formally, the transition function is of the form

$$\delta : Q \times \Gamma^k \to Q \times \Gamma^k \times \{L, R\}^k.$$

Thus, given state q and scanned symbols $a_1, \ldots, a_k$, on tapes $1, \ldots, k$, respectively, $\delta(q, a_1, \ldots, a_k) = (p, b_1, \ldots, b_k, D_1, \ldots, D_k)$, where $b_1, \ldots, b_k$ are the new symbols to be written, $D_1, \ldots, D_k$ are the directions (left or right) in which the heads should move, and p is the next state.

Definition 2.3. Two Turing machines are *equivalent* if they accept the same language.

Two Turing machines might accept the same language L, and the first might be a decider for L, while the second does not even halt on all inputs. We will prove that every multitape Turing machine is equivalent to some ordinary (one-tape) Turing machine. Our interest in this result is twofold. First, showing that adding features does not increase a Turing machine's computational power helps us to convince ourselves that the Turing machine is a natural model of computing. Second, the multitape Turing machine is in fact the model that we will accept as our standard, and as such is the one to be used in the remainder of the course. This is a matter of efficiency. The multitape Turing machine is more efficient and easier to program than single-tape Turing machines. Also, there are efficient simulations between the multitape Turing machine and all other known models of computation.

Example 2.2. This example illustrates the efficiency of multitape Turing machines over single-tape Turing machines. We can easily design a two-tape Turing machine to accept the language $L = \{ww^R \mid w \in \{0,1\}^*\}$. Namely, given an input word that is placed on tape 1, the machine copies the input word onto the second tape. This requires one sweep of both reading heads from left to right. Next, move the reading head on tape 1 back to the left end. Then, compare the word claimed to be w^R with the word claimed to be w by moving the two heads in opposite directions, moving the head on tape 1 from left to right and on tape 2 from right to left. At each step, if the symbols on the scanned cells are identical, then continue, else halt without accepting. Finally, after the input word passes these tests, determine whether the length of the input word is even and if it is, then accept.

Observe that this machine requires no more that a few scans of its heads from one end of the input word to the other. Hence, the number of steps is $O(n)$, where $n = |w|$. In general, we will measure the complexity of computational problems as a function of the length of the input word.

In contrast, consider your solution to Homework 2.1. First, the above solution is probably simpler. Second, your solution probably compares the first symbol of the input word with the last, placing markers to detect that they were visited. Then the machine compares the second symbol with the next-to-last symbol, and so on. The first comparison requires n steps, the second comparison requires $n - 1$ steps, and so forth, until we reach the last comparison, which requires only one step. Thus, the total number of comparisons is $O(n^2)$. Indeed, one can prove that every single-tape Turing machine that accepts L must take at least $O(n^2)$ steps.

Homework 2.2 *In the above example, why do you need to check whether the input word is even before accepting?*

Theorem 2.1. *Every multitape Turing machine has an equivalent one-tape Turing machine.*

Track k	a_{k1}	$\uparrow a_{k2}$		a_{kd}	
Track 2	$\uparrow a_{21}$	a_{22}		a_{2d}	
Track 1	a_{11}	a_{12}		a_{1d}	

Fig. 2.3 d cells of one-tape Turing machine N with k tracks

Proof. Let M be a k-tape Turing machine. The single tape of N is viewed as consisting of k "tracks," one track for each work tape of M. This is accomplished by enlarging the tape alphabet of N so that each cell of N contains a symbol that represents k symbols of M and possibly a marker $\uparrow$ to indicate M's head position on the ith tape head. The tape alphabet of N is sufficiently large so that each tape symbol of N uniquely denotes such an array of M's tape symbols and head indicator. (For example, in the illustration given in Fig. 2.3, the second cell of N contains a symbol that uniquely denotes the array $(a_{12}, a_{22}, \ldots, \uparrow a_{k2})$.)

The one-tape Turing machine N simulates a move of M as follows: Initially N's head is at the leftmost cell containing a head marker. N sweeps right, visiting each of the cells with head markers, and stores in its control the symbol scanned by each of the k heads of M.[2] When N crosses a head marker, it updates the count of head markers to its right. When no more head markers are to the right, N has enough information to determine the move of M. Next, N sweeps left until it reaches the leftmost head marker. While doing so, it updates the tape symbols of M scanned by the head markers and moves the head markers one cell left or right as required. Finally, N changes M's current state, which is stored in N's control. N accepts its input word if and only if the new state of M is accepting.   □

In this proof, if M is a decider for a language L, then so is N, for we need only to stipulate that N rejects if and only if the new state of M is rejecting. Also, note that N must make many moves in order to simulate one move of M. This is frequently true of simulations. Since one head of M might be moving to the left while another is moving to the right, it can take about $\Sigma_{i=1}^{n} 2i = O(n^2)$ moves of N to simulate n moves of M.

By definition, two Turing machines are equivalent if they accept the same language, and this definition will continue to be useful for us. You might think it more natural to have defined "equivalent" to mean that the two machines compute the same partial function. Clearly, this is the stronger notion, for it is possible for two different partial computable functions to have the same domain. The simulation

---

[2]By increasing the number of states, a Turing machine can always store a fixed number of symbols in its finite control. The technique is to let each new state uniquely represent a combination of stored symbols.

given in the proof of Theorem 2.1 holds for the stronger notion as well. Thus, we state the following corollary:

Corollary 2.1. *For every multitape Turing machine there is a one-tape Turing machine that computes the same partial computable function.*

The following theorem is an important characterization of the decidable sets and pinpoints the distinction between decidable and acceptable. Its proof is a good illustration of the usefulness of multitape Turing machines.

Theorem 2.2. *A language L is decidable if and only if both L and $\overline{L}$ are acceptable.*

Proof. If L is decidable, then it is acceptable, by definition. Let M be a decider for L. A Turing machine that is exactly like M, but with the states q_{accept} and q_{reject} reversed, is a decider for $\overline{L}$ (which, in passing, proves Proposition 2.1) and so $\overline{L}$ is acceptable. For the proof of the converse, let M_L and $M_{\overline{L}}$ be Turing machines that accept L and $\overline{L}$, respectively. Design N so that on an input word w, N copies the input to a second tape and then simulates M_L on some of its tapes while simultaneously simulating $M_{\overline{L}}$ on others of its tapes. N is to accept w if the simulation of M_L accepts, and is to reject w if the simulation of $M_{\overline{L}}$ accepts. Clearly, N accepts L. Since every word w belongs to either L or $\overline{L}$, either the simulation of M_L eventually accepts or the simulation of $M_{\overline{L}}$ eventually accepts. Thus, N halts on every input, which proves that L is decidable.   □

Homework 2.3 *Using either a 2-adic or binary representation for numbers, describe multitape Turing machines that compute the following functions:*

1. $\lceil \log_2 n \rceil$;
2. $n!$;
3. n^2.

2.3.2   Nondeterministic Turing Machines

A nondeterministic Turing machine allows for the possibility of more than one next move from a given configuration. If there is more than one next move, we do not specify which next move the machine makes, only that it chooses one such move. This is a crucial concept for our study of complexity. Unlike deterministic computing machines, we do not design nondeterministic machines to be executed. Rather, one should understand nondeterministic Turing machines to be a useful device for describing languages, and later, when we study complexity theory, for classifying computational problems.

Formally, a nondeterministic Turing machine M is the same as a multitape Turing machine, except that the transition function has the form

$$\delta : Q \times \Gamma^k \to \mathscr{P}(Q \times \Gamma^k \times \{L, R\}^k).$$

Recall that for any set A, $\mathscr{P}(A)$ denotes the power set of A. To keep the notation manageable, let us assume for the moment that $k = 1$, so that M is a nondeterministic single-tape Turing machine. Then, given state q and scanned symbol a, $\delta(q,a) = \{(p_1, b_1, D_1), \ldots, (p_n, b_n, D_n)\}$, for some $n \geq 1$. We interpret this to mean that in state q reading the symbol a, M may make any of the possible moves indicated by one of the triples (p_i, b_i, D_i), $1 \leq i \leq n$. Thus, for some $1 \leq i \leq n$, M will write the symbol b_i in the cell that is currently scanned, move in the direction D_i, and change to state p_i.

There are two additional subtle but important distinctions between deterministic and nondeterministic Turing machines: First, it is possible that $\delta(q,a) = \emptyset$, in which case there is no next move and the machine halts without accepting. Second, we do not include the state q_{reject}, so there are no *rejecting* computations.

A nondeterministic Turing machine M and input word w specify a *computation tree* as follows: The *root* of the tree is the initial configuration of M. The *children* of a node are the configurations that follow in one move. Note that a node is a *leaf* if there is no next move. A path from the root to a leaf is an accepting computation if and only if the leaf is an accepting configuration. In general, some computation paths might be infinite, some might be accepting, and others might halt in nonaccepting states. By definition, M accepts w if and only if there is an accepting computation of M on w (in which case, the other possibilities are irrelevant). Recall that M accepts the language $L(M) = \{w \mid M \text{ accepts } w\}$. Thus, $w \in L(M)$ if and only if there is an accepting computation of M on w. This is the important point to remember. It does not matter whether certain computations run forever or whether there is a computation that halts without accepting. All that matters is that at least one computation of M on w accepts, in which case $w \in L(M)$. Conversely, w does *not* belong to $L(M)$ if and only if every computation of M on w is *not* an accepting computation. Presumably, one cannot know whether this is so without executing all possible computations of M on w.

Now we prove that nondeterministic Turing machines are not more powerful than deterministic ones after all.

Theorem 2.3. *Every nondeterministic Turing machine has an equivalent deterministic Turing machine.*

The idea of the proof is a familiar one: Given a nondeterministic Turing machine N, design a deterministic Turing machine M that on an input word w builds the computation tree of N on input w and performs a standard tree-search algorithm that halts and accepts if and only if it finds a leaf that is accepting. Implementation is not difficult, but notice one possible pitfall. Suppose that M implements a depth-first search of the computation tree. Suppose that M has an infinite computation path that is to the left of some accepting computation. Then M will descend the infinite computation path, running forever, without ever finding the accepting computation. The solution to this difficulty is to implement a breadth-first search. Then the computation tree is searched one level at a time, so, if there is a leaf that is accepting, the simulation will find it. The proof to follow gives the details.

Proof. We assume that N is a single-tape nondeterministic Turing machine. The Turing machine M will have three tapes. Tape 1 contains the input word and is never changed. Tape 2 contains a copy of N's tape on some branch of its nondeterministic computation. Tape 3 records M's location in the computation tree.

Let b be the largest number of choices given by N's transition function. Assign each node an address that is a string in $\{1, 2, \ldots, b\}$. A node has address $a_1 \ldots a_k$ if the node is at level $k+1$, a_1 is the a_1th child of the root, and for $i = 2, \ldots, k$, $a_1 \ldots a_i$ is the a_ith child of the node with address $a_1 \ldots a_{i-1}$. The address of the root is the empty word λ. Tape 3 will contain addresses.

The computation of M proceeds as follows:

1. Initially, tape 1 contains the input word w and tapes 2 and 3 are empty.
2. M copies tape 1 to tape 2.
3. On tape 2, M simulates N on w using the string on tape 3 to determine which choices to make. If tape 3 does not contain symbols for a choice or the symbol gives an invalid choice, then M aborts this branch and goes to step 4. If this simulation reaches an accepting configuration, then M accepts, but if it reaches a halting configuration that is nonaccepting, then M aborts this branch and goes to step 4.
4. M replaces the string on tape 3 with the lexicographically next string. Then M returns to step 2.

It is self-evident that M correctly simulates N. $\square$

Corollary 2.2. *If every computation path of a nondeterministic Turing machine N halts on every input word, then there is a deterministic Turing machine M that decides the language $L(N)$.*

For the proof, notice that M must be able to determine when an input word w does not belong to $L(N)$. This occurs if and only if every computation path is nonaccepting. Since, by hypothesis, no computation paths are infinite, the breadth-first search will eventually search the entire computation tree and visit every leaf node, thereby gaining the information that it needs.

Example 2.3. Given a graph G, a *clique* H is a complete subgraph of G, meaning that every two vertices in H are connected by an edge. Consider the following nondeterministic algorithm that accepts the set

$$C = \{(G, k) \mid G \text{ is a graph, } k \text{ is a positive integer, and } G \text{ has a clique with } k \text{ vertices}\}:$$

The procedure on an input pair (G, k) nondeterministically chooses a subset of k vertices. Then the procedure tests whether there is an edge between every two vertices in the subset. If so, then the procedure accepts.

If the procedure accepts, then it has chosen a clique with k vertices, so the pair (G, k) belongs to C. Conversely, if $(G, k) \in C$, then G contains a clique H of size k. The computation path of the nondeterministic procedure that selects H is an accepting computation. Hence, the procedure has an accepting computation on input (G, k) if and only if (G, k) has a clique with k vertices.

We can easily implement this procedure on a nondeterministic Turing machine. However, in order to do so we would have to make decisions about how to represent graphs as words over a finite alphabet (because an input to a Turing machine is a word and not a graph). We postpone this discussion of representation to a later chapter. Then we would need to tend to the tedious details of Turing-machine programming. Without exercising this distraction, let us simply note that some nondeterministic Turing machine accepts a suitable representation of the set C.

A deterministic Turing machine to decide the same language, following the idea of the proof of Theorem 2.3, systematically searches all subsets of k vertices of G and accepts if and only if one of these is a complete subgraph.

2.4 Church's Thesis

Church's thesis states that every "effective computation," or "algorithm," can be programmed to run on a Turing machine. Every "computational device" can be simulated by some Turing machine. In 1936, the same year as Turing introduced the Turing machine [Tur36], Emil Post created the Post machine [Pos65], which he hoped would prove to be the "universal algorithm machine" sought after. Also that year, Alonzo Church [Chu36] developed the *lambda calculus*. Slightly *before* Turing invented his machine, Church proposed the thesis that every function that can be computed by an algorithm can be defined using his lambda calculus. That is, he identified effective computability, a heretofore imprecise notion, with a specific mathematical formulation. Then, independently, Turing posited the thesis that every algorithm can be programmed on a Turing machine. The Church–Post–Turing formulations are provably equivalent, so these theses express the same belief. Several factors contributed to the general acceptance of Church's thesis. Turing's paper contains a convincing analysis of the basic steps of calculation and he demonstrated how this analysis led to the definition of the Turing machine. That is one important factor. Another important factor is the simplicity and naturalness of the Turing-machine model. A third factor is that the formulations of Church, Post, and Turing have been proven to be equivalent. This is no small matter, for each was independently invented from different considerations and perspectives. We should rightfully write the "Church–Turing" thesis, or even the "Church–Post–Turing" thesis, but for brevity we will continue to refer to "Church's" thesis.

Church's thesis cannot be "proven" because concepts such as "effective process" and "algorithms" are not part of any branch of mathematics. Yet evidence for the correctness of Church's thesis abounds. Two points are important to understand with regard to the notion of "algorithm" or "machine" as used here. The first is that every machine must have a "finite description." For example, even though there is no bound on the size of a Turing-machine tape, the description of the Turing machine as a tuple, including the transition function δ, has a finite length. The second is the notion of *determinacy*. For example, once a Turing machine is defined, for every input word, the transition function *determines* uniquely what sequence of IDs will occur. This never changes. Run the machine once or one hundred times, and the same sequence of IDs will occur.

In Chap. 3 we will learn about languages L that are Turing-machine-undecidable. (There exists no Turing machine that halts on every input and accepts L.) Using Church's thesis, we can understand results of this kind more broadly: There is no computational procedure (of any kind) that halts on every input and that for every input word w correctly determines whether w belongs to L.

In this course we are studying both computability theory and complexity theory. The basic model of computation for complexity theory is the multitape Turing machine. However, complexity measures should not depend too much on the choice of computational model. To this end, we introduce an *expanded version of Church's thesis*. Church's thesis states that every computational device can be simulated by a Turing machine. Our expanded Church's thesis is even stronger. It asserts that every computational device can be simulated by a multitape Turing machine with the simulation taking at most polynomial time. (That is, if M is some computational device, then there is a Turing machine T_M that simulates M such that programs run at most a polynomial number of additional steps on T_M than on M.)

This thesis is particularly fortunate because of another assertion known as Cobham's thesis (1964). Cobham's thesis asserts that computational problems can be feasibly computed on some computational device only if they can be computed in polynomial time. Truth be told, an n^{100}-time algorithm is not a useful algorithm. It is a remarkable phenomenon, though, that problems for which polynomial algorithms are found have such algorithms with small exponents and with small coefficients. Thus, combining the two theses, a problem can be feasibly computed only if it can be computed in polynomial time on some multitape Turing machine.

We are neglecting to describe the intellectual fervor that existed at the turn of the last century. What was in the air to cause brilliant scientists to converge on equivalent formulations of universal computing in 1936? This story is told extremely well in a collection of articles edited by Herken [Her94]. Alan Turing, if not the father of computer science, is frequently credited for being the father of theoretical computer science and artificial intelligence. His work in cryptography has been credited in recent years for being instrumental in enabling the Allied forces to win the Second World War. The extraordinary story of his life and work is described in the biography by Hodges [Hod83].

The next section will provide further evidence for the correctness of Church's thesis.

2.5   RAMs

A *random access machine* (RAM) is a conceptual model of a digital computer. A RAM contains registers that serve as the computer's memory and there is random access to the registers. The basic model, as a general model of computation, is due to Shepherdson and Sturgis [SS63]. The variation that we will describe here is due to Machtey and Young [MY78]. Random access machines are important models for the analysis of concrete algorithms [CR73].

For each finite alphabet Σ, there is a RAM for that alphabet. Thus, let us fix a finite alphabet $\Sigma = \{a_1, \ldots, a_k\}$ with $k > 1$ letters. The RAM consists of a potentially infinite set of registers $R1, R2, \ldots$, each of which can store any word of Σ^*. Any given program uses only the finite set of registers that it specifically names, and any given computation that halts uses only a finite set of words of Σ^*. (Thus, any such computation needs only a finite amount of "hardware.") RAM instructions have available an infinite set of *line names* $N0, N1, \ldots$.

RAM instructions are of the following seven types:

1_j	X **add**$_j$ Y,
2	X **del** Y,
3	X **clr** Y,
4	X $Y \leftarrow Z$,
5	X **jmp** X',
6_j	X Y **jmp**$_j$ X',
7	X **continue**,

where X is either a line name or nothing, Y and Z are register names, X' is a line name followed by an "a" or a "b" (e.g., $N6a$), and $1 \leq j \leq k$.

Instructions of types 1 through 4 affect the contents of registers in obvious ways: Type 1_j adds a_j to the right end of the word in register Y. Type 2 deletes the leftmost letter of the word in Y, if there is one. Type 3 changes the word in Y to λ. Type 4 copies the word in Z into Y and leaves Z unchanged.

Types 5 and 6 are jump instructions. Normally instructions are executed in the order in which they are written. When a **jmp** Nia is executed, the next instruction to be executed is the closest instruction above bearing the line name Ni; **jmp** Nib goes to the closest instruction below bearing line name Ni. Several different instructions in a program may have the same line name. Type 6_j are conditional jumps that are performed only if the first letter of the word in Y is a_j. Type 7 are "no-ops" instructions. Table 2.1 summarizes the actions of some of these instructions.

A RAM *program* is a finite sequence of instructions such that each jump has a place to go and such that the last line is a **continue**. A program *halts* if and when it reaches the final **continue** instruction.

A program P *computes* the partial function ϕ if when the initial contents of registers $R1, R2, \ldots, Rn$ are $w_1, w_2, \ldots, w_n$, respectively, and the initial contents of all other registers named in P are λ, then

1. P eventually halts if and only if $\phi(w_1, \ldots, w_n) \downarrow$, and
2. If and when P halts, the final contents of $R1$ are $\phi(w_1, \ldots, w_n)$.

Every RAM program P and $n \geq 1$ determines the partial function ϕ_P^n of n arguments such that P halts with $\phi_M^n(w_1, \ldots, w_n)$ as the final contents of $R1$ if and

Table 2.1 Summary of
RAM instructions

1	**add**$_j$ $R1$	
	before	*boy*
	after	*boya*$_j$
2	**del** $R1$	
	before	*boy*
	after	*oy*
3	**clr** $R1$	
	before	*boy*
	after	λ
4	$R2 \leftarrow R1$	
	$R1$ before	*dog*
	$R2$ before	*cat*
	$R1$ after	*dog*
	$R2$ after	*dog*

only if P halts after being run on inputs $w_1, \ldots, w_n$ initially in $R1, \ldots, Rn$, with the rest of the registers empty.

A partial function ϕ is RAM-*computable* if some RAM program computes it.

Homework 2.4 *Assume that h and g are RAM-computable. Define f as follows, where $a \in \Sigma$, $y \in \Sigma^*$, and $z \in \Sigma^*$:*

$$f(\lambda, z) = g(z);$$
$$f(ya, z) = h(y, a, f(y, z), z).$$

Then f is said to be defined by recursion *from h and g. Show that f is RAM-computable.*

We defined RAM programs with a rich instruction set in order to make programming relatively easy and to demonstrate the naturalness of this model.

Two RAM programs are *equivalent* if they compute the same partial function.

Theorem 2.4. *Every RAM program can be effectively transformed into an equivalent one that uses only instructions of types 1, 2, 6, and 7.*

We will show how to replace type 4 instructions and leave the remaining steps as a homework exercise.

Replace each instruction of the form

$$X \quad Y \leftarrow Y$$

by

$$X \quad \textbf{continue}.$$

Replace an instruction of the form

$$X \quad Rf \leftarrow Rg,$$

where f is different from g by the following code of Machtey and Young [MY78]:

Let Rm be a register that is not named in the original program and let $Nh, Ni, Nj_1, \ldots, Nj_k$ be line names that are not used in the original program.

X	**clr**	Rf	
	clr	Rm	
	jmp	Nib	
Nh	**del**	Rg	
Ni	Rg **jmp$_1$**	$Nj_1 b$	[copy Rg into Rm]
	$\cdots$		
	Rg **jmp$_k$**	$Nj_k b$	
	jmp	Nib	
Nj_1	**add$_1$**	Rm	
	jmp	Nha	
	$\cdots$		
Nj_k	**add$_k$**	Rm	
	jmp	Nha	
Nh	**del**	Rm	
Ni	Rm **jmp$_1$**	$Nj_1 b$	[copy Rm into Rf and Rg]
	$\cdots$		
	Rm **jmp$_k$**	$Nj_k b$	
	jmp	Nib	
Nj_1	**add$_1$**	Rf	
	add$_1$	Rg	
	jmp	Nha	
	$\cdots$		
Nj_k	**add$_k$**	Rf	
	add$_k$	Rg	
	jmp	Nha	
Ni	**continue**		

Homework 2.5 *Complete the proof by showing how to replace type 3 and 5 instructions.*

Homework 2.6 *Show that type 1, 2, 6, and 7 instructions form a minimal set of instructions for the RAM by showing that if we eliminate any one of these types of instructions, then we will no longer have programs for computing all of the RAM-computable functions.*

Observe carefully how many instructions are used to replace instructions of types 3, 4, and 5. That is, observe that a RAM with the minimal instruction set executes at most a polynomial number of additional instructions than the RAM with the full instruction set.

2.5.1   Turing Machines for RAMS

Here we will show that every RAM program can be simulated by a Turing machine. (It is true also that every Turing machine can be simulated by a RAM program, but as it is the generality of Turing machines that we are seeking evidence of, we will not include the proof in this direction.)

Theorem 2.5. *Every RAM-computable function is Turing-machine-computable. In particular, there is an effective procedure[3] that given a RAM program outputs a Turing machine that computes the same partial function.*

Proof. Let P be a RAM program that uses only the registers $R1, \ldots, Rm$. We design an m-tape Turing machine M that simulates P. Let $r1, \ldots, rm$ denote the contents of the registers $R1, \ldots, Rm$, respectively. If the input registers are $R1, \ldots, Rt$ with $R(t+1), \ldots, Rm$ empty, for some $1 \leq t \leq m$, then the input to M is $r1Br2B \ldots Brt$. M begins with an initialization phase that writes ri on tape i, for each $1 \leq i \leq t$, leaves tapes $t+1, \ldots, m$ empty, and then erases $r2, \ldots, rm$ on tape 1 so that only $r1$ remains.

By Theorem 2.4, we need to show how to simulate instructions 1, 2, 6, and 7. If P consists of n instructions, then M will consist of n simulating blocks of instructions. Each block begins with a unique state. M uses these unique states to connect the blocks for the same flow of control as the instructions of P. Except for jump instructions, the last instruction of each block moves M into the state that begins the next block.

To simulate instruction 1, an instruction of the form **add**$_j$ Rq, M writes the symbol a_j to the right end of rq on tape q. M simulates instruction 2, of the form **del** Rq, by shifting the symbol in the second cell of tape q one cell to the left, then the symbol in the third cell one cell to the left, and so on, until it has shifted the last symbol of rq to the left and replaced the contents of the cell that contained rq with the blank symbol B.

To simulate a type 6 instruction, of the form Rq **jmp**$_j$, if the first symbol on tape q is a_j, then M moves to the state that begins the block to which the jump instruction refers; otherwise, it moves to the next block. Finally, M simulates the final **continue** statement by entering its accepting state and halting.

It should be clear that M is equivalent to P. Furthermore, the proof provides instructions for constructing M from P, which proves the second claim as well.   □

---

[3]As all students are familiar with compilers, you are familiar with programs that take a program written in one programming language as its input and outputs an equivalent program in another programming language.

Chapter 3
Undecidability

3.1 Decision Problems

A *decision problem* is a general question to be answered, usually possessing
several parameters, or free variables, whose values are left unspecified. An *instance*
of a problem is obtained by specifying particular values for all of the problem
parameters.

Example 3.1. The Hamiltonian Circuit problem.

HAMILTONIAN CIRCUIT
> **instance** A graph $G = (V, E)$.
> **question** Does G contain a Hamiltonian circuit?

A "problem" is not the same as a "question." For example, "Does the graph in
Fig. 1.1 have a Hamiltonian circuit?" is a question. It refers to a specific instance.

A *solution* to a decision problem is an algorithm that answers the question that
results from each instance. A decision problem is *decidable* if a solution exists and
is *undecidable* otherwise.

We will be concerned with the question of whether certain decision problems are
decidable. For those that are, in general, computer science is concerned with finding
efficient solutions. Later in the course we will address the question of whether
certain decidable decision problems have efficient solutions.

According to Church's thesis, every computational device can be simulated by
some Turing machine that solves the problem. To show that a decision problem
is undecidable, we take the point of view that it suffices to show that no Turing
machine solves the problem. Conversely, to show that a Turing machine exists to
solve a decision problem, it suffices to present an informal algorithm. It should take
you no effort to find an algorithm that solves the Hamiltonian Circuit problem in
Example 3.1, but one of the central open questions that drives research in complexity
theory is the question of whether the Hamiltonian Circuit, and hundreds of similar
decision problems, has an efficient solution.

S. Homer and A.L. Selman, *Computability and Complexity Theory*,
Texts in Computer Science, DOI 10.1007/978-1-4614-0682-2_3,
© Springer Science+Business Media, LLC 2011

Recalling that input to a Turing machine must be presented as a word over a finite alphabet, we must address our first technical issue of *encodings*. For example, in order for a Turing machine to solve a decision problem about graphs, graphs must be encoded as words over some finite alphabet. If we cared only about whether or not decision problems are decidable, then this would be enough. However, since we will be concerned also with the question of whether decision problems are feasible, meaning that they have an efficient solution, then we must insist that encodings are *reasonable*. Encodings must be reasonable in the sense that the length of the word that represents the graph must be no more than a polynomial in the length of whatever is considered to be a natural presentation of a graph.

Reasonable encodings should be concise and not "padded" with unnecessary information or symbols. For example, numbers should be represented in 2-adic, binary, or any other concise representation, but should not be represented in unary. If we restrict ourselves to encoding schemes with these properties, then the particular choice of representation will not affect whether a given decision problem has a feasible solution. For example, the natural presentation of a graph $G = (V, E)$ may be either by a vertex list, edge list, or an adjacency matrix. For our purpose either is acceptable. Once such a decision is made, it is straightforward to encode the natural presentation as a word over a finite alphabet. Now let us do this. We will show how to represent a graph as a string over the finite alphabet $\{1, 2, \ldots, [,], (,)\}$. Suppose that $V = \{1, \ldots, k\}$ and E consists of pairs of the form (e_1, e_2). Then:

1. Denote each integer by its 2-adic representation. Let $C_2(i)$ denote the 2-adic representation of the number i;
2. For each i, $i = 1, \ldots, k$, let $[C_2(i)]$ represent the vertex i;
3. In general, if $x_1, \ldots, x_n$ represent the objects $X_1, \ldots, X_n$, let $(x_1, \ldots, x_n)$ represent the object $(X_1, \ldots, X_n)$. Thus, in particular, the string $([C_2(e_1)], [C_2(e_2)])$ represents the edge (e_1, e_2).

In this manner, every graph is representable as a string. Any other data structure can be encoded in a similar manner.

3.2 Undecidable Problems

In this chapter we will assume that all Turing machines compute partial computable functions. Thus, a Turing machine halts on an input word if and only if it accepts the input word, so we no longer need to distinguish halting from accepting. The characteristic function of a set S is the function f_S defined by $f_S(x) = 0$ if $x \in S$, and $f_S(x) = 1$ if $x \notin S$. By the following easy-to-prove Proposition, restricting to Turing machines that compute partial functions does not limit our ability to decide languages.

Proposition 3.1. *A set S is decidable if and only if its characteristic function is computable.*

Now we turn our attention to the existence of undecidable problems. We will show that a number of decision problems about Turing machines themselves are undecidable. For example, we will see that the following Program Termination problem for Turing machines is undecidable.

Example 3.2. The Program Termination problem for Turing machines

PROGRAM TERMINATION
    instance A Turing machine M
    question Does M eventually halt on every input?

First we must encode Turing machines as words so that Turing machines can be presented as input strings to other Turing machines. This is straightforward using the efficient encoding method that we gave in the last section. Let us note just a few of the details. Suppose we want to encode Turing machine

$$M = \langle Q, \Sigma, \Gamma, \delta, q_0, B, q_{\text{accept}} \rangle.$$

Assume that $Q = \{q_0, q_1, \ldots, q_{k-1}\}$. Represent the state q_i by $c(q_i) = [C_2(i)]$, and represent the set of states Q by the string $\{c(q_0), c(q_1), \ldots,\}$. Similarly, represent Σ and Γ as strings. Write a move $\delta(q_i, a_j) = (q_k, a_l, D)$, where $D = 1$, for a shift left, and $D = 2$, for a shift right, as a five-tuple (q_i, a_j, q_k, a_l, D). Then, of course, we represent the five-tuple by the string

$$(c(q_i), c(a_j), c(q_k), c(a_l), D).$$

Then δ is a sequence of such five-tuples, so we can represent the sequence as a string as well. Finally, represent the entire seven-tuple that defines M as a string.

Observe that the current representation of a Turing machine M is a word w over the language $\{1, 2, ,, \{, \}, [,], (,)\}$ consisting of nine symbols. We will make one more refinement. Identify this alphabet with the symbols $\{1, \ldots, 9\}$. Then, for each word w over the alphabet $\{1, \ldots, 9\}$, let $T(w) = C_2(N_9(w))$. (Recall that $N_9(w)$ is the natural number n whose 9-adic representation is w, and that $C_2(n)$ is the 2-adic representation of n.) $T(w)$ is the result of inputting w to an algorithm that converts 9-adic notation to 2-adic notation, and $T(w)$ is a word over the two-letter alphabet $\{1, 2\}$. For a Turing machine M, where w is the representation of M as a word over the nine-letter alphabet, we call the word $T(w)$ the *encoding* of M.

For each Turing machine M, w_M will denote the word that encodes M. We will say that a problem about Turing machines is *decidable* if the set of words corresponding to Turing machines that satisfy the problem is decidable. Thus, the Program Termination decision problem, stated in Example 3.2, is decidable if and only if $\{w_M \mid M \text{ halts on every input}\}$ is a decidable set. Given M one can effectively find w_M; conversely, given a word w one can effectively determine whether $w = w_M$ for any M and if so, then effectively find M.

Since every word is a number and vice versa, we may think of a Turing-machine code as a number. The code for a Turing machine M is called the *Gödel number* of M. If e is a Gödel number, then M_e is the Turing machine whose Gödel number is e.

Let U be a Turing machine that computes on input e and x and that implements the following algorithm:

if e is a code
    then simulate M_e on input x
    else output 0.

(Why are you convinced that a Turing machine with this behavior exists?) U is a *universal* Turing machine. To put it differently, U is a general-purpose, stored-program computer: U accepts as input two values: a "stored program" e, and "input to e," a word x. If e is the correct code of a program M_e, then U computes the value of M_e on input x.

Early computers had their programs hard-wired into them. Several years after Turing's 1936 paper, von Neumann and co-workers built the first computer that stored instructions internally in the same manner as data. Von Neumann knew Turing's work, and it is believed that von Neumann was influenced by Turing's universal machine. Turing's machine U is the first conceptual general-purpose, stored-program computer.

For every natural number e, define

$$\phi_e = \lambda x.\, U(e,x).^1$$

If e is a Gödel number, then ϕ_e is the partial function of one argument that is computed by M_e. If e is not the code of any Turing machine, then by the definition of U, $\phi_e(x) = 0$ for all x.

Let's use the Program Termination problem to illustrate all of this new notation: The Program Termination problem is decidable if and only if

$$\{w_M \mid M \text{ halts on every input}\} = \{e \mid e \text{ is a Gödel number and } \phi_e$$

$$\text{halts on every input}\}$$

is decidable, which holds if and only if

$$\{e \mid \phi_e \text{ is total computable}\} = \{e \mid L(M_e) = \Sigma^*\}$$

is decidable. Note that there is an algorithm to determine whether a natural number e is a Gödel number; in case it is not, then, by definition, ϕ_e is total.

---

[1]This denotes the function of one variable that one obtains by holding the value of e fixed and letting x vary. Lambda-notation is familiar, for example, to students who have studied the programming language Lisp.

Observe that every partial computable function of one argument is ϕ_e for some e, and conversely, every ϕ_e is a partial computable function. Thus, $\{\phi_e\}_{e \geq 0}$ is an *effective enumeration* of the set of all partial computable functions.

Now comes our first undecidability result. We will show that the Program Termination problem is undecidable.

Theorem 3.1. *The Program Termination problem (Example 3.2) is undecidable. There is no algorithm to determine whether an arbitrary partial computable function is total. Thus, there is no algorithm to determine whether a Turing machine halts on every input.*

We need to show that no such algorithm exists. We use the diagonalization technique that we introduced in Chap. 1 in order to show that every proposed algorithm must fail on some input.

Proof. Suppose there is an algorithm TEST such that, for every i,

$$\text{TEST}(i) = \text{"yes" if } \phi_i \text{ halts on every input value, and}$$

$$\text{TEST}(i) = \text{"no" otherwise.}$$

Define a function δ by

$$\delta(k) = \phi_k(k) + 1 \text{ if TEST}(k) = \text{"yes" and}$$

$$\delta(k) = 0 \text{ if TEST}(k) = \text{"no."}$$

By definition, δ is defined on every input and δ is computable, so δ is a total computable function. Let e be the Gödel number of a Turing machine that computes δ. Thus, $\delta = \phi_e$ and $\text{TEST}(e) = \text{"yes."}$ However, in this case, $\delta(e) = \phi_e(e) + 1$, which contradicts the assertion that $\delta = \phi_e$. Thus, the initial supposition must be false. $\qquad\square$

3.3 Pairing Functions

Before continuing with our discussion of undecidability, we digress here to introduce an encoding of ordered pairs of natural numbers and of k-tuples of natural numbers that will remain fixed and that we will use for the remainder of this book.

Definition 3.1. A *pairing function* is a computable one-to-one mapping

$$< , >: N \times N \to N.$$

whose inverses

$$\tau_1(< x, y >) = x \text{ and } \tau_2(< x, y >) = y,$$

are computable also.

Fig. 3.1 Enumeration of
ordered pairs

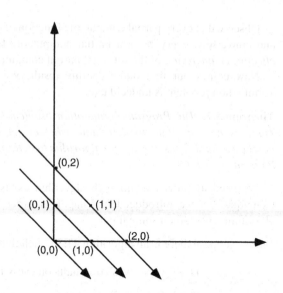

Observe that for every z,

$$< \tau_1(z), \tau_2(z) >= z.$$

We claim that the function $< \ , \ >$ defined by

$$<x,y>= \frac{1}{2}\left(x^2 + 2xy + y^2 + 3x + y\right)$$

is a pairing function. Clearly, $< \ , \ >$ is computable. We claim that $< \ , \ >$ maps $N \times N$ one-to-one and onto N by the correspondence that lists ordered pairs in the order

$$< 0,0 >, < 0,1 >, < 1,0 >, < 0,2 >, < 1,1 >, < 2,0 >, < 0,3 >, < 1,2 >, \dots$$

as given in Fig. 3.1.

Homework 3.1 *Use the fact that $x+y=k$ is the equation of the kth line in Fig. 3.1, together with the identity*

$$1+2+\cdots+k = \frac{1}{2}k(k+1),$$

to verify that $< \ , \ >$ gives this correspondence.

It follows immediately that $< \ , \ >$ is one-to-one and onto.

Homework 3.2 *Show how to compute τ_1 and τ_2.*

We can use this pairing function to define tuples of any size: Inductively define

$$< x > = x$$

$$< x_1, \ldots, x_{n+1} > = << x_1, \ldots, x_n >, x_{n+1} >.$$

Let $\tau_k(x_1, \ldots, x_k)$ denote the computable function that outputs $< x_1, \ldots, x_k >$, and let the inverses be $\tau_{k1}, \ldots, \tau_{kk}$, so that $\tau_{ki}(< x_1, \ldots, x_k >) = x_i$ for all $i = 1 \ldots k$.

3.4 Computably Enumerable Sets

Recall that a nonempty set S is enumerable if some function f maps N onto S, in which case we say that f enumerates S. Indeed, $S = \{f(0), f(1), \ldots, \}$.

Definition 3.2. A set S is *computably enumerable (c.e.)* if $S = \emptyset$ or $S = range(f)$, for some total computable function f.

A collection of Turing machines is *effectively* enumerable if the corresponding set of Gödel numbers is c.e., so, in particular, the set of all Turing machines is effectively enumerable.

Let $\mathscr{C}$ be any set of partial computable functions. Let $P_\mathscr{C} = \{e \mid \phi_e \in \mathscr{C}\}$ be the set of all programs that compute partial functions belonging to $\mathscr{C}$. $P_\mathscr{C}$ is called an *index* set.

Example 3.3. Let $\mathscr{C}$ be the set of all total computable functions. Then

$$P_\mathscr{C} = \{e \mid \phi_e \text{ is total computable}\}.$$

A set of partial computable functions is decidable (effectively enumerable) if its index set is decidable (c.e.). So the set of all partial computable functions $\{\phi_0, \phi_1, \ldots\}$ is effectively enumerable. A subtlety: Every partial computable function has infinitely many programs. (Think about why this is true.) Hence, if an index set is nonempty, then it must be infinite.

Homework 3.3 *(i)   Use Theorem 3.1 directly to show that the following problem is undecidable: Given two Turing machines M and N, determine whether they are equivalent. That is, show that the set*

$$\{(e, j) \mid L(M_e) = L(M_j)\}$$

is not decidable.

(ii)   Use the result of part (i) to show that the function that maps a program e to its smallest equivalent program is not computable.

The next theorem shows that the Program Termination problem is not computably enumerable.

Theorem 3.2. $\{e \mid \phi_e$ *is total computable*$\}$ *is not computably enumerable.*

Proof. Let $S = \{e \mid \phi_e$ is total computable$\}$, and suppose that S is c.e. As $S \neq \emptyset$, there is a total computable function g such that $range(g) = S$. Next, we can use g in order to define a "universal function U_S for S." For all e and all x, define $U_S(e,x) = \phi_{g(e)}(x)$. U_S is a total computable function: To compute $U_S(e,x)$, first compute $g(e) = k$, and then compute $\phi_k(x) = y$. Note that both $g(e)$ and $\phi_k(x)$ must converge.

Now define $h(x) = U_S(x,x) + 1$ for all x. So h is a total computable function. Thus, there is a program $k \in S$ so that $h = \phi_k$ and for some e, $k = g(e)$. Finally,

$$\phi_k(e) = h(e)$$
$$= U_S(e,e) + 1$$
$$= \phi_{g(e)}(e) + 1$$
$$= \phi_k(e) + 1,$$

which is impossible. Thus, the original supposition that S is computably enumerable is false. □

Now we will prove several useful properties and characterizations of the computably enumerable sets. After doing so, we will easily and quickly derive several more undecidable problems. (We could do so now, but developing some tools first will make things easier later.)

Lemma 3.1. *The graph of a total computable function is decidable.*

The proof is easy. Let f be a total computable function. Let

$$G = \{(x,y) \mid f(x) = y\}.$$

Design a Turing machine that on input (x,y), computes $f(x)$ and then if $f(x) = y$ accepts and otherwise rejects.

Theorem 3.3. *A set S is computably enumerable if and only if there is a decidable relation $R(x,y)$ such that*

$$x \in S \Leftrightarrow \exists y R(x,y). \tag{3.1}$$

Proof. If $S = \emptyset$, then

$$x \in S \Leftrightarrow \exists y[x = x \wedge y \neq y]$$

and the relation $[x = x \wedge y \neq y]$ is decidable.

If $S \neq \emptyset$ is computably enumerable, then S is the range of a total computable function f. Thus,

$$x \in S \Leftrightarrow \exists y[f(y) = x].$$

By Lemma 3.1, the relation $[f(y) = x]$ is decidable.

Conversely, suppose that there is a decidable relation $R(x,y)$ such that

$$x \in S \Leftrightarrow \exists y R(x,y).$$

If $S = \emptyset$, then S is c.e. by definition. So assume that S is not empty. Let a be a fixed member of S. Now we will use the pairing function that we defined in the last section. Define

$$f(x) = \begin{cases} a & \text{if } R(\tau_1(x), \tau_2(x)) \text{ is false,} \\ \tau_1(x) & \text{if } R(\tau_1(x), \tau_2(x)) \text{ is true.} \end{cases}$$

Then f is a total computable function and clearly, $range(f) \subseteq S$. If $x \in S$, consider a value y such that $R(x,y)$. Then $f(\langle x,y \rangle) = x$. So $S \subseteq range(f)$. $\square$

The next theorem demonstrates that the c.e. sets are none other than the acceptable sets. The two basic concepts, acceptable and computably enumerable, are identical!

Theorem 3.4. *A set S is computably enumerable if and only if it is Turing-machine-acceptable.*

Given a Turing machine M, recall that an accepting computation of M is a sequence of configurations $I_0, I_1, \ldots, I_n$ such that I_0 is an initial configuration, I_n is an accepting configuration, and for each $i < n$, $I_i \vdash_M I_{i+1}$. Thus, a computation is a word over the finite alphabet that defines M.

Proof. Assume that S is Turing-machine-acceptable and let M be a Turing machine that accepts S. Define the relation R_M by

$$R_M(x,y) \Leftrightarrow [x \text{ is an input word to } M \text{ and } y \text{ is an accepting computation of } M \text{ on } x].$$
$$(3.2)$$

It should be clear that R_M is a decidable relation. Moreover,

$$x \in S \Leftrightarrow \exists y R_M(x,y).$$

Thus, by Theorem 3.3, S is computably enumerable.

Conversely, suppose that S is c.e. and let R be a decidable relation such that (3.1) holds. A Turing machine M will accept S in the following manner: M contains a counter y and initializes y to 0. On input x, M writes the pair $(x,y) = (x,0)$ and then determines whether $R(x,y)$ holds. If so, M accepts x. If not, then M increments the value y and repeats the test. Observe that if $x \in S$, then for some value of y, $R(x,y)$ holds. In this case M eventually accepts. (However, if $x \notin S$, then M runs forever.) Thus, M accepts S, and this completes the proof. $\square$

Corollary 3.1. *A set S is decidable if and only if S and $\overline{S}$ are both computably enumerable.*

The corollary follows immediately from Theorem 2.2 and Theorem 3.4. In particular, every decidable set is c.e., so Theorem 3.2 is a more general result than Theorem 3.1.

Corollary 3.2. *A set S is computably enumerable if and only if S is the domain of some partial computable function.*

Proof. Surely, the domain of a partial computable function is Turing-machine-acceptable and, therefore, c.e. Conversely, if S is c.e., then S is the domain of the partial computable function f_S defined by $f_S(x) = 0$ if $x \in S$, and $f_S(x) \uparrow$ otherwise. □

Suppose that S is a c.e. set and R is a decidable relation such that (3.1) holds. Define a total computable function f by

$$f(x,y) = \begin{cases} 0 & \text{if } R(x,y), \\ 1 & \text{otherwise.} \end{cases}$$

Let $g(x) = \min\{y \mid f(x,y) = 0\}$. Then g is a partial computable function with domain S. This is an alternative proof of one direction of Corollary 3.2.

Define $W_e = dom(\phi_e)$. Then, $\{W_e\}_{e \in \mathbb{N}}$ provides us with a standard effective enumeration of the computably enumerable sets.

Every programmer knows that the purpose of sorting a (finite) set S is to make searching efficient. Searching is simply the problem, given a possible element w of S, to determine whether $w \in S$, that is, "searching" is the decision problem for S. The next homework problem is to demonstrate that this phenomenon holds for infinite sets as well.

Homework 3.4 *Prove that an infinite set is decidable if and only if it can be enumerated in increasing order by a one-to-one total computable function.*

Homework 3.5 *Show that if A and B are c.e., then $A \cup B$ and $A \cap B$ are c.e.*

Homework 3.6 *Prove that every infinite c.e. set contains an infinite decidable subset.*

3.5   Halting Problem, Reductions, and Complete Sets

In this section we will learn that the famous Halting problem for Turing machines is undecidable. Along the way, we will build more useful tools.

Example 3.4. The Halting problem for Turing machines

HALTING PROBLEM
>   **instance** A Turing machine M and input word w
>   **question** Does M eventually halt on input w?

We begin by considering the "diagonal" set

$$K = \{x \mid \phi_x(x) \downarrow\} = \{x \mid U(x,x) \downarrow\}.$$

Observe that the function $\lambda x. U(x,x)$ is partial computable. It follows from Corollary 3.2 that K is computably enumerable.

Theorem 3.5. *K is not decidable. In particular, $\overline{K}$ is not c.e.*

Thus, K is an example of a set that is c.e. but not decidable.

Proof. We prove that $\overline{K}$ is not c.e., for the two assertions are equivalent.

Suppose that $\overline{K}$ is c.e., then for some Gödel number e,

$$\overline{K} = W_e = dom(\phi_e).$$

In particular,

$$e \in \overline{K} \Leftrightarrow \phi_e(e) \downarrow$$

$$\Leftrightarrow e \in K.$$

This is a contradiction. Thus, the supposition that $\overline{K}$ is c.e. must be false. □

No diagonalization argument is more fundamental than the one we have just seen. Next we will introduce a tool that plays an important role in both computability theory and complexity theory. This is the notion of reductions. We have seen the idea in an informal way already. In some of your homework problems you showed that certain problems are undecidable by demonstrating that a solution would yield a solution to a problem that you already knew to be undecidable. In other words, you "reduced" one problem to another.

Definition 3.3. A set A is *many-one reducible* to a set B, denoted by $A \leq_m B$, if there is a total computable function such that

$$x \in A \Leftrightarrow f(x) \in B.$$

Lemma 3.2. *1. If $A \leq_m B$ and B is c.e., then A is c.e.*
2. If $A \leq_m B$ and B is decidable, then A is decidable.

Proof. By hypothesis, $x \in A \Leftrightarrow f(x) \in B$ for some total computable function f.

To prove the first assertion, $x \in B \Leftrightarrow \exists y R(x,y)$. So $x \in A \Leftrightarrow \exists y R(f(x),y)$. Finally, $R(f(x),y)$ is a decidable relation. Thus, A is c.e.

To prove the second assertion, the following algorithm determines whether an input word x belongs to A: If $f(x) \in B$, then "accept" else "reject." □

Homework 3.7 *Show that $\leq_m$ is reflexive and transitive.*

Our interest will be primarily in the contrapositive of Lemma 3.2, item 2: Suppose that A is some set that we know is undecidable, for example, A might be the set K, and suppose that B is some set that we want to show is undecidable. If we can demonstrate that $A \leq_m B$, then it follows immediately that B is undecidable. This is the "reduction method" that we will employ.

Now we will use the reduction method to show that the Halting problem is undecidable. Define the set

$$L_U = \{(e, w) \mid M_e \text{ accepts } w\}.$$

Since L_U is the language accepted by the universal Turing machine U, L_U is computably enumerable. We will show that L_U is not decidable. Thus, there is no algorithm that, given an arbitrary Turing machine M and input w, determines whether M will accept w. Thus, the Halting problem for Turing machines is undecidable.

Theorem 3.6. *The Halting problem is undecidable. Specifically, the set L_U is not decidable.*

Proof. Note that

$$x \in K \Leftrightarrow (x, x) \in L_U.$$

The mapping $x \mapsto (x, x)$ is total computable. So $K \leq_m L_U$, from which it follows that L_U is not decidable.   □

3.5.1 Complete Problems

Let A be any c.e. set whatsoever. For some e, $A = W_e$. Recall that

$$x \in W_e \Leftrightarrow (e, x) \in L_U.$$

Since the mapping $x \mapsto (e, x)$ is total computable, $A \leq_m L_U$.

Thus, L_U is c.e., and every c.e. set many-one reduces to L_U. This observation leads to the following definition.

Definition 3.4. A language L is *many-one complete* for the computably enumerable sets if

1. L is computably enumerable, and
2. For every c.e. set A, $A \leq_m L$.

Thus, L_U is a many-one complete set.

Homework 3.8 *Show that K is a many-one complete set. Note that it suffices to show that $L_U \leq_m K$. This is not an easy problem. (Do not use the s-m-n theorem.)*

The question of whether there exist c.e. sets that are neither decidable nor complete was posed by Post [Pos44] in 1944. This problem has since become known as Post's problem. It was solved independently by Friedberg and Muchnik in 1956. The proof, known as a priority argument, is beyond the scope of this text.

3.5.1.1   Summary

At this point we know that the decidable sets are a proper subclass of the set of all c.e. sets. K and L_U are examples of c.e. sets that are not decidable; they are many-one complete. The sets $\overline{K}$ and $\{e \mid L(M_e) = \Sigma^*\}$ are not even c.e.

3.6   *S-m-n* Theorem

Suppose that you have program e, that is, a Turing machine M_e, to compute the product of two natural numbers x and y. Namely, $M(x,y) = x * y$. Obviously, you could modify this program to obtain one to compute $2 * y$. The new Turing machine will store the value 2 in its finite control. On input y, the new machine will shift y to the right, write $2By$ on its input tape, and then proceed to simulate M. In this manner, knowing a program e to perform multiplication, for any constant value x, you can *compute* a new program $f(e,x)$ that for each value y computes the function $\lambda y.\ (x * y)$. In symbols, there is a total computable function f so that for every x and y,

$$\phi_{f(e,x)}(y) = \phi_e(x,y).$$

In general, any program that computes a function of some $m + n$ variables can easily be modified to hold m of the variables fixed. Furthermore, the modification can be obtained effectively. This is the gist of the *s-m-n* theorem.

Theorem 3.7. *For every $m,n \geq 1$, there is a total computable function $s_n^m : \mathbb{N}^{m+1} \to \mathbb{N}$ such that for all values $e, x_1, \ldots, x_m, x_{m+1}, \ldots, x_{m+n}$,*

$$\phi_{s_n^m(e,x_1,\ldots,x_m)}(x_{m+1},\ldots,x_{m+n}) = \phi_e(x_1,\ldots,x_m,x_{m+1},\ldots,x_{m+n}).$$

Taking $m = n = 1$, the theorem states that

$$\phi_{s_1^1(e,x)}(y) = \phi_e(x,y).$$

Corollary 3.3. *For every partial computable function $\lambda e,x.\ \psi(e,x)$, there is a total computable function f so that*

$$\phi_{f(e)}(x) = \psi(e,x).$$

First we give the proof of the Corollary.

Proof. For some Gödel number i, $\psi = \phi_i$. So

$$\psi(e,x) = \phi_i(e,x)$$
$$= \phi_{s_1^1(i,e)}(x).$$

Define $f = \lambda e.\, s_1^1(i,e)$.   □

Now we present the proof of Theorem 3.7 for the case $m = n = 1$.

Proof. Given a natural number i, let $[i]$ denote the 2-adic representation of i. For each e and x, let $S(e,x)$ be a Turing machine that, given an input value y, performs the following actions:

1. Computes the pair $< x,y >$ (i.e., writes $[< x,y >]$ on the otherwise empty tape);
2. Writes $[e]B[< x,y >]B$ on the otherwise empty tape;
3. Behaves like the universal machine U on the current tape (i.e., computes $\phi_e(x,y)$).

Let $s_1^1(e,x,)$ be the Gödel number of $S(e,x)$. So, for each number e and x, $s_1^1(e,x,)$ is the Gödel number of a program that, for each y, computes $\phi_e(x,y)$.

We need to show that the mapping

$$e,x \mapsto s_1^1(e,x)$$

is total computable.

We could (and probably should) construct a Turing machine that implements the mapping. As usual, though, we will take the easier route, sketch the procedure, and yield to Church's thesis[2]: There is an effective procedure that, given e and x, produces the Turing machine program $S(e,x)$. Second, there is an effective procedure that, given any Turing machine, produces its Gödel number. Thus (here is where we use Church's thesis) there is a total computable function that, given e and x, has value $s_1^1(e,x)$.   □

Our first application of the *s-m-n* theorem formalizes the comment we just made. We demonstrate that there is a compiler that translates programs from any "acceptable" programming system into a Turing-machine program. To this end, we present the following definitions. A *programming system* is an effectively enumerable listing $\psi_0, \psi_1, \ldots$ that includes *all* of the partial computable functions of one argument. A programming system is *universal* if the partial function ψ_{univ} such that $\psi_{\text{univ}}(i,x) = \psi_i(x)$, for all i and x, is itself a partial computable function. (In this case, there is a program k that computes the partial computable function

---

[2]Church's thesis, remember, is a statement of philosophical belief and so should not be cited as part of the proof of the theorem. For this reason, let us clarify our position. We are not yielding to Church's thesis as much as we are to our reader's ability as trained programmers. We take it for granted that if we understand a procedure, then we can program a Turing machine to implement the procedure.

$\psi'(\langle i,x\rangle) = \psi_{\text{univ}}(i,x)$; i.e., $\psi_k(\langle i,x\rangle) = \psi_i(x)$ for all i and x.) A programming system is *acceptable* if it is universal and it satisfies the *s-m-n* theorem.

Theorem 3.8. *Let* $\phi_0, \phi_1, \ldots$ *and* $\psi_0, \psi_1, \ldots$ *be any two acceptable programming systems. There is a total computable function* t *that translates the system* $\psi_0, \psi_1, \ldots$ *into the system* $\phi_0, \phi_1, \ldots,$ *that is,* $\psi_i = \phi_{t(i)}$ *for all* i.

Proof. Let ψ_{univ} be a universal partial computable function for the system ψ_0, $\psi_1, \ldots$. Let $\psi'(\langle i,x\rangle) = \psi_{\text{univ}}(i,x)$ for all i and x. Since the system $\phi_0, \phi_1, \ldots$ contains all partial computable functions of one variable, there is a program k such that $\psi' = \phi_k$. Then, by Theorem 3.7,

$$\phi_{s_1^1(k,i)}(x) = \phi_k(\langle i,x\rangle)$$

$$= \psi'(\langle i,x\rangle)$$

$$= \psi_{\text{univ}}(i,x)$$

$$= \psi_i(x)$$

for all i and x. We complete the proof by defining $t(i) = s_1^1(k,i)$ for all i. □

The following is a typical application of the *s-m-n* theorem.

Theorem 3.9. *There is a total computable function* f *such that*

$$\text{range } \phi_{f(e)} = \text{dom } \phi_e.$$

Proof. We want a partial computable function ψ of two variables such that

$$\psi(e,x) = \begin{cases} x & \text{if } x \in \text{dom } \phi_e, \\ \uparrow & \text{otherwise,} \end{cases}$$

for then, for each e, $\text{range}[\lambda x.\ \psi(e,x)] = \text{dom } \phi_e$. To see that ψ exists, define a Turing machine on input e and x to simulate the universal Turing machine and to output x if it eventually halts.

By Corollary 3.3, there is a total computable function f such that $\phi_{f(e)}(x) = \psi(e,x)$. Thus, $\text{range } \phi_{f(e)} = \text{dom } \phi_e$. □

Homework 3.9 *Prove that there is a total computable function* g *such that*

$$\text{dom } \phi_{g(e)} = \text{range } \phi_e.$$

The definition of computably enumerable sets states that a nonempty set S is computably enumerable if and only if S is the range of a *total* computable function. However, we learn as a corollary to Homework 3.9 that a set is computably enumerable even if it is the range of a partial computable function.

Corollary 3.4. *A set S is computably enumerable if and only if S is the range of some partial computable function.*

Proof. If $S = \emptyset$, then S is the range of the empty function, which is computed by a Turing machine that on arbitrary input runs forever. If S is nonempty, then the definition applies directly.

We need to prove that if S is the range of some partial computable function, then S is c.e. Suppose that $S = range\ \phi_e$. Then, by Homework 3.9, $S = dom\ \phi_{g(e)}$. By Corollary 3.2, S is c.e. $\square$

3.7   Recursion Theorem

The *recursion theorem* is a deep and powerful result with several important applications. In this section we will content ourselves with studying only one version of this result and only a limited number of applications. Other forms of the recursion theorem justify the use of recursion in programming by guaranteeing appropriate solutions to recursive procedures. These will appear in a later section.

Theorem 3.10. *For every total computable function f there is a number n such that*

$$\phi_n = \phi_{f(n)}.$$

A number n with this property is called a *fixed point* of f.

Proof. We define the function $\theta(e,x) = U(U(e,e),x)$. Observe that

$$\theta(e,x) = \phi_{\phi_e(e)}(x),$$

if $\phi_e(e)$ is defined. By our standard corollary of the *s-m-n* theorem, Corollary 3.3, there is a total computable function g such that

$$\phi_{g(e)}(x) = \theta(e,x).$$

Let f be any total computable function. The composition $f \circ g$ is total computable. Thus, there is a program k such that for all e,

$$\phi_k(e) = f(g(e)).$$

Thus, for all e,

$$\phi_{f(g(e))} = \phi_{\phi_k(e)}.$$

Set $e = k$ so that for all x,

$$\phi_{f(g(k))}(x) = \phi_{\phi_k(k)}(x)$$
$$= \theta(k,x)$$
$$= \phi_{g(k)}(x).$$

We conclude that $\phi_{f(g(k))} = \phi_{g(k)}$. Let $n = g(k)$. It follows that

$$\phi_{f(n)} = \phi_n.$$

$\square$

With regard to this proof, observe that $\phi_e(e)$ cannot be defined for all values of e. Since $\phi_e(e)$ is a partial computable function, so is the function $\phi_e(e)+1$. Thus, some program i computes this function, that is,

$$\phi_i(e) = \phi_e(e)+1.$$

It follows immediately that $\phi_i(i)$ is not defined.

Corollary 3.5. *There is a number (i.e., program) n such that ϕ_n is the constant function with output n.*

Hence, n is a "self-reproducing" program – the Turing machine whose code is n does nothing on any input value other than print its own code.

Proof. Consider the total computable function ψ defined by $\psi(e,x) = e$, for all e and x. By Corollary 3.3, there is a total computable function f such $\phi_{f(e)}(x) = \psi(e,x)$.

By Theorem 3.10, let n be a fixed point of f. Then, for all x,

$$\phi_n(x) = \phi_{f(n)}(x)$$
$$= \psi(n,x)$$
$$= n.$$

$\square$

Homework 3.10 *Write a program in Lisp that prints itself and nothing else.*

Corollary 3.6. *For every total computable function f, there exists n such that*

$$W_n = W_{f(n)}.$$

As an application, we can see that there is a program n such that $W_n = \{n\}$. To see this, first define a partial computable function ψ such that for all e, $\psi(e,e) = e$ and $\psi(e,x)$ is undefined for all other values of x. Now, use Corollary 3.3 to obtain a total computable function f such that $\phi_{f(e)}(x) = \psi(e,x)$. Then, $dom \, \phi_{f(e)} = \{e\}$ for all e. So $W_{f(e)} = \{e\}$. Thus, by Corollary 3.6, there exists n such that

$$W_n = W_{f(n)} = \{n\}.$$

We are seeing that programs can be self-referencing.

Theorem 3.11. *For every partial computable function $\psi(e,x)$, there is a value e_0 such that*
$$\psi(e_0,x) = \phi_{e_0}(x).$$

For example, there is a program e_0 such that $\phi_{e_0}(x) = e_0 * x$.

Proof. Given ψ, obtain as usual, using Corollary 3.3, a total computable function f such that $\psi(e,x) = \phi_{f(e)}(x)$. Then, by Theorem 3.10, there exists e_0 such that $\phi_{f(e_0)} = \phi_{e_0}$. So, for all x,

$$\phi_{e_0}(x) = \phi_{f(e_0)}(x) = \psi(e_0,x).$$

$\square$

Observe that there is a standard pattern to the proof of these results. First, we use the *s-m-n* theorem or its corollary to obtain a total computable function f with whatever property we find useful. Then, we use the recursion theorem or its corollary to select a fixed point of f.

Homework 3.11 *Show that there is no algorithm that given as input a Turing machine M, where M defines a partial function of one variable, outputs a Turing machine M' such that M' defines a different partial function of one variable.*

Homework 3.12 *Show that there is a program e such that $W_e = \{e^2\}$.*

3.8   Rice's Theorem

Recall that the set of all Gödel numbers of some collection of partial computable functions is called an *index set*. That is, if $\mathscr{C}$ is any set of partial computable functions, then the set $P_{\mathscr{C}} = \{e \mid \phi_e \in \mathscr{C}\}$ is an index set. Here we will learn that *every* nontrivial index set is undecidable. This remarkable theorem tells us that undecidability is not an exception – it is the rule.

Theorem 3.12. *An index set $P_{\mathscr{C}}$ is decidable if and only if $P_{\mathscr{C}} = \emptyset$ or $P_{\mathscr{C}} = N$.*

Proof. If $P_{\mathscr{C}} = \emptyset$ or $P_{\mathscr{C}} = N$, then, of course, $P_{\mathscr{C}}$ is decidable. We need to prove the converse.

Suppose that $P_{\mathscr{C}} \neq \emptyset$ and $P_{\mathscr{C}} \neq N$. Let $j \in P_{\mathscr{C}}$ and $k \in \overline{P_{\mathscr{C}}}$. Define the function f by

$$f(x) = \begin{cases} k & \text{if } x \in P_{\mathscr{C}}, \\ j & \text{if } x \notin P_{\mathscr{C}}. \end{cases}$$

Suppose that $P_{\mathscr{C}}$ is decidable. Then f is a total computable function. Thus, by Theorem 3.10, the recursion theorem, f has a fixed point. That is, there is a number n such that $\phi_n = \phi_{f(n)}$. Since n and $f(n)$ are programs for the same partial computable function, either they both belong to $P_{\mathscr{C}}$ or they both belong to $\overline{P_{\mathscr{C}}}$. However, this is impossible because we defined f so that for all x, $x \in P_{\mathscr{C}} \Leftrightarrow f(x) \notin P_{\mathscr{C}}$. Thus, the supposition that $P_{\mathscr{C}}$ is decidable is false. $\qquad\square$

Recall that a set S is computably enumerable if $S = \emptyset$ or $S = range(f)$, for some total computable function f. Given a collection $\mathscr{C}$ of computably enumerable sets, the corresponding index set is the set $P_{\mathscr{C}} = \{e \mid range(\phi_e) \in \mathscr{C}\}$, and $\mathscr{C}$ is decidable if and only if $P_{\mathscr{C}}$ is decidable.

Corollary 3.7. *The following properties of computably enumerable sets are not decidable:*

1. *Emptiness;*
2. *Finiteness;*
3. *Regularity;*
4. *Context-freedom.*

Proof. We will give details for item 1. For the other items, we will just indicate the set $\mathscr{C}$, from which we can easily note that there exist sets that have the specified property and there exist sets that do not have the specified property.

1. In this case, $\mathscr{C} = \{\emptyset\}$ and

$$P_{\mathscr{C}} = \{e \mid range\ \phi_e = \emptyset\}$$
$$= \{e \mid e \text{ computes the totally undefined function}\}.$$

So $P_{\mathscr{C}} \neq \emptyset$ and $P_{\mathscr{C}} \neq N$. (The same proof demonstrates that one cannot decide whether a Turing machine program e will halt on some input.)
2. $\mathscr{C}$ is the set of all finite computably enumerable sets.
3. $\mathscr{C}$ is the set of all regular sets.
4. $\mathscr{C}$ is the set of all context-free languages. $\qquad\square$

To use Rice's theorem to show that a set A is not decidable, the set A must be an index set. Therefore, if one program e to compute ϕ_e belongs to A, then every program i such that $\phi_i = \phi_e$ must also belong to A. Thus, Rice's theorem only applies to machine-independent properties. For an example of a *machine-dependent* property, consider the following important property of Turing machines. We say that a Turing machine M *operates in polynomial time* if there is a polynomial p such that for every input word x, M on x halts within $p(|x|)$ steps. In Chap. 6 we will study this property of Turing machines in some detail, and in Sect. 6.3 we will prove that the set

$$S = \{i \mid M_i \text{ operates in polynomial time}\}$$

of all (encodings of) Turing machines that operate in polynomial time is not even computably enumerable. However, S is not an index set, so the result cannot be obtained using Rice's theorem.

3.9   Turing Reductions and Oracle Turing Machines

Suppose that $A \leq_m B$ for two sets A and B. Then there is a total computable function f such that $x \in A \Leftrightarrow f(x) \in B$. This reduction can be used to define an algorithm for an acceptor for A that makes a subroutine call to the set B:

begin
input x;
if $f(x) \in B$ **then** accept **else** reject;
end.

Let us consider the most general possible set of programs that contain subroutine calls to B. We want to be able to write a program that is an acceptor for A and allow it to make subroutine calls of the form "$y \in B$." These calls should return *true* if the Boolean test is true and should return *false* otherwise. Such a program is called a *reduction procedure* and the set B is called an *oracle*.

Since our programming language is the Turing machine, we make these ideas precise by extending the notion of Turing machine to enable Turing machines to make subroutine calls – only they are not called subroutine calls; they are called *oracle calls*.

An *oracle* Turing machine is a Turing machine with a distinguished oracle tape and three special states, Q, YES, and NO. When the Turing machine enters state Q, the next state is YES or NO depending on whether or not the word currently written on the oracle tape belongs to the oracle set. (In this way, the machine receives an answer to a Boolean test of the form "$y \in B$" in one move.) Also, we assume that the word written on the oracle tape is immediately erased.

Consider the reduction procedure given in Fig. 3.2. First, it should be clear that this reduction procedure can be implemented by an oracle Turing machine. Observe that for every choice of oracle set, this procedure will halt on every input. (This is not always the case; given an arbitrary oracle Turing machine M, there are three possibilities: (i) For every choice of oracle set, there exist inputs on which M does not eventually halt; (ii) there are some oracle sets A such that M with oracle A halts on every input, and there exist other oracles B such that M with oracle B does not

Fig. 3.2 A reduction procedure

```
begin
  read x in {0,1}*;
  z := x;
  while |z| < 2 * |x| do
    if z ∈ B then z := z1 else z := z0
  if z ∈ B then ACCEPT else REJECT
end.
```

halt on every input; (iii) for every choice of oracle, M halts on every input.) Also observe that this reduction procedure is *adaptive*. This means that queries made to the oracle at a later stage of a computation depend on what answers were given to queries made at earlier stages of the computation.

We let M^A denote an oracle Turing machine M with A as its oracle.

Definition 3.5. A is *decidable in* B if $A = L(M^B)$, where M^B halts on every input.

Definition 3.6. A is *Turing-reducible to* B if and only if A is decidable in B. In notation: $A \leq_T B$.

Homework 3.13 *Prove each of the following properties:*

1. $\leq_T$ *is transitive;*
2. $\leq_T$ *is reflexive;*
3. *For all sets A, $A \leq_T \overline{A}$;*
4. *If B is decidable and $A \leq_T B$, then A is decidable;*
5. *If A is decidable, then $A \leq_T B$ for all sets B;*
6. $A \leq_m B \Rightarrow A \leq_T B$;
7. $\exists A, B[A \leq_T B$ and $A \not\leq_m B]$;
8. $\exists A, B[A \leq_T B$ and B is c.e. and A is not c.e. $]$.

Definition 3.7. A is *Turing-acceptable in* B if $A = L(M^B)$ for some M^B.

Definition 3.8. A partial function ψ^A is *partial computable in* A if ψ^A is computable by some oracle Turing machine with oracle A.

Definition 3.9. A set A is *computably enumerable in* B if $A = \emptyset$ or $A = range(f^B)$, where f^B is a total computable in B function.

Theorem 3.13. *A is c.e. in B if and only if A is Turing-acceptable in B.*

The proof is the same as the proof for Turing machines without oracles. In particular, since an oracle Turing machine is just a certain kind of Turing machine, oracle Turing machines have Gödel numbers and there is an effective enumeration of oracle Turing machines.

As before, ϕ_i^A denotes the partial computable function in A that is computed by the oracle Turing machine M_i^A with Gödel number i and oracle A (and denotes the constant 0 function if i is not the Gödel number of any oracle Turing machine). Let $W_i^A = dom(\phi_i^A)$.

Definition 3.10. For each set A,

$$
\begin{aligned}
K^A &= \{x \mid \phi_x^A(x) \text{ converges}\} \\
&= \{x \mid x \in W_x^A\} \\
&= \{x \mid M_x^A \text{ accepts } x\}.
\end{aligned}
$$

One of the goals of computability theory is to classify undecidable sets and undecidable problems. The answer to the question "are some undecidable problems more undecidable than other undecidable sets?" is "yes." We will see that some undecidable problems are "harder" than others.

Theorem 3.14. $K^A \not\leq_T A$.

The proof that follows is the same diagonalization as in the corresponding non-oracle result.

Proof. If $K^A \leq_T A$, then $\overline{K^A}$ is accepted by some oracle Turing machine M_e^A that halts on every input. Then $e \in \overline{K^A} \Leftrightarrow M_e^A$ accepts $e \Leftrightarrow e \in K^A$. □

Thus, $K^{(1)} = K = K^\emptyset, K^{(2)} = K^K, \ldots, K^{(n+1)} = K^{K^n}$ forms an infinite hierarchy of undecidable sets – each more undecidable than the one before it.

Proposition 3.2. *Neither $K^{(2)}$ nor $\overline{K^{(2)}}$ are computably enumerable.*

Proof. If $K^{(2)}$ is c.e., then $K^{(2)} \leq_m K$, because K is a complete c.e. set. Thus, if $K^{(2)}$ is c.e., then $K^{(2)} \leq_T K$, which contradicts Theorem 3.14. Thus, $K^{(2)}$ is not computably enumerable.

If $\overline{K^{(2)}}$ is c.e., then $\overline{K^{(2)}} \leq_m K$, which implies that $\overline{K^{(2)}} \leq_T K$, because $\overline{K^{(2)}} \leq_T K^{(2)}$. Again, this is a contradiction. Thus, $\overline{K^{(2)}}$ is not computably enumerable. □

The next theorem says that for each set A, K^A is a complete set for the collection of all sets that are c.e. in A.

Theorem 3.15. *1. K^A is c.e. in A.*
2. If B is c.e. in A, then $B \leq_m K^A$.

The proof of 1 is the same as the proof that shows that K is c.e. and the proof of 2 is the same as the proof of your homework problem to show that K is complete, except that now we will simplify the proof by using the corollary to the *s-m-n* Theorem, Corollary 3.3.

Proof. Let B be c.e. in A. For some oracle Turing machine M^A with oracle A, $B = L(M^A)$. We want to show that $B \leq_m K^A$, and thus we want a total computable function f such that $x \in B \Leftrightarrow f(x) \in K^A$.

We claim that the following function ψ^A is partial computable in A:

$$
\psi^A(x,y) = \begin{cases} y & \text{if } M \text{ with oracle } A \text{ accepts } x, \\ \uparrow & \text{otherwise} \end{cases}
$$

To compute $\psi^A(x,y)$, simulate M with oracle A on input x and output y if this simulation eventually accepts. If M^A does not converge, then neither will the simulation.

Notice that the computation ignores the second input string y. By Corollary 3.3 (which still holds in the relativized version), there is a total computable function f such that $\phi^A_{f(x)}(y) = \psi^A(x,y)$. Moreover,

- If M^A accepts x, then for all y, $\phi^A_{f(x)}(y) = y$;
- If M^A does not accept x, then for all y, $\phi^A_{f(x)}(y)$ is undefined.

Thus,

$$x \in B \Leftrightarrow M^A \text{ accepts } x$$

$$\Leftrightarrow \text{ for all } y, \phi^A_{f(x)}(y) \text{ is defined}$$

$$\Leftrightarrow \phi^A_{f(x)}(f(x)) \text{ is defined}$$

$$\Leftrightarrow f(x) \in K^A.$$

Thus, f is a many-one reduction from B to K^A. $\square$

Recall that $K \equiv_m L_U$. Thus, K has the same difficulty as the halting problem. By the previous theorem, $K^{(2)}$ is more difficult than the halting problem. We will demonstrate a natural decision problem that is equivalent to $K^{(2)}$ and therefore that is harder than the halting problem. But first it may be useful to derive still more machinery.

For any class of languages $\mathscr{C}$, define

$$co\text{-}\mathscr{C} = \{\overline{L} \mid L \in \mathscr{C}\}$$

to be the class of all complements of languages that belong to $\mathscr{C}$. Next, we define an infinite hierarchy of classes of sets called the Kleene–Mostowksi *arithmetical hierarchy*.

Definition 3.11. The *arithmetical hierarchy* is the collection of all classes $\{\Sigma_k, \Pi_k\}_{k \geq 0}$, where these classes are defined inductively as follows:
Define $\Sigma_0 = \Pi_0$ to be the class of all decidable sets.
For any class of sets $\mathscr{C}$, define

$$\Sigma_1(\mathscr{C}) = \{B \mid B \text{ is c.e. in some set belonging to } \mathscr{C}\}.$$

Then, by induction, for each $k \geq 0$, define

$$\Sigma_{k+1} = \Sigma_1(\Sigma_k),$$

and, for each $k \geq 1$, define
$$\Pi_k = co\text{-}\Sigma_k.$$

By the definition, Σ_1 is the class of all computably enumerable sets and Π_1 is the class of complements of c.e. sets.

Note that $\Sigma_0 \subset \Sigma_1 \cup \Pi_1$, that $\Sigma_0 \neq \Sigma_1$, and that $\Sigma_1 \neq \Pi_1$. Also note that $K^{(2)}$ is not in $\Sigma_1 \cup \Pi_1$.

Now let's focus attention on the class Σ_2. By definition,

$$\Sigma_2 = \Sigma_1(\Sigma_1)$$

$$= \{B \mid B \text{ is c.e. in some c.e. set}\}.$$

That is,

$$B \in \Sigma_2 \Leftrightarrow \exists \text{ c.e. } C[B \text{ c.e. in } C]].$$

In particular, $K^{(2)} \in \Sigma_2$.

Recall that a set B is c.e. if and only if $B \leq_m K$ and if and only if B is expressible in the form $\exists y R(x, y)$, for some decidable relation $R(x, y)$. The next theorem gives a similar result for Σ_2.

Theorem 3.16.

$$B \in \Sigma_2 \Leftrightarrow B \text{ is c.e. in } K$$

$$\Leftrightarrow B \leq_m K^{(2)}$$

$$\Leftrightarrow B \text{ is expressible in the form } \exists y \forall z R(x, y, z),$$

where R is a decidable relation.

Proof. We begin by proving the first equivalence. Suppose that B is c.e. in K. Since K is a c.e. set, $B \in \Sigma_2$ by definition. Now suppose that $B \in \Sigma_2$. Then, by definition, there is a c.e. set A such that B is c.e. in A. So, for some oracle Turing machine M^A, $B = L(M^A)$. Let f be a total computable function that gives $A \leq_m K$. Here is an oracle Turing machine M_1^K that accepts B with K as the oracle: on input x simulate M except whenever M goes into its query state with a word y on its query tape, instead, M_1 should write $f(y)$ on its query tape, and then M_1 should enter its query state. Obviously, a query of y to A is equivalent to a query of $f(y)$ to K. So, B is c.e. in K. Thus, the first equivalence holds.

Now we prove the second equivalence. If B is c.e. in K, then $B \leq_m K^{(2)}$ by the previous theorem. Suppose $B \leq_m K^{(2)}$, and let f be a total computable function that gives this reduction. By the previous theorem $K^{(2)}$ is c.e. in K. So there is an oracle Turing machine M^K such that $K^{(2)} = L(M^K)$. We have $x \in B \Leftrightarrow f(x) \in K^{(2)} \Leftrightarrow M^K$ accepts $f(x)$. Let M_1 be an oracle Turing machine that on input x computes $f(x)$ and then simulates M^K on $f(x)$. Obviously, $x \in B \Leftrightarrow M_1^K$ accepts x. Thus, B is c.e. in K. We proved the second equivalence.

To prove the third equivalence, suppose there is a decidable relation R such that

$$x \in B \Leftrightarrow \exists y \forall z R(x, y, z).$$

Consider the set $S = \{\langle x, y \rangle \mid \forall z R(x, y, z)\}$. S is the complement of a c.e. set. Thus, S is decidable in a c.e. set (namely, in its own complement). So B is c.e. in a c.e. set. Thus, $B \in \Sigma_2$.

In order to prove the third equivalence in the other direction, we make some general observations first. Let z be an arbitrary computation on an arbitrary oracle Turing machine. By this we mean that z is a sequence of configurations. A *query configuration* is a configuration in which the current state is Q, the query state. If C_i is a query configuration, then the next configuration C_{i+1} has state either YES or NO. Let $y_1, \ldots, y_k$ denote the words on the query tape of each query configuration of z for which the next state is YES. Let $n_1, \ldots, n_l$ denote the words on the query tape of each query configuration of z for which the next state is NO. Observe that the list of words $y_1, \ldots, y_k, n_1, \ldots, n_l$ is effectively found from z.

Now suppose that B is c.e. in K and let M be an oracle Turing machine such that $B = L(M^K)$.

$$x \in B \Leftrightarrow \exists z[(z \text{ is an accepting computation of } M \text{ on } x)$$
$$\wedge y_1 \in K \wedge y_2 \in K \wedge \cdots \wedge y_k \in K$$
$$\wedge n_1 \notin K \wedge n_2 \notin K \wedge \cdots \wedge n_l \notin K].$$

Observe that the expression (z is an accepting computation of M on x) defines a decidable relation. Call this relation $S(x, z)$. Of course, K is c.e. and so is expressible in the form $\exists u R(x, u)$ for some decidable relation $R(x, u)$. Thus, we may rewrite the above equivalence as

$$x \in B \Leftrightarrow \exists z[S(x, z)$$
$$\wedge \exists u_1 R(y_1, u_1) \wedge \exists u_2 R(y_2, u_2) \wedge \cdots \wedge \exists u_k R(y_k, u_k)$$
$$\wedge \forall v_1 \overline{R}(n_1, v_1) \wedge \forall v_2 \overline{R}(n_2, v_2) \wedge \cdots \wedge \forall v_l \overline{R}(n_l, v_l)].$$

Then, by placing this expression in prenex normal form, we get

$$x \in B \Leftrightarrow \exists z \exists u_1 \ldots u_k \forall v_1 \ldots v_l [S(x, z)$$
$$\wedge R(y_1, u_1) \wedge R(y_2, u_2) \wedge \cdots \wedge R(y_k, u_k)$$
$$\wedge \overline{R}(n_1, v_1) \wedge \overline{R}(n_2, v_2) \wedge \cdots \wedge \overline{R}(n_l, v_l)].$$

We are almost there: What is inside the brackets is a decidable relation and the quantifiers are in the right order; there are just too many of them. For brevity, call the bracketed expression $R(x, z, u_1, \ldots, u_k, v_1, \ldots, v_l)$. Then, we have

$$x \in B \Leftrightarrow \exists z \exists u_1 \ldots u_k \forall v_1 \ldots v_l R(x, z, u_1, \ldots, u_k, v_1, \ldots, v_l).$$

Now pairing functions come in handy:

$$x \in B \Leftrightarrow \exists y \forall z R(x, \tau_{k+1,1}(y), \tau_{k+1,2}(y), \ldots, \tau_{k+1,k+1}(y), \tau_{l1}(z_1), \ldots, \tau_{ll}(z_l)).$$

We're done.   □

Homework 3.14 *Prove that*

$$\Sigma_2 \cap \Pi_2 = \{A \mid A \text{ is decidable in some language belonging to } \Sigma_1\}.$$

Although we will not do so, Theorem 3.16 and this homework exercise generalize. That is, we could, by induction, prove the following properties of the arithmetical hierarchy.

1. For all $n \geq 1$, $K^{(n)} \in \Sigma_n$, $K^{(n)} \notin \Sigma_{n-1}$, and $K^{(n)}$ is $\leq_m$-complete for Σ_n.
2. For all $n \geq 1$, A belongs to Σ_n if and only if A is expressible in Σ_n-quantifier form, where this means that there is a decidable relation $R(x, y_1, \ldots, y_n)$ such that

$$x \in A \Leftrightarrow \exists y_1 \forall y_2 \ldots Q_n y_n R(x, y_1, \ldots, y_n),$$

where the quantifiers alternate ($Q_n = \forall$ if n is even, and $Q_n = \exists$ if n is odd). Dually, A belongs to Π_n if and only if A is expressible in Π_n-quantifier form, which means that

$$x \in A \Leftrightarrow \forall y_1 \exists y_2 \ldots Q'_n y_n R(x, y_1, \ldots, y_n).$$

3. For all $n \geq 1$,

$$\Sigma_{n+1} \cap \Pi_{n+1} = \{A \mid A \text{ is decidable in some language belonging to } \Sigma_n\}.$$

Consider the problem of determining, for an arbitrary Turing machine M, whether $L(M) = \Sigma^*$. We will show that this problem is Turing-equivalent to $K^{(2)}$. The way to get insight about what level of the arithmetical hierarchy a problem belongs is to express it in quantifier form: $L(M) = \Sigma^*$ if and only if *for every* input x *there exists* an accepting computation y of M on x. Clearly, this is expressible in Π_2 form. So we should expect the following to be true.

Theorem 3.17. *The problem for an arbitrary Turing machine M, whether $L(M) = \Sigma^*$, is Turing-equivalent to $K^{(2)}$. In particular,*

$$\overline{\{e \mid L(M_e) = \Sigma^*\}} \equiv_m K^{(2)}.$$

Proof. Let $B = \overline{\{e \mid L(M_e) = \Sigma^*\}}$. Then $x \in B \Leftrightarrow \exists w \langle x, w \rangle \notin L_U$. So B is c.e. in L_U. (Observe how we obtained this from the form of the expression that relates B to L_U.) Since $L_U \equiv_m K$, B is c.e. in K. Thus, $B \leq_m K^{(2)}$.

Conversely, we show that $K^{(2)} \leq_m B$. We need a total computable function f such that

$$\phi_x^K(x) \downarrow \ \Leftrightarrow \ \exists w \phi_{f(x)}(w) \uparrow.$$

The value $f(x)$ is to be the Gödel number of the following partial computable function ψ. Given x, try for w steps to find a valid converging computation of $\phi_x^K(x)$, but do not use the oracle and do not check for correct oracle usage. If unsuccessful, set $\psi(w) = w$. If successful, then for each query q that is claimed to be in K, use w steps to try to check. If unsuccessful, set $\psi(w) = w$. If all steps are successful, consider queries for which it is claimed that $q \notin K$. Begin an enumeration of K and if and when it is shown that such a q in fact belongs to K, set $\psi(w) = w$. Otherwise, $\psi(w)$ diverges.

It should be clear that this f does the job. □

3.10 Recursion Theorem: Continued

Now we continue our study of the recursion theorem. We must explain first that the recursion theorem is not just one theorem, but rather a collection of slightly varying results. All forms of the recursion theorem are due to Kleene.

We begin our discussion with the following example:

Example 3.5. Consider the computation rule defined by

if $x = 1$ **then** $\psi(x) = 2$
  else if even(x) **then** $\psi(x) = 2\phi(x \div 2)$.

This rule defines a function ψ in terms of a known function ϕ and value for x. Think of the rule as a definition of a *type 2* function F that maps a function ϕ and number x to the integral value $\psi(x)$ of another function ψ.

In general, a computation rule F that takes as parameters a partial computable function ϕ and integer values $x_1, \ldots, x_n$ of the form

$$F(\phi; x_1, \ldots, x_n) = \psi(x_1, \ldots, x_n)$$

is called a *functional*. We say that a functional F is partial computable if given a program s for computing ϕ, we can compute the value of ψ. That is, F is a *partial computable functional* if there is a partial computable function η such that

$$\eta(s, x_1, \ldots, x_n) = F(\phi; x_1, \ldots, x_n),$$

where s is any Gödel number of ϕ. Observe that a computation of η, i.e., a computation of F on inputs ϕ_s and $x_1, \ldots, x_n$, might involve using s in order to compute some values of ϕ_s, but there can exist at most some finitely many numbers $n_1, \ldots, n_k$ for which $\phi(n_1), \ldots, \phi(n_k)$ are required.

The forms of the recursion theorem that we study next, which explains why the result is so named, addresses the question of whether, for every partial computable functional F, the *recursive definition*

$$F(\xi;x_1,\ldots,x_n) = \xi(x_1,\ldots,x_n) \tag{3.3}$$

is guaranteed a solution.

Example 3.6. Does the rule

> **if** $x = 1$ **then** $\phi(x) = 2$
>   **else if** even(x) **then** $\phi(x) = 2\phi(x \div 2)$

define a partial computable function ϕ?

Given two partial functions ϕ and ψ, we say that ψ is an *extension* of ϕ, in symbols $\phi \subseteq \psi$, if $graph(\phi) \subseteq graph(\psi)$. If ψ extends ϕ, F is a partial computable functional, and $F(\phi;x)$ converges, then $F(\psi;x)$ converges and $F(\psi;x) = F(\phi;x)$.

Theorem 3.18. *Let $F(\xi;x_1,\ldots,x_n)$ be a partial computable functional, in which ξ is a function variable that ranges over partial functions of n variables. Then there is a solution ϕ of (3.3) such that*

1. $F(\phi;x_1,\ldots,x_n) = \phi(x_1,\ldots,x_n)$,
2. ϕ *is partial computable, and*
3. *If $F(\psi;x_1,\ldots,x_n) = \psi(x_1,\ldots,x_n)$ is any other solution of (3.3), then $\phi \subseteq \psi$.*

Given any recursive definition, the theorem guarantees the existence of a partial computable solution. The function that is implicitly computed, whose existence is guaranteed, is called the *least fixed point* of F.

Proof. (For ease of notation, we assume that $n = 1$.) Let ϕ_0 be the completely undefined function. Then inductively define

$$\phi_{i+1}(x) = F(\phi_i;x)$$

for $i \geq 0$.

Lemma 3.3. *For all $i \geq 0$, ϕ_{i+1} extends ϕ_i. That is, $\phi_i(x) = y$ implies $\phi_{i+1}(x) = y$.*

Given Lemma 3.3, we define ϕ to be the "limit" function. That is, for each x, $\phi(x)$ converges if and only if for some i, $\phi_i(x)$ converges, in which case, $\phi(x)$ is the common value of $\phi_i(x)$ for all i greater than or equal to the least such i.

Proof. The proof is by induction on i. Since ϕ_0 is completely undefined, clearly ϕ_1 extends ϕ_0. Let $i \geq 1$ and assume as induction hypothesis that ϕ_{j+1} extends ϕ_j for $j < i$.

Suppose that $\phi_i(x) = y$. Then $\phi_i(x) = F(\phi_{i-1};x) = y$. By induction hypothesis, ϕ_i extends ϕ_{i-1}. Since the computation of F on ϕ_{i-1} and x converges with output y, so must F on ϕ_i and x. That is, since ϕ_{i-1} is already sufficiently defined to determine a value for $F(\phi_{i-1};x)$, extending ϕ_{i-1} to ϕ_i cannot change F's computation. Thus, $F(\phi_i;x) = y$ also. That is, $\phi_{i+1}(x) = y$. $\square$

Now we prove that assertion 1 holds.

Lemma 3.4. *For all x,*

$$\phi(x) = F(\phi;x).$$

Proof. Suppose $\phi(x) \downarrow$. Then, for some i, $\phi(x) = F(\phi_i;x)$. Since ϕ extends ϕ_i, $F(\phi;x) = F(\phi_i;x) = \phi(x)$.

Conversely, suppose that $F(\phi;x)$ is defined. The computation of F on ϕ and x is of finite length; i.e., there are some finitely many values $n_1,\ldots,n_k$ such that $\phi(n_1),\ldots,\phi(n_k)$ are required. There exist $i_1,\ldots,i_k$ such that $\phi(n_1) = \phi_{i_1}(n_1),\ldots,\phi(n_k) = \phi_{i_k}(n_k)$. Let $i = \max\{i_1,\ldots,i_k\}$. Then $\phi(n_1) = \phi_i(n_1),\ldots,$ $\phi(n_k) = \phi_i(n_k)$. So, $F(\phi;x) = F(\phi_i;x)$, and the value of $F(\phi_i;x)$, by definition, is $\phi(x)$. $\square$

Lemma 3.5. *ϕ is partial computable.*

Proof. We indicate a proof by using Church's thesis. To compute $\phi(x)$, one needs to compute $F(\phi;x)$. To compute $F(\phi;x)$, at most some finitely many values $\phi(n_1),\ldots,\phi(n_k)$ are required. If no such values are required, then $\phi(x) = \phi_1(x) = F(\phi_0;x)$. Otherwise, assume as induction hypothesis that for some i, $\phi(n_1) = \phi_i(n_1),\ldots,\phi(n_k) = \phi_i(n_k)$ and that each of these can be obtained. Then compute $F(\phi;x)$ using these values. $\square$

Lemma 3.6. *If $F(\psi;x) = \psi(x)$, then ψ extends ϕ.*

Proof. We show by induction on i that ψ extends each ϕ_i. Clearly, ψ extends ϕ_0. By induction hypothesis, assume that ψ extends ϕ_i. Let $\phi_{i+1}(x) = y$. Then

$$y = \phi_{i+1}(x)$$
$$= F(\phi_i;x)$$
$$= F(\psi;x), \text{ because } \psi \text{ is an extension of } \phi_i,$$
$$= \psi(x).$$

So ψ is an extension of ϕ_{i+1}. $\square$

This completes the proof of Theorem 3.18. $\square$

Theorem 3.18 gives a partial computable solution ϕ to (3.3) so that for any $x_1,\ldots,x_n$, the value of $\phi(x_1,\ldots,x_n)$ can be computed in terms of ϕ and $x_1,\ldots,x_n$. A program e to compute ϕ is not explicitly given.

The following consequence of Theorem 3.11 is closely related to Theorem 3.18; in some ways it is stronger, in other ways weaker.

Theorem 3.19. *Let $F(\xi;x_1,\ldots,x_n)$ be a partial computable functional in which ξ is a function variable that ranges over partial functions of n variables. Then there is a number e such that*

$$\phi(x_1,\ldots,x_n) = F(\phi;e,x_1,\ldots,x_n).$$

Proof. There is a partial computable function η such that

$$\eta(s,x_1,\ldots,x_n) = F(\phi;z,x_1,\ldots,x_n)$$

for any Gödel number s of ϕ. That is,

$$\eta(s,x_1,\ldots,x_n) = F(\phi_s;z,x_1,\ldots,x_n).$$

Now let us consider the function ψ defined by $\psi(s,x_1,\ldots,x_n) = \eta(s,s,x_1,\ldots,x_n)$. By Theorem 3.11, there is a number e such that

$$\begin{aligned}
\phi_e(x_1,\ldots,x_n) &= \psi(e,x_1,\ldots,x_n)\\
&= \eta(e,e,x_1,\ldots,x_n)\\
&= F(\phi_e;e,x_1,\ldots,x_n).
\end{aligned}$$

$\square$

Theorem 3.19 is stronger than Theorem 3.18 in that F is permitted to depend not only on ϕ but also on the Gödel number of a Turing machine for computing ϕ, but it is also weaker in that there is no reason to suppose that the solution ϕ_e is a least fixed point. That is, there is no reason to suppose that all other solutions are extensions of the one that Theorem 3.19 obtains.

Does Theorem 3.18 essentially reduce to Theorem 3.11 in the case that we do not include a Gödel number in the recursion? In that case, there is a partial computable function η such that

$$\eta(s,x_1,\ldots,x_n) = F(\phi_s,x_1,\ldots,x_n).$$

So, by Theorem 3.19, there is a number e such that

$$\begin{aligned}
\phi_e(x_1,\ldots,x_n) &= \eta(e,x_1,\ldots,x_n)\\
&= F(\phi_e;x_1,\ldots,x_n).
\end{aligned}$$

Again, we do not know whether ϕ_e is the least fixed point.

3.11 References

Chapters 1 and 2 of this text contain material on computability and undecidability that was developed prior to 1960. For students wishing to pursue a deeper study of computability theory, we cite the classic text by Rogers [Rog67] and the seminal paper of Post [Pos44]. Davis' source book [Dav65] contains many of the original papers on undecidability. For developments in computability theory since 1960, consult the text by Soare [Soa80].

3.12 Additional Homework Problems

Homework 3.15 *Show that every infinite decidable set has an undecidable c.e. subset.*

Homework 3.16 *Let A be an undecidable c.e. set and let B be an infinite decidable subset of A. Show that $A - B$ is an undecidable c.e. set.*

Homework 3.17 *Show that if A is a decidable language, then so is the concatenation AA. Provide an example to demonstrate that the converse is false.*

Homework 3.18 *The* graph *of a partial function f is the set $\{\langle x, f(x) \rangle \mid f(x) \downarrow\}$. Show that a partial function f is partial computable if and only if its graph is c.e.*

Homework 3.19 *Prove that it is decidable to determine whether a Turing machine ever writes a nonblank symbol when started on a blank tape.*

Homework 3.20 *Prove that it is undecidable to determine whether a Turing machine halts on every input word that has an even number of symbols.*

Homework 3.21 *Give an example of a nontrivial language L (i.e., $L \neq \Sigma^*$ and $L \neq \emptyset$) such that L is not many-one reducible to $\overline{L}$. That is, $L \not\leq_m \overline{L}$. (Observe, therefore, using Homework 3.13, item 3, that many-one and Turing reducibilities are different relations on $\mathscr{P}(N)$.)*

Homework 3.22 *Let A and B be disjoint c.e. sets. Show that $A \leq_T A \cup B$ and $B \leq_T A \cup B$.*

Homework 3.23 *Given disjoint sets A and B, we say that a set C separates A and B if $A \subseteq C$ and $C \cap B = \emptyset$. Show that if A and B are disjoint sets such that both $\overline{A}$ and $\overline{B}$ are c.e., then there is a decidable set that separates them.*

Homework 3.24 *1. Give an example of sets A, B, and C such that $A \subseteq B$, $B \subseteq C$, A and C are decidable, and B is undecidable.*

2. *Give an example of sets A, B, and C such that $A \subseteq B$, $B \subseteq C$, A and C are undecidable, and B is decidable.*

Homework 3.25 *Show that the set*

$$L = \{(e, w) \mid \text{the head of } M_e \text{ shifts left at some point during}$$
$$\text{the computation of } M_e \text{ on input } w\}$$

is decidable.

Homework 3.26 *Prove that the set*

$$L = \{e \mid M_e \text{ accepts the input string } 11\}$$

is undecidable.

Homework 3.27 *Prove that the set*

$$L = \{< i, j > \mid \text{ there is some input } x \text{ on which both } M_i(x) \text{ and } M_j(x) \text{ halt }\}$$

is undecidable.

Homework 3.28 *One of the following languages is computably enumerable and the other is not. Answer which is which, demonstrate that the language you claim to be c.e. is, and prove that the other language is not c.e.*

$$L_1 = \{e \mid M_e \text{ accepts at least 20 different inputs}\}.$$

$$L_2 = \{e \mid M_e \text{ accepts at most 20 different inputs}\}.$$

Homework 3.29 *A c.e. set is* simple *if its complement is infinite but does not have any infinite c.e. subset.*

1. *Explain whether a simple set can be decidable.*
2. *Prove that simple sets exist by constructing one. (This is a difficult problem.)*

Homework 3.30 *A c.e. set A is* creative *if there is a total computable function f such that for all m, if $W_m \subseteq \overline{A}$, then $f(m) \in \overline{A} - W_m$.*

1. *Show that K is creative.*
2. *Show that no creative set is simple.*

Homework 3.31 *Construct a computably enumerable, undecidable set B of pairs of natural numbers with the property that for each natural number x, both sets $\{y \mid (x, y) \in B\}$ and $\{y \mid (y, x) \in B\}$ are decidable.*

Homework 3.32 *Let us define the set $K^{(\omega)}$ as follows:*

$$K^{(\omega)} = \{\langle i, j \rangle \mid i \in K^{(j)}\}.$$

1. Show for every $j \geq 1$ that $K^{(j)}$ is many-one reducible to $K^{(\omega)}$.
2. Show that $K^{(\omega)}$ is not Turing reducible to $K^{(j)}$ for any $j \geq 1$.

Chapter 4
Introduction to Complexity Theory

The remaining chapters of this book are concerned with complexity theory. The goal of complexity theory is to provide mechanisms for classifying combinatorial problems and measuring the computational resources necessary to solve them. Complexity theory provides an explanation of why certain problems have no practical solutions and provides a way of anticipating difficulties involved in solving problems of certain types. The classification is quantitative and is intended to investigate what resources are necessary (lower bounds) and what resources are sufficient (upper bounds) to solve various problems.

This classification should not depend on a particular computational model but rather should measure the intrinsic difficulty of a problem. The basic model of computation for our study is the multitape Turing machine, but the measurement mechanisms are essentially machine-independent, up to the exactitude required. Cobham's thesis and the expanded version of Church's thesis summarize the fact that all reasonable general models of computation give rise to essentially the same classification. Let's recapitulate: We will be interested primarily in the class of problems that can be computed in polynomial time (Cobham's thesis), and any computational device that operates in polynomial time can be simulated by a Turing machine that runs in polynomial time (expanded version of Church's thesis). Thus, especially for polynomial time, the theory we provide is a robust one whose definition does not depend on a single machine or its technical features.

Many of the techniques of Chaps. 2 and 3 will serve us well as we proceed. However, the most difficult and interesting facets of complexity theory appear exactly where the older mathematical theories lend no guiding hand and where new methods, particular to this study, must be developed.

Complexity theory today addresses issues of contemporary concern: cryptography and data security, probabilistic computation (those that depend on random number generators), parallel computation, circuit design, quantum computing, biological computing, development of efficient algorithms. Moreover, complexity theory is interested not in the merely computable but in problems that are *efficiently* computable. Algorithms whose running times are n^2 in the size of their inputs can be

S. Homer and A.L. Selman, *Computability and Complexity Theory*,
Texts in Computer Science, DOI 10.1007/978-1-4614-0682-2_4,
© Springer Science+Business Media, LLC 2011

implemented to execute efficiently even for fairly large values of n, but algorithms that require an exponential running time can be executed only for small values of n. It is common today to identify efficiently computable problems with those that have polynomial-time algorithms.

A complexity measure quantifies the use of a particular computational resource during execution of a computation. The two most important measures, and the two most common measures, are *time*, the time it takes a program to execute, and *space*, the amount of storage used during a computation. However, other measures are considered as well, and we will introduce other resources as we proceed.

Complexity theory forms a basis for the classification and analysis of combinatorial algorithms. To illustrate this, consider the Hamiltonian Circuit problem, the problem of determining whether an arbitrary graph possesses a Hamiltonian circuit. Currently it is not known whether this problem has a feasible solution, and all known solutions are equivalent to a sequential search of all paths through the graph, testing each in turn for the Hamiltonian property. Since complexity will be measured by time and/or space in Turing-machine computations, it becomes clear why it is important to be able to efficiently encode data structures such as graphs into words over Σ so that what is intuitively the size of the graph differs from the length of the input by no more than a polynomial. Then, we must demand that the theory is capable of classifying the intrinsic complexity of this problem in a precise way and is capable of elucidating the difficulty in finding an efficient solution to this problem.

To summarize the discussion so far, we conclude that the use of the multitape Turing machine as the basic model of computation is robust over all possible models of computation and is robust via standard encodings for all standard data types.

Nondeterminism will play an important role in this study. We do not design nondeterministic machines to be executed, as are ordinary computing devices. Rather, one should understand nondeterministic Turing machines to be a useful mode for classification of computational problems. For example, whereas it is not known whether there is a deterministic polynomial-time-bounded Turing machine to solve (an encoding of) the Hamiltonian Circuit problem, it is easy to design a nondeterministic polynomial-time-bounded Turing machine that solves this problem. This is what makes it possible to give an exact classification of the Hamiltonian Circuit problem. Indeed, this problem is known to be NP-complete, which places it among hundreds of other important computational problems whose deterministic complexity is still open.

We will return to nondeterminism and to a precise definition of NP-complete in Chap. 6.

4.1 Complexity Classes and Complexity Measures

In order to define time complexity, we consider on-line Turing machines. An *online* Turing machine is a multitape Turing machine whose input is written on one of the work tapes, which can be rewritten and used as an ordinary work tape. The machine may be either deterministic or nondeterministic. Let M be an on-line Turing machine, and let T be a function defined on the set of natural numbers. M is a $T(n)$ *time-bounded* Turing machine if for every input of length n, M makes at most $T(n)$ moves before halting. If M is nondeterministic, then every computation of M on words of length n must take at most $T(n)$ steps. The language $L(M)$ that is accepted by a deterministic $T(n)$ time-bounded M has *time complexity* $T(n)$.

By convention, the time it takes to read the input is counted, and every machine is entitled to read its input. This takes $n + 1$ steps. So when we say a computation has time complexity $T(n)$, we really mean $\max(n + 1, \lceil T(n) \rceil)$.

Denote the length of a word x by $|x|$. We might be tempted to say that a nondeterministic Turing machine is $T(n)$ time-bounded, if for every input word $x \in L(M)$, the number of steps of the shortest accepting computation of M on x is at most $T(|x|)$. In Chap. 5 we will see that the formulations are equivalent for the specific time bounds that we write about. But they are not equivalent for arbitrary time bounds.

A complexity class is a collection of sets that can be accepted by Turing machines with the same resources. Now we define the time-bounded complexity classes: Define DTIME($T(n)$) to be the set of all languages having time complexity $T(n)$. Define NTIME($T(n)$) to be the set of all languages accepted by nondeterministic $T(n)$ time-bounded Turing machines.

In order to define space complexity, we need to use off-line Turing machines. An *off-line* Turing machine is a multitape Turing machine with a separate read-only input tape. The Turing machine can read the input but cannot write over the input. Let M be an off-line multitape Turing machine and let S be a function defined on the set of natural numbers. M is an $S(n)$ *space-bounded* Turing machine if, for every word of length n, M scans at most $S(n)$ cells over all storage tapes. If M is nondeterministic, then every computation must scan no more than $S(n)$ cells over all storage tapes. The language $L(M)$ accepted by a deterministic $S(n)$ space-bounded Turing machine has *space complexity* $S(n)$.

Observe that the space the input takes is not counted. Every Turing machine is permitted to use at least one work cell, so when we say that a problem has space complexity $S(n)$, we always mean $\max(1, \lceil S(n) \rceil)$. For example, space complexity $\log(n)$ can never be 0.

One might be tempted to say that a nondeterministic Turing machine is $S(n)$ space-bounded, if for every word of length n that belongs to $L(M)$, there is an accepting computation that uses no more than $S(n)$ work cells on any work tape. As is the case for nondeterministic time, we will show in the next chapter that the two formulations are equivalent for the time bounds that interest us.

Now, we define the space-bounded complexity classes: Define DSPACE($S(n)$) to be the set of all languages having space complexity $S(n)$. Define NSPACE($S(n)$) to be the set of all languages accepted by nondeterministic $S(n)$ space-bounded Turing machines.

The study of time complexity begins with the paper [HS65] of Hartmanis and Stearns. The title of this paper contains the first usage of the phrase "computational complexity." The study of space complexity begins with the paper [HLS65] of

Hartmanis, Lewis, and Stearns. These seminal papers introduced some of the issues that remain of concern even today. These include time/space trade-offs, inclusion relations, hierarchy results, and efficient simulation of nondeterministic computations.

We will be primarily concerned with classes defined by logarithmic, polynomial, and exponential functions. As we proceed to relate and discuss various facts about complexity classes in general, we will see their impact on the following list of *standard* complexity classes. These classes are well-studied in the literature and each contains important computational problems. The classes are introduced with their common notations.

1. $L = \text{DSPACE}(\log(n))$[1]
2. $NL = \text{NSPACE}(\log(n))$
3. $\text{POLYLOGSPACE} = \bigcup \{\text{DSPACE}((\log n)^k) \mid k \geq 1\}$
4. $\text{DLBA} = \bigcup \{\text{DSPACE}(kn) \mid k \geq 1\}$
5. $\text{LBA} = \bigcup \{\text{NSPACE}(kn) \mid k \geq 1\}$
6. $P = \bigcup \{\text{DTIME}(n^k) \mid k \geq 1\}$
7. $NP = \bigcup \{\text{NTIME}(n^k) \mid k \geq 1\}$
8. $E = \bigcup \{\text{DTIME}(k^n) \mid k \geq 1\}$
9. $NE = \bigcup \{\text{NTIME}(k^n) \mid k \geq 1\}$
10. $\text{PSPACE} = \bigcup \{\text{DSPACE}(n^k) \mid k \geq 1\}$
11. $\text{EXP} = \bigcup \{\text{DTIME}(2^{p(n)}) \mid p \text{ is a polynomial} \}$
12. $\text{NEXP} = \bigcup \{\text{NTIME}(2^{p(n)}) \mid p \text{ is a polynomial} \}$

The study of the computational complexity of specific computational problems on specific models of computation is called *concrete complexity*. The concrete-complexity literature provides a rich source of examples of problems in our standard list. The following is merely an introduction to a vast subject.

NL contains the problem of determining for arbitrary directed graphs G and vertices u and v, whether there is a path from u to v. This problem is not known to belong to L. The class L contains the restriction of this problem to the case that no vertex has more than one directed edge leading from it. [Jon73,Jon75]. P is identified with the class of feasibly computed problems. The corresponding nondeterministic class NP will be discussed in a later chapter. We will easily see that P is a subset of NP, but it is not known whether P is equal to NP, and many consider the question of whether these two classes differ to be the most important open question of either mathematics or computer science. Chapters 6 and 7 will focus almost entirely on this question.

The class $\bigcup \{\text{NSPACE}(kn) \mid k \geq 1\}$ is denoted LBA because it is known to be identical to the class of languages accepted by linear-bounded automata, otherwise known as the context-sensitive languages [Myh60, Kur64]. This explains the notation for the corresponding deterministic class as well.

---

[1]All logarithms in this book are binary.

The class E characterizes the complexity of languages accepted by writing push-down automata [Mag69], and NE characterizes the complexity of a well-known computational problem in finite model theory [JS74]. PSPACE contains many computational games, such as generalized HEX [ET76]. These results are beyond the scope of this text.

4.1.1 Computing Functions

Occasionally we will need to discuss the computational complexity of computing functions. We are already familiar with partial computable functions and the Turing machines that compute them already. However, for our study of complexity theory, let us agree on the following particular formalism. A Turing-machine *transducer* M is a multitape Turing machine, either deterministic or nondeterministic, with a distinguished write-only output tape and with accepting and rejecting states in the usual manner. A transducer M computes a value y on an input string x if there is an accepting computation of M on x for which y is the final contents of M's output tape. In general, such transducers compute partial multivalued functions – partial because transducers do not typically accept all input strings, and multivalued because different accepting computations of a nondeterministic transducer may produce different output values. We will see important examples of this phenomena in Chap. 4. For now, we will not be concerned with partial functions.

Let f be a function defined on Σ^*. A deterministic Turing-machine transducer M *computes f* if for all x, M on input x halts in its accepting state with $f(x)$ written on the output tape. A nondeterministic Turing-machine transducer M *computes f* if (i) there is an accepting computation of M on x, and (ii) every accepting computation of M on x has $f(x)$ written on the output tape. Time-bounded transducers are defined as above. A transducer M is $S(n)$ space-bounded if M is an off-line transducer (i.e., M has a separate read-only input tape) that never uses more than $S(n)$ storage cells on any computation on an input word of length n. The space the input and output words takes is not counted.

4.2 Prerequisites

Before proceeding, let us review the main points that students should know from the earlier chapters:

- Students should know that multitape Turing machines and RAMs have identical computing power.
- Students should know how to represent data structures as words over a finite alphabet with no more than a polynomial blowup in size.

- Students should know the capabilities of Turing machines (for example, understand that a finite table can be stored in a Turing machine's finite control).
- Students should be comfortable with the universal Turing machine and believe
  that there exists a compiler that will translate any algorithm written in pseudo-
  code into a Turing machine.

In addition, complexity theory will borrow the methods of relative computability
that we learned in the last chapter.

Finally, we invite students to read some discussion of Cobham's thesis such as
the excellent one in the first paragraph of Garey and Johnson's monograph [GJ79].

Chapter 5
Basic Results of Complexity Theory

We begin our study of complexity theory by examining the fundamental properties of complexity classes. These results apply to all complexity classes and show that the definitions of these classes are invariant under small changes in the time or space bounds of the Turing machines that define them. We will prove general relationships between time- and space-bounded complexity classes. These consist of inclusions between some classes and separations of other classes. Then we will apply the methods and results of these general relationships to important specific cases in order to establish relationships between the central standard complexity classes we defined in the previous chapter. In order to begin this study we need to understand some simple assertions that involve the behavior of functions at limits, so let's review these now.

Let f be a function that is defined on the set of all natural numbers, and recall that by definition

$$\sup_{n \to \infty} f(n) = \lim_{n \to \infty} \text{l.u.b.} \{ f(m) \mid m \geq n \},$$

and

$$\inf_{n \to \infty} f(n) = \lim_{n \to \infty} \text{g.l.b.} \{ f(m) \mid m \geq n \}.$$

Then, the limit $\lim_{n \to \infty} f(n)$ is defined to exist if and only if $\inf_{n \to \infty} f(n) = \sup_{n \to \infty} f(n)$, in which case,

$$\lim_{n \to \infty} f(n) = \inf_{n \to \infty} f(n) = \sup_{n \to \infty} f(n).$$

Example 5.1. Consider the function $f(n)$ defined by

$$f(n) = \begin{cases} 1/n & n \text{ is even,} \\ n & n \text{ is odd,} \end{cases}$$

S. Homer and A.L. Selman, *Computability and Complexity Theory*,
Texts in Computer Science, DOI 10.1007/978-1-4614-0682-2_5,
© Springer Science+Business Media, LLC 2011

Observe that l.u.b.$\{f(n), f(n+1), \ldots\} = \infty$ for every n. Hence,

$$\sup_{n \to \infty} f(n) = \lim_{n \to \infty} \text{l.u.b.}\{f(m) \mid m \geq n\} = \infty.$$

For any n, g.l.b.$\{f(n), f(n+1), \ldots\} = 0$. So, $\inf_{n \to \infty} f(n) = 0$. Thus, the limit $\lim_{n \to \infty} f(n)$ does not exist.

Example 5.2. Consider the function $f(n)$ defined by $f(n) = n/(n+1)$. We have l.u.b.$\{n/(n+1), (n+1)/(n+2), \ldots\} = 1$, for all n, and g.l.b.$\{n/(n+1), (n+1)/(n+2), \ldots\} = n/(n+1)$, from which we arrive at $\lim_{n \to \infty} 1 = \lim_{n \to \infty} n/(n+1) = 1$. Thus, the limit exists, and $\lim_{n \to \infty} f(n) = 1$.

We will need to understand the assertion

$$\inf_{n \to \infty} f(n) = \infty.$$

Let $g(n) = $ g.l.b.$\{f(n), f(n+1), \ldots\}$. Then the following are immediate:

$$\inf_{n \to \infty} f(n) = \infty \Leftrightarrow \lim_{n \to \infty} g.l.b\{f(n), f(n+1), \ldots\} = \infty$$

$$\Leftrightarrow \lim_{n \to \infty} g(n) = \infty$$

$$\Leftrightarrow (\forall c > 0)(\exists N)(\forall n \geq N)(g(n) > c).$$

Then $(\forall c > 0)(\exists N)(\forall n \geq N)(f(n) > c)$, because $f(m) \geq g(n)$ for all $m \geq n$. Thus,

$$\inf_{n \to \infty} f(n) = \infty \text{ implies } \lim_{n \to \infty} f(n) = \infty.$$

We can use this assertion to define "little-oh" notation. Namely,

$$g(n) \in o(f(n)) \Leftrightarrow \inf_{n \to \infty} f(n)/g(n) = \infty$$

$$\Leftrightarrow (\forall c > 0)(\exists N)(\forall n \geq N)(cg(n) < f(n)).$$

Example 5.3. $\log n \in o(n)$ and $n \in o(n \log n)$. The second statement holds as, given a constant $c > 0$, we can choose N such that $\log N > c$. Then $cn < n \log n$ for any $n > N$.

Homework 5.1 *Prove that $\log n \in o(n)$ and that $n \in o(n^{1+\varepsilon})$ for any $\varepsilon > 0$.*

5.1 Linear Compression and Speedup

The proofs of the results in the next few sections involve clever and sometimes tricky algorithms. The algorithms tell us how one Turing machine can efficiently simulate another when it has slightly less computational power, either having less space or less time. In Sect. 5.3 we consider the question of efficient simulations of k-tape Turing machines by one-tape and two-tape Turing machines. Since complexity classes are defined in terms of multitape Turing machines – not in terms of one-tape or two-tape machines – one might view this as a digression from our main purpose, which is to elucidate properties of complexity classes. However, the results proved will turn out to be important in later sections of this chapter.

The first results are of the following form: If a language can be accepted with resource $f(n)$, then it can be accepted with resource $cf(n)$ for any $c > 0$. These results justify use of "big-oh" notation for complexity functions. To review this notation, $g(n) \in O(f(n))$ if there is a constant $c > 0$ such that, for all n, $g(n) \le cf(n)$. We define the class DTIME($O(T(n))$) as follows:

$$\text{DTIME}(O(T(n))) = \bigcup \{\text{DTIME}(g(n)) \mid g(n) \in O(T(n))\}.$$

DSPACE($O(S(n))$), NTIME($O(T(n))$), and NSPACE($O(S(n))$) are defined similarly. It follows readily that DTIME($O(T(n))$) = $\bigcup\{\text{DTIME}(cT(n)) \mid c > 0\}$. Similar identities hold for the other classes.

The first example of a theorem of this form is the *space compression theorem* [HLS65]. This theorem asserts that if L is accepted by a k-tape $S(n)$ space-bounded Turing machine, then for any $c > 0$, L is accepted by a k-tape $cS(n)$ space-bounded Turing machine. If the $S(n)$ space-bounded Turing machine is nondeterministic, then so is the $cS(n)$ space-bounded Turing machine. In the following theorem, we combine space compression with tape reduction – the result is a one-tape $cS(n)$ Turing machine. The proof is essentially the same simple simulation that we used in the proof of Theorem 2.1. We repeat it in part to note that it applies to nondeterministic Turing machines as well to as deterministic ones. As a corollary, it follows that DSPACE($S(n)$) = DSPACE($O(S(n))$) and NSPACE($S(n)$) = NSPACE($O(S(n))$).

Theorem 5.1 (Space Compression with Tape Reduction). *For every k-tape $S(n)$ space-bounded off-line Turing machine M and constant $c > 0$, there exists a one-tape $cS(n)$ space-bounded off-line Turing machine N such that $L(M) = L(N)$. Furthermore, if M is deterministic, then so is N.*

Proof. Let M be a k-tape $S(n)$ space-bounded off-line Turing machine, and let $c > 0$. Choose an integer d such that $2 \le cdk$. As in the proof of Theorem 2.1, view the single work tape of N as consisting of k tracks, one track for each work tape of M. (This is pictured in Fig. 5.1.) The difference is that now each cell of N contains a "composite symbol" that represents a k by d matrix, where the ith row contains d tape symbols of the ith tape of M, and possibly an indicator $\uparrow$ of the head position of the ith tape head. Formally, the tape alphabet of N is sufficiently large so that each tape symbol of N uniquely denotes such a k by d matrix of M's tape and with head indicators.

Since d symbols of each of M's work tapes are encoded in a single cell of N, N uses at most $\lceil S(n)/dk \rceil$ cells to encode all of M's work tapes.

track 1	a_{11}	a_{12}	a_{13}		a_{1d}	
track 2	a_{21}	$\uparrow a_{22}$	a_{23}		a_{2d}	
track k	a_{k1}	a_{k2}	a_{k3}		a_{kd}	

Fig. 5.1 A single cell of N

N simulates a move of M as follows: Beginning at the leftmost cell containing a head marker, N "sweeps right" until it has visited all cells containing head markers and then "sweeps left" to its start position. A *neighborhood* of M consists of those cells of M that either are scanned by some tape head or are adjacent to such a scanned cell. On the sweep right, N records all the current neighborhoods of M in its finite control. On the left sweep, it updates the neighborhoods to reflect the changes that M would have made.

It is clear that N uses no more than

$$\lceil S(n)/dk \rceil \leq 2(S(n)/dk) \leq cS(n)$$

cells.   □

Corollary 5.1. *The following identities hold:*

$$\mathrm{DSPACE}(S(n)) = \mathrm{DSPACE}(O(S(n)))$$

and

$$\mathrm{NSPACE}(S(n)) = \mathrm{NSPACE}(O(S(n))).$$

Since a "linear bounded automaton" is just a one-tape n space-bounded Turing machine, it follows from this corollary that the formal language class DLBA = DSPACE(n), and LBA = NSPACE(n).

Linear speedup of time is possible, too, but not quite as readily as is linear compression of space.

Theorem 5.2 (Linear Speedup [HS65]). *If L is accepted by a k-tape $T(n)$ time-bounded Turing machine M, $k > 1$, and if $n \in o(T(n))$, then for any $c > 0$, L is accepted by a k-tape $cT(n)$ time-bounded Turing machine N. Furthermore, if M is deterministic, then so is N.*

Proof. Let M be a k-tape $T(n)$ time-bounded Turing machine, where $k \geq 2$, let $c > 0$, and assume that $n \in o(T(n))$.

Choose m so that $mc \geq 16$. The ith tape of N will encode the contents of the ith tape of M using composite symbols (i.e., using a large tape alphabet), and eight moves of N will simulate at least m moves of M.

To begin, N scans the input of M and copies the input onto a storage tape, encoding m symbols of M into one symbol of N. After this, N moves the head of the storage tape containing the input back to the left end. This routine takes

$$n + \lceil n/m \rceil$$

moves. Henceforth, N will use its original input tape as a storage tape and use the tape containing the compressed input as an input tape.

N simulates moves of M as follows: Define a *neighborhood* of N to be those cells of N currently being scanned together with their adjacent cells. Let us say that the head of tape i is currently scanning cell j. First, N makes four moves (left to $j-1$, right to j, right to $j+1$, left to j) to determine the contents of its current neighborhood. Using its finite control, N determines the contents of all of M's cells represented by this neighborhood and determines what the contents will be the very next time, say t_0, that the head of tape i is not scanning one of the cells represented by the region $j-1, j, j+1$. If M accepts its input before any tape head of M moves outside the region corresponding to the current neighborhood of N, then N accepts immediately. Similarly, if M halts, so does N. Otherwise, N uses four more moves to update the contents of its neighborhood to correspond correctly with the contents of M's cells at time t_0, and N completes its sequence of eight moves by positioning its heads over the cells that represent the region M is in at time t_0. (For example, suppose N is to change its neighborhood on tape i from $j-1, j, j+1$ to $j+1, j+2, j+3$ with the head scanning $j+2$. Then N updates cells $j-1, j, j+1$ by moving left one cell from j and then updating $j-1, j, j+1$ in that order, and then moves to $j+2$.)

M must make at least m moves in order to move out of a region, so N takes eight moves to simulate at least m moves of M.

Now we calculate the running time of N. Let this be denoted by T_N. We have

$$T_N \leq n + \lceil n/m \rceil + 8 \lceil T(n)/m \rceil.$$

Since $\lceil x \rceil \leq x + 1$, for all x,

$$T_N \leq n + n/m + 8T(n)/m + 9.$$

By the hypothesis that $n \in o(T(n))$, $(\forall d)(\exists N_d)(\forall n \geq N_d)(dn < T(n))$. That is,

$$(\forall d)(\exists N_d)(\forall n \geq N_d)(n < T(n)/d).$$

Also, for all $n \geq 9$, $n + 9 \leq 2n$. Thus, for all $d > 0$ and all $n \geq \max(9, N_d)$,

$$\begin{aligned}
T_N &\leq 2T(n)/d + T(n)/md + 8T(n)/m \\
&= T(n)[2/d + 1/md + 8/m] \\
&\leq T(n)[32/16d + c/16d + 8c/16] \quad \text{(because } cm \geq 16\text{)}.
\end{aligned}$$

We want to choose d so that $32/16d + c/16d + 8c/16 \leq c$: Because,

$$32/16d + c/16d + 8c/16 \leq c \Leftrightarrow 32 + c + 8cd \leq 16cd$$

$$\Leftrightarrow 32 + c \leq 8cd$$

$$\Leftrightarrow (32 + c)/8c \leq d$$

$$\Leftrightarrow 4/c + 1/8 \leq d,$$

it suffices to choose d in accordance with the last inequality. Then, for all $n \geq \max(9, N_d)$, N makes at most $cT(n)$ moves.

To decide words in $L(M)$ whose length is less than $\max(9, N_d)$, store these words in the finite control on N. $\qquad\qquad\qquad\qquad\qquad\qquad\qquad\qquad\qquad\qquad\qquad\qquad\qquad$ □

Corollary 5.2. *If $n \in o(T(n))$, then*

$$\mathrm{DTIME}(T(n)) = \mathrm{DTIME}(O(T(n)))$$

and

$$\mathrm{NTIME}(T(n)) = \mathrm{NTIME}(O(T(n))).$$

The condition $n \in o(T(n))$ stipulates that $T(n)$ grows faster than every linear function. For this reason, the linear speedup theorem does not apply if $T(n) = cn$ for some constant c. Instead, we have the following result.

Corollary 5.3. *For all $\varepsilon > 0$,*

$$\mathrm{DTIME}(O(n)) = \mathrm{DTIME}((1+\varepsilon)n)$$

and

$$\mathrm{NTIME}(O(n)) = \mathrm{NTIME}((1+\varepsilon)n).$$

Proof. The same simulation applies. Let M be a k-tape cn time-bounded Turing machine, where $k > 1$ and $c > 0$. Let $\varepsilon > 0$. Recall from the proof of the linear speedup theorem that $T_N \leq n + n/m + 8T(n)/m + 9$. Using the hypothesis, we derive the following estimates to T_N:

$$T_N \leq n + n/m + 8T(n)/m + 9$$

$$\leq n + n/m + 8cn/m + 9$$

$$= n[1 + (1 + 8c)/m + 9/n]$$

$$< (1+\varepsilon)n$$

if n and m are chosen so that $(1 + 8c)/m < \varepsilon/2$ and $9/n < \varepsilon/2$. Thus, the result holds for all $n > 18/\varepsilon$, and with $m > 2(1 + 8c)/\varepsilon$ as an additional condition.

For $n \leq 18/\varepsilon$, store the words in $L(M)$ in the finite control of N. $\qquad\qquad$ □

This result cannot be improved for deterministic linear-time complexity classes, because Rosenberg [Ros67] showed that

$$\text{DTIME}(n) \neq \text{DTIME}(2n).$$

However, a stronger result is known for nondeterministic linear-time complexity classes: A Turing machine that accepts inputs of length n in time $n + 1$ (the time it takes to read the input) is called *real time*. Nondeterministic Turing machines that accept in time $n + 1$ are called *quasi-real time*. The class of quasi-real-time languages is $\text{NTIME}(n + 1)$. Book and Greibach [BG70] showed that NTIME $(n + 1) = \text{NTIME}(O(n))$. This result is a corollary of the next theorem.

Theorem 5.3 ([BG70]). *Let M be a k-tape $T(n)$ time-bounded Turing machine, $T(n) \geq n$. Let $c > 0$. Then, there is a nondeterministic $(k + 3)$-tape Turing machine N such that $L(M) = L(N)$ with the property that for every word $x \in L(M), |x| = n$, there is an accepting computation of N that accepts x in time*

$$\max(n + 1, cT(n)).$$

Proof. Choose an integer d (according to specifications to be given later). As before, one symbol of N will compress d symbols of M. For $i = 2, \ldots, k$, tape i will contain in compressed form the contents of tape i of M. Tape $k + 1$ will contain in compressed form an initial segment of the input string of M. Tapes $k + 2$ and $k + 3$ will contain certain guesses of the input string. Remember that the simulation in the proof of the linear speedup theorem, Theorem 5.2, first writes the input of M onto one of its tapes in compressed form, which requires $n + \lceil n/d \rceil$ steps, and then enters a process that uses eight moves of N to simulate d moves of M. This simulation will use nondeterminism and even parallel processing to cleverly reduce the time of these processes.

N simulates M in two phases, and each phase consists of two simultaneous processes. In the initial phase execute the following processes 1 and 2 in parallel:

1. Nondeterministically copy a prefix x_1 of the input word x onto tape $k + 1$ in compressed form. (This takes $|x_1|$ steps.)
2. N writes onto tapes $k + 2$ and $k + 3$ some guessed string y from the input alphabet of M in compressed form. Then the heads of $k + 2$ and $k + 3$ move synchronously leftward over y and nondeterministically stop while scanning y.

For any word w from the tape alphabet of M, let $\overline{w}$ denote the compressed version of w. The initial phase ends when both processes halt. At this point, on tape 1, the input tape, is $x = x_1 x_2$, where x_1 is the initial segment of x that is copied in compressed form onto tape $k + 1$. On tapes $k + 2$ and $k + 3$ are $\overline{y} = \overline{y_1} \overline{y_2}$. Note that $x_1, y_1,$ or y_2 may be empty. Figure 5.2 illustrates the current situation.

The final phase consists of the following processes executed in parallel:

3. The input head scans the rest of the input (i.e., x_2) comparing it to $\overline{y_2}$, the compressed copy of y_2, on tape $k + 2$. It is important to note that both input

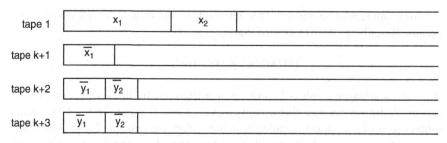

Fig. 5.2 The initial phase

heads began at the left end of x_2 and y_2, respectively. If $x_2 \neq y_2$ is discovered, N
halts without accepting. Otherwise, process 3 stops when it confirms that $x_2 = y_2$.
4. Use $\overline{x_1}$ on tape $k+1$ and $\overline{y_1}$ on tape $k+3$ to check whether $x_1 = y_1$. If $x_1 \neq y_1$ is
discovered, then N rejects. Otherwise, the head of $k+3$ is placed at the beginning
of y, and the "8-move simulation" of the linear speedup theorem begins.

Observe that process 4 may be executing the "8-move simulation" even while
step 3 is still verifying the input on tape $k+2$. Clearly, $x \in L(M)$ if and only if there
is a computation of N for which $x_2 = y_2$, $x_1 = y_1$, and N accepts x.

Assume that $d \geq 3$. Let $n = |x|$, and consider an accepting computation of N for
which $|x_1| = \lceil 3n/d \rceil$. Recall that process 1 took $|x_1| = \lceil 3n/d \rceil$ steps. Since process 2
actually wrote $\overline{x}$, process 2 took $\lceil n/d \rceil$ steps to guess y and $\lceil |y_2|/d \rceil$ steps to position
heads $k+2$ and $k+3$. Thus, the initial phase takes

$$\max(|x_1|, (n+|y_2|)/d + O(1)) = |x_1|$$

steps for sufficiently large n.

Process 3 takes $\leq |x_2|$ steps. Process 4 takes $\leq \lceil |x_1|/d \rceil$ steps to check that $x_1 =
y_1$, and, of course, the 8-move simulation takes $\lceil 8T(n)/d \rceil$ steps. So, process 4 takes
$\leq \lceil |x_1|/d \rceil + \lceil 8T(n)/d \rceil$ steps. Thus, the final phase takes,

$$1 + \max(|x_2|, |x_1|/d + 8T(n)/d + O(1))$$

steps. (Note that it takes one step at the end to enter an accepting or nonaccepting
state.)

Now, let us calculate, for sufficiently large n, the total time T_N:

$$T_N \leq |x_1| + 1 + \max(|x_2|, |x_1|/d + 8T(n)/d + O(1))$$
$$\leq 1 + \max(n, |x_1| + |x_1|/d + 8T(n)/d + O(1))$$
$$\leq 1 + \max(n, 3n/d + |x_1|/d + 8T(n)/d + O(1))$$
$$(\text{because } |x_1| \leq \lceil 3n/d \rceil)$$
$$\leq 1 + \max(n, 12T(n)/d + O(1)).$$

The last inequality holds because $|x_1| \leq n \leq T(n)$.

Thus, we choose $d > 12/c$ in order to obtain

$$\max(n+1, cT(n))$$

for all sufficiently large n.   □

Corollary 5.4. $\text{NTIME}(n+1) = \text{NTIME}(O(n))$.

Proof. We know already that $\text{NTIME}(O(n)) = \text{NTIME}(2n)$. Let $c = 1/2$. If M is any $2n$ time-bounded Turing machine, Theorem 5.3 gives a nondeterministic Turing machine N that accepts a word x if and only if *some* computation of N accepts x within $\max(n+1, n) = n+1$ steps. This by itself does not yield our result because we need to know that *all* computations of N terminate in $n+1$ steps. We can obtain this condition for the special case that $T(n) = 2n$ and $c = 1/2$. In fact, observing that the input head of N moves to the right only, let us stipulate that the input head moves one cell to the right every step and that the computation of N halts when the input head reads the first blank after the input word. This stipulation does not affect N's computation on the correct nondeterministically guessed accepting computation. Thus, $L(N) = L(M)$ and N runs in time $n+1$.   □

5.2 Constructible Functions

A function $S(n)$ is *space-constructible* if there is an $S(n)$ space-bounded Turing machine M such that for each n there is some input of length n on which M uses exactly $S(n)$ cells. A function $S(n)$ is *fully space-constructible* if, in addition, on every input of length n, M uses exactly $S(n)$ cells.

A function $T(n)$ is *time-constructible* if there is a $T(n)$ time-bounded Turing machine M such that for each n there is some input of length n on which M runs for exactly $T(n)$ steps. A function $T(n)$ is *fully time-constructible* if, in addition, on every input of length n, M runs for exactly $T(n)$ steps.

The usefulness of constructible functions will become clear as we proceed. The following homework exercise demonstrates that the functions in which we are interested primarily (those that are either space bounds or time bounds for the complexity classes that we named in the previous chapter) are constructible.

Homework 5.2 *Show the following:*

1. The functions

$$\log(n), n^k, 2^n, \text{ and } n!$$

are space-constructible and, with the exception of $\log n$, time-constructible;
2. If $S_1(n)$ and $S_2(n)$ are space-constructible, then so are $S_1(n)S_2(n)$, $2^{S_1(n)}$, and $S_1(n)^{S_2(n)}$;
3. If $T_1(n)$ and $T_2(n)$ are time-constructible, then so are $T_1(n)T_2(n)$, $2^{T_1(n)}$, and $T_1(n)^{T_2(n)}$.

Homework 5.3 *Show that space-constructible implies fully space-constructible for space bounds $S(n)$ such that $S(n) \geq n$. Hint: On an input word of length n, use a separate tape to cycle through all input words of length n.*

5.2.1 Simultaneous Simulation

Here we will show that the decisions we made when defining nondeterministic complexity classes do not matter for the classes that we are most interested in. At the same time, we will illustrate the usefulness of constructible functions. First we show that if $S(n)$ is a fully space-constructible function, then, in the definition of NSPACE($S(n)$), it does not matter whether we insist that all paths are $S(n)$ space-bounded or whether only some path must be $S(n)$ space-bounded. More precisely, we claim that the following proposition holds.

Proposition 5.1. *If $S(n)$ is fully space-constructible, then $L \in$ NSPACE($S(n)$) if and only if there is a nondeterministic Turing machine N that accepts L such that for every word x of length n that belongs to L, there is an accepting computation of N on input x that uses no more than $S(n)$ cells on any work tape.*

Proof. The proof from left to right is trivial: Namely, if $L \in$ NSPACE($S(n)$), then, by definition, there is a nondeterministic Turing machine N that accepts L that uses at most $S(n)$ tape cells in every computation. Thus, the restriction that N uses no more than $S(n)$ cells on words x of length n that belong to L certainly holds.

Now assume that L is accepted by a nondeterministic Turing machine for which this property holds. We will prove that $L \in$ NSPACE($S(n)$) by showing that there is another nondeterministic Turing machine N' that accepts L that uses no more than $S(n)$ space on every computation: Using the proof technique of Theorem 5.1 (enlarge the tape alphabet to replace k tapes by one tape with k tracks), there is a one-tape Turing machine N that accepts L such that the same property holds. Define N' so that on an input word x of length n, it first runs the space constructor on x and marks on its work tape all the cells that the space constructor visits on this input. Then N' simulates N on input x within the marked region of the work tape. However, if N' ever attempts to leave the marked region, then it halts without accepting. Thus, since the space constructor is $S(n)$ space-bounded, so is N'. If N reaches an accepting state without leaving the marked region, then N' accepts. Since the space constructor marks $S(n)$ cells and since, for every word x of length n that belongs to L, there is an accepting computation of N on input x that uses no more than $S(n)$ cells, N' accepts L.　　　□

If $T(n)$ is fully time-constructible, then we can make the analogous claim for NTIME($T(n)$) but we need a more complicated analysis. Recall that a function $T(n)$ is fully time-constructible if there is a $T(n)$ time-bounded Turing machine M that on every input of length n runs for exactly $T(n)$ steps. A Turing machine that runs for exactly $T(n)$ steps on every input of length n is called a "$T(n)$-clock," and we denote this by C_T.

Let $T(n)$ be a fully time-constructible function and let M be an arbitrary Turing machine. In several applications we will want to construct a Turing machine $M' = M\|C_T$ that simultaneously simulates M and a $T(n)$-clock C_T. M' should have the property that it is $T(n)$ time-bounded and that it accepts an input word x if and only if M accepts x within $T(|x|)$ steps. The difficulty in constructing M' is that C_T and M might access the input word differently. That is, at some ith step $(i > 0)$ of a computation C_T might expect its read/write head to be acting on a different symbol of the input word than M is currently acting on. The simplest solution to this problem is to have two copies of the input word available. M' begins its computation with the input word x in cells 1 through $|x|$ on tape 1 with the head scanning cell 1. Tape 2 is blank and its head is also scanning cell 1. M' begins its computation by copying x from tape 1 to tape 2, moving both heads from left to right, and then returns both heads to the starting position. This takes $2(|x| + 1)$ steps. Then M' begins its simultaneous simulation of C_T and M. Thus, in order to simulate $T(n)$ moves of M, M' may require $2(|x| + 1) + T(n)$ steps. Since by convention, $T(n) \geq n + 1$, we see that for some constant $c > 0$, M' is $cT(n)$ time-bounded. If $n \in o(T(n))$, then Theorem 5.2 yields a Turing machine M'' that is $T(n)$ time-bounded and that accepts the same language as M'. If $T(n)$ is bounded by a linear function, then Corollary 5.4 yields a machine M'' that accepts the same language as M' and that runs in time $n + 1$. In either case, since M' accepts a word x if and only if M accepts x within $T(|x|)$ steps, so does M''. Suppose that $T(n)$ is a fully time-constructible function such that either $n \in o(T(n))$ or $T(n)$ is bounded by a linear function, and suppose that N is a nondeterministic Turing machine that accepts a language L such that for every word x of length n that belongs to L, the number of steps in the shortest accepting computation of N on input x is at most $T(n)$. Let $N' = N\|C_T$. Then, the Turing machine N'' that results either from Theorem 5.2 or Corollary 5.4 is $T(n)$ time-bounded and accepts an input word x if and only if some computation of N accepts x within $T(|x|)$ steps. That is, N'' accepts L.

All the time bounds in which we are interested satisfy one of the conditions, either $n \in o(T(n))$ or $T(n)$ is bounded by a linear function. For these, the construction that we just described works fine. However, fully time-constructible functions that do not satisfy either of these properties exist.

Homework 5.4 *Give examples of fully time-constructible functions $T(n)$ that do not satisfy these properties.*

The following theorem asserts the result we want for all fully time-constructible functions. This result is probably known, but it was communicated to the authors by Regan [Reg].

Theorem 5.4. *If $T(n)$ is fully time-constructible, then $L \in \mathrm{NTIME}(T(n))$ if and only if there is a nondeterministic Turing machine N that accepts L such that for every word x of length n that belongs to L, the number of steps in the shortest accepting computation of N on input x is at most $T(n)$.*

Proof. As was the case for Proposition 5.1, the proof of this result from left to right is trivial. We describe the proof from right to left. Noting that the extra cost incurred in the fundamental simultaneous simulation is the cost of copying the input to a new tape, the idea of the proof is to use the technique in the proof of Theorem 5.3 to guess and verify a copy of the input in compressed form while the simultaneous simulation is taking place. Specifically, let M be a nondeterministic Turing machine that accepts L such that, for every word x of length n that belongs to L, the number of steps in the shortest accepting computation of M on input x is at most $T(n)$. We will show that $L \in \text{NTIME}(T(n))$. Let $C = C_T$ be a Turing-machine "clock" that runs exactly $T(n)$ steps on every input of length n. Let $c = 1/3$ and, as in the proof of Theorem 5.3, choose $d > 12/c$ (i.e., choose $d > 36$). Now we will implement a variation of the construction in the proof of Theorem 5.3 in order to define a new machine N in which one symbol of N will compress d symbols of M. N simulates M and C simultaneously in compressed form, in two stages and possibly a little bit more.

Let x be an input word to N. In stage 1, N uses three new tapes to guess the compressed input word $\bar{x}$. With one addition, N does this exactly as before. The addition is that N also writes its guess of the input word on tape $k+4$. Thus, at the end of Stage 1, tape $k+1$ contains a prefix $\overline{x_1}$ of the input word in compressed form and tapes $k+2$, $k+3$, and $k+4$ contain a string $\overline{y_1 y_2}$.

In stage 2, N runs the following processes simultaneously:

1. As before, N uses tapes 1, $k+1$, $k+2$, and $k+3$ to verify that the guess $\overline{y_1 y_2}$ is correct.
2. After verifying that $\overline{x_1} = \overline{y_1}$, N begins the "8-move simulation" of the linear speedup theorem of M with the compressed input string on tape $k+3$ and N begins the "8-move simulation" of the linear speedup theorem of C with the same compressed input string on tape $k+4$.

We stipulate that stage 2 of N ends when the input head reaches the first blank after reading the input. That is, stage 2 ends when its first process is complete. Recall that this takes exactly $n+1$ steps.

If the simulation of C halts by the end of stage 2, then, because $c = 1/3$, $T(|x|) \leq 3|x|$. Thus, in this case, N halts. If M accepts x and N has guessed well, then N will have found an accepting computation of M. Now comes the little bit more: Otherwise, N continues the "8-move simulations" of both C and M until C halts, and then N halts. Observe, in this case, that N is simultaneously simulating M and C for $T(n)$ steps. As in the previous case, if M accepts x and N has guessed well, then N will have found an accepting computation of M. Moreover, the running time of N in this case is only $cT(|x|)$.

Finally, let us observe that N runs for no more than $T(n)$ steps on every input of length n, and this completes the proof.   □

A central and unifying theme in complexity theory is the problem of determining the exact power of nondeterminism. For most of the time bounds and space bounds we study, the question is open, but for linear time the following results are known. Since $\text{DTIME}(n)$ is a proper subset of $\text{DTIME}(2n)$, and $\text{DTIME}(2n) \subseteq \text{NTIME}(2n) = \text{NTIME}(n)$, it follows that $\text{DTIME}(n) \neq \text{NTIME}(n)$. In 1983, Paul et al. [PPST83] obtained the striking and deep result that $\text{DTIME}(O(n)) \neq \text{NTIME}(O(n))$.

5.3   Tape Reduction

In this section we present results on tape reduction for time-bounded Turing machines. The first theorem is proved using the same "k tracks for k tapes" technique as in the Space Reduction theorem.

Theorem 5.5 ([HS65]). *Let M be a k-tape $T(n)$ time-bounded Turing machine such that $n \in o(T(n))$. There is a one-tape $T^2(n)$ time-bounded Turing machine N such that $L(N) = L(M)$. Furthermore, if M is deterministic, then so is N.*

Proof. We use the one-tape simulation given in the proof of the space compression theorem: N has one tape; this tape is viewed as consisting of k tracks, with one composite symbol of N representing k symbols of M.

Since all heads of M begin at the leftmost cell of M's tapes, after i moves of M, the heads of M can be at most i cells apart. Recall that a "move" of N consists of a sweep left followed by a sweep right. We see that it takes at most $2(i+1)$ steps of N to simulate the $(i+1)$st move of M. Thus, for every positive integer t, it takes

$$\sum_{i=1}^{t} 2i = O(t^2)$$

moves of N to simulate t moves of M.

At this point, we see that M can be replaced by an equivalent $O(T^2(n))$ one-tape Turing machine. However, we may apply the linear speedup theorem to M before applying the above simulation so that the resulting one-tape Turing machine N is $T^2(n)$ time-bounded.   □

This is the best result possible, for it is known that the language

$$L = \{wcw^r \mid w \in \{0,1\}^*\},$$

where c is a symbol not belonging to $\{0,1\}^*$, cannot be accepted by any one-tape Turing machine of time complexity $T(n)$ unless $\sup_{n \to \infty} T(n)/n^2 > 0$.

Homework 5.5 *Show that L can be decided by a deterministic two-tape Turing machine in linear time.*

On the one hand, Theorem 5.5 is an important result because it is part of the illustration that computing models are equivalent within polynomial time. On the other hand, because of the quadratic slowdown, one-tape Turing machines are frequently considered of limited interest. If we restrict ourselves to two tapes, there is a classic simulation of k tapes by a two-tape Turing machine due to Hennie and Stearns [HS66], where the simulation is slower by a logarithmic factor. The following result of Pippenger and Fischer [PF79] yields a two-tape "oblivious" Turing machine with the same time bound as the result of Hennie and Stearns. The proof is long, but the algorithm is clever and the result is important.

Definition 5.1. A Turing machine is *oblivious* if the sequence of head moves on the Turing machine's tapes is the same for all input words of the same length. That is, for $t \geq 1$, the position of each of the heads after t moves on an input word x depends on t and $|x|$, but not on x.

Oblivious Turing machines idealize certain kinds of oblivious algorithms, for example, searching a file sequentially, which depends on the size of the file but not its contents.

Theorem 5.6 ([PF79]). *If L is accepted by a k-tape $T(n)$ time-bounded Turing machine M, then L is accepted by an oblivious two-tape Turing machine N in time $O(T(n) \log T(n))$. Furthermore, if M is deterministic, then so is N.*

Before describing the proof, we state the following corollary, which is the result of Hennie and Stearns [HS66].

Corollary 5.5. *If L is accepted by a k-tape $T(n)$ time-bounded Turing machine M, then L is accepted by a two-tape Turing machine N' in time $T(n) \log T(n)$. Furthermore, if M is deterministic, then so is N'.*

The proof of the corollary is immediate. As $n \in o(T(n) \log T(n))$, we obtain N' by applying to N the linear speedup theorem, Theorem 5.2. Of course, N' is no longer oblivious. In this chapter we will require only the corollary. However, the fact that N is oblivious will be useful in Chap. 8 for the study of families of Boolean circuits.

Homework 5.6 *The proof of the next theorem constructs a Turing machine with a two-way infinite tape. Show that if a language L is accepted in time $T(n)$ by a Turing machine M with a two-way infinite tape, then L is accepted in time $T(n)$ by a Turing machine with a one-way infinite tape.*

Proof. We assume that M contains two-way infinite tapes, and so will N. One tape of N will consist of tracks that encode the k tapes of M. The other tape of N will support various bookkeeping and auxiliary memory activities. Let us focus on tape 1 of N. Tape 1 has $3k$ tracks, three tracks for each tape of M. We introduce a new symbol # that does not belong to M's tape alphabet Γ. # will be used as a marker. Each cell of tape 1 of N holds a composite symbol that represents $3k$ symbols of $\Gamma \cup \{\#\}$. The cells of tape 1 are labeled by the integers. Unlike all previous simulations, N does not simulate M by moving head markers; rather, N moves data. In particular, the storage symbols that are scanned by M's heads are always in cell 0. When the head of one of M's tapes moves left (say), the entire contents of this tape, on its tracks in tape 1 of N, are shifted right, so that the scanned symbol on M's tape is in cell 0 of N's tape 1. This, by itself, would still result in an $O(T^2(n))$ simulation. The clever idea that improves the running time is to divide the information on the tape into blocks. Blocks near the origin (cell 0) are small, but they double in size as they get farther from the origin. The information in the small blocks that are close to the origin will be moved often, but the data in larger blocks that are far from the origin will rarely be moved.

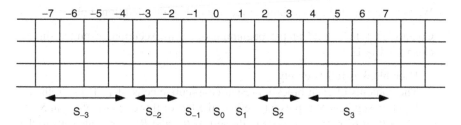

Fig. 5.3 Three tracks of N grouped into segments

First we divide the tape into segments S_i. The length of each segment grows exponentially in size, with $\|S_i\| = \|S_{-i}\| = 2^{i-1}$. There is a marker between each segment, but it does not actually appear until the segment is used. Segment S_0 is cell 0 of N. Segment S_1 is cell 1 of N. Segment S_2 consists of cells 2 and 3 of N. In general, segment S_j consists of cells

$$[2^{j-1}, 2^j) = \{2^{j-1}, 2^{j-1} + 1, \ldots, 2^j - 1\},$$

and segment S_{-j} consists of $(-2^j, -2^{j-1}]$. This is illustrated in Fig. 5.3.

Now we are ready to say what the blocks are. Consider the three tracks of N's tape 1 that represent some work tape T of M. Given a segment S_i, let block B_i^1 be the lower track of S_i, let block B_i^2 be the middle track of S_i, and let block B_i^3 be the upper track of S_i. A segment, therefore, is the union of its three blocks. A block is called *empty* if it contains only #'s and is called *full* if it contains no #. We define a segment to be *clean* if the number of its full blocks is either one or two.

Initially, when N begins its simulation, tracks 2 and 3 contain the marker # and track 1 contains the contents of T. Thus, when N scans the symbol a of M for the first time, it reads the composite symbol $(a, \#, \#)$. Initially all blocks are either full or empty, and all segments are clean.

We will define a procedure sim that simulates one step of the computation of M on an input of length n. Because M is $T(n)$ time-bounded, N stops operating after it executes sim $T(n)$ times. N's operation, however, is more complicated than this. In order to move data in blocks efficiently, we need to use empty blocks as buffers. For this reason certain segments need to be clean prior to executions of sim. Execution of sim might not leave segments clean, so we have to define a procedure clean(k) with an integer parameter k. Clean(k) cleans segments S_{-k} and S_k. For each t, $1 \leq t < T(n)$, the tth execution of sim is followed by clean(1),...,clean(l_t), for $l_t = \max\{m \mid 2^{m-1} \text{ divides } t\}$, prior to the next execution of sim. Think of the simulation as a sequence of *stages*, where, for $1 \leq t < T(n)$, stage t consists of the tth execution of sim followed by execution of clean(1),...,clean(l_t). We manage this requirement by using one track on tape 2 to count executions of sim in binary. Observe that it easy to determine from this value which clean(k) procedures need to be performed: Just count the number of rightmost zeros and add 1. Note also that these actions on tape 2 are oblivious.

We assume as induction hypotheses that the following conditions hold:

- Conditions 1 to 3 hold at the beginning of each execution of either sim or clean(k), $k \geq 1$.

  1. Each block is full or empty.
  2. The contents of each block represent consecutive cells of T. If $i < j$, then a block in segment S_i represents cells to the left of those in any block in S_j. If $i \geq 0$, then B_i^1 represents cells to the left of B_i^2, and B_i^2 represents cells to the left of B_i^3. If $i < 0$, then the opposite holds, that is, B_i^3 represents cells to the left of B_i^2, and B_i^2 represents cells to the left of B_i^1.
  3. The head of N scans cell 0, which is segment S_0. Block B_0^1 contains the symbol that M's head is scanning on tape T. Block B_0^3 is empty.

- For $1 \leq t < T(n)$, at the beginning of the tth execution of sim, segments

$$S_{-l_{(t-1)}}, \ldots, S_{l_{(t-1)}}$$

  are clean.
- An execution of clean(k) visits at most segments $S_{-(k+1)}, \ldots, S_{(k+1)}$ and increases or decreases the number of full blocks of $S_{-(k+1)}$ and $S_{(k+1)}$ by at most 1.

Note that the induction hypotheses hold before the first execution of sim.

Sim operates as follows. Suppose that the current state of M is q, that the head of tape T is scanning symbol a, and that $\delta_M(q, a) = (q', a', D)$. N has state q stored in its finite control before this execution of sim and replaces this with q'. If $D = L$, then N needs to move data to the right, and if $D = R$, then N needs to move data to the left. Nevertheless, it it will be easy to see that sim can perform its tasks obliviously. Suppose that $D = L$. By the induction hypotheses, segments S_{-1}, S_0, and S_1 are clean. N copies the symbol in block B_0^2 into B_0^3, and then writes a' into B_0^2. Next, N writes the symbol in the full block of S_{-1} that is closest to the origin into B_0^1, and replaces the symbol in that block with #. (That is, if B_{-1}^j, $1 \leq j \leq 3$, is the only full block in segment S_{-1} that is full, or if B_{-1}^j and $B_{-1}^{j'}$ are both full and $1 \leq j < j' \leq 3$, then N writes the symbol in B_0^j into B_0^1, and writes # into B_0^j.) Finally, to ensure that B_0 is clean after execution of sim, if segment S_0 is now full, then N copies the symbol in B_1^2 into B_1^3, copies the symbol in B_0^1 into B_0^2, copies the symbol in B_0^3 into B_1^1, and writes # into B_0^3. If $D = R$, then N moves similarly to shift data to the left. This completes the description of sim, except that in order to have the procedure oblivious, the head will simulate the actions that need to take place for both $D = L$ and $D = R$, but N will perform only the actions that are correct. Observe that S_{-1}, S_0, and S_1 are the only segments that are visited during execution of sim. After execution, S_0 is clean, but S_{-1} and S_1 might not be clean.

Now we explain clean(k). Using a separate track on tape 2, N counts the distance to the first cell of S_k. When it completes its work at S_k, it moves to the first cell of S_{-k}, cleans that segment, and then returns to the origin. The actions that take place at S_k depend on whether the segment is already clean, empty, or full. However, in order to make the procedure oblivious, the head simulates all cases. If S_k is clean, nothing is done. If all blocks of S_k are empty, then the procedure *moves* the contents of the full block of S_{k+1} that is closest to S_k into blocks B_k^1 and B_k^2. Let us note some details: We prove as a separate claim below that clean(k) can carry out the actions that it needs to, so there is a full block B_{k+1}^j to move. B_{k+1}^j contains twice the number of cells as the blocks of S_k, so this action leaves S_k with two full blocks. Finally, we stress that moving symbols from a block leaves the block empty. If all blocks of S_k are full, then N concatenates the contents of blocks B_k^2 and B_k^3 and moves them into B_{k+1}^1. In order to do this, N first copies the contents of B_{k+1}^2 into B_{k+1}^3 and then copies the contents of B_{k+1}^1 into B_{k+1}^2.

To copy the contents of a block from one segment into another, N copies the data to a separate track of tape 2 (just as they would appear in tape T) and then copies from tape 2 to the target segment. The three tracks of tape 2 that we have described and the different actions that take place on these tracks occur during the execution of different procedures, so all head movements on tape 2 are oblivious.

It is straightforward to see that the relevant induction hypotheses hold after execution of clean(k). Now we will show that clean(k) can perform the steps that it needs to:

Claim. For each t, $1 \leq t < l_t$, if clean(k) is executed at stage t, then

(i) if S_k (S_{-k}) is empty, then S_{k+1} ($S_{-(k+1)}$) contains a full block, and
(ii) if S_k (S_{-k}) is full, then S_{k+1} ($S_{-(k+1)}$) contains an empty block.

Proof. Since all segments are clean before N begins its simulation, the conditions clearly hold at time $t = 1$. Suppose that $t \geq 1$, that N executes clean(k) at stage t, and that clean(k) successfully carries out it actions at this stage. We need to prove that conditions (i) and (ii) hold the next time that clean(k) is executed.

Note that $k \leq l_t$. If $k < l_t$, then N executes clean$(k+1)$ immediately after executing clean(k), so S_{k+1} will be clean the next time that N executes clean(k). Therefore, assume that $k = l_t$. By definition of l_t, $t = m2^{k-1}$, where m is odd. N next executes clean(k) at stage

$$t_1 = t + 2^{k-1}$$
$$= m2^{k-1} + 2^{k-1}$$
$$= (m+1)2^{k-1}.$$

However, $m + 1$ is even, so N executes clean(k) at stage t_1 also. We need to show that conditions (i) and (ii) hold when N attempts to clean S_k at stage t_1. Consider the actions that take place when N cleans S_k at stage t that might interfere with conditions (i) and (ii) holding at stage t_1. If S_k is full prior to execution of clean(k) at stage t, then, after execution, S_k has one full block and two empty blocks, and S_{k+1} might be full. This can be a problem only if S_k is full at stage t_1, but that cannot happen: It requires at least 2^k executions of sim to fill two blocks of S_k, but N simulates only 2^{k-1} moves of M between stages t and t_1. The other possibility that we must eliminate is that S_k and S_{k+1} are both empty at stage $t+1$. If S_{k+1} is empty at stage $t+1$, it is because S_k is empty is stage t, for which reason N moves one full block from S_{k+1} into two full blocks of S_k. Thus, in this case, after execution of clean(k) at stage t, S_k has two full blocks. Now, just as in the previous case, we see that it is impossible for S_k to be empty at stage $t+1$: It requires at least 2^k simulations of sim to empty two blocks of S_k.

The argument for S_{-k} is identical, so the proof of the claim is complete.   □

Our discussion demonstrates that N accepts L and that N is oblivious. Now we must determine N's running time. Each execution of sim takes time $O(1)$ and sim executes $T(n)$ times. An execution of clean(k) takes $O(2^k)$ steps, because moving takes a number of steps proportional to the number of symbols moved. As we have seen already, there must be at least 2^{k-1} stages between consecutive executions of clean(k). (If clean(k) executes at stage t, then $k \leq l_t$, so N executes clean(k) next at stage $k+2^{k+1}$.) Also, N does not perform clean(k) for the first time until stage 2^{k-1}. Thus, for each k, N executes clean(k) at most $T(n)/2^{k-1}$ times, and each costs $O(2^k)$. The largest value of k such that N executes clean(k) is

$$m = \log T(n) + 1.$$

Thus, the number $T_N(n)$ of moves N makes is given as follows:

$$T_N(n) \leq \sum_{i=1}^{m} \frac{T(n)O(2^i)}{2^{i-1}}$$

$$\leq c2T(n)[\log T(n) + 1]$$

$$\leq 4cT(n)\log T(n),$$

where c is a constant. This completes the proof of the theorem.   □

Homework 5.7 *Let M be a Turing machine, the details of which are unnecessary to specify, except to say that on one of its tapes M always moves left, replaces the symbol a that it currently scans by the symbol a', and remains in the same state. Give N's simulation for this tape of the first four stages. Present your answer as a sequence of drawings.*

The next result [BGW70] shows that a two-tape nondeterministic machine can simulate a k-tape machine with a time loss of only a multiplicative constant. The proof we give here is due to Seiferas, Fischer, and Meyer [SFM78].

Theorem 5.7 ([BGW70]). *If L is accepted by a k-tape $T(n)$ time-bounded non-deterministic Turing machine M, then there are a constant $c > 0$ and a two-tape nondeterministic Turing machine N that accepts L such that for each word $x \in L$, the number of steps in the shortest computation of N on x is at most $cT(n)$.*

Proof. Define the "display" of a configuration of a k-tape Turing machine M to be a $k+1$-tuple consisting of the current state and the k tape symbols scanned in the configuration. The display of a configuration determines whether the configuration is an accepting one and if it is not, determines what actions of M are legal as the next move. We design N to behave as follows: N nondeterministically guesses on its second tape an alternating sequence of displays and legal actions by M. Observe that this sequence describes a legal computation by M on the given input if and only if the symbols that are actually scanned on each tape when the actions are taken agree with the guessed displays. This can be checked independently for each tape in turn by letting the first tape of N play the role of the tape to be checked while running through the guessed sequence of displays and actions. Clearly, each check takes time proportional to the length of the guessed sequence. Since there are k checks, the total running time of N is proportional to the length of the guessed check. □

5.4 Inclusion Relationships

Now we survey the known inclusion relationships between time-bounded and space-bounded, deterministic, and nondeterministic classes.

Our first theorem requires no proof.

Theorem 5.8. *For every function f,*

$$\text{DTIME}(f) \subseteq \text{DSPACE}(f)$$

and

$$\text{NTIME}(f) \subseteq \text{NSPACE}(f).$$

A Turing machine might enter an infinite loop and still use only bounded space. Nevertheless, the next theorem shows that if a language L is accepted by an $S(n)$ space-bounded Turing machine, where $S(n) \geq \log(n)$, then L is accepted by an $S(n)$ space-bounded Turing machine that halts on every input. The proof depends on the observation that within space $S(n)$ a Turing machine can enter at most an exponential in $S(n)$ possible distinct configurations. A machine enters an infinite loop by repeating one of these configurations, thus making loop detection possible.

Lemma 5.1. *Let M be a one-tape $S(n)$ space-bounded Turing machine, where $S(n) \geq \log n$. Define the length of a configuration I of M to be the length of the work tape of M in configuration I. There exists a constant k such that for each n and each l, $\log n \leq l \leq S(n)$, the number of different configurations of M having length l on any input of length n is at most k^l. In particular, the number of different configurations of M on any input of length n is at most $k^{S(n)}$.*

Proof. Assume that M has s states and t tape symbols. A configuration I of M of length l consists of

(i) the input head position (at most $n + 1$),
(ii) the tape head position (at most l),

(iii) the current state (at most s), and
(iv) the tape contents (at most t^l).

Thus, M has at most $(n+1)slt^l$ different configurations.

We claim that there is a constant k such that for all $n \geq 1$ and $\log n \leq l \leq S(n)$,

$$k^l \geq (n+1)slt^l.$$

We will not prove the claim in detail, but simply note that the key is the following sequence of inequalities: Suppose c and d are constants;

$$\begin{aligned}
n^c d^l &= 2^{c\log n} d^l \\
&= 2^{c\log n} 2^{d_1 l}, \quad \text{for some } d_1 \\
&= 2^{c\log n + d_1 l} \\
&\leq 2^{cl + d_1 l}, \quad \text{since } \log n \leq l \\
&= k^l, \quad \text{for some } k.
\end{aligned}$$

$\square$

Using Lemma 5.1, the following theorem is obtained easily.

Theorem 5.9 ([HU69]). *If L is accepted by an $S(n)$ space-bounded Turing machine, $S(n) \geq \log n$, then L is accepted by an $S(n)$ space-bounded Turing machine that halts on every input.*

Proof. Let M be a one-tape $S(n)$ space-bounded off-line Turing machine that accepts L. Let k be the constant guaranteed by Lemma 5.1. We design a Turing machine N to simulate M but to shut off after $k^{S(n)}$ moves. N simulates M on one track and at the same time counts in base k on another track, thereby using no more than $S(n)$ space to count to $k^{S(n)}$. More generally, for each length $\log n \leq l \leq S(n)$, N uses no more than space l to count to k^l.

N initially assigns $\log n$ space to the counter. Whenever M scans a new cell beyond the cells containing the counter, increase the counter length by 1. Suppose M repeats some configuration. Then, this must occur with M using only some l cells, where $l \leq S(n)$. Thus, by Lemma 5.1, this looping will eventually be detected because the counter will not be large enough to hold the count. Since M is $S(n)$ space-bounded, the largest the counter can be is $S(n)$, which is large enough to hold the count of all of M's accepting computations. Thus, $L(N) = L(M)$. $\square$

Corollary 5.6.

$$\mathrm{DSPACE}(S(n)) \subseteq \bigcup \{\mathrm{DTIME}(c^{S(n)}) \mid c \geq 1\},$$

for $S(n) \geq \log(n)$.

The next result improves one of the assertions of Theorem 5.8.

Theorem 5.10.

$$\text{NTIME}(T(n)) \subseteq \text{DSPACE}(T(n)).$$

Recall the breadth-first search in the proof of Theorem 2.3: To prove Theorem 5.10, we need to observe that if we are given a $T(n)$ time-bounded nondeterministic Turing machine, then the deterministic Turing machine that performs the breadth-first search simulation is $T(n)$ space-bounded.

Proof. Let L be accepted by k-tape Turing machine N in time $T(n)$. As in the proof of Theorem 2.3, let b be the largest number of choices given by N's transition function. Assign addresses to each node of N's computation tree as we did earlier. Since each computation path of N on an input of length n is bounded by $T(n)$, all computation paths will terminate within $T(n)$ steps, and every address has length less than or equal to $T(n)$.

Define M to be a $(k+2)$-tape off-line Turing machine. In order for the breadth-first search algorithm to terminate correctly, it needs to recognize two cases: when N has an accepting path, and when all paths terminate in a nonaccepting configuration. The first case is straightforward. The algorithm uses a Boolean flag to detect the second case. The flag is initialized to 0. When the breadth-first search visits the address of a nonterminating configuration, then the flag is changed to 1. After M visits all nodes at a given level in the computation tree, it continues to the next level if the value of the flag is 1 and terminates in the reject state if the flag is set to 0. (The details of how the flag is implemented are not important. We could keep this stored in the finite control of M or on a separate tape. Let's not allow implementation details get in the way of understanding or appreciating the algorithm. With this in mind, we continue as follows.) Turing machine M uses tape $k+1$ to record N's location in the computation tree. The only use of tape $k+2$ will be to contain the value of the Boolean flag in square one that will help us to determine when the simulation is complete. The computation proceeds as follows:

1. Initially the input tape contains the input word w and all other tapes are empty.
2. M copies the input w to tape 1, and writes the symbol 0 onto square one of tape $k+2$.
3. M simulates N on tapes 1 through k using the string on tape $k+1$ to determine which choices to make. If this string does not provide M with a valid simulation, then M aborts this branch and goes to step 4. Otherwise, the string on tape $k+1$ provides M with a valid simulation. If this simulation reaches an accepting configuration, then M halts and accepts. If the simulation reaches a nonaccepting halting configuration, then M aborts this branch and goes to step 4. If the simulation terminates in a nonhalting configuration, then M sets the flag to 1, aborts this branch, and goes to step 4.
4. Let x be the current string on tape $k+1$, let $l = |x|$, and let $x+1$ denote the lexicographically next string after x. If the length of $x+1$ is greater than l and the flag is set to 0, then M halts and rejects, for in the case there are no computation paths of length greater than l. If the length of $x+1$ is greater than l and the flag is

set to 1, then M sets the flag to 0, replaces the string on tape $k+1$ with $x+1$, and returns to step 2. If the length of $x+1$ is equal to l, then M replaces the string on tape $k+1$ with $x+1$ and returns to step 2.

It is clear that M correctly simulates N. Since N is $T(n)$ time-bounded, tapes 1 through k use no more than $T(n)$ cells. Furthermore, since all computation paths terminate within $T(n)$ steps, tape $k+1$ uses no more than $T(n)$ cells. Therefore (using Corollary 5.1), $L \in \mathrm{DSPACE}(T(n))$.   □

Corollary 5.7. $\mathrm{NP} \subseteq \mathrm{PSPACE}$.

The following theorem is a corollary of Theorem 5.10, because there are at most $b^{T(n)}$ distinct computation paths and each path takes at most $T(n)$ steps. Nevertheless, it is instructive to give a proof that is based on a depth-first search of the computation tree, because this will introduce ideas that we will continue to use in later proofs.

Theorem 5.11.

$$\mathrm{NTIME}(T(n)) \subseteq \bigcup \{\mathrm{DTIME}(c^{T(n)}) \mid c \geq 1\}.$$

Proof. Let L be accepted by M in time $T(n)$. Assume that M is a k-tape on-line nondeterministic Turing machine with s states and t tape symbols. A configuration of M consists of

(i)   the current state (at most s),
(ii) the position of each tape head (at most $(T(n)+1)^k$), and
(iii) the tape contents (at most $t^{kT(n)}$).

Thus, M has at most $s(T(n)+1)^k t^{kT(n)}$ different configurations. A computation similar to the one in the proof of Lemma 5.1 shows that there exists a constant d such that

$$s(T(n)+1)^k t^{kT(n)} \leq d^{T(n)}$$

for all $n > 0$.

We design a Turing machine N to behave as follows. Let I_0 denote the initial configuration of M. N executes the following procedure in order to make a list of all configurations that M can reach from I_0:

> place I_0 on the list;
> **repeat**
>> **for** each configuration I on the list **do**
>>> place all configurations I' on the list
>>> that M can reach in one move
>>> and that are not already on the list
>> **until** for each I on the list, no such I' exists.

This procedure can be carried out in time $O((\text{length of the list})^2)$ on a RAM, so for some constant c, we can design N to carry out this procedure in time $(\text{length of the list})^c$. The length of the list is $\leq d^{T(n)} * (\text{the length of a configuration})$, and the length of a configuration is bounded by some polynomial in $T(n)$. Finally, $O(1)^{T(n)} T(n)^{O(1)} = O(1)^{T(n)}$.

N is to accept its input if and only if it places an accepting configuration on the list. Since, N makes no more than $O(1)^{T(n)}$ moves on any input, the result is proved.   □

Observe that N in this way computes the transitive closure $\vdash_M^*$ of M's next-move relation $\vdash_M$.

Theorem 5.12 ([Coo71a]). *Let $S(n) \geq \log n$. Let M be a nondeterministic off-line Turing machine such that for every word $x \in L(M)$ there is an accepting computation of M on x that scans at most $S(n)$ cells on any work tape. There is a deterministic on-line Turing machine N such that $L(N) = L(M)$ and there is a constant c such that for every $x \in L(N)$, N on input x makes at most $c^{S(n)}$ moves.*

Corollary 5.8 ([Coo71a]). *If S is fully time-constructible and $S(n) \geq \log(n)$, then $\text{NSPACE}(S(n)) \subseteq \bigcup \{ \text{DTIME}(c^{S(n)}) \mid c \geq 1 \}$.*

Homework 5.8 *Prove the corollary. (Observe, for each constant c, that $c^{S(n)}$ is fully time-constructible when S is. Also, observe that $n \in o(c^{S(n)})$, so the construction in Sect. 5.2.1 can be made to work.)*

Proof. Much as in the proof of the previous theorem, we want to construct N so that N can find all configurations I that are reachable from I_0, the initial configuration of M. Since M on input x has an $S(n)$ space-bounded computation if M accepts x, it suffices to consider only those configurations whose work-tape strings have length bounded by $S(n)$. The problem is, we are not assuming that S is space-constructible, so we may not be able to compute $S(n)$. Instead, N uses a parameter l stored on one of its work tapes to guess at $S(n)$. Initially, $l = 1$. In general, if N finds all configurations I such that $I_0 \vdash_M^* I$ for which M's work tapes are l-bounded, and if none of these is accepting, then l is incremented by 1. The process may run forever, but if M accepts x, then N will find an accepting I for some $l \leq S(n)$.

Let $V_{x,l}$ denote the set of all configurations of M on input x with work tapes restricted to length l. Assume the configurations in $V_{x,l}$ are ordered in some canonical way so that 0 is the number of the initial configuration of M on input x, and consider the $\|V_{x,l}\| \times \|V_{x,l}\|$ Boolean matrix $A_{x,l}$ that represents the next-move relation $\vdash_M$ of M restricted to configurations in $V_{x,l}$. In other words, for $1 \leq i, j \leq \|V_{x,l}\|, A_{x,l}(i,j) = 1$ if and only if $I_i \vdash_M I_j$.

It is well known (assuming you know the Floyd–Warshall algorithm [War62]) that transitive closure of an $n \times n$ matrix can be computed in time $O(n^3)$ on a RAM. Hence, N can compute $A_{x,l}^*$ in $\|V_{x,l}\|^{O(1)}$ steps.

Clearly, M accepts an input word x if and only if there are $l \leq S(n)$ and $j \leq \|V_{x,l}\|$ such that I_j is an accepting configuration and $A_{x,l}^*(0,j) = 1$. Thus, if M accepts x, then N accepts x within

$$\sum_{l=1}^{S(n)} \|V_{x,l}\|^{O(1)}$$

steps. Finally, there is a constant d such that for all l, $\|V_{x,l}\| \leq d^{S(n)}$. Thus,

$$\sum_{l=1}^{S(n)} \|V_{x,l}\|^{O(1)} = O(1)^{S(n)},$$

which proves our result.   □

The theorems we have studied thus far are proved by reasonably straightforward simulations. The next theorem involves a deep recursion in the simulation. The result is due to Savitch [Sav70] and is widely known as Savitch's Theorem. Our formulation of the proof is due to Hopcroft and Ullman [HU79].

Theorem 5.13 (Savitch [Sav70]). *If S is fully space-constructible and $S(n) \geq \log(n)$, then*
$$\mathrm{NSPACE}(S(n)) \subseteq \mathrm{DSPACE}(S^2(n)).$$

This is an important result. Observe that a standard depth-first search simulation, as in the previous theorems, would only provide an exponential upper bound.

Corollary 5.9.

$$\mathrm{PSPACE} = \bigcup \{\mathrm{DSPACE}(n^c) \mid c \geq 1\}$$

$$= \bigcup \{\mathrm{NSPACE}(n^c) \mid c \geq 1\}$$

and

$$\mathrm{POLYLOGSPACE} = \bigcup \{\mathrm{DSPACE}(\log(n)^c) \mid c \geq 1\}$$

$$= \bigcup \{\mathrm{NSPACE}(\log(n)^c) \mid c \geq 1\}.$$

For this reason, we did not define nondeterministic versions of PSPACE and POLYLOGSPACE as standard complexity classes.

Corollary 5.10.

$$\mathrm{NSPACE}(n) \subseteq \mathrm{DSPACE}(n^2)$$

and

$$\mathrm{NL} \subseteq \mathrm{POLYLOGSPACE}.$$

Proof. To begin the proof of Theorem 5.13, Let S be a fully space-constructible function such that $S(n) \geq \log(n)$, and let $L = L(M)$, where M is an $S(n)$ space-bounded one-tape nondeterministic Turing machine with s states and t tape symbols.

Using Lemma 5.1, recall that there is a constant c so that $c^{S(n)}$ is greater than or equal to the number of configurations for an input of length n. If M accepts an input word w, $|w| = n$, then a shortest accepting computation will not have any configuration repeated. Thus, if M accepts w, there is an accepting computation of length $\leq c^{S(n)}$.

Let $m = \lceil \log c \rceil$. The value $c^{S(n)}$ in binary notation has length at most

$$\lceil \log c^{S(n)} \rceil \leq S(n) \lceil \log c \rceil = mS(n).$$

Also, $2^{mS(n)} \geq c^{S(n)}$.

Let w be an input word of length n. Recall that we defined the length of a configuration I to mean the length of the work tape of M in configuration I. If M accepts w, then there is a sequence of at most $2^{mS(n)}$ moves from the initial configuration I_0 to some accepting configuration I_f of length at most $S(n)$. Moreover, each intermediate configuration must have length at most $S(n)$.

In Fig. 5.4 we introduce a computable function

$$\text{TEST}(I_1, I_2, i) : \text{Boolean};$$

that returns true if and only if there is a sequence of at most 2^i moves from I_1 to I_2 such that each intermediate move has length at most $S(n)$. Then we can determine membership of w in L by the following procedure that makes calls to TEST:

> **for** each accepting configuration I_f
> of length at most $S(n)$ **do**
> **if** TEST$(I_0, I_f, mS(n))$
> **then** accept;
> reject;

FUNCTION TEST(I_1, I_2, i): Boolean;
var I': configuration;
begin
if $(i = 0)$ and $(I_1 = I_2$ or $I_1 \vdash_M I_2)$
    then return true;
if $i \geq 1$
    then for each I' of length at most $S(n)$ **do**
        if TEST$(I_1, I', i-1)$ and TEST$(I', I_2, i-1)$
           then return true;
return false;
end;

Fig. 5.4 The recursive procedure TEST

We claim that these procedures can be implemented by an $S^2(n)$ space-bounded deterministic Turing machine. First, let us observe that each of the configurations I_1, I_2, and I' requires no more than $O(S(n))$ space. This is certainly true of the storage tape and head positions. Since we are assuming that $\log n \leq S(n)$, the input head position can be written in binary in no more than $S(n)$ space. Also, since $i \leq mS(n)$, i in binary takes $\leq O(S(n))$ space. So the active variables in a call to TEST takes space $O(S(n))$.

TEST can be implemented by a stack of activation records for the calls. The activation record contains the values of all global and local variables at the current incarnation of the recursion. Although students of computer science should be familiar with the implementation of recursive procedures, let's visit the implementation of TEST, because we want to see that the depth of the stack is never more than $mS(n)$. The initial call to TEST has $i = mS(n)$, each successive call decrements the value of i by 1, and no call is made with $i = 0$. Each call to TEST generates two new recursive calls to TEST. However, we do not make the second call until the first call is returned, and we make the second call only if the first call is positive.

Implement the recursive procedure as follows: Use a tape of the Turing machine we are constructing as a stack. To execute $\text{TEST}(I_1, I_2, i)$, if $i \geq 1$, then begin an enumeration of the configurations I' of length at most $S(n)$. Given such a configuration I', to call TEST from within the current incarnation, write the activation record, which consists of the calling arguments I_1, I_2, I', and i onto the stack. Continue recursively from there. On return from this recursive call, if the return is positive, and if this is the first call to TEST from the current incarnation, then make the second call. Now, it should be clear how to proceed. It should be clear that the value of i in successive activation records on the stack decreases by 1 and therefore that the depth of the stack never exceeds $mS(n)$.

We showed above that each activation record has size $O(S(n))$. Thus, the total stack size is $O(S^2(n))$. Finally, $O(S^2(n))$ space can be compressed to $S^2(n)$, and this proves the theorem. $\square$

The following corollary is a generalization of Theorem 5.13. Note that we do not even assume that $S(n)$ is space-constructible.

Corollary 5.11. *Let $S(n) \geq \log(n)$. If L is accepted by a nondeterministic Turing machine with* simultaneous *bounds of space $S(n)$ and time $T(n)$, then L is accepted by a deterministic Turing machine that accepts every word in L within space $S(n) \log T(n)$.*

Proof. For each $s \geq 1$, let $C(s)$ be the set of all configurations I of M of length $\leq s$. For $I_1, I_2 \in C(s)$, and $t \geq 1$, define $\text{TEST}(I_1, I_2, t, s)$ if and only if there is a computation of M from I_1 to I_2 of length $\leq 2^t$ such that each intermediate configuration belongs to $C(s)$.

Recursive implementation of TEST is as above; however, if the process ever tries to exceed a stack depth of $\log t$, then stop. Observe that the total stack size does not exceed $s \log t$.

We determine membership in L by the following procedure that contains nested loops:

for $t = 1, 2, \ldots$
      for $s = 1, \ldots, t$
            for each accepting configuration I_f
                of length at most s
                    if $\text{TEST}(I_0, I_f, \log t, s)$
                        then accept;
reject;

If M accepts x, then there is an accepting computation that uses space at most $s = S(n)$ and time at most $t = T(n)$. For these values of s and t, the procedure will return and accept – and will use no more than $S(n) \log T(n)$ space. $\square$

Observe that our assertion applies only to words x that belong to L; we make no claim about words that do not belong to L.

The following example illustrates an application of Corollary 5.11. Although in the sequel we will not be concerned with languages that can be accepted by simultaneous resource-bounded Turing machines, let us define

$$\text{N-}SPACE\text{-}TIME(S(n), T(n))$$

to be the set of languages L that are accepted by a nondeterministic Turing machine with *simultaneous* bounds of space $S(n)$ and time $T(n)$. (One could define corresponding deterministic classes similarly.)

Example 5.4.

$$\text{N-SPACE-TIME}(n, n^2) \subseteq \text{DSPACE}(n \log n).$$

Corollary 5.11 yields a deterministic Turing machine that accepts every word in L within space $n \log n$. Even though the corollary does not provide any bound on words that do not belong to L, $n \log n$ is a fully space-constructible function. Thus, we can ensure that no more than $n \log n$ space is used on every input word.

5.4.1   *Relations Between the Standard Classes*

Figures 5.5 and 5.6 show the inclusion relations that emerge by application of the results just presented. In these figures, a complexity class C is included in complexity class D if there is a path from C to D reading upward.

The following consequences follow from Corollary 5.6: $L \subseteq P$, $PSPACE \subseteq EXP$, and $DLBA \subseteq E$.

Corollary 5.7 states that $NP \subseteq PSPACE$.

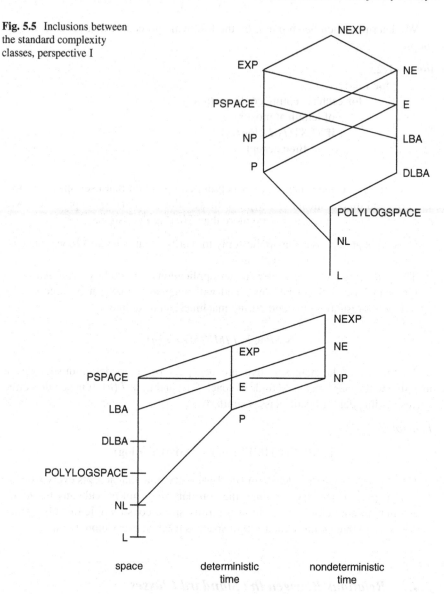

Fig. 5.5 Inclusions between the standard complexity classes, perspective I

Fig. 5.6 Inclusions between the standard complexity classes, perspective II

By Corollary 5.9, we know that LBA ⊆ PSPACE. Corollary 5.10 states than NL ⊆ POLYLOGSPACE.

Corollary 5.8 is used to conclude that NL ⊆ P and LBA ⊆ E.

All other inclusions in the figures are straightforward.

5.5 Separation Results

In this section we consider which of these classes are the same and which are not equal. First though, we present an improvement of Theorem 5.9 due to Sipser that does not require the assumption that $S(n) \geq \log n$. The reader might observe that we could have presented this theorem earlier. However, the main results of the previous section cannot take advantage of Theorem 5.14 because they require Lemma 5.1.

Theorem 5.14 ([Sip78]). *For every one-tape off-line deterministic Turing machine M, there is a Turing machine N such that for all input strings x:*

1. *N accepts if and only if M accepts;*
2. *N uses no more space than does M; and*
3. *N does not loop using a finite amount of tape.*

Proof. Let M be a one-tape off-line Turing machine. We assume without loss of generality that when M accepts an input string it completely erases its work tape, returns the heads to their starting points, and then halts in a unique accepting state. Thus, M has a unique accepting configuration. N will execute a procedure to determine whether M's starting configuration reaches the accepting configuration by a computation that uses at most space l, where $l \geq 1$. Think of the configurations of M using at most space l to be the nodes of a finite directed graph. The edges of the graph "point backward one step in M's computation." That is, if (I, J) is an edge in the digraph, then I and J are configurations of M and $J \vdash_M I$. Because M is deterministic, the component of this graph that contains the accepting configuration is a tree rooted at the accepting configuration. Our procedure begins at the accepting configuration and performs a depth-first search of this tree to determine if the starting configuration is a member. We will say that the procedure is searching *backward* if it is moving backward through a computation (a sequence of configurations) of M; that is, if it is searching down the tree (from the root toward a leaf). For any configuration I', there may be several configurations I such that $I \vdash_M I'$. These are ordered in some canonical way and N selects them one at a time in the usual depth-first search manner. If, however, there is no way to search backward from a current configuration I', either because I' has no predecessor or because the predecessors use space $l + 1$, then a leaf of the tree is reached and the search instead proceeds *forward*. N easily implements a forward search by simulating execution of M one step from the current configuration.

A difficulty arises in using the above reverse-search procedure because N has no advance knowledge of the amount of space used by M, so N will need to execute the procedure iteratively for $l = 1, 2, 3, \ldots$ until an accepting computation is found. If M accepts its input, then this uses exactly as much space as M. However, if M does not accept, then this will run forever (risking the possibility that N uses more space than M). To prevent this, N ensures that M uses at least space $l + 1$ before beginning an $l + 1$ search. N does so by cycling through all configurations using space l and selecting those that are about to use a $(l + 1)$st cell on the next step. (N's read-only input tape contains the same input word as M, so N simulates a move of M from a configuration I of M by writing the contents of I on its work tape, moving its heads to the positions given by I, and entering the state of I. Then N makes the move that M's next-move relation indicates. N can cycle through all configurations of M that use space l by ordering these configurations in some canonical way. After testing a configuration I of length l, N can enter the successor configuration by moving its heads, changing state, or incrementing the word of length l that is written on the work tape in accordance with the canonical ordering.) For each configuration that uses space l and that is about to use an $(l+1)$st cell on the next step, N performs the reverse search for the initial configuration. If none of these reverse searches is successful, then N rejects since it knows that M does not use space $l+1$. If, however, one of these succeeds, then N continues its iteration and performs an $l+1$ search from the accepting configuration as before.   □

Corollary 5.12. *If L is accepted by an $S(n)$ space-bounded Turing machine, then L is accepted by an $S(n)$ space-bounded Turing machine that halts on every input.*

Our first separation result, the *space hierarchy theorem*, asserts that if two space bounds differ by even a small amount, then the corresponding complexity classes differ. The second separation result, the *time hierarchy theorem*, requires that the time functions differ by a logarithmic factor. There are technical reasons for this. The intuition that makes results for time harder to obtain than for space is straightforward though. Time marches relentlessly forward, but space can be reused.

Theorem 5.15 (Space Hierarchy Theorem [HLS65]). *Let $S(n)$ be fully space-constructible. There is a language $L \in \mathrm{DSPACE}(S(n))$ such that for every function $S'(n)$, if $S'(n) \in o(S(n))$, then $L \notin \mathrm{DSPACE}(S'(n))$.*

For each one-tape Turing machine M, let w_M denote the result of encoding M as a word over a two-letter alphabet (Sect. 3.2). Here, however, we assume the two-letter alphabet is $\{0,1\}$. It is possible to pad codes w_M with arbitrarily many extraneous bits in order to obtain a code w for M of every sufficiently large length. To do this, we let the string $w = 0^i 111 w_M$, for each $i \geq 0$, be a pad of the code w_M. If w is a code (padded or otherwise) for some Turing machine, we let M_w denote the Turing machine encoded by w. However, given a Turing machine M, w_M will denote the minimum-length, unpadded, code for M.

The simplest way to obtain a language L that does not belong to $\mathrm{DSPACE}(S'(n))$, in direct analogy to the set $\overline{K}$, which we earlier showed is not accepted by *any* Turing machine, is to define

$$L = \{w_M \mid M \text{ does not accept } w_M \text{ and } M \text{ is } S'(n) \text{ space-bounded}\}.$$

Using diagonalization, L does not belong to $\mathrm{DSPACE}(S'(n))$. However, this language does not satisfy the condition of belonging to $\mathrm{DSPACE}(S(n))$. (It is not even decidable.) To solve this difficulty, the proof to follow defines a language L so that for *each* $S'(n)$ space-bounded Turing machine M, L will contain *some sufficiently large* code w of M if and only if M does not accept w.

Proof. Let C be a one-tape Turing machine that uses exactly $S(n)$ space on every input of length n. We will design a two-tape off-line Turing machine D, whose tape alphabet includes that of C, to behave as follows on an input word w: If w is a code of some one-tape Turing machine M, then first D simulates C on input w on both tapes, marking every cell that it visits. In this manner, D marks $S(|w|)$ cells on both tapes. Then D copies w_M onto one of the tapes, assuming that it is possible. If not, D halts and rejects. On the other tape, using the copy of w_M and the input word w, D attempts to simulate M on input w within the marked region. (It should be clear why D needs a copy of w_M in order to perform its simulation. To see this, recall that D is an off-line Turing machine. So it is not possible to write on the input tape.) If D ever attempts to leave the marked region, D halts and rejects. D accepts w if and only if it can complete its simulation within the allotted space and M halts without accepting w.

Clearly, $L(D)$ is in DSPACE($S(n)$). Let $S'(n)$ be any function such that $S'(n) \in o(S(n))$. Now we show that $L(D)$ is *not* in DSPACE($S'(n)$). Suppose that $L(D) \in$ DSPACE($S'(n)$) and, using Corollary 5.12, that M is a one-tape, $S'(n)$ space-bounded Turing machine with t tape symbols that halts on all its inputs (because M does not loop on a finite amount of space) and that accepts $L(D)$. Recall that strings of length $\lceil \log t \rceil$ can represent the t tape symbols of M. It follows that D can simulate M on input any code w of M in space $\lceil \log t \rceil S'(|w|) + |w_M|$. Since $S'(n) \in o(S(n))$, we know that

$$(\forall c > 0)(\exists N > 0)(\forall n > N)(cS'(n) < S(n)).$$

Thus,

$$(\exists N > 0)(\forall n > N)(\lceil \log t \rceil S'(n) + |w_M| < S(n)). \tag{5.1}$$

Choose N so that (5.1) is satisfied, and let w be a code of M of length greater than N. Then, on input w, D has sufficient space to simulate M. However, by definition, D accepts w if and only if M does not accept w. Thus, $L(D) \neq L(M)$, which is what we wanted to prove. Thus, $L(D) \notin$ DSPACE($S'(n)$). $\qquad \square$

Let $\subset$ denote *proper* inclusion.

Corollary 5.13. L $\subset$ POLYLOGSPACE, POLYLOGSPACE $\subset$ DLBA, *and* DLBA $\subset$ PSPACE.

Proof. We prove only the second assertion, for the others are straightforward.

$$\text{POLYLOGSPACE} = \bigcup \{\text{DSPACE}((\log n)^k) \mid k \geq 1\}$$

$$\subseteq \text{DSPACE}(n^{\frac{1}{2}})$$

$$\subset \text{DLBA}.$$

$\qquad \square$

Corollary 5.14. LBA $\subset$ PSPACE.

Proof.

$$\text{LBA} = \text{NSPACE}(n), \quad \text{by Corollary 5.1}$$

$$\subseteq \text{DSPACE}(n^2), \quad \text{by Theorem 5.13}$$

$$\subset \text{DSPACE}(n^3), \quad \text{by Theorem 5.15}$$

$$\subseteq \text{PSPACE}.$$

$\square$

The proof of Theorem 5.15 requires that $S(n)$ is fully space-constructible. It is possible to prove this result assuming only that $S(n)$ is space-constructible, but, since the space bounds in which we are interested are fully space-constructible, we will not burden ourselves with the technical intricacies that the extension requires.

While it is immediate that DTIME($T(n)$) is a subset of DSPACE($T(n)$), in 1977, Hopcroft, Paul, and Valiant [HPV77] showed that space is strictly more powerful than time as a resource for deterministic multitape Turing machines. Their theorem is that for all time-bounds $T(n)$, DTIME($T(n)$) $\subseteq$ DSPACE($T(n)/\log T(n)$). By Theorem 5.15, it follows, for all fully space-constructible $T(n)$, that DTIME($T(n)$) is a proper subset of DSPACE($T(n)$).

Theorem 5.16 (Time Hierarchy Theorem [HS65]). *Let T be a fully time-constructible function and assume that there exists a function $T'(n)$ so that*

$$T'(n)\log(T'(n)) \in o(T(n)).$$

Then there is a language $L \in$ DTIME($T(n)$) such that for every function $T'(n)$ such that $T'(n)\log(T'(n)) \in o(T(n))$, $L \notin$ DTIME($T'(n)$).

Proof. Now the goal is to construct a Turing machine D so that D is $T(n)$ time-bounded and simultaneously, for each T', diagonalizes over all T' time-bounded Turing machines. More exactly, $L(D)$ will belong to DTIME($T(n)$), but for every T' and every language $L' \in$ DTIME($T'(n)$), D will diagonalize over some Turing machine that accepts L'. Let us observe that if a word w is a code of a multitape Turing machine M_w, then w must encode the number k of tapes of M_w. The details of how are not important.

We adapt the construction in Sect. 5.2.1: We design D so that on an input word w, D simultaneously does the following: (1) D executes a Turing machine that fully time-constructs $T(|w|)$, and (2) if w is a code of a two-tape Turing machine M_w, then D attempts to simulate M_w on input w. D completes its simulation of M_w on input w only if it can do so within $T(|w|)$ steps. If the simulation is successful within $T(|w|)$ steps, then D accepts w if and only if M_w does not accept w. (If w is not the code of a two-tape Turing machine or the simulation is not successful, then D rejects w.)

Recall from Sect. 5.2.1 that D runs for at most $2(n+1) + T(n)$ steps on inputs of length n. (Therefore, $L(D) \in \text{DTIME}(O(T(n)))$.) We are assuming that $T'(n)$ is a function with the property that $T'(n)\log(T'(n)) \in o(T(n))$. Then, since for all n, $n+1 \leq T'(n)$, it follows that $n+1 \in o(T(n))$. Thus, Theorem 5.2, the linear speedup theorem, applies, from which we conclude that $L(D) \in \text{DTIME}(T(n))$.

Now let us show that $L(D)$ is not in $\text{DTIME}(T'(n))$ if $T'(n)\log(T'(n)) \in o(T(n))$. Suppose otherwise. Then, by Corollary 5.5, there is a two-tape Turing machine M such that $L(M) = L(D)$ and M runs in time $T'(n)\log(T'(n))$. As in the proof of the previous theorem, choose n sufficiently large so that M has a code w of length n and such that

$$\lceil \log t \rceil T'(n)\log(T'(n)) \leq T(n),$$

where t is the number of M's tape symbols. On this input w, D completes its simulation of M and D accepts w if and only if M rejects w. Thus, we have a contradiction; $L(M) \neq L(D)$. So, $L(D)$ is not in $\text{DTIME}(T'(n))$. $\square$

Corollary 5.15. *For every constant $c > 0$, $\text{DTIME}(n^c) \subset \text{DTIME}(n^{c+1})$ and* $\text{DTIME}(2^{cn}) \subset \text{DTIME}(2^{(c+1)n})$.

Corollary 5.16. $\text{P} \subset \text{E}$ *and* $\text{E} \subset \text{EXP}$.

5.6   Translation Techniques and Padding

Using Savitch's theorem and the space hierarchy theorem, it is easy to see that $\text{NSPACE}(n^2)$ is properly included in $\text{DSPACE}(n^5)$, so we may conclude immediately that $\text{NSPACE}(n^2)$ is properly included in $\text{NSPACE}(n^5)$. Using the following theorem, we can show that $\text{NSPACE}(n^2)$ is properly included in $\text{NSPACE}(n^3)$. The theorem states that inclusions "translate" upward. The proof is based on the simple idea of padding, which we illustrate with the observation that if L is a language in $\text{DSPACE}(n^2)$, then the language of "padded" words

$$\left\{ w10^{|w|^2-|w|-1} \mid w \in L \right\}$$

is in $\text{DSPACE}(n)$.

Lemma 5.2. *Let $S(n)$ and $f(n)$ be fully space-constructible functions, where $S(n) \geq n$ and $f(n) \geq n$. For a language L, define*

$$p(L) = \{x10^i \mid x \in L \text{ and } |x10^i| = f(|x|)\}.$$

Then $L \in \text{NSPACE}(S(f(n))) \Leftrightarrow p(L) \in \text{NSPACE}(S(n))$.

Proof. Let $L \in \text{NSPACE}(S(f(n)))$ and let M be a nondeterministic $S(f(n))$ space-bounded Turing machine that accepts L. We need to define an $S(n)$ space-bounded Turing machine N to accept $p(L)$. On an input $x10^i$, N marks $|x10^i|$ cells. Then N identifies x and within the marked cells N attempts to mark $f(|x|)$ cells. If N discovers that $f(|x|)$ is less than $|x10^i|$, or if attempting to mark $f(|x|)$ cells wants to use more than $|x10^i|$ cells, then N halts without accepting, for the two lengths are not equal. Next, N uses these cells to mark $S(f(|x|))$ cells. Since $S(n) \geq n$, we have $S(f(n)) \geq f(n)$; so N uses at most $S(f(|x|))$ cells for this. Then N simulates a computation of M on x and accepts its input if and only if the computation is accepting and stays within the marked cells. It is clear that N accepts $p(L)$ and, letting $n = |x10^i|$, since $|x10^i| = f(|x|)$, it is clear that N operates in space $S(n)$.

To prove the converse, suppose $p(L) \in \text{NSPACE}(S(n))$ and let M be a nondeterministic $S(n)$ space-bounded Turing machine that accepts $p(L)$. We define an $S(f(n))$ space-bounded Turing machine N that accepts L: On an input word x, N marks $f(|x|)$ cells and then writes $x10^i$ on the marked cells, where $|x10^i| = f(|x|)$. Then N simulates a computation of M on $x10^i$ and accepts its input if and only if the computation is accepting. A computation of M on $x10^i$ uses space at most $S(|x10^i|) = S(f(|x|))$. Thus, N accepts L and N is $S(f(n))$ space-bounded.   □

Theorem 5.17. *Let $S_1(n)$, $S_2(n)$, and $f(n)$ be fully space-constructible functions, where $S_1(n) \geq n$, $S_2(n) \geq n$ and $f(n) \geq n$. Then*

$$\text{NSPACE}(S_1(n)) \subseteq \text{NSPACE}(S_2(n)) \text{ implies } \text{NSPACE}(S_1(f(n)))$$

$$\subseteq \text{NSPACE}(S_2(f(n))).$$

Proof. Let $L \in \text{NSPACE}(S_1(f(n)))$. By Lemma 5.2, $p(L) \in \text{NSPACE}(S_1(n))$. So, $p(L) \in \text{NSPACE}(S_2(n))$. Use the lemma again to conclude that $L \in \text{NSPACE}$ $(S_2(f(n)))$.   □

Similar arguments show analogous results for DSPACE, DTIME, and NTIME.

Example 5.5. $\text{NSPACE}(n^2)$ is properly included in $\text{NSPACE}(n^3)$.

Suppose that $\text{NSPACE}(n^3) \subseteq \text{NSPACE}(n^2)$. Apply Theorem 5.17 with $f(n) = n^2$ to get $\text{NSPACE}(n^6) \subseteq \text{NSPACE}(n^4)$, and with $f(n) = n^3$ to get $\text{NSPACE}(n^9) \subseteq \text{NSPACE}(n^6)$. Then combine these inclusions to derive the following:

$$\text{NSPACE}(n^9) \subseteq \text{NSPACE}(n^6)$$

$$\subseteq \text{NSPACE}(n^4)$$

$$\subseteq \text{DSPACE}(n^8), \text{ by Theorem 5.13}$$

$$\subset \text{DSPACE}(n^9)$$

$$\subseteq \text{NSPACE}(n^9),$$

which is a contradiction. Thus, our assumption that $\text{NSPACE}(n^3)$ is included in $\text{NSPACE}(n^2)$ is false.

Using a similar line of reasoning, Ibarra [Iba72] proved that $\text{NSPACE}(n^r) \subset$ $\text{NSPACE}(n^{r+\varepsilon})$ for all $\varepsilon > 0$ and $r \geq 0$. We will not prove this result because a tight hierarchy theorem for nondeterministic space will follow immediately from a result, Theorem 5.21, that we will obtain in a later section. Nevertheless, translation techniques remain important, as the next example, due to Hopcroft and Ullman [HU79], demonstrates.

Example 5.6. We use the analog of Theorem 5.17 for deterministic time to show that
$$\text{DTIME}(2^n) \subset \text{DTIME}(n2^n).$$
This does not follow from Theorem 5.16 because
$$\inf_{n \mapsto \infty} \frac{2^n \log 2^n}{n2^n} = \inf_{n \mapsto \infty} \frac{n2^n}{n2^n} = 1.$$

Suppose $\text{DTIME}(n2^n) \subseteq \text{DTIME}(2^n)$. Apply the translation theorem with $f(n) = 2^n$ to get
$$\text{DTIME}(2^n 2^{2^n}) \subseteq \text{DTIME}(2^{2^n})$$
and with $f(n) = n + 2^n$ to get
$$\text{DTIME}((n+2^n)2^{n+2^n}) \subseteq \text{DTIME}(2^{n+2^n}).$$

Combining these inclusions, we arrive at
$$\text{DTIME}((n+2^n)2^n 2^{2^n}) \subseteq \text{DTIME}(2^{2^n}).$$
However,
$$\inf_{n \mapsto \infty} \frac{(n+2^n)2^n 2^{2^n}}{2^{2^n} \log 2^{2^n}} = \inf_{n \mapsto \infty} \frac{(n+2^n)2^n 2^{2^n}}{2^{2^n} 2^n}$$
$$= \inf_{n \mapsto \infty}(n + 2^n) = \infty.$$

Thus, $\text{DTIME}((n+2^n)2^n 2^{2^n}) \subseteq \text{DTIME}(2^{2^n})$ is false, from which it follows that our assumption $\text{DTIME}(n2^n) \subseteq \text{DTIME}(2^n)$ is false.

There are hierarchy theorems for nondeterministic time, and these are harder to obtain than for nondeterministic space because Savitch's theorem, Theorem 5.13, is not available. The results that are known use translation techniques in exceedingly clever ways. Observe that straightforward diagonalization does not work because we do not know how to detect in time $T(n)$ when a nondeterministic $T(n)$ time-bounded Turing machine does not accept its input. Cook [Coo73] obtained the first hierarchy theorem for nondeterministic time, and Seiferas, Fischer, and Meyer [SFM78] wrote a thorough study of such hierarchy theorems. The strongest hierarchy theorem for nondeterministic time that is currently known is due to Žák [Ž83]. Žák proved that if T_1 and T_2 are fully time-constructible functions such that $T_1(n+1) \in o(T_2(n))$, then $\text{NTIME}(T_2(n))$ contains a set that is not in $\text{NTIME}(T_1(n))$.

5.6.1 Tally Languages

A *tally* string is a word over the alphabet $\{1\}^*$, and a tally language is a subset of $\{1\}^*$. We have seen already that natural numbers n can be represented succinctly as a word $n(w)$ in 2-adic notation. Unlike such an acceptable representation, the tally string $1^{n(w)}$ is a verbose representation of the information $n(w)$ that w represents. Here we will exploit this observation in order to obtain another interesting translation result. For $L \subseteq \Sigma^*$, let $\text{Tally}(L) = \{1^{n(w)} \mid w \in L\}$.

Theorem 5.18 ([Boo74]). NE $\subseteq$ E *if and only if every tally language in* NP *belongs to* P.

Proof. Let Σ be a two-letter alphabet and let L denote a language in Σ^*. The proof proceeds by establishing the following four claims:

1. $L \in$ NE $\Rightarrow$ Tally$(L) \in$ NP;
2. Tally$(L) \in$ P $\Rightarrow L \in$ E;
3. Tally$(L) \in$ NP $\Rightarrow L \in$ NE;
4. $L \in$ E $\Rightarrow$ Tally$(L) \in$ P.

Assume that the claims are correct. Let $L \in$ NE and assume that every tally language in NP belongs to P. By claim 1, Tally$(L) \in$ NP, so Tally$(L) \in$ P. Then, by claim 2, $L \in$ E. Thus, NE $\subseteq$ E. To prove the converse, let T be a tally language in NP and assume that NE $\subseteq$ E. Let $L = \{w \in \Sigma^* \mid 1^{n(w)} \in T\}$. By claim 3, $L \in$ NE, so $L \in$ E. Then, by claim 4, Tally$(L) = T \in$ P. Thus, every tally language in NP belongs to P.

We present the proof of the first claim: Let $L \in$ NE, and let M_1 be a 2^{cn} time-bounded nondeterministic multitape Turing machine that accepts L. From M_1 we construct a Turing machine M_2 that operates as follows: Given an input string 1^m, M_2 writes onto a storage tape the unique word w such that $n(w) = m$. M_2 does this by adding 1 in dyadic notation for each symbol 1 read as input. Then, M_2 simulates M_1's computation on w and M_2 accepts $1^{n(w)}$ if and only if M_1 accepts w. Thus, $L(M_2) = \text{Tally}(L(M_1)) = \text{Tally}(L)$. We need to calculate the running time of M_2 as a function of the length of its input word, i.e., as a function of m. The number of steps taken by M_2 is $O(m \log m + 2^{c|w|})$. For some constant c_2, $|w| \le c_2 \log m$, so M_2 runs in time $O(m \log m + m^{c_3})$ for some constant c_3. Since M_1 is nondeterministic, so is M_2, and M_2 runs in polynomial time. Thus, Tally$(L) \in$ NP, which establishes claim 1.

Homework 5.9 *Prove claims 2, 3, and 4.*

And this completes the proof. $\square$

Corollary 5.17. P $=$ NP *implies* E $=$ NE.

Homework 5.10 *Prove the following: For every* $L \in$ NP, Tally$(L) \in$ P *if and only if* NP $\subseteq$ E.

5.7   Relations Between the Standard Classes: Continued

All known inclusions between the standard classes have been given. Book [Boo72, Boo76] has shown that none of the complexity classes POLYLOGSPACE, DLBA, and LBA is equal to either P or NP. However, to this date, it is not known which of these classes contains a language that does not belong to the other. The following theorem shows that DLBA $\neq$ P, and we leave the others as exercises. The lemma uses a padding argument.

Lemma 5.3. *If* DSPACE$(n) \subseteq$ P, *then* PSPACE $=$ NP $=$ P.

Proof. It suffices to show, for each integer $k > 1$, that DSPACE$(n^k) \subseteq$ P. Let $L \in$ DSPACE(n^k) and define the language $p(L)$ as follows:

$$p(L) = \{w10^m \mid w \in L \text{ and } |w10^m| = |w|^k\}.$$

Since $L \in$ DSPACE(n^k), it follows that $p(L) \in$ DSPACE(n). Thus, by hypothesis, $p(L) \in$ P. However, this implies that $L \in$ P as well, because to accept L, simply pad each input word w to $w10^m$ and use the polynomial-time algorithm for $p(L)$ to determine whether $w10^m \in p(L)$. $\square$

Theorem 5.19 ([Boo72]). DLBA $\neq$ P.

Proof. Recall that DLBA $=$ DSPACE(n). If DSPACE$(n) =$ P, then by Lemma 5.3, PSPACE $=$ P. Combining these, we have PSPACE $\subseteq$ DSPACE(n). However, by the space hierarchy theorem, Theorem 5.15, this inclusion is false. Thus, our assumption that DSPACE$(n) =$ P is false.

Homework 5.11 *Show that* LBA $\neq$ P *and that* DLBA $\neq$ NP

Equality (or inequality) of all other inclusion relationships given in Figs. 5.5 and 5.6 is unknown. Amazingly, proper inclusion of each inclusion in the chain

$$L \subseteq NL \subseteq P \subseteq NP \subseteq PSPACE$$

is an open question even though the ends of the chain are distinct (L $\neq$ PSPACE). Similarly, equality of each inclusion in the chain

$$P \subseteq NP \subseteq PSPACE \subseteq EXP$$

is open, yet P $\neq$ EXP.
Also, it is not known whether any of the inclusions in the chain

$$DLBA \subseteq LBA \subseteq E \subseteq NE$$

are proper.

5.7.1   Complements of Complexity Classes: The Immerman–Szelepcsényi Theorem

It is always important to know whether complexity classes are closed under natural operations. Here we discuss closure under complements. The complement of a language L over the finite alphabet Σ is the language $\overline{L} = \Sigma^* - L$. For any complexity class $\mathscr{C}$, $co\text{-}\mathscr{C} = \{\overline{L} \mid L \in \mathscr{C}\}$.

It is easy to see that $\text{DTIME}(T(n)) = co\text{-}\text{DTIME}(T(n))$ for any time bound $T(n)$. If M is a deterministic $T(n)$ time-bounded Turing machine, we can easily define a deterministic $T(n)$ time-bounded N that accepts $\overline{L(M)}$. N simply accepts if and only if M halts in a nonaccepting state, but in every other respect N behaves exactly as M.

The above trick of reversing the roles of accepting and nonaccepting states is insufficient for showing that deterministic space-bounded complexity classes are closed under complements, because space-bounded Turing machines may enter infinite loops. However, it follows immediately from Sipser's theorem, Theorem 5.14, that this difficulty can be eliminated. Thus, as a corollary of Theorem 5.14 it follows that $\text{DSPACE}(S(n)) = co\text{-}\text{DSPACE}(S(n))$ for all S.

It is not known whether nondeterministic time-bounded complexity classes are closed under complements, and we will discuss the question of whether $\text{NP} = co\text{-}\text{NP}$ in the next chapter.

In 1987 Immerman [Imm88] and Szelepcsényi [Sze88] independently proved that nondeterministic $S(n)$ space-bounded complexity classes are closed under complements for $S(n) \geq \log(n)$. It follows immediately that context-sensitive languages are closed under complements, thus settling a question raised by Kuroda in 1964 [Kur64]. We prove this theorem next.

Theorem 5.20. *For any $S(n) \geq \log(n)$, $\text{NSPACE}(S(N)) = co\text{-}\text{NSPACE}(S(n))$.*

First we will prove Theorem 5.20 with the additional assumption that $S(n)$ is fully space-constructible. Then we will indicate how to remove this condition.

The proof consists of two lemmas. The first lemma says that the exact number of configurations that are reachable from an initial configuration of an $S(n)$ space-bounded nondeterministic Turing machine can be computed in $\text{NSPACE}(S(n))$. The second lemma says that once this number is calculated, rejection as well as acceptance can be detected.

Given an $S(n)$ space-bounded Turing machine M, $S(n) \geq \log(n)$, define the function COUNT_M as follows: For any input word x of M, $\text{COUNT}_M(x) =$ the number of configurations of M that are reachable from I_0^x, the initial configuration of M on input x.

Lemma 5.4. *There is a nondeterministic $S(n)$ space-bounded Turing machine transducer N that computes COUNT_M.*

Proof. By Lemma 5.1, there is a constant k such that the number of different configurations of M on any input of length n is $\leq k^{S(n)}$. Thus, for any input x

of length n, $\text{COUNT}_M(x)$ can be written in space $O(S(n))$. Define the relation $\text{REACH}_M(x,I,d)$, where I is a configuration of M that uses space $S(n)$ and $d \leq k^{S(n)}$ by

$$\text{REACH}_M(x,I,d) \equiv I \text{ is reachable from } I_0^x \text{ in at most } d \text{ steps.}$$

The set of yes-instances of the relation $\text{REACH}_M(x,I,d)$ can be accepted nondeterministically in space $S(n)$ by guessing a computation C of at most d steps from I_0^x, and accepting if and only if I is the final configuration of C.

Let $N(x,d)$ denote the number of configurations that are reachable from I_0^x in at most d steps. We show by induction on d that $N(x,d)$ can be computed nondeterministically in space $S(n)$. This will prove the lemma for $\text{COUNT}_M(x) = N(x,k^{S(n)})$. Obviously, $N(x,0) = 1$. A naive approach to computing $N(x,d+1)$ would be to cycle through all configurations that use space $S(n)$ and to increment a counter for each configuration that is found to be reachable from I_0^x in at most $d+1$ steps (i.e., for which $\text{REACH}_M(x,I,d+1)$). It is possible that the nondeterministic algorithm that implements $\text{REACH}_M(x,I,d+1)$ does not execute an accepting computation even though the relation is true. Thus, this approach cannot be correct. Observe that a configuration TARGET is reachable from I_0^x in at most $d+1$ steps if and only if there is a configuration TEST such that $\text{REACH}_M(x,\text{TEST},d)$ and TARGET = TEST or TEST leads to TARGET in one step. By induction hypothesis we know the number $N(x,d)$ of different configurations such that $\text{REACH}_M(x,\text{TEST},d)$ holds. In order to have a correct procedure, we only need to know that TEST is one of these. To summarize, we cycle through all configurations TARGET that use space $S(n)$. For each, we cycle through all configurations TEST, and for each such that $\text{REACH}_M(x,\text{TEST},d)$, we increment a counter if TARGET = TEST or TEST leads to TARGET in one step.

The procedure to compute $N(x,d+1)$ is given in Fig. 5.7. In this procedure, if I is a configuration that uses space $S(n)$, we let $I+1$ denote the next configuration in the lexicographic ordering of all configurations that use space $S(n)$. In order to properly initialize the program, let $\perp$ denote the predecessor of the lexicographically smallest configuration that uses space $S(n)$, and let us stipulate that $\text{REACH}_M(x,\perp,d)$ is false for all x and d.

Since each configuration uses space $S(n)$, the counters never exceed $k^{S(n)}$, and REACH_M is accepted in nondeterministic space $S(n)$, it follows that the procedure can be implemented by a nondeterministic $S(n)$ space-bounded Turing machine transducer.

To see that the procedure is correct, in an accepting computation each execution of the inner loop terminates without causing the procedure to halt. Thus, either TARGET is reachable and C is incremented, or we can be sure that TARGET is not reachable because all $N(x,d)$ values of TEST have been found. $\square$

Lemma 5.5. *There is a nondeterministic $S(n)$ space-bounded Turing machine N' that, given input words x and $\text{COUNT}_M(x)$, accepts if and only if M does not accept x.*

$C := 0$; {C is a counter that will hold $N(x, d+1)$ }
for each configuration $TARGET$ that uses space $S(n)$ **do**
{cycle through all such configurations in lexicographic order}
>   **begin**
> $D := 0$;
>   {D is a counter that will increment to $N(x, d)$ }
>   TEST $:= \perp$;
>   **repeat**
>   >   TEST $:=$ TEST $+ 1$;
>   >   **if** $REACH_M(x, TEST, d)$ **then**
>   >   > $D := D + 1$;
>   >
>   >   **until** $(D = N(x, d))$ or $(REACH_M(x, TEST, d)$ and
>   > $(TARGET = TEST$ or TEST leads to TARGET in one step))
>   >   or (all configurations that use space $S(n)$ have been tested);
>   >   **if** $REACH_M(x, TEST, d)$ and $(TARGET = TEST$ or
>   >   TEST leads to TARGET in one step)
>   >   >   **then** $C := C + 1$; { $REACH_M(x, TARGET, d+1)$ }
>   >   >   **else if** $(D \neq N(x, d))$ **then**
>   >   >   >   halt without accepting;
>   >   >   >   {all configurations that use space $S(n)$ have been
>   >   >   >   tested but the nondeterministic implementations of
>   >   >   > $REACH_M$ have not found $N(x, d)$ reachable configurations }
>   **end**
> $N(x, d+1) := C$

Fig. 5.7 Procedure to compute $N(x, d+1)$

Proof. Cycle through all configurations that use space $S(n)$. For each such configuration TARGET, nondeterministically determine whether TARGET is reachable from I_0^x (i.e., whether $REACH_M(x, TARGET, k^{S(n)})$) and whether TARGET is an accepting configuration. If this iterative procedure finds an accepting configuration of M on x, then it should halt without accepting. Every time the procedure finds a configuration TARGET for which

$$REACH_M(x, TARGET, k^{S(n)})$$

is true, it iterates a counter. If the counter eventually reaches $COUNT_M(x)$, and none of these $COUNT_M(x)$ configurations is accepting, then the procedure accepts its input, for in this case it has discovered that none of M's reachable configurations on input x has an accepting configuration.

The procedure is given in greater detail in Fig. 5.8. As in the proof of Lemma 5.4, there is an $S(n)$ space-bounded nondeterministic Turing machine N' that implements the procedure. Suppose M accepts. Then at least one of the $COUNT_M(x)$ reachable configurations is accepting, so N' rejects. On the other hand, if M does not accept, then none of the $COUNT_M(x)$ reachable configurations is accepting, so in this case N' accepts. □

$D := 0$; {D is a counter that will increment to $\text{COUNT}_M(x)$ }
$\text{TARGET} := \perp$;
repeat
    $\text{TARGET} := \text{TARGET} + 1$;
    if $\text{REACH}_M(x, \text{TARGET}, k^{S(n)})$ **then**
        $D := D + 1$;
until $(D = \text{COUNT}_M(x))$
    or $(\text{REACH}_M(x, \text{TARGET}, k^{S(n)})$ and TARGET is an accepting configuration)
    or (all configurations that use space $S(n)$ have been tested);
if $\text{REACH}_M(x, \text{TARGET}, k^{S(n)})$ and TARGET is an accepting configuration
    then halt without accepting {because M accepts x}
    else if $D = \text{COUNT}_M(x)$
        then {all reachable configurations of M have
            been found and none of them is accepting}
            accept and halt
        else {all configurations have been tested but the nondeterministic tests
            did not find all $\text{COUNT}_M(x)$ reachable configurations}
            halt without accepting

Fig. 5.8 Procedure to accept $\overline{L(M)}$, given COUNT_M

The proof of Theorem 5.20, with the assumption that $S(n)$ is fully space-constructible, follows immediately from the lemmas. We only need to observe that the value $\text{COUNT}_M(x)$ computed in Lemma 5.4 uses no more than $O(S(n))$ space.

Now that we have mastered the proof, do not assume that $S(n)$ is fully space-constructible. Instead we will initialize a counter S for the space bound to $\log(n)$ and increment the space bound as needed. We need to show that we never exceed $S(n)$ and we need to see that if our algorithm claims that no reachable configuration (within space S) is accepting, then, in fact, the input word x does not belong to $L(M)$. The technique follows:

At some stage of the inductive counting, S has some value and we nondeterministically compute the number of configurations that are reachable within the space bound S and within some d steps. Call this $N(x, S, d)$. (Remember that the procedure to compute $N(x, S, d)$ is nondeterministic; that if the procedure computes a value, the value it computes is correct, and that if no value is returned, the procedure halts.) Suppose that $N(x, S, d)$ is not 0. Then nondeterministically compute $N(x, S + 1, d + 1)$ and $N(x, S, d + 1)$. If the difference is non zero, i.e., M uses space $S + 1$ to reach configurations in $d + 1$ steps that it cannot reach using space S, then continue the process with $S = S + 1$. that is, continue with $N(x, S + 1, d + 1)$. Otherwise, do not increment S; That is, continue with $N(x, S, d + 1)$.

Since no computation path of M on any input x of length n uses more than $S(n)$ space, our procedure does not exceed the space bound $S(n)$, except by a constant. Second, if no computation of M on input x is accepting, then this process will discover that. The point is that for all $S \leq S(n)$ and all $d \leq k^{S(n)}$, all possible routes to reachable configurations are checked.

Counting plays an important role in many aspects of complexity theory, which the interested student can learn more about from the survey article by Schöning [Sch90]. We will introduce certain counting classes in Chap. 11.

Theorem 5.21. *If S_2 is fully space-constructible, $S_1(n) \in o(S_2(n))$ and $S_1 \geq \log n$, then there is a language in NSPACE$(S_2(n))$ that is not in NSPACE$(S_1(n))$.*

Recall that the proof of the hierarchy theorem for deterministic space, Theorem 5.15, required us to show that looping in finite space can be detected. More precisely, if w is the code for some $S_1(n)$ space-bounded deterministic Turing machine, the diagonalizing $S_2(n)$ space-bounded Turing machine D needs to determine whether M_w halts *without accepting* w. This is the information that Theorem 5.20 provides for nondeterministic space.

Proof. Given any Turing machine M_w, let M_w^c denote the nondeterministic Turing machine that is constructed in the proof of Theorem 5.20. Thus, M_w^c uses no more space on any input word than M_w, and M_w^c accepts an input x if and only if $x \notin L(M_w)$. As in the proof of Theorem 5.15, design a nondeterministic Turing machine D to mark $S_2(|w|)$ cells on two tapes, and if D ever attempts to leave the marked region, then D halts and rejects. Next, if w is a code, then D simulates M_w^c on input word w. D accepts w if and only if it completes its simulation within the allotted space and M_w^c accepts w. As a consequence, in the case that D completes its simulation of M_w^c within its allotted space, observe that D accepts w if and only if M_w does not accept w. This is the point we needed to demonstrate; the rest of the proof proceeds exactly as in the proof of Theorem 5.15.

There is one detail that we thus far have glossed over. D must simulate M_w^c from the code for M_w. Thus D must implement the algorithms that comprise the proof of Theorem 5.20. It should be clear that D does so without using any more space on any input word than M_w.

5.8   Additional Homework Problems

Homework 5.12 *If one of the following classes is included in another, state which and explain why. If one of the inclusions is a proper inclusion, then state that and explain why. Find as many inclusions and proper inclusions as possible:* DTIME(n^2), DSPACE(n^8), NTIME(n^2), NSPACE(n^5).

Homework 5.13 *Do the same for the following classes:* DTIME(2^n), DTIME(3^n), NSPACE(2^n), DSPACE(5^n).

Homework 5.14 *Show that if* L $=$ NL, *then* DLBA $=$ LBA. *Use a padding argument.*

Homework 5.15 *Define* ESPACE $= \bigcup\{$DSPACE$(k^n) \mid k \geq 1\}$ *and* NESPACE $= \bigcup\{$NSPACE$(k^n) \mid k \geq 1\}$. *Prove that* ESPACE $=$ NESPACE.

Homework 5.16 *Prove that* NP *is not included in* DTIME(n^k) *for any fixed $k \geq 1$.*

Chapter 6
Nondeterminism and NP-Completeness

Several different additions to the basic deterministic Turing machine model are often considered. These additions add computational power to the model and so allow us to compute certain problems more efficiently. Often these are important problems with seemingly no efficient solution in the basic model. The question then becomes whether the efficiency the additional power provides is really due to the new model or whether the added efficiency could have been attained without the additional resources.

The original and most important example of this type of consideration is nondeterminism. For each of the standard nondeterministic complexity classes we have been considering, it is an open question whether the class is distinct from its deterministic counterpart. We will concentrate our study of nondeterminism on the class NP, for this is the most important nondeterministic complexity class. Recall that

$$\text{NP} = \bigcup \{\text{NTIME}(n^k) \mid k \geq 1\}$$

is the class of languages that can be solved nondeterministically in polynomial time. NP plays a central role in complexity theory as many important problems from computer science and mathematics that are not known to be solvable deterministically in polynomial time are in NP. The most central and well-known open problem in complexity theory is whether P = NP. All that is known about NP with respect to deterministic time is that NP $\subseteq$ EXP. A given problem in NP might be solvable in deterministic polynomial time, or it might require exponential time, but a middle ground is conceivable as well: A function g *majorizes* a function f if there exists $N > 0$ such that, for all $n \geq N, g(n) \geq f(n)$. The function $n^{\log n} = 2^{\log^2(n)}$ is subexponential but majorizes all polynomials. Thus, a given problem in NP might be solvable in, and require, deterministic time $n^{\log n}$. These are general remarks only; unfortunately, little is actually known.

S. Homer and A.L. Selman, *Computability and Complexity Theory*,
Texts in Computer Science, DOI 10.1007/978-1-4614-0682-2_6,
© Springer Science+Business Media, LLC 2011

6.1   Characterizing NP

Recall that a nondeterministic Turing machine is one with a multivalued transition function, and recall that such a machine M accepts an input word x if there is a computation path of M on x that terminates in an accepting state.

Homework 6.1 *Given a Turing machine M, recall that an accepting computation of M is defined to be a sequence of configurations $I_0, I_1, \ldots, I_n$ such that I_0 is an initial configuration, I_n is an accepting configuration, and for each $i < n$, $I_i \vdash_M I_{i+1}$. Thus, a computation is a word over the finite alphabet that defines M. Consider the binary relation R defined as follows:*

$$R(x,y) \Leftrightarrow [x \text{ is an input word to } M \text{ and } y \text{ is an accepting computation of } M \text{ on } x].$$
(6.1)

Show that $\{(x,y) \mid R(x,y)\}$ is in the complexity class L.

The following theorem gives an important machine-independent characterization of NP.

Theorem 6.1. *A set A belongs to* NP *if and only if there exist a polynomial p and a binary relation R that is decidable in polynomial time such that for all words in Σ^*,*

$$x \in A \Leftrightarrow \exists y[|y| \leq p(|x|) \wedge R(x,y)].$$
(6.2)

Proof. Assume that $A \in$ NP, and let M be a nondeterministic polynomial time-bounded Turing machine that accepts A. Since L $\subseteq$ P, it follows from Homework 6.1, that the relation R defined in (6.1) satisfies (6.2).

Conversely, if there exist a polynomial p and a polynomial-time decidable relation R such that (6.2) holds, then a nondeterministic Turing machine N will accept A in the following two-stage manner: On input x, (1) N nondeterministically writes a string y on its work tape whose length is at most $p(|x|)$; (2) N deterministically verifies in polynomial time that $R(x,y)$ holds. Thus, $A \in$ NP.   □

Given a set A in NP together with a corresponding polynomial p and relation R for which (6.2) holds, for any word x in A, a string y such that $R(x,y)$ holds is called a *witness* or *proof* that x belongs to A. Let us reflect on Turing machine N's two-stage process. Informally, stage (1) comprises a "guess" of a witness y to the fact that $x \in A$, and stage (2) comprises a deterministic "verification" that y is a correct guess. Theorem 6.1 demonstrates that "guessing" and "verifying" completely characterize nondeterminism. We can make these observations a bit more formal as follows: Define a *verifier* for a language A to be an algorithm V such that

$$A = \{x \mid \exists y[V \text{ accepts } \langle x,y \rangle]\}.$$

A *polynomial-time verifier* is a verifier that runs in polynomial time in the length of x. Then, the following elegant and useful characterization of NP follows immediately from Theorem 6.1.

Corollary 6.1. NP *is the class of all languages A having a polynomial-time verifier.*

The proof follows by taking V to be the polynomial-time algorithm that accepts the relation $R(x,y)$ in (6.2). Since the length of the witness y is a polynomial in the length of x, V runs in polynomial time in the length of x.

Example 6.1. Recall (Example 3.1) that the Hamiltonian Circuit problem is the problem of determining whether a graph has a Hamiltonian circuit. It is easy to show that the Hamiltonian Circuit problem belongs to NP: A nondeterministic Turing machine in polynomial time can, given as input a graph G, guess a sequence of vertices, and then accept if and only if it verifies that the sequence is a Hamiltonian circuit.

It is just as easy to show that the Hamiltonian Circuit problem belongs to NP by using Corollary 6.1: A verifier V for this problem should, given as input a graph G and a path p in G, accept if p is a Hamiltonian circuit, and reject otherwise.

6.2 The Class P

Before continuing with our detailed discussion of nondeterminism, since the question of whether $P = NP$ drives so much of this development, let us say a few words about the class P. Recall that we identify P with the problems that are feasibly computable and that we do so based on the evidence supporting Church's and Cobham's theses. The simple distinction that makes theory of computing crucial to computing practice, and independent of the current state of technology, is seen by comparing a typical polynomial running time with an exponential one on modest-size input strings: An algorithm whose running time is n^3 on strings of length 100 takes one million (100^3) steps. However, an algorithm whose running time is 2^n would require 2^{100} steps, which is greater than the number of atoms in the universe. Contrary to naive intuition, improvements in hardware technology make this difference more dramatic, not less. As hardware gets faster, computers can handle larger input instances of problems having polynomial-time algorithms, but the number of steps required for an exponential-time algorithm remains unfathomably large.

We present two typical decision problems that belong to P. One's experience as a student of computer science presents many more (everything that you compute). Our examples here are quite simple, but our intent is to illustrate that it is not usually apparent whether a problem has an efficient algorithm, and finding good algorithms is a challenging intellectual endeavor.

First we show that the following GRAPH ACCESSIBILITY PROBLEM (GAP) problem belongs to P.

GRAPH ACCESSIBILITY PROBLEM (GAP)

    instance A digraph $G = (V,A)$, and vertices s and t in V.

    question Is there a path from s to t?

It is obvious that GAP belongs to NP: Just guess a sequence of vertices p beginning with s and ending at t. However, the following straightforward algorithm shows that this problem is in P:

1.   input G, s, and t;
2.   mark node s;
3.   **repeat**
        for all nodes b of G
            if there is an arc (a,b), where a is marked
                then mark b
        until no new nodes are marked;
4.   **if** t is marked **then** accept **else** reject.

Clearly, the algorithm is correct. We only need to see that it operates in polynomial time: Steps 2 and 4 execute once. Let m be the number of nodes in G. The repeat-until loop marks at least one new node every time it executes. Thus, step 3 runs no more than m times. Searching all nodes takes m steps. Marking a node takes constant time. So the algorithm runs in $O(m^2)$ steps. Recalling how we encode graphs as an input string, the length of the input is a polynomial in m. Thus, the algorithm can be implemented on a Turing machine in time a polynomial in the length of the input.

Homework 6.2 *Show that* GAP *belongs to* NL.

The next example demonstrates that the set of relatively prime pairs of integers

$$\text{RELPRIME} = \{(x,y) \mid x \text{ and } y \text{ are relatively prime}\}$$

belongs to P. We learned in Sect. 1.7 that the Euclidean Algorithm computes $\gcd(x,y)$. Thus, all that we need to do is demonstrate that this algorithm runs in polynomial time. Recall that the Euclidean Algorithm proceeds by computing a sequence of remainders $r_1, r_2, \ldots$.

Claim. For each $j \geq 1$, $r_{j+2} < \frac{1}{2}r_j$.

Proof. If $r_{j+1} \leq \frac{1}{2}r_j$, then $r_{j+2} < r_{j+1} \leq \frac{1}{2}r_j$ immediately. Suppose that $r_{j+1} > \frac{1}{2}r_j$. Then the next division gives $r_j = 1 \cdot r_{j+1} + r_{j+2}$, so $r_{j+2} = r_j - r_{j+1} < \frac{1}{2}r_j$.   □

Hence, every two steps cuts the size of the remainder at least in half. Therefore, there are at most $2\log x$ divisions. That is, the loop executes $O(\log x)$ times. Since $\log x$ is essentially the length of x, the loop executes $O(n)$ times, where n is the length of the input, and this completes our demonstration.

6.3 Enumerations

Definition 6.1. A class of sets $\mathscr{C}$ is *effectively presentable* if there is an effective enumeration $\{M_i\}_i$ of Turing machines such that every Turing machine in the enumeration halts on all inputs and $\mathscr{C} = \{L(M_i) \mid i \geq 0\}$.

The key feature in this definition is that the Turing machines halt on all inputs, so an effectively presentable class must be a class of decidable sets. Let $\{DM_i\}_i$ be the standard effective enumeration of all deterministic Turing machines from Chap. 3, and let $\{NM_i\}_i$ be a standard effective enumeration of all nondeterministic Turing machines. (We can obtain this easily by encoding nondeterministic Turing machines in the same way that we encoded deterministic Turing machines.) We want to start with these enumerations and develop effective presentations of the languages in P and NP, respectively. A naive approach would be to scan the machines in each list, select those that are polynomial time-bounded, and discard the others. However, this is not possible, for we are stymied by the following theorem.

Theorem 6.2. *There is no effective enumeration of the class of all deterministic Turing machines that operate in polynomial time. That is,*

$$S = \{i \mid DM_i \text{ operates in polynomial time}\}$$

is not a computably enumerable set.

The analogous result holds for nondeterministic machines as well. Intuitively, the problem is that one cannot decide whether a Turing machine is polynomial time-bounded. The exact difficulty of the set S is given by Hájek [Háj79].

Proof. The set $L_U = \{\langle i, w \rangle \mid$ Turing machine DM_i on input w converges$\}$ is a computably enumerable, undecidable set. Thus, the complement of L_U, the set

$$D = \{\langle i, w \rangle \mid DM_i \text{ on input } w \text{ diverges}\}$$

is not computably enumerable, because it is the complement of a computably enumerable, undecidable set.

Now, we will give an effective procedure that, given a Turing machine code i and input word w, produces a Turing machine $F(i, w)$ such that $\langle i, w \rangle \in D$ if and only if $F(i, w)$ operates in polynomial time. It follows that any effective enumeration of the class of all deterministic Turing machines that operate in polynomial time would yield one for D.

$F(i, w)$ on an input word x is to operate as follows: Simulate DM_i on w for at most $|x|$ steps. If DM_i on w does not halt within $|x|$ steps, then accept input x. Otherwise, let $F(i, w)$ run forever on x.

If DM_i diverges on input w, then $F(i, w)$ will accept every word x in linear time. If DM_i converges on input w, then it will do so after some N steps. So $F(i, w)$ will run forever, and therefore not operate in polynomial time, on all inputs of length greater than N. Thus, $\langle i, w \rangle \in D \Leftrightarrow F(i, w)$ operates in polynomial time.

The proof is essentially complete. For each Turing-machine code i and input word w, define $f(i, w)$ to be the code for the Turing machine $F(i, w)$. Then

$$\langle i, w \rangle \in D \Leftrightarrow f(i, w) \in S.$$

Observe that f is a computable function. Thus, by Lemma 3.2, S is not c.e.   □

Nevertheless, it is possible to enumerate a list of deterministic Turing machines, $\{P_i\}_i$, each of which is polynomial time-bounded, so that $\{L(P_i) \mid i \geq 0\} = P$ and a list of nondeterministic Turing machines, $\{NP_i\}_i$, each of which is polynomial time-bounded, so that $\{L(NP_i) \mid i \geq 0\} = NP$. By the previous theorem, neither of these lists will contain *all* of the polynomial time-bounded machines, but we don't care.

We will use the pairing function of Sect. 3.3. Observe that the function $<, >$ and its inverses τ_1 and τ_2 are computable in polynomial time, and that $\langle x, y \rangle = z$ implies $x < z$ and $y < z$.

Let $p_j(n) = n^j + j$. Observing that each p_j is fully time-constructible, let C_j be a p_j-clock Turing machine. Let P_k (NP_k) be the Turing machine $DM_i \| C_j$ ($NM_i \| C_j$, respectively), where $k = \langle i, j \rangle$. Then, P_k is a polynomial-time-bounded Turing machine with p_j as its time bound. Furthermore, since $j < k$, p_k is a strict upper bound on the running time of P_k. Thus, each P_k is a polynomial-time-bounded Turing machine and each P_k operates in time p_k. Now we need to show that these classes of machines provide effective presentations of P and NP.

Theorem 6.3. P *and* NP *are effectively presentable:*

$$NP = \{L(NP_i) \mid i \geq 0\};$$

$$P = \{L(P_i) \mid i \geq 0\}.$$

Proof. We give the proof for NP only, as the argument for P is the same. Clearly,

$$\{L(NP_i) \mid i \geq 0\} \subseteq NP.$$

If $L \in NP$, then there is some nondeterministic Turing machine NM_i that accepts L, and there is some polynomial p_j such that NM_i accepts L in time p_j. Thus, the Turing machine $NP_{\langle i,j \rangle} = NM_i \| C_j$ accepts L also. So, $NP \subseteq \{L(NP_i) \mid i \geq 0\}$.   □

Recall that a *function f is computable in time* $T(n)$ if there is a deterministic multitape Turing-machine transducer with a distinguished output tape such that if x is any input of length n, then the Turing machine halts within $T(n)$ moves with $f(x)$ written on the output tape. A function f is *computable in polynomial time* if it is computable in time $p(n)$ for some polynomial p. A class of functions $\mathscr{F}$ is *effectively presentable* if there is an effective enumeration $\{M_i\}_i$ of Turing-machine transducers such that every Turing machine in the enumeration halts on all inputs and $\mathscr{F} = \{f \mid \text{for some } i \geq 0, f \text{ is computed by } M_i\}$. Using the same argument as above, it follows that the class of polynomial-time-computable functions is effectively presentable, and, for each k, the kth Turing-machine transducer in the enumeration operates in time p_k.

6.4 NP-Completeness

The concept of NP-completeness gives us a method of locating problems in NP whose deterministic complexity is as difficult as any problem in NP. One intuition for defining the notion of NP-completeness would be that a problem A in NP is NP-complete if any problem in NP could be computed efficiently using an efficient algorithm for A as a subroutine. In Sect. 3.9, without consideration of time-bounds, this intuition led us to define oracle Turing machines and Turing reductions. However, we will take a stronger condition, leaving this intuition as a necessary condition for NP-completeness, and we will return to consideration of time-bounded oracle Turing machines in Chap. 7. Instead, here we define a polynomial-time-bounded version of many-one reducibility. We say that a problem A in NP is NP-complete if every other problem in NP can be transformed into A by a polynomial-time-bounded function. Thus, A will be as difficult as any problem in NP for the simple reason that A encodes the information in every problem in NP. These remarks are informal, and precise definitions follow.

Definition 6.2. A set A is *many-one reducible in polynomial time* to a set B (notation: $A \leq_m^P B$) if there exists a function f that is computable in polynomial time so that

$$x \in A \Leftrightarrow f(x) \in B.$$

The function f transforms A into B. Polynomial-time many-one reducibility is the time-bounded restriction of *many-one reducibility* (Definition 3.3), which played an important role in our study of the computably enumerable sets. Polynomial-time many-one reducibility is frequently called "Karp reducibility" in honor of its usage in a seminal paper by Karp [Kar72] that demonstrated NP-completeness of a wide variety of important combinatorial problems. Observe that $\leq_m^P$ is a binary relation over Σ^*.

Homework 6.3 *Prove the following facts.*

1. $\leq_m^P$ *is reflexive.*
2. $\leq_m^P$ *is transitive.*
3. $A \leq_m^P B$ *if and only if* $\overline{A} \leq_m^P \overline{B}$.
4. $A \leq_m^P B$ *and* $B \in P$ *implies* $A \in P$. *($\leq_m^P$ preserves membership in P.)*
5. $A \leq_m^P B$ *and* $B \in NP$ *implies* $A \in NP$. *($\leq_m^P$ preserves membership in NP.)*
6. *If* $A \in P$, *then for all* B, $B \neq \Sigma^*$ *and* $B \neq \emptyset$, $A \leq_m^P B$.

In the following theorem we use statement 5 of Homework 6.3 to show that $NP \neq E$. Unfortunately, the proof does not inform us whether $NP \not\subseteq E$, $E \not\subseteq NP$, or both.

Theorem 6.4. $NP \neq E$.

Proof. We know that $\leq_m^P$ preserves membership in NP. We will use a padding argument to show that $\leq_m^P$ does not preserve membership in E. Let A be any set that belongs to $\text{DTIME}(2^{n^2}) - E$. Then let

$$B = \{w10^{|w|^2-|w|-1} \mid w \in A\}.$$

It is easy to see that the padded set B belongs to E. Define a function f by $f(w) = w10^{|w|^2-|w|-1}$, and observe that f is computable in polynomial time. Finally, observe that $w \in A \Leftrightarrow f(w) \in B$. Thus, $A \leq_m^P B$. Since $B \in E$ but $A \notin E$, we see that $\leq_m^P$ does not preserve membership in E, so $NP \neq E$. □

Homework 6.4 $NP \neq NE$.

Homework 6.4 can be solved using a padding argument as in Theorem 6.4. A different proof can be obtained directly using the nondeterministic time hierarchy theorem of Žák [Ž83] stated on page 115. This yields the stronger result $NP \subset NE$.

Homework 6.5 *Show that there exist decidable sets A and B so that $A \leq_m^P B$ and $B \not\leq_m^P A$, and A, B, $\overline{A}$, and $\overline{B}$ are all infinite sets.*

Definition 6.3. A set A is $\leq_m^P$-*complete* for NP (commonly called NP-*complete*) if

1. $A \in NP$;
2. for every set $L \in NP$, $L \leq_m^P A$.

Let A be NP-complete. This definition captures the intuitive notion that every problem in NP is transformable into A. Furthermore, we see readily that any efficient algorithm for A could be used as a subroutine to efficiently determine membership in any set L in NP. An efficient procedure for determining whether x belongs to L is to compute $f(x)$ and then input $f(x)$ to a subroutine for determining membership in A. This observation yields the salient fact about NP-complete problems, which is that $NP = P$ if and only if P contains an NP-complete problem. Thus, each NP-complete problem captures the complexity of the entire class.

Theorem 6.5. *If A is NP-complete, then $A \in P$ if and only if $P = NP$.*

Proof. Let A be NP-complete and let $L \in NP$. By definition, $L \leq_m^P A$. Since A belongs to P, so does L. Thus, $NP \subseteq P$. The converse is trivial. □

Now we prove, rather swiftly, that NP-complete languages exist. We do so by defining a *universal set* for NP. Define

$$\mathcal{U} = \{\langle i,x,0^n\rangle \mid \text{some computation of } NP_i \text{ accepts } x \text{ in fewer than } n \text{ steps}\}. \quad (6.3)$$

Homework 6.6 *Show that $\mathcal{U} \in NP$.*

Observe that it is necessary to write n in unary in (6.3).

Theorem 6.6. $\mathcal{U}$ *is* NP-*complete.*

Proof. We know from Homework 6.6 that $\mathcal{U} \in$ NP, so we have to show that every set $S \in$ NP is $\leq_m^P$-reducible to $\mathcal{U}$. For each $S \in$ NP, there is some i such that $S = L(NP_i)$. Given $S = L(NP_i)$, define f so that for every word x,

$$f(x) = \langle i, x, 0^{p_i(|x|)} \rangle.$$

Clearly, f is computable in polynomial time. Also,

$$x \in S \Leftrightarrow NP_i \text{ accepts } x$$
$$\Leftrightarrow NP_i \text{ accepts } x \text{ in } p_i(|x|) \text{ steps}$$
$$\Leftrightarrow \langle i, x, 0^{p_i(|x|)} \rangle \in \mathcal{U}$$
$$\Leftrightarrow f(x) \in \mathcal{U}.$$

So $S \leq_m^P$ U. $\qquad\qquad\qquad\qquad\qquad\qquad\qquad\qquad\qquad\qquad\qquad\qquad\qquad$ □

Homework 6.7 *Explain why* $\{\langle i, x \rangle \mid NP_i \text{ accepts } x\}$ *is not* NP-*complete.*

Homework 6.8 *Show that*

$$\{\langle i, x, 0^n \rangle \mid \text{ some computation of } NM_i \text{ accepts } x \text{ in fewer than } n \text{ steps}\}$$

is NP-*complete.*

6.5 The Cook–Levin Theorem

Now we know that NP-complete sets exist, but the theory of NP-completeness is important outside the domain of complexity theory because of its practical significance. There exist hundreds of natural[1] NP-complete problems. These include the Hamiltonian Circuit problem, various scheduling problems, packing problems, nonlinear programming, and many others. Many of these NP-complete problems are catalogued in Garey and Johnson's excellent guide to NP-completeness [GJ79]. The first to discover natural NP-complete problems were Cook [Coo71b] and Levin [Lev73]. Moreover, working independently, they were the first to formulate the notion and recognize its importance. Cook proved that the problem of determining, given a formula F of propositional logic, whether F is satisfiable, is NP-complete. The proof we will give of this result is a slight modification of the exposition of Garey and Johnson [GJ79].

---

[1] By "natural" we mean a problem whose definition has intrinsic independent interest, and one that does not arise by a complexity-theoretic construction.

The satisfiability problem SAT is the following problem of determining, for an arbitrary propositional formula F, whether F is satisfiable.

SATISFIABILITY (SAT)
 instance A propositional formula F.
 question Is F satisfiable?

We will focus attention on the problem CNF-SAT of determining whether a cnf-formula is satisfiable. A *cnf-formula* is a propositional formula in conjunctive normal form. Recall that a formula is a cnf-formula if it is a conjunction of clauses, and a clause is a disjunction of literals.

CNF-SAT
 instance A cnf-formula F.
 question Is F satisfiable?

The length N of an instance F of SAT is the length of an acceptable encoding of the instance as a word x over a finite alphabet. Suppose that F has n occurrences of variables. Since we represent each variable in binary (or dyadic), $N = O(n \log(n))$. Depending on whether there are multiples occurrences of variables, F might have 2^n different truth assignments. All known deterministic algorithms are equivalent to a sequential search of each of the assignments to see whether one of them leads to satisfaction (i.e., evaluates to the truth value True). Clearly, an exhaustive search algorithm for checking satisfaction takes 2^n steps. Thus, there is an exponential upper bound on the deterministic complexity of SAT.

Theorem 6.7. SAT *belongs to* NP.

The following nondeterministic algorithm for SAT, which follows the typical two-stage pattern that we described in Sect. 6.1, proves Theorem 6.7: (1) Guess an assignment to the Boolean variables of F. This takes $O(n)$ steps. (2) Verify that the assignment evaluates to True. A straightforward deterministic algorithm takes $O(N^2)$ time. Thus, SAT belongs to the class NP.

Homework 6.9 *Give an $O(N \log(N))$-time algorithm to determine whether an assignment satisfies an instance of SAT. Hint: The difficult part is to make the assignment to the variables. An input instance F is written on a Turing machine tape. Copy the literals in F onto another tape, but double-index each literal so that $u[i][j]$ ($\overline{u}[i][j]$) denotes the fact that u_i ($\overline{u}_i$, respectively) is the jth occurrence of a literal in F. Merge-sort the double-indexed literals on the first index. Then replace each variable name by 1 or 0 in accordance with the assignment, but keep the indexing. Finally, merge-sort again, this time on the second index in order to regain the original ordering. Now, with one scan from left to right, it is possible to give each literal in F its correct truth assignment.*

Theorem 6.8. CNF-SAT *is an* NP-*complete problem.*

Proof. A formula belongs to CNF-SAT if and only if it is in conjunctive normal form and belongs to SAT. Thus, CNF-SAT belongs to NP. We show that every

Table 6.1 Variables in $f_L(x)$ and their intended meaning

Variable	Intended meaning	Range
$Q[i,k]$	At time i, M is in state q_k.	$0 \le i \le p(n)$
		$0 \le k \le r$
$H[i,j]$	At time i, the read–write head is	$0 \le i \le p(n)$
	scanning tape square j.	$1 \le j \le p(n)+1$
$S[i,j,k]$	At time i, the contents of tape	$0 \le i \le p(n)$
	square j is symbol s_k.	$1 \le j \le p(n)+1$
		$0 \le k \le v$

Table 6.2 The six Cnf-formulas

Cnf-formula	Restriction imposed
G_1	At each time i, M is in exactly one state.
G_2	At each time i, the read-write head is scanning exactly one tape square.
G_3	At each time i, each tape square contains exactly one symbol from Γ.
G_4	At time 0, the computation is in the initial configuration.
G_5	By time $p(n)$, M has entered the accepting state q_1.
G_6	For each time i, $0 \le i \le p(n)$, the configuration of M at time $i+1$ follows by a single application of M's next-move relation from the configuration at time i.

language L in NP is many-one reducible in polynomial time to CNF-SAT. Let L in NP. By Theorem 6.1, there exist a polynomial q and a polynomial-time decidable binary relation R that, for all words in Σ^*, satisfy

$$x \in L \Leftrightarrow \exists y[|y| \le q(|x|) \land R(x,y)]. \tag{6.4}$$

Without loss of generality, we may assume that $|y| = q(|x|)$. To see this, define $R'(x,y)$ if and only if $R(x,z)$ for some prefix z of y. Then R' is decidable in polynomial time and $R(x,y)$, where $|y| \le q(|x|)$, implies $R'(x,y0^{q(|x|)-|y|})$.

Let M be a deterministic single-tape Turing machine that decides R in polynomial time. Let r be a polynomial so that for all x and y, M runs in at most $r(|x| + |y| + 1)$ steps. Let $p(n) = r(n + q(n) + 1)$. Then, for each string y, where $|y| = q(|x|)$, M on input (x,y) runs no more than $p(|x|)$ steps. Clearly, $x \in L$ if and only if there is a string y, $|y| = q(|x|)$, such that M accepts the input pair (x,y) in $p(|x|)$ steps. For any such string y, a computation of M uses at most tape squares 1 through $p(n) + 1$.

Assume that M's set of states is $Q = \{q_0, q_1, \ldots, q_r\}$, where q_0 is the initial state and $q_1 = q_{\text{accept}}$ is the unique accepting state. Let $\Gamma = \{s_0, \ldots, s_v\}$ be the tape alphabet, and let $s_0 = B$ be the blank symbol.

Now we give the transformation f_L: Table 6.1 lists the set of variables U of $f_L(x)$ with their intended meanings. (Tables 6.1 and 6.2 are adapted from Garey and Johnson [GJ79]).

Table 6.3 Clauses in G_2 and G_3

Cnf-formulas	Clauses
G_2	$(H[i,1] \vee \cdots \vee H[i, p(n)+1]), 0 \le i \le p(n)$
	$(\overline{H[i,j]} \vee \overline{H[i,j']}), 0 \le i \le p(n), i \le j < j' \le p(n)+1$
G_3	$(S[i,j,0] \vee S[i,j,1] \vee \cdots \vee S[i,j,v]), 0 \le i \le p(n), 1 \le j \le p(n)+1$
	$(\overline{S[i,j,k]} \vee \overline{S[i,j,k']}), 0 \le i \le p(n), 1 \le j \le p(n)+1, 0 \le k < k' \le v$

The set of variables U of $f_L(x)$ is given by Table 6.1. Note that these are just Boolean variables. The subscript notation is for convenience only, to help us remember the intended meaning of the various variables.

The formula $f_L(x)$ is the conjunction of six cnf-formulas: $G_1, \ldots, G_6$. Each of these individual cnf-formulas imposes a restriction on any satisfying assignment, as given in Table 6.2.

Given an accepting computation of M on x, it should be clear that if each individual cnf-formula performs as intended, then a satisfying assignment to $f_L(x)$ will correspond to the accepting computation.

Now we describe the six cnf-formulas. To make our formulas more readable, we begin by allowing the implication connective $\rightarrow$ in our formulas. The exact meaning of implication is given by the following truth-table:

$$
\begin{array}{ccc}
A & B & (A \rightarrow B) \\
1 & 1 & 1 \\
1 & 0 & 0 \\
0 & 1 & 1 \\
0 & 0 & 1
\end{array}
$$

Formula G_1 is to mean that "At each time i, M is in exactly one state," so this can be expressed by the following formula:

$$
\begin{aligned}
&(Q[i,0] \vee Q[i,1] \vee \cdots \vee Q[i,r]) \\
&\wedge (Q[i,0] \rightarrow \overline{Q[i,1]}) \wedge (Q[i,0] \rightarrow \overline{Q[i,2]}) \wedge \cdots \wedge (Q[i,0] \rightarrow \overline{Q[i,r]}) \\
&\wedge \cdots \wedge (Q[i,r] \rightarrow \overline{Q[i,r-1]}),
\end{aligned}
$$

which is equivalent to

$$
\begin{aligned}
&(Q[i,0] \vee Q[i,1] \vee \cdots \vee Q[i,r]) \\
&\wedge (\overline{Q[i,0]} \vee \overline{Q[i,1]}) \wedge (\overline{Q[i,0]} \vee \overline{Q[i,2]}) \wedge \cdots \wedge (\overline{Q[i,0]} \vee \overline{Q[i,r]}) \\
&\wedge \cdots \wedge (\overline{Q[i,r]} \vee \overline{Q[i,r-1]}).
\end{aligned}
$$

Formulas G_2 and G_3 are similar to formula G_1, so these are the conjunction of the clauses listed in Table 6.3.

The cnf-formula G_4 is to mean that "At time 0, M is in the initial configuration." Thus, G_4 is the conjunction of the following components:

(i) The input word $x = s_{k_1} \ldots s_{k_n}$ is written in squares 1 through n, square $n+1$ contains the blank symbol, and a word y, $|y| = q(n)$, is written in squares $n+2, \ldots, n+q(n)+1$. The blank symbol is written in squares $n+q(n)+2$ through $p(n)+1$. This can be expressed as

$$S[0,1,k_1] \wedge S[0,2,k_2] \wedge \cdots S[0,n,k_n] \wedge S[0,n+1,0]$$
$$\wedge \overline{S[0,n+2,0]} \wedge \cdots \wedge \overline{S[0,n+q(n)+1,0]}$$
$$\wedge S[0,n+q(n)+2,0] \cdots \wedge S[0,p(n)+1,0].$$

(ii) The head scans square 1, which is expressed by the clause $H[0,1]$.
(iii) The state is q_0, which is expressed by Q[0,0].

G_5 should state that at time $p(n)$, M is in the accepting state, which we assume is q_1, so G_5 is given by $Q[p(n),1]$.

G_6 should mean that the configuration at time $i+1$ should be obtained by a legal move of M from the configuration at time i. We need to express the changes that are made if the head is scanning square j at time i, and we need to express the fact that if the head is not scanning square j at time i, then the symbol in square j does not change. The latter is expressed by formulas of the form

$$S[i,j,l] \wedge \overline{H[i,j]} \to S[i+1,j,l].$$

Thus, for each i, $0 \leq i < p(n)$, each j, $1 \leq j \leq p(n)+1$, and each l, $0 \leq l \leq v$, G_6 contains clauses

$$(\overline{S[i,j,l]} \vee H[i,j] \vee S[i+1,j,l]).$$

If the head at time i is scanning square j, then we need to know the current state and symbol scanned as well: Suppose that q_k is not the accepting state, and that in state q_k scanning symbol s_l, M writes $s_{l'}$, moves to square $j+\Delta$, and enters state $q_{k'}$. This is expressible by the formula

$$(H[i,j] \wedge Q[i,k] \wedge S[i,j,l])$$
$$\to (H[i+1,j+\Delta] \wedge Q[i+1,k'] \wedge S[i+1,j,l']).$$

Thus, for every i,j, k, and l, $0 \leq i < p(n)$, $1 \leq j \leq p(n)+1$, $0 \leq k \leq r$, $0 \leq l \leq v$, corresponding to the instruction "in state q_k scanning symbol s_l, write $s_{l'}$, move to square $j+\Delta$, and enter state $q_{k'}$," G_6 contains the conjunctions

$$(\overline{H[i,j]} \vee \overline{Q[i,k]} \vee \overline{S[i,j,l]} \vee H[i+1,j+\Delta])$$
$$\wedge (\overline{H[i,j]} \vee \overline{Q[i,k]} \vee \overline{S[i,j,l]} \vee Q[i+1,k'])$$
$$\wedge (\overline{H[i,j]} \vee \overline{Q[i,k]} \vee \overline{S[i,j,l]} \vee S[i+1,j,l']).$$

For the accepting state q_1, we stipulate that

$$(H[i,j] \wedge Q[i,1] \wedge S[i,j,l])$$
$$\rightarrow (H[i+1,j] \wedge Q[i+1,1] \wedge S[i+1,j,l]).$$

This case adds the following additional conjunctions to G_6:

$$(\overline{H[i,j]} \vee \overline{Q[i,1]} \vee \overline{S[i,j,l]} \vee H[i+1,j])$$
$$\wedge (\overline{H[i,j]} \vee \overline{Q[i,1]} \vee \overline{S[i,j,l]} \vee Q[i+1,1])$$
$$\wedge (\overline{H[i,j]} \vee \overline{Q[i,1]} \vee \overline{S[i,j,l]} \vee S[i+1,j,l]).$$

This completes the construction of $f_L(x)$. To see that f_L can be computed in time some polynomial in $|x|$, we make two observations. One, the number of variables U and the size of $G_1, \ldots, G_6$ are no more than a polynomial in $|x|$. Second, only G_4 depends on input x, as the other clauses depend on M alone. Finding G_4, given x, is just a matter of filling values into a formula for G_4. A satisfying assignment corresponds uniquely to a value of y, $|y| = q(|x|)$, for which M accepts (x,y). Thus, $x \in L$ if and only if $f_L(x)$ is satisfiable. $\square$

We wish to make another observation about this important result. Let M be any nondeterministic polynomial-time-bounded Turing machine, and let $L = L(M)$. Let $q(n)$ be a polynomial bound on the running time of M. As in Homework 6.1, consider the relation $R(x,y)$ defined by "x is an input word to M and y is an accepting computation of M on x." Since computations are paddable, we may assume that M has an accepting computation on an input word x if and only if M has an accepting computation y on input x such that $|y| = q(|x|)$. Now consider the construction of f_L from R and q. Focus attention on G_4: Different satisfying assignments of $f_L(x)$ are due to the different values of y that at time 0 are written in squares $n+2, \ldots, n+q(n)+1$. Moreover, each satisfying assignment encodes, by assigning the value 1 to variables of the form $S[0,j,k]$, $n+2 \le j \le n+q(n)+1$, $1 \le k \le v$, a unique value of y. Thus, every satisfying assignment of $f_L(x)$ encodes an accepting computation of M on x. In this case, the number of distinct accepting computations of M on x is equal to the number of different satisfying assignments of $f_L(x)$.

6.6   More NP-Complete Problems

Now that we know two NP-complete problems, additional NP-problems can be found using the following proposition.

Proposition 6.1. *If A is NP-complete, $A \le_m^P B$, and $B \in NP$, then B is NP-complete.*

Thus, given a language B, to show that B is NP-complete, we need to

(i) show that B belongs to NP, and
(ii) show that $A \leq_m^P B$, where it is already known that A is NP-complete.

Corollary 6.2. SAT *is* NP-*complete.*

Homework 6.10 *Use Proposition 6.1 to prove Corollary 6.2.*

In this section we will apply this technique in order to obtain other interesting NP-complete problems.[2] First, we digress to set down the following homework exercises, which concern the open question of whether NP is closed under complements.

Homework 6.11 *Prove the following:* co-NP $=$ NP *if and only if some* NP-*complete set has its complement in* NP.

Homework 6.12 *A set A in* co-NP *is* $\leq_m^P$-*complete for* co-NP *if for all* $L \in$ co-NP, $L \leq_m^P A$. *Show the following:*

1. *A is* $\leq_m^P$-*complete for* co-NP *if and only if* $\overline{A}$ *is* $\leq_m^P$-*complete for* NP.
2. *The problem of determining whether a formula of propositional logic is a tautology is* $\leq_m^P$-*complete for* co-NP.

We conclude that NP is closed under complements if and only if the set of all tautologies is in NP, which remains an open question.

6.6.1   The Diagonal Set Is NP-Complete

Define
$$K = \{i \mid NP_i \text{ accepts } i \text{ within } |i| \text{ steps}\}.$$

We will show that K is NP-complete.

Homework 6.13 *Show that K belongs to* NP.

Theorem 6.9. K *is* NP-*complete.*

We will show that $\mathscr{U} \leq_m^P K$. Since, by Theorem 6.6, we know that $\mathscr{U}$ is NP-complete, this is all that is required.

Let M be a Turing machine that takes two strings x and y as input and that accepts x and y if and only if $x \in \mathscr{U}$. (Thus, M acts independently of y.) For each string x, consider the Turing machine M^x that operates as follows: M^x has x stored in its finite control. On an input string y, M^x simulates M on inputs x and y, and M^x accepts y if

---

[2]It should be apparent that we have been confusing "problem" with "language." Recall that we are free to do so because we identify a decision problem with the set of its yes-instances – those instances for which the answer to the question is "yes." Also, we are relying on the fact that there are polynomial-time encodings of the standard data structures into strings over the two-letter alphabet.

and only if M accepts x and y. Notice that M^x operates in constant time since M^x's computation on any input string y is independent of its input.

There is a procedure that for each input word x outputs the Turing machine M^x, and this procedure requires at most a polynomial in $|x|$ number of steps. (This procedure builds the code of M, and thus of $\mathscr{U}$, into the finite control of M^x – it does not run $\mathscr{U}$ on x.) Also, there is a procedure that takes as input a Turing machine M^x and outputs its index i in the standard enumeration $\{NM_i\}_i$ of all nondeterministic Turing machines. (As the index i is just a code for the Turing machine NM_i, this is true in general.) Finally, as M^x runs in constant time, $L(M^x) = L(NP_{\langle i,2 \rangle})$, where the pair $\langle i, 2 \rangle$ is an index in the enumeration $\{NP_i\}_i$ of nondeterministic Turing machines with clocks that effectively presents NP. Combining these procedures, we see that there is a function g that is computable in polynomial time so that for each word x, $g(x) = \langle i, 2 \rangle$ is an index in the enumeration $\{NP_i\}_i$ for which $L(M^x) = L(NP_{\langle i,2 \rangle})$. The salient fact about g is that

$$NP_{g(x)} \text{ accepts an input string } y \Leftrightarrow x \in \mathscr{U}.$$

We claim that $x \in \mathscr{U} \Leftrightarrow g(x) \in K$. First, observe that

$$x \in \mathscr{U} \Leftrightarrow L(NP_{g(x)}) = \Sigma^*, \text{ and}$$
$$x \notin \mathscr{U} \Leftrightarrow L(NP_{g(x)}) = \emptyset.$$

Thus,

$$x \in \mathscr{U} \Leftrightarrow NP_{g(x)} \text{ accepts } g(x)$$
$$\Leftrightarrow NP_{g(x)} \text{ accepts } g(x) \text{ in } |g(x)| \text{ steps}$$
$$\Leftrightarrow g(x) \in K.$$

Thus, g is an $\leq_m^P$-reduction from $\mathscr{U}$ to K, so K is NP-complete. ∎

6.6.2 Some Natural NP-Complete Problems

3SAT is the restriction of CNF-SAT to instances for which every clause contains three literals.

3SAT
>   **instance** A cnf-formula F such that each clause contains three literals.
>   **question** Is there a satisfying truth assignment for F?

Theorem 6.10. 3SAT *is* NP-*complete.*

We know already that CNF-SAT belongs to NP, so 3SAT belongs to NP. Thus, to prove Theorem 6.10 it suffices to show that CNF-SAT $\leq_m^P$ 3SAT. Consider the mapping g whose input is an arbitrary conjunction of clauses F and whose output is given as follows: Replace each clause of F

$$(x_1 \vee \ldots \vee x_n) \tag{6.5}$$

with the following conjunction of clauses:

$$(x_1 \vee x_2 \vee y_1) \wedge (x_3 \vee \overline{y_1} \vee y_2) \wedge (x_4 \vee \overline{y_2} \vee y_3) \wedge \cdots \wedge (x_{n-1} \vee x_n \vee \overline{y_{n-3}}), \tag{6.6}$$

where $y_1, \ldots, y_{n-3}$ are new variables that do not occur in $\mathrm{VAR}(F)$. We leave it to the reader to verify that the formula F is satisfiable if and only if the output formula $g(F)$ is satisfiable. The following observations will help in this task. Let t be an arbitrary assignment to $\mathrm{VAR}(F)$ that satisfies the clause in (6.5). Then there is an assignment t' to $\mathrm{VAR}(F) \cup \{y_1, \ldots, y_{n-3}\}$ agreeing with t on $\mathrm{VAR}(F)$ (That is, if u is a variable in $\mathrm{VAR}(F)$, then $t(u) = t'(u)$.) that satisfies the formula in (6.6). Conversely, any assignment that satisfies (6.6) must also satisfy (6.5).

Since g is a polynomial-time reduction from CNF-SAT to 3SAT, we conclude that 3SAT is NP-complete.

Example 6.2 (k = 4). Let $x_1, \ldots, x_4$ be variables and let t be an assignment that assigns the value 1 to at least one of these variables, so that t satisfies the clause $(x_1 \vee x_2 \vee x_3 \vee x_4)$. Then some extension of t to the variables $\{x_1, \ldots, x_4, y_1\}$ satisfies the formula

$$(x_1 \vee x_2 \vee y_1) \wedge (x_3 \vee x_4 \vee \overline{y_1}).$$

Conversely, every satisfying assignment to this formula must assign the value 1 to at least one of the x_i, $1 \le i \le 4$.

Example 6.3 (k = 5). The same properties as in the previous example apply to the clause $(x_1 \vee x_2 \vee x_3 \vee x_4 \vee x_5)$ and the corresponding conjunction of clauses

$$(x_1 \vee x_2 \vee y_1) \wedge (x_3 \vee \overline{y_1} \vee y_2) \wedge (x_4 \vee x_5 \vee \overline{y_2}).$$

Some of the most famous NP-complete problems are about graphs. The following problem, VERTEX COVER, is NP-complete and is an important tool for showing NP-completeness of other NP-complete problems. A *vertex cover* of a graph $G = (V, E)$ is a subset V' of V that, for each edge $(u, v) \in E$, contains at least one of the adjacent vertices u and v. The *size* of a vertex cover V' is the number of distinct vertices it contains. These notions are illustrated in Fig. 6.1.

VERTEX COVER
    instance A graph $G = (V, E)$ and a positive integer $k \le \|V\|$.
    question Is there a vertex cover of size $\le k$ for G?

Theorem 6.11. VERTEX COVER *is NP-complete.*

Fig. 6.1 A graph G: $\{1,3,5\}$ and $\{1,2,4\}$ are vertex covers. Does G have a vertex cover of size 2?

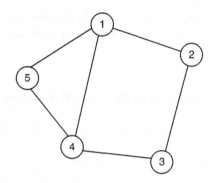

Proof. It is easy to see that VERTEX COVER belongs to NP: Given a graph $G = (V,E)$, guess a set of vertices V', and check whether V' is a vertex cover. This test can be performed deterministically in polynomial time.

Now we show that 3SAT $\leq_m^P$ VERTEX COVER. We will describe a polynomial-time-bounded construction that maps an instance F of 3SAT to some graph $G = (V,E)$ and positive integer k such that F is satisfiable if and only if G has a vertex cover of size $\leq k$. The construction of G consists of the following three steps, each of which adds a different component to the graph:

1. Let $U = \mathrm{VAR}(F)$. For each variable $u_i \in U$, put vertices u_i and $\overline{u}_i$ into V and put the edge $(u_i, \overline{u}_i)$ into E. We call this the *truth-setting* component. Note that any vertex cover must contain at least one of u_i and $\overline{u}_i$.
2. Let C be the set of clauses in F; that is, $F = \bigwedge_{c_j \in C} c_j$. For each clause $c_j \in C$, put three vertices v_1^j, v_2^j, and v_3^j into V and three edges into E that join these vertices to make a triangle:

$$(v_1^j, v_2^j), (v_2^j, v_3^j), (v_3^j, v_1^j).$$

   This is the *satisfaction-testing* component. Note that any vertex cover must contain at least two vertices from each triangle.
3. This step creates the *communications* component, which adds edges connecting the satisfaction-testing and truth-setting components. This is the only component that depends on which literals are contained in which clauses. Each clause $c_j \in C$ is a conjunction of literals $c_j = (x_j \vee y_j \vee z_j)$. For each such c_j, put the edges

$$(v_1^j, x_j), (v_2^j, y_j), (v_3^j, z_j)$$

   into E.

This completes the definition of G. Define the constant k to be

$$k = \|U\| + 2\|C\|.$$

Clearly, the construction takes polynomial time.

Fig. 6.2 The instance of
VERTEX COVER that
results from the instance
$(\overline{u_1} \vee u_2 \vee \overline{u_3}) \wedge (\overline{u_1} \vee \overline{u_2} \vee u_3)$
of 3SAT, with the vertex
cover that corresponds to the
satisfying assignment
$t(u_2) = 1$ and
$t(u_1) = t(u_3) = 0$

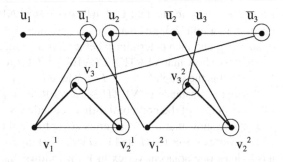

We need to show that G has a vertex cover of size $\leq k$ if and only if F is satisfiable. Suppose V' is a vertex cover for G and $\|V'\| \leq k$; then, as we have noted, V' has at least one vertex for each variable (i.e., at least one of u_i and $\overline{u_i}$) and has at least two vertices for each clause (i.e., at least two vertices from each triangle). Thus, $\|V'\| = k$. Define an assignment $t : U \to \{0,1\}$ by $t(u_i) = 1$ if $u_i \in V'$, and by $t(u_i) = 0$ if $u_i \notin V'$. We claim that this assignment satisfies each clause $c_j \in C$. Consider the triangle in the satisfaction-testing component that corresponds to c_j. Exactly two of the vertices of this triangle belong to V'. The third vertex does not belong to V', so the communications component edge between this vertex and a vertex in the truth-setting component must be covered by the vertex in the truth-setting component. By definition of the communications component, this means that c_j contains a literal $x \in \{u_i, \overline{u_i}\}$ and that $t(x) = 1$. Thus, t satisfies c_j.

Conversely, suppose that an assignment t satisfies each clause c_j in C. For each variable $u_i \in U$, either $t(u_i) = 1$ or $t(\overline{u_i}) = 1$. Place the vertex u_i into V' if $t(u_i) = 1$, and place the vertex $\overline{u_i}$ into V' if $t(\overline{u_i}) = 1$. Then V' contains one vertex of each edge in the truth-setting component. In particular, if $x \in \{u_i, \overline{u_i}\}$ is a literal in c_j that is assigned the value 1, then x is a vertex that is placed into V'. By definition of the communications component, one vertex of the triangle in the satisfaction-testing component that corresponds to c_j is covered by the edge that connects the triangle to the vertex x. For each clause c_j, place the other two vertices of the corresponding triangle into V'. It follows that $\|V'\| \leq k$ and that V' is a vertex cover. This completes the proof.   □

Figure 6.2 shows the graph that is obtained by applying the construction to the instance $(\overline{u_1} \vee u_2 \vee \overline{u_3}) \wedge (\overline{u_1} \vee \overline{u_3} \vee u_3)$ of 3SAT, and shows the vertex cover that corresponds to the satisfying assignment $t(u_2) = 1$ and $t(u_1) = t(u_3) = 0$.

For any graph G, recall from Example 2.3 that a *clique* is a complete subgraph of G. Now that we know that VERTEX COVER is NP-complete, it is rather easy to show that the following CLIQUE problem is NP-complete.

CLIQUE
> **instance** A graph $G = (V, E)$ and a positive integer $j \leq \|V\|$.
> **question** Does G contain a clique of size j or more?

Theorem 6.12. CLIQUE *is NP-complete.*

Proof. It is easy to see that CLIQUE belongs to NP: To summarize the approach given in Example 2.3, given a graph G and integer $j \leq \|V\|$, guess a subgraph of G of size $\geq j$, and then determine whether it is a clique.

Now we show that VERTEX COVER $\leq_m^P$ CLIQUE. The *complement* of a graph $G = (V, E)$ is the graph $G^c = (V, E^c)$, where $E^c = \{(u, v) \mid u \in V, v \in V, \text{and } (u, v) \notin E\}$. Given an instance of VERTEX COVER, a graph G, and positive integer $k \leq \|V\|$, the output of the polynomial-time reduction is G^c and integer $\|V\| - k$.

First we show that if V' is a vertex cover for G, then $V - V'$ is a clique of G^c. Let V' be a vertex cover for G, and let u and v belong to $V - V'$. Since every edge of G has at least one adjacent vertex in V', it follows that $(u, v) \notin E$. Thus, $(u, v) \in E^c$, and this proves the claim. It follows from the same line of reasoning that if V' is a clique in G^c, then $V - V'$ is a vertex cover for G.   □

Homework 6.14 *Show the natural reduction from* CLIQUE *to* VERTEX COVER.

We conclude this chapter with mention of two additional NP-complete problems: 3-DIMENSIONAL MATCHING and PARTITION.

3-DIMENSIONAL MATCHING
> **instance** A set $M \subset W \times X \times Y$, where W, X, and Y are disjoint sets having the same number q of elements.
> **question** Is there a subset M' of M, called a *matching*, such that $\|M'\| = q$ and no two elements of M' agree in any coordinate?

PARTITION
> **instance** A finite set A and a positive integer "size" $s(a)$ for each $a \in A$.
> **question** Is there a subset A' of A such that $\sum_{a \in A'} s(a) = \sum_{a \in A-A'} s(a)$?

The VERTEX COVER problem is used to show completeness of HAMILTONIAN CIRCUIT; i.e., VERTEX COVER $\leq_m^P$ HAMILTONIAN CIRCUIT.

We refer to a source such as Garey and Johnson's guide [GJ79] for the reductions showing that these problems are NP-complete and for in-depth study of NP-completeness. The intent of this section has been to provide a sense of the importance of NP-completeness as a tool for classifying seemingly intractable problems and to provide an understanding of the methods for proving NP-completeness. However, this is but one stopping point in our continuing development of complexity theory.

6.7   Additional Homework Problems

Homework 6.15 *Define the function maxclique by, for any graph G,*

$$maxclique(G) = \max\{k \mid G \text{ contains a clique of size } k\}.$$

Show that $P = NP$ *if and only if the function maxclique is polynomial-time computable.*

Homework 6.16 *Show that some infinite subset of* CLIQUE *belongs to* P.

Homework 6.17 *Show that the set*

$$L = \{F \mid F \text{ is a propositional formula that has as least two satisfying assignments}\}$$

is NP-*complete.*

Homework 6.18 *Show that* NTIME(n) *contains an* NP-*complete language. (Hint: Use padding.)*

Homework 6.19 *Let S be a nonempty set and let $\mathscr{C}$ be a collection of nonempty subsets of S. A* hitting set *for $\mathscr{C}$ is a subset H of S such that H has a nonempty intersection with every set in $\mathscr{C}$. Show that the following* HITTING SET *problem is* NP-*complete. (Hint: Reduce* VERTEX COVER *to* HITTING SET.*)*

HITTING SET
    instance *A nonempty set S, a collection of nonempty subsets $\mathscr{C}$, and positive integer $k \geq 1$.*
    question *Is there a hitting set for $\mathscr{C}$ of size at most k?*

Homework 6.20 *Define a partial function f by*

$$f(\phi) = \text{ some satisfying assignment of } \phi, \text{ if one exists,}$$

where ϕ is a formula of propositional logic (i.e., ϕ is an instance of the satisfiability problem). Show that f is polynomial-time computable if and only if $P = NP$.

Homework 6.21 *Define a set $A \subseteq \Sigma^*$ to be* p-selective *[Sel79] if there is a polynomial-time-computable function $f : \Sigma^* \times \Sigma^* \to \Sigma^*$ such that*

(i) for all strings x and y, $f(x,y) = x$ or $f(x,y) = y$, and
(ii) if $x \in A$ or $y \in A$, then $f(x,y) \in A$.

1. *Show that every nonempty set in* P *is p-selective.*
2. *Show that if the set of all satisfiable formulas* SAT *is p-selective, then* SAT *belongs to* P.

Homework 6.22 *A probabilistic polynomial-time Turing machine [Gil77] N is a nondeterministic polynomial-time-bounded Turing machine, but the set of words that N accepts is defined differently. Assume that N's computation tree is binary. Assign a probability to each accepting path in N's computation tree by raising $1/2$ to a power equal to the number of nondeterministic choices along it. For an input string x, let $\Pr(x)$ be the sum of the probabilities of all accepting paths. Then define $L(N)$ to be the set of all input strings x that are accepted with probability at least $1/2$.*

1. *Show that $L(N) \in$ PSPACE.*
2. *Suppose, in addition, that $\Pr(x) = 0$ for all $x \notin L(N)$. Show that $L(N) \in$ NP.*

Homework 6.23 *Define a partial function f to be* honest *if there is a polynomial p such that for all $y \in range(f)$, there exists x such that $f(x) = y$ and $|x| \leq p(|f(x)|)$. Which of the following partial functions are honest?*

1. *Let M be a deterministic polynomial-time-bounded Turing machine. Define $f(x) = y$ if M accepts x and y is an accepting computation of M on x.*
2. *Let M be a nondeterministic polynomial-time-bounded Turing machine. Define $f(x) = y$ if x is an accepting computation of M and y is the input string that is accepted.*
3. *Define $f(x) = 0^{\log|x|}$.*

Homework 6.24 *Let f be an honest, polynomial-time-computable partial function. We say that f is* invertible *if there exists a polynomial-time-computable partial function g so that for all $y \in range(f)$, $f(g(y)) = y$.*

1. *Prove that if $P = NP$, then every honest, polynomial-time-computable partial function f is invertible. Hint: Consider the following set pre-f, and observe that pre-f belongs to NP.*

$$pre\text{-}f = \{u\#y \mid \exists v[|v| \leq p(|y|) \text{ and } f(uv) = y]\}.$$

2. *Prove that if every honest, polynomial-time-computable partial function is invertible, then $P = NP$.*

Homework 6.25 *Prove that if there exists an NP-complete tally language, then $P = NP$ [Ber78].*

Chapter 7
Relative Computability

In this chapter we expand more broadly on the idea of using a subroutine for one problem in order to efficiently solve another problem. By doing so, we make precise the notion that the complexity of a problem B is related to the complexity of A – that there is an algorithm to efficiently accept B *relative to* an algorithm to efficiently decide A. As in Sect. 3.9, this should mean that an acceptor for B can be written as a program that contains subroutine calls of the form "$x \in A$," which returns True if the Boolean test is true and returns False otherwise. Recall that the algorithm for accepting B is called a *reduction procedure* and the set A is called an *oracle*. The reduction procedure is *polynomial time-bounded* if the algorithm runs in polynomial time when we stipulate that only one unit of time is to be charged for the execution of each subroutine call. Placing faith in our modified Church's thesis and in Cobham's thesis, these ideas, once again, are made precise via the oracle Turing machine.

Let M be an oracle Turing machine, let A be an oracle, and let T be a time-complexity function. We define an oracle Turing machine M with oracle A to be $T(n)$ *time-bounded* if, for every input of length n, M makes at most $T(n)$ moves before halting. If M is a nondeterministic oracle Turing machine, then every computation of M with A on words of length n must make at most $T(n)$ moves before halting. The language accepted by M with oracle A is denoted $L(M,A)$.

Let us consider once again the reduction procedure given in Fig. 3.2. For each input word x, the procedure makes a total of $|x|$ queries to the oracle set B. This reduction procedure can be implemented on an oracle Turing machine that operates in time cn^2 for some constant c. Suppose the input word is 110. The string 110 is the first query to B. The second query to the oracle is either 1101 or 1100, depending on whether or not 110 belongs to B. There is a potential of 2^n different queries as B ranges over all possible oracles.

Definition 7.1. A set A is *Turing-reducible to B in polynomial-time* $(A \leq^P_T B)$ if there exists a deterministic polynomial-time-bounded oracle Turing machine M such that $A = L(M,B)$.

Polynomial-time Turing reducibility is frequently called "Cook reducibility" in honor of its usage by Cook [Coo71b], who defined NP-completeness and proved

S. Homer and A.L. Selman, *Computability and Complexity Theory*, Texts in Computer Science, DOI 10.1007/978-1-4614-0682-2_7, © Springer Science+Business Media, LLC 2011

that the satisfiability problem is NP-complete. Also, polynomial-time reducibility is the restriction to polynomial time of Turing reducibility (Definition 3.6).

Homework 7.1 *Prove the following facts:*

1. $\leq_T^P$ *is reflexive.*
2. $\leq_T^P$ *is transitive.*
3. $A \leq_T^P B$ *and* $B \in P$ *implies* $A \in P$.
4. *If* $A \in P$ *then, for all* B, $A \leq_T^P B$.
5. $\overline{A} \leq_T^P A$.
6. $A \leq_m^P B$ *implies* $A \leq_T^P B$.

Homework 7.2 *Prove the following: If* $A \leq_T^P B$ *and* $B \in NP \cap co\text{-}NP$, *then* $A \in NP \cap co\text{-}NP$.

Homework 7.3 *Prove that* $\leq_T^P$ *reducibility preserves membership in NP if and only if* $NP = co\text{-}NP$.

A *reducibility*, in general, is a reflexive, transitive binary relation defined on $\mathscr{P}(\Sigma^*)$. Let $\leq_r$ denote an arbitrary reducibility. It is immediate that $\leq_r \cap \leq_r^{-1}$ is an equivalence relation, which is denoted as $\equiv_r$. The equivalence classes of this relation are called *r-degrees*. Let us use $\leq_T^P$ to illustrate these notions. The relation $\equiv_T^P$ defined by $A \equiv_T^P B$ if and only if $A \leq_T^P B$ and $B \leq_T^P A$ is an equivalence relation. Two sets A and B such that $A \equiv_T^P B$ have the same $\leq_T^P$-degree. In this case, we say that they are $\leq_T^P$-equivalent or, informally, that they are "polynomially equivalent." For example, Homework 7.1 states that $\overline{A} \leq_T^P A$, for all A. Thus, A and $\overline{A}$ are polynomially equivalent. As another example, all $\leq_m^P$-complete sets for NP are $\leq_m^P$-equivalent.

Consider again the property that $\overline{A} \leq_T^P A$ for all A. We saw in Homework 6.3 that $\leq_m^P$ preserves membership in NP. If a reducibility were to satisfy both of these properties, then NP would be closed under complements. Indeed, we show next that sets are not in general $\leq_m^P$-reducible to their own complements. Thus, $\leq_m^P$ and $\leq_T^P$ are different reducibilities.

Theorem 7.1. *There is a decidable set* A *such that* $\overline{A} \not\leq_m^P A$ *(and* $A \neq \Sigma^*$ *and* $A \neq \emptyset$).

Proof. Let $\{F_i\}_i$ be an effective presentation of the class of polynomial-time-computable functions. Let f_i denote the function computed by F_i. We define a set A so that, for each i,

$$\exists n \neg [0^n \in \overline{A} \Leftrightarrow f_i(0^n) \in A].$$

From this, it follows that, for each i, $\overline{A}$ is not many-one reducible to A by f_i.

A is defined inductively in a sequence of "stages." At stage 0, A is completely undefined. At stage i, $i > 0$, we assume for some n that A is already defined for all words of length less than n, and we call this set $A(n)$. That is, for every word w of length less than n, a decision has already been made concerning whether or not w belongs to A, and no decision has been made for any words of length n or higher.

We do the following at stage i: Compute $f_i(0^n)$. If $f_i(0^n) \in A(n)$, then define $A(n+1) = A(n) \cup \{0^n\}$. (In this case both 0^n and $f_i(0^n)$ will belong to A.) Note that $A(n+1)$ contains exactly one word of length n and that all other words of length n will not belong to A. However, if $f_i(0^n)$ does not belong to $A(n)$, either because its length is greater than or equal to n or because at an earlier stage it was excluded from A, then extend the definition of A to all words of length less than $m = 1 + \max\{n, |f_i(0^n)|\}$ as follows: Put 0^n and $f_i(0^n)$ into $\overline{A}$ and put all other words of length n through $m-1$ into $A(m)$. (In this case, both 0^n and $f_i(0^n)$ will belong to $\overline{A}$.) This completes stage i.

At each stage A is defined on a larger initial segment of Σ^*, so A is eventually defined for every finite length. Both A and $\overline{A}$ are infinite sets, so $A \neq \Sigma^*$ and $A \neq \emptyset$. A is a decidable set because the inductive definition gives an effective procedure for determining membership in A. $\square$

By carefully "padding out" the definition of A, we can make A belong to the complexity class E. This refinement is due to M. Machtey [LLS75].

7.1 NP-Hardness

In the previous chapter we studied NP-completeness, learned of the fundamental role of NP-complete sets, and examined several specific NP-complete problems. Now we will study sets that are as hard as NP, but do not necessarily belong to NP.

Definition 7.2. A set A is NP-*hard* if, for every $L \in$ NP, $L \leq_T^P A$.

There are two very important differences between this notion and NP-completeness. The first is that an NP-hard set does not need to belong to NP. The second is that we use Turing reducibility this time instead of many-one reducibility. Intuitively, a set is NP-hard if it is at least as difficult to accept as every problem in NP. The proof of the following proposition is straightforward.

Proposition 7.1. *If A is NP-hard and $A \in$ P, then NP = P.*

The notion is of interest only if NP $\neq$ P, for otherwise every set is NP-hard. Namely, if NP = P, so that every set $L \in$ NP belongs to P, by Homework 7.1, for every set A, if $L \in$ NP, then $L \leq_T^P A$.

Trivially, every NP-complete set is NP-hard. By Homework 7.1, the complement of every NP-complete set is NP-hard, but only one call to the oracle is needed in order to Turing-reduce a set to its complement, so in a sense this example is trivial also. Let us consider the following example.

Kth LARGEST SUBSET
> **instance** A finite set A, a positive integer size $s(a)$ for each $a \in A$, and two nonnegative integers $B \leq \sum_{a \in A} s(a)$ and $K \leq 2^{\|A\|}$.
> **question** Are there at least K distinct subsets $A' \subseteq A$ that satisfy $s(A') \leq B$, where $s(A') = \sum_{a \in A'} s(a)$?

The size of an instance is $O(\|A\| \log s(A))$, where $s(A) = \sum_{a \in A} s(a)$. This problem does not appear to belong to NP, for the natural way to solve it nondeterministically involves guessing K subsets of A, and there is no way to write down such a guess using only a polynomial number of symbols in the size of an instance. There is no known polynomial-time many-one reduction from any NP-complete problem to Kth LARGEST SUBSET. However, we show next that the NP-complete PARTITION problem is $\leq_T^P$-reducible to Kth LARGEST SUBSET. This was shown by Johnson and Kashdan [JK76], and our proof follows the exposition of Garey and Johnson [GJ79].

Theorem 7.2. PARTITION $\leq_T^P$ *Kth* LARGEST SUBSET.

Proof. We show that PARTITION can be solved in polynomial time relative to an oracle O for Kth LARGEST SUBSET. (Given an instance (A, s, b, K) of Kth LARGEST SUBSET, the oracle O answers "yes," if (A, s, b, K) is a yes-instance and answers "no" otherwise.)

Let A and s be an instance of the PARTITION problem that is given as input to the following reduction procedure:

1. Compute $s(A) = \sum_{a \in A} s(a)$.
2. If $s(A)$ is not divisible by 2, then halt and do not accept; else $b := s(A)/2$.
3. Determine the number n of subsets $A' \subseteq A$ such that $s(A') \leq b$. This is accomplished by the following binary search procedure.

> MIN := 0;
> MAX := $2^{\|A\|}$; {in binary}
> **while** MAX − MIN > 1 **do**
> > **begin**
> > $K := [\text{MAX} + \text{MIN}]/2$;
> > Query O with instance (A, s, b, K);
> > **if** the answer is "yes"
> > > **then** MIN := K
> > > **else** MAX := K
> > **end**;
> $n := \text{MIN}$

To see that the binary search procedure finds n, observe that there are always at least MIN subsets A' such that $s(A') \leq b$ and there are never at least MAX subsets A' such that $s(A') \leq b$. Initially, this is true because MIN = 0 and $s(A) > b$.

4. Query O with instance $(A, s, b - 1, n)$. If the answer is "yes," then every subset for which $s(A') \leq b$ also satisfies $s(A') \leq b - 1$. Thus, in this case, A cannot be partitioned. If the answer is "no," then there is a subset A' such that $s(A') = b$, so, in this case, we accept.

As step 3 uses $\|A\|$ calls to the oracle, and only one additional call is used in step 4, the reduction procedure is polynomial-time-bounded.   □

The procedure we just described uses the adaptiveness of Turing reducibility to full advantage and suggests that many-one reducibility could not properly capture the intended notion of NP-hardness. This intuition is confirmed by the corollary to the following theorem. In order to make comparisons properly, we introduce the following uniform notation. Let $\leq_r^P$ denote a polynomial-time reducibility (such as $\leq_m^P$ or $\leq_T^P$) and let $\mathscr{C}$ denote an arbitrary complexity class (such as NP). Define a set A to be $\leq_r^P$-*hard* for $\mathscr{C}$ if for all $L \in \mathscr{C}, L \leq_r^P A$. Define a set A to be $\leq_r^P$-*complete* for $\mathscr{C}$ if $A \in \mathscr{C}$ and A is $\leq_r^P$-hard for $\mathscr{C}$. So, $\leq_T^P$-hard for NP is the same as NP-hard, and $\leq_m^P$-complete for NP is the same as NP-complete. Assuming that P $\neq$ NP, we prove the existence of sets that are NP-hard but not $\leq_m^P$-hard for NP.

Theorem 7.3 ([SG77]). *For each decidable set $A \notin$ P, there is a decidable set B such that $A \leq_T^P B$ but $A \nleq_m^P B$. In particular, $A \leq_T^P B$ by a reduction procedure that on every input makes* two *queries to the oracle.*

Corollary 7.1. *If* P $\neq$ NP, *then there exists a set that is $\leq_T^P$-hard for* NP *but not $\leq_m^P$-hard for* NP.

Proof of Corollary 7.1. If P $\neq$ NP, then the NP-complete language SAT is not in P. By Theorem 7.3, there is a decidable set B such that SAT $\leq_T^P B$ but SAT $\nleq_m^P B$. That is, B is $\leq_T^P$-hard for NP but not $\leq_m^P$-hard for NP. ∎

Now we prove the theorem.

Proof. Let A be a decidable set that is not in P. As in the proof of Theorem 7.1, we will construct B in stages. We will ensure that $A \nleq_m^P B$ by diagonalization, and we will ensure that $A \leq_T^P B$ by preserving the condition

$$x \in A \Leftrightarrow \text{exactly one of } x0 \text{ and } x1 \text{ belongs to } B. \tag{7.1}$$

Recall that $\{F_i\}_i$ is an effective presentation of the class of polynomial-time-computable functions, and let f_i denote the function computed by F_i. At stage 0, B is completely undefined, and at stage $i, i > 0$, we assume for some n that B is already defined for all words of length less than n and we call this set $B(n)$.

The construction at stage i consists of the following steps:

1. Find the smallest x such that either

   (a) $|f_i(x)| < n$ and $x \in A \Leftrightarrow f_i(x) \notin B(n)$, or
   (b) $|f_i(x)| \geq n$.

   If (a) holds for the x that is found, then go directly to step 3 (in this case f_i clearly does not $\leq_m^P$-reduce A to B), and if (b) holds, then go to step 2.
2. Let $f_i(x) = za$, where $a \in \{0,1\}$, and let $\bar{a}$ denote the complement of a ($\bar{0} = 1$ and $\bar{1} = 0$). Decide membership of $f_i(x) = za$ in B so that $x \in A \Leftrightarrow f_i(x) \notin B$ (hence, f_i does not $\leq_m^P$-reduce A to B). Then decide membership of $z\bar{a} \in B$ so that if $z \in A$, then exactly one of $z0$ and $z1$ belongs to B, and if $z \notin A$, then either both or none of $z0$ and $z1$ belongs to B (hence, Condition 7.1 is preserved).

3. Let $m = 1 + \max\{n, |f_i(x)|\}$ and extend the definition of B to all words of length less than m in a manner that is consistent with Condition 7.1.

This completes the construction.

Step 1 always finds a string x, for otherwise A is many-one reducible in polynomial time to the finite set $B(n)$, which would imply that $A \in P$. Steps 2 and 3 can be carried out because membership of a string za is decided if and only if membership of $z\bar{a}$ is decided. At each stage B is defined on a larger initial segment of Σ^*, so B is eventually defined for every finite length. B is a decidable set because the inductive definition gives an effective procedure for determining membership in B. The construction ensures that $A \leq_T^P B$ and that $A \not\leq_m^P B$. $\square$

What can we say about sets that are $\leq_T^P$-complete for NP? By Proposition 7.1, $\leq_T^P$-complete sets capture the complexity of NP in the same manner as do $\leq_m^P$-complete sets. That is, the following theorem holds.

Theorem 7.4. *If A is $\leq_T^P$-complete for* NP*, then $A \in P$ if and only if* P $=$ NP.

The proof follows immediately from Proposition 7.1.

It is not known whether there exist sets that are $\leq_T^P$-complete for NP that are not $\leq_m^P$-complete for NP. Whereas we have provided technical justification to support the use of $\leq_T^P$ in the definition of NP-hard, no such technical justification exists to support the use of $\leq_m^P$ in the definition of NP-complete. It works! Thousands of NP-complete problems have been discovered and they are all $\leq_m^P$-equivalent. Also, whether there exist sets A and B in NP such that $A \leq_T^P B$ but $A \not\leq_m^P B$ is an open question.

7.2   Search Problems

Many of the combinatorial decision problems we have examined arise more naturally as problems that involve computing output values that are more useful than accept or reject. For example, one does not care to know merely whether a graph has a Hamiltonian circuit, but one wants a Hamiltonian circuit to be output, if in fact one exists. A given graph might have no Hamiltonian circuit, or there might be several, or even exponentially many. Thus, it is natural to think of the Hamiltonian Circuit problem as a partial multivalued function. Moreover, this function has an obvious nondeterministic algorithm: Guess a path; if it is a Hamiltonian circuit, then output the path.

The problem of computing a Hamiltonian circuit is one example of the more general question of whether witnesses can be computed for sets in NP. The problem of computing witnesses for a set in NP is called a *search* problem. We formalize this as follows: Recall (Theorem 6.1) that a set L belongs to NP if and only if there are a polynomial-time decidable relation R_L and a polynomial p_L such that, for all x,

$$x \in L \Leftrightarrow \exists y[|y| \leq p_L(|x|) \text{ and } R_L(x,y)].$$

```
begin
    input x in {0,1}*;
    y := λ; {the empty string}
    while |y| ≤ pₗ(|x|) and ¬Rₗ(x,y) and ⟨x,y⟩ ∈ Prefix(Rₗ,pₗ) do
    if ⟨x,y1⟩ ∈ Prefix(Rₗ,pₗ)
        then y := y1
        else if ⟨x,y0⟩ ∈ Prefix(Rₗ,pₗ)
            then y := y0;
    if Rₗ(x,y), then accept and output y
end.
```

Fig. 7.1 A polynomial time-bounded reduction procedure that reduces search for L to $\text{Prefix}(R_L, p_L)$

We say that R_L and p_L *define* L. Given a set L, relation R_L, and polynomial p_L that define L, the *search problem* for L (*search problem* for R_L and p_L) is the problem of finding an algorithm that for each instance x computes a string y such that $|y| \leq p_L(|x|)$ and $R_L(x,y)$ if $x \in L$. Obviously, L can be decided in polynomial time from any oracle for solving the search problem for L. We are interested in the converse question. As an important application of $\leq_T^P$-reducibility, we will prove that the search problem for every $\leq_T^P$-complete set L has an algorithm that is polynomially equivalent to L.

Definition 7.3. Let $L \in \text{NP}$ and let R_L and p_L define L.

$$\text{Prefix}(R_L, p_L) = \{\langle x, u \rangle \mid u \text{ is a prefix of a witness } y \text{ such that}$$

$$|y| \leq p_L(|x|) \text{ and } R_L(x,y)\}.$$

Proposition 7.2. *1.* $\text{Prefix}(R_L, p_L) \in \text{NP}$.
2. $L \leq_m^P \text{Prefix}(R_L, p_L)$.
3. If L is NP-complete, then $\text{Prefix}(R_L, p_L)$ is NP-complete.
4. If L is $\leq_T^P$-complete for NP, then $\text{Prefix}(R_L, p_L)$ is $\leq_T^P$-complete for NP.

Theorem 7.5. *The search problem for R_L and p_L is Turing-reducible in polynomial time to $\text{Prefix}(R_L, p_L)$.*

Proof. Figure 7.1 gives an adaptive reduction procedure that accesses $\text{Prefix}(R_L, p_L)$ as an oracle. It is obvious that the procedure is correct – for each input word x, the procedure outputs a string y if and only if y is a witness for $x \in L$ – and it is obvious that the procedure runs in polynomial time. □

The following corollary follows immediately.

Corollary 7.2. *If $L \equiv_T^P \text{Prefix}(R_L, p_L)$, then the search problem for R_L and p_L is Turing-reducible in polynomial time to L.*

Corollary 7.3. *If L is $\leq_T^P$-complete for NP, then the search problem for L (i.e., for R_L and p_L) is Turing-reducible in polynomial time to L.*

Proof. If L is $\leq_T^P$-complete for NP, then $L \equiv_T^P \mathrm{Prefix}(R_L, p_L)$ follows from Proposition 7.2. So the result follows from Corollary 7.2. $\qquad\square$

Thus, for every $\leq_T^P$-complete set L, it is no harder to compute witnesses for L than it is to decide membership in L. Especially, for any $\leq_T^P$-complete set L, the search problem for L is solvable in polynomial time if and only if $L \in P$ if and only if $NP = P$.

The following notion of *self-reducibility* is important in many complexity theory studies, but we give the definition at this time only to develop the following homework exercises. Loosely speaking, a set is self-reducible if the membership question for any element can be reduced in polynomial-time to the membership question for a number of shorter elements, and a set is *disjunctively* self-reducible if there is a polynomial-time-computable transducer that for any element computes a number of smaller elements $x_1, \ldots, x_n$ such that $x \in L$ if and only if at least one of the smaller elements $x_1, \ldots, x_n$ belongs to L. The classic example is SAT: SAT is disjunctive self-reducible because a Boolean formula $\phi(x_1, \ldots, x_n)$ is satisfiable if and only if at least one of the "shorter" formulas $\phi(0, x_2, \ldots, x_n)$ or $\phi(1, x_2, \ldots, x_n)$ is satisfiable. The formal definition, due to Meyer and Paterson [MP79], follows.

Definition 7.4. A polynomial-time-computable partial order $<$ on Σ^* is *OK* if and only if there exist polynomials p and q such that

1. each strictly decreasing chain is finite and every finite decreasing chain is shorter than p of the length of its maximum element, and
2. for all $x, y \in \Sigma^*$, $x < y$ implies that $|x| \leq q(|y|)$.

Definition 7.5. A set L is *self-reducible* if there is an OK partial order $<$ and a deterministic polynomial-time-bounded machine M such that M accepts L with oracle L and, on any input x, M asks its oracle only about words strictly less than x in the partial order. L is *disjunctive* self-reducible if, in addition, on every input word x, the query machine either

(i) computes a set of queries $x_1, \ldots, x_n$ in polynomial time so that

$$x \in L \Leftrightarrow \{x_1, \ldots, x_n\} \cap L \neq \emptyset$$

  or

(ii) decides membership of x in L in polynomial time without queries to the oracle.

Homework 7.4 *1. If L is self-reducible, then $L \in PSPACE$.*
2. If L is disjunctive self-reducible, then $L \in NP$. ([Ko83])
3. For every polynomial-time decidable relation R and polynomial p, $\mathrm{Prefix}(R, p)$ is disjunctive self-reducible. ([Sel88])
4. If L is disjunctive self-reducible, then there are a relation R_L and polynomial p_L that define L such that $L \equiv_T^P \mathrm{Prefix}(R_L, p_L)$. ([Sel88])

7.3   The Structure of NP

In this section we will continue to look more closely at the complexity class NP. Thus far, we know that P is a subset of NP and that all complete sets (either $\leq^P_m$-complete or $\leq^P_T$-complete) belong to NP and, by Theorem 7.4, capture the complexity of NP. We want to discover whether there are problems in NP whose complexity lies strictly between P and the complete sets.

Recall that the $\leq^P_T$-degree of a set A consists of all sets B that are $\leq^P_T$-equivalent to A. If $A \in$ NP, then we will say that the $\leq^P_T$-degree of A is "contained in" NP. This does not imply that every set in the $\leq^P_T$-degree of A belongs to NP. For example, suppose that A is an NP-complete set. Then $\overline{A}$ belongs to the $\leq^P_T$-degree of A, but, since we do not expect that co-NP $=$ NP, by Homework 6.11, we do not expect that $\overline{A}$ belongs to NP.

At this point in the course, three logical possibilities may occur:

1. P $=$ NP, in which case all sets in NP are $\leq^P_T$-complete for NP, and therefore, NP contains exactly one $\leq^P_T$-degree. (Indeed, in this case, with the exception of $\emptyset$ and Σ^*, all sets in NP would be $\leq^P_m$-complete. However, we choose to carry out this exercise for $\leq^P_T$-reducibility.)
2. P $\neq$ NP, and NP contains exactly two different $\leq^P_T$-degrees; one of them is P and the other is the collection of all $\leq^P_T$-complete sets.
3. P $\neq$ NP, and there exists a set in NP $-$ P that is not $\leq^P_T$-complete.

We will prove that case 2 cannot occur. Thus, if P $\neq$ NP, then there exist sets in NP that are neither in P nor $\leq^P_T$-complete. The theorem is due to Ladner [Lad75], but we will see the result as a corollary to a more general theorem that was proved by Schöning [Sch82].

Definition 7.6. Two sets A and B are *equal almost everywhere* ($A = B$ a.e.) if the symmetric difference of A and B, $A \triangle B$, is a finite set. A class of sets $\mathscr{C}$ is closed under *finite variations* if $A \in \mathscr{C}$ and $A = B$ a.e. implies $B \in \mathscr{C}$.

Since every Turing machine can be made to change its acceptance behavior on a finite set by storing a finite table in its control, without changing its use of computational resources, the complexity classes P and NP are closed under finite variation.

Given a deterministic Turing machine M that halts on every input, let T_M denote the running time of M. We will be interested in certain total computable functions and their Turing-machine computations. Define a function $f : N \to N$ to be *fast* if the following two properties hold:

1. For all $n \in N$, $f(n) > n$, and
2. There is a Turing machine M that computes f in unary notation such that M writes a symbol on its output tape every move of its computation. In particular, for every n, $f(n) = T_M(n)$.

Proposition 7.3. *For every total computable function f, there is a fast function f' such that, for all n, $f'(n) > f(n)$.*

Proof. Since f is computable, there is a Turing machine M that on input 1^n halts after a finite number of steps with $1^{f(n)}$ written on its output tape. Modify M to M' such that M' has one additional tape, which will be M''s write-only output tape, and such that M', on any input of the form 1^n, behaves like M on input 1^n and, in addition, writes the symbol 1 on its output tape every time it moves. When M' completes its simulation of M, then M' makes one additional move, writing one additional symbol on its output tape. Then M' computes a fast function f', and since on every input M' is simulating M, $f'(n) > f(n)$ must hold for all n.   □

For any function f, define $f^n(x)$ to be the n-fold iteration of f on x ($f^0(x) = x$, $f^1(x) = f(x)$, and $f^{n+1}(x) = f(f^n(x))$). For any function f defined on the set of natural numbers, define

$$G[f] = \left\{ x \in \Sigma^* \mid f^n(0) \le |x| < f^{n+1}(0), \text{ for even } n \right\}.$$

Lemma 7.1. *If f is fast, then $G[f] \in$ P.*

Proof. On input x, compute $0, f(0), f(f(0)), \ldots$, in unary notation, until a word of length at least $|x|$ is obtained, and determine whether the number of f-applications is even or odd. Clearly, at most $|x|$ iterations are needed. The running time is calculated as follows: It takes $f(0)$ steps to compute $f(0)$; it takes $f(f(0))$ steps to compute $f(f(0))$; and so on. As long each of these values is $\le |x|$, so is the running time to compute each value. We would use more than $|x|$ steps only when trying to compute $f^{n+1}(0)$ such that $|x| < f^{n+1}(0)$, but there is no need to complete a computation of $f^{n+1}(0)$. Instead, permit at most $|x| + 1$ steps on the computation of each value. If some computation uses $|x| + 1$ steps, then stop the iteration. There are at most $|x|$ values and each uses at most $|x| + 1$ steps, so the total running time is $O(|x|^2)$.   □

Theorem 7.6. *Let A and B be decidable sets and let $\mathscr{C}_1$ and $\mathscr{C}_2$ be classes of decidable sets with the following properties:*

1. *$A \notin \mathscr{C}_1$ and $B \notin \mathscr{C}_2$;*
2. *$\mathscr{C}_1$ and $\mathscr{C}_2$ are effectively presentable; and*
3. *$\mathscr{C}_1$ and $\mathscr{C}_2$ are closed under finite variations.*

Then there exists a decidable set C such that

1. *$C \notin \mathscr{C}_1$ and $C \notin \mathscr{C}_2$, and*
2. *If $A \in$ P and $B \ne \emptyset$ and $B \ne \Sigma^*$, then $C \le_m^P B$.*

First we show how to obtain from Theorem 7.6 the result in which we are interested. In order to apply the theorem, we need to show that the class of $\le_T^P$-complete sets for NP is effectively presentable. The demonstration of this is significantly more sophisticated than simply attaching polynomial-time Turing-machine clocks, as has worked thus far.

Lemma 7.2. *The class of all $\le_T^P$-complete sets for NP is effectively presentable.*

Proof. Let $\{NP_i\}_i$ be the effective presentation of NP. Let $\{M_i\}_i$ be an effective enumeration of oracle Turing machines such that machine M_i runs in time

$p_i(n) = n^i + i$ and such that every polynomial-time-bounded reduction procedure can be implemented by some M_i. (Simply attach a polynomial clock to each oracle Turing machine, as in Section 3.2.) To construct an effective presentation $\{Q_i\}_i$ of the $\leq_T^P$-complete sets for NP, define Q_n, $n = \langle i, j \rangle$, to be the machine that behaves as follows: On input x, for each string y such that $|y| < |x|$, test whether

$$y \in \text{SAT} \Leftrightarrow y \in L(M_j, L(NP_i)),$$

that is, test whether M_j is correctly reducing SAT to $L(NP_i)$. If this test is true for all such y, then Q_n is to accept x if and only if NP_i accepts x. Otherwise, Q_n is to accept x if and only if $x \in \text{SAT}$.

Suppose X is a $\leq_T^P$-complete set for NP. Then, for some i, $X = L(NP_i)$ and for some j, $\text{SAT} = L(M_j, X)$. Thus, the test will always be true, from which it follows that $L(Q_{\langle i,j \rangle}) = L(NP_i) = X$. Now we need to show for each n that $L(Q_n)$ is $\leq_T^P$-complete for NP. If the test is true for each input x, then $L(Q_n) = L(NP_i)$ is $\leq_T^P$-complete because SAT $\leq_T^P$-reduces to it. However, if for some input x the test fails, then it fails for all strings z such that $|x| \leq |z|$. In this case $L(Q_n) = \text{SAT}$ a.e. Thus, in either case $L(Q_n)$ is $\leq_T^P$-complete for NP. Thus, $\{Q_i\}_i$ is an effective presentation of the $\leq_T^P$-complete sets for NP.   □

Homework 7.5 *Let $B \in \text{NP}$. Show that $\{C \in \text{NP} \mid B \leq_T^P C\}$ is effectively presentable.*

Corollary 7.4. *If $P \neq \text{NP}$, then there exists a set C in $\text{NP} - P$ that is not $\leq_T^P$-complete for NP.*

Proof. Let $A = \emptyset$ and $B = \text{SAT}$, and let $\mathscr{C}_1$ be the collection of all $\leq_T^P$-complete sets for NP, and $\mathscr{C}_2 = P$. If $P \neq \text{NP}$, then A is not $\leq_T^P$-complete and $B \notin P$. The complexity class P is effectively presentable, and by Lemma 7.2 the class of all $\leq_T^P$-complete sets for NP is effectively presentable. Thus, Theorem 7.6 is applicable, so there is a decidable set C that satisfies both consequences. The first consequence yields $C \notin P$ and C is not $\leq_T^P$-complete for NP. By the second consequence of Theorem 7.6, $C \leq_m^P \text{SAT}$, from which it follows that $C \in \text{NP}$. Thus, C has all the desired properties.   □

Now we will turn to the proof of Theorem 7.6. If R is a unary relation on Σ^*, then $\min\{z \mid R(z)\}$ denotes the lexicographically smallest string z such that $R(z)$, if such a z exists, and is undefined otherwise.

Proof. Let $\{M_i\}_i$ and $\{N_i\}_i$ be effective presentations of $\mathscr{C}_1$ and $\mathscr{C}_2$, respectively. Define functions

$$f_1(n) = \max\{|\min\{z \mid |z| \geq n \text{ and } z \in L(M_i) \triangle A\}| \mid i \leq n\} + 1, \text{ and}$$

$$f_2(n) = \max\{|\min\{z \mid |z| \geq n \text{ and } z \in L(N_i) \triangle B\}| \mid i \leq n\} + 1.$$

We prove that f_1 and f_2 are total computable functions. Since $A \notin \mathscr{C}_1$, for all i, $A \neq L(M_i)$. As $\mathscr{C}_1$ is closed under finite variations, for all i, $L(M_i) \triangle A$ is an infinite set. Thus, for all i, and for all $n \geq i$, there is a string z such that $|z| \geq n$ and $z \in L(M_i) \triangle A$.

Observe that the relation defined by "$z \in L(M_i) \triangle A$" is decidable, because A is decidable and M_i halts on all inputs. Min is a computable operator and taking the maximum over a finite set is a computable operator, so f_1 is computable. The same argument applies to f_2.

Since $\max(f_1, f_2)$ is a total computable function, by Proposition 7.3 there exists a fast function f such that for all n, $f(n) > \max(f_1(n), f_2(n))$, and, by Lemma 7.1, $G[f] \in P$. We prove that the set $C = (G[f] \cap A) \cup (\overline{G[f]} \cap B)$ has the desired properties. (The intuition is this: In order to have $C \notin \mathscr{C}_1$, make C look like A for all strings in $G[f]$. In order to have $C \notin \mathscr{C}_2$, make C look like B for all strings that are not in $G[f]$.)

The definition of f_1 implies the following:

$$j \leq n \rightarrow \exists z(n \leq |z| < f_1(n) \text{ and } z \in L(M_j) \triangle A). \tag{7.2}$$

Suppose that $C \in \mathscr{C}_1$. Then, there is an index j such that $C = L(M_j)$. Select n to be an even positive integer such that $f^n(0) \geq j$. Substituting $f^n(0)$ for n in (7.2), there is a string z such that $f^n(0) \leq |z| < f_1(f^n(0)) < f^{n+1}(0)$ and $z \in L(M_j) \triangle A$. Thus, $z \in G[f]$ and $z \in L(M_j) \triangle A$, which implies, using the definition of C, that $z \in L(M_j) \triangle C$. This is a contradiction. We conclude that $C \notin \mathscr{C}_1$. A similar argument shows that $C \notin \mathscr{C}_2$.

Now we show that the second consequence holds. Suppose that $A \in P$ and $B \neq \emptyset$ and $B \neq \Sigma^*$. Let u and v be fixed words that belong to B and $\overline{B}$, respectively. Then $C \leq_m^P B$ via the following polynomial-time-computable function g:

$$g(x) = \begin{cases} x & \text{if } x \in \overline{G[f]}, \\ u & \text{if } x \in G[f] \text{ and } x \in A, \\ v & \text{if } x \in G[f] \text{ and } x \notin A. \end{cases}$$

This completes the proof.   □

Homework 7.6 (i) Give the argument to show that $C \notin \mathscr{C}_2$.
(ii) Show that $x \in C \Leftrightarrow g(x) \in B$.

Homework 7.7 Let $C_0 = (G[f] \cap A) \cup (\overline{G[f]} \cap B)$ be the set constructed in the proof of Theorem 7.6, and let $C_1 = (\overline{G[f]} \cap A) \cup (G[f] \cap B)$. Show that C_1 satisfies all the consequences of Theorem 7.6 as well.

Consider the proof of Theorem 7.6 as specialized to the proof of Corollary 7.4. Since $A = \emptyset$ in the proof of Corollary 7.4, $C = \overline{G[f]} \cap \text{SAT}$. Also, recall that $\overline{G[f]}$ belongs to P. We see that C is the intersection of SAT with a set that can be decided in polynomial time. Thus, if $P \neq NP$, there is a set of formulas of propositional logic that can be decided in polynomial time, but the restriction of the satisfiability problem to this set of formulas is a set in $NP - P$ that is not $\leq_T^P$-complete for NP.

For any set X and Y, define

$$X \oplus Y = \{0x \mid x \in X\} \cup \{1x \mid x \in Y\}.$$

Homework 7.8 *Prove the following:*

  (i) $X \leq_T^P X \oplus Y$ and $Y \leq_T^P X \oplus Y$;
 (ii) $X \leq_T^P Z$ and $Y \leq_T^P Z$ implies $X \oplus Y \leq_T^P Z$;
(iii) $X \leq_T^P Y$ and $Z \leq_T^P X \oplus Y$ implies $Z \leq_T^P Y$.

Corollary 7.5. *If* $P \neq NP$, *then there exist* $\leq_T^P$-*incomparable members of* NP. *That is, there exist sets* C_0 *and* C_1 *in* NP *such that* $C_0 \not\leq_T^P C_1$ *and* $C_1 \not\leq_T^P C_0$.

Proof. As in the proof of Corollary 7.4, let $A = \emptyset$ and $B = $ SAT, and let $\mathscr{C}_1$ be the collection of all $\leq_T^P$-complete sets for NP, and $\mathscr{C}_2 = $ P. From the proof of Theorem 7.6, and by Homework 7.7, $C_0 = \overline{G[f]} \cap $ SAT and $C_1 = G[f] \cap $ SAT belong to NP $-$ P and neither C_0 nor C_1 is $\leq_T^P$-complete for NP. Thus, SAT $\not\leq_T^P C_0$ and SAT $\not\leq_T^P C_1$. It is straightforward that SAT $\leq_T^P C_0 \oplus C_1$. So it follows from Homework 7.8, item (iii), that $C_0 \not\leq_T^P C_1$ and $C_1 \not\leq_T^P C_0$. □

Corollary 7.6. *If* $P \neq NP$, *then for every set* $B \in$ NP $-$ P, *there is a set* $C \in$ NP $-$ P *such that* $C \leq_T^P B$ *and* $B \not\leq_T^P C$.

By repeated application of Corollary 7.6, if $P \neq NP$, then NP contains countably many distinct $\leq_T^P$-degrees that form an infinite descending hierarchy.

Proof. Let $A = \emptyset$ and $B = $ SAT. Let $\mathscr{C}_1 = \{C \in $ NP $\mid B \leq_T^P C\}$ and $\mathscr{C}_2 = $ P. By Homework 7.5, we may apply Theorem 7.6, and the result is a set C that satisfies the asserted conditions. □

It is instructive to know that there are reasonable classes of sets that are not effectively presentable. We demonstrate this in the next corollary.

Corollary 7.7. *If* $P \neq NP$, *then* NP $-$ P *is not effectively presentable.*

Proof. Suppose that $P \neq NP$ and NP $-$ P is effectively presentable. Then $A = \emptyset$, $B = $ SAT, $\mathscr{C}_1 = $ NP $-$ P, and $\mathscr{C}_2 = $ P satisfy the hypotheses of Theorem 7.6. It follows that there is a set C that is not in $\mathscr{C}_1$ and not in $\mathscr{C}_2$, hence not in NP, but $\leq_m^P$-reducible to SAT, hence in NP, a contradiction. □

Homework 7.9 *Show the following: If* $P \neq NP$, *then* NP $- \{\leq_T^P$-*complete sets for* NP$\}$ *is not effectively presentable.*

7.3.1   Composite Number and Graph Isomorphism

The most famous combinatorial problem that is still believed to be an intermediate problem in NP $-$ P (with greater or lesser conviction) is the following GRAPH ISOMORPHISM problem:

GRAPH ISOMORPHISM
>   **instance** Two graphs $G_1 = (V_1, E_1)$ and $G_2 = (V_2, E_2)$.
>   **question** Are G_1 and G_2 isomorphic? That is, is there a one-to-one onto
>   function $f : V_1 \mapsto V_2$ such that $\{u, v\} \in E_1 \Leftrightarrow \{f(u), f(v)\} \in E_2$?

It is obvious that this problem belongs to NP. No polynomial-time algorithm for the GRAPH ISOMORPHISM problem is known, but polynomial-time algorithms are known when this problem is restricted to important classes of graphs. Schöning [Sch88] has shown that the GRAPH ISOMORPHISM problem is "nearly" in NP ∩ co-NP. The technical result provides strong evidence that GRAPH ISOMORPHISM is not NP-complete. We will present this result in Sect. 10.5, because we are lacking the background to present the result here.

COMPOSITE NUMBER is the following decision problem:

COMPOSITE NUMBER
>   **instance** A positive integer n, given in binary.
>   **question** Are there positive integers $j, k > 1$ such that $n = j \cdot k$?

This problem clearly belongs to NP also. The complement of the COMPOSITE NUMBER problem is the famous PRIMALITY problem: Given a positive integer n, is n a prime number? In 1975, Pratt [Pra75] demonstrated that PRIMALITY belongs to NP. Thus, if n is a prime number, there exists a short proof of this that can be verified in polynomial time. Pratt's result implies that the COMPOSITE NUMBER problem belongs to NP ∩ co-NP, so COMPOSITE NUMBER cannot be NP-complete unless NP is closed under complements. This is fairly strong evidence that COMPOSITE NUMBER is not NP-complete. In 1976 Miller [Mil76] proved that testing whether a positive integer is composite or prime can be done deterministically in polynomial time if the "extended Riemann hypothesis" of number theory is true. Also, there exist very good probabilistic algorithms for primality that operate in polynomial time. (This is merely an allusion to an important topic that we will take up in Chap. 10.) However, the exact complexity of these problems remained open until the year 2004, at which time Agrawal et al. [AKS04] obtained the outstanding result that PRIMALITY belongs to P.

The result of Agrawal et al. is beyond our scope; here we present Pratt's result, for it is not obvious that PRIMALITY belongs to NP. We begin with the following theorems of number theory. Recall from Definition 1.15 that for any positive integer n, if $1 < x < n$, the *order* of x (mod n), which we will denote $\mathrm{ord}_n(x)$, is the least positive integer j such that $x^j \equiv 1$ (mod n).

Theorem 7.7. *A positive integer $n > 2$ is prime if and only if there is an integer x, $1 < x < n$, of order $n - 1$ (mod n).*

Proof. Assume n is prime. By Corollary 1.3, Fermat's theorem, $x^{n-1} \equiv 1$ (mod n) for all $x < n$. By Theorem 1.17 and Corollary 1.17, since n is prime, Z_n, the set of integers modulo n, is a finite field and the multiplicative group of nonzero elements is cyclic. Thus, the multiplicative group of nonzero elements has a generator x. By definition, x is an element of order $n - 1$.

If n is not prime, then $(Z_n - \{0\}, \cdot_n)$ is not a group, from which it follows that no element of Z_n can have order $n - 1$ (mod n).   □

Theorem 7.8. $x^s \equiv 1$ (mod n) *if and only if s is a multiple of* $\mathrm{ord}_n(x)$.

Proof. If s is a multiple of $\mathrm{ord}_n(x)$, then trivially, for some k, $x^s \equiv x^{k(\mathrm{ord}_n(x))} \equiv 1^k \equiv 1$ (mod n).

1. Input $n > 2$.
2. Nondeterministically guess x, where $1 < x < n$.
3. Verify that $x^{n-1} \equiv 1 \pmod{n}$. If not, then halt without accepting.
4. Nondeterministically guess a multiset of positive integers $p_1, p_2, \ldots, p_k$ and verify that $p_1 \cdots p_k = n - 1$. If not, then halt without accepting.
5. Recursively, verify that each p_i, $1 \leq i \leq k$, is a prime number. If not all are prime, then halt without accepting.
6. For each $1 \leq i \leq k$, verify that $x^{(n-1)/p_i} \not\equiv 1 \pmod{n}$. If not, then halt without accepting.
7. Accept.

Fig. 7.2 A recursive nondeterministic algorithm for PRIMALITY

Assume s is not a multiple of $\mathrm{ord}_n(x)$ and $x^s \equiv 1 \pmod{n}$. Without loss of generality, we may assume that $\mathrm{ord}_n(x) < s < 2(\mathrm{ord}_n(x))$. For, if $s \geq 2(\mathrm{ord}_n(x))$, then we can reduce s by $\mathrm{ord}_n(x)$ and still have $x^s \equiv 1 \pmod{n}$. (That is, $x^{s - \mathrm{ord}_n(x)} \equiv x^s x^{-\mathrm{ord}_n(x)} \equiv x^s 1 \equiv 1 \pmod{n}$.) With this assumption, $x^s \equiv 1 \equiv x^{\mathrm{ord}_n(x)} \pmod{n}$. Thus, $x^{s - \mathrm{ord}_n(x)} \equiv 1 \pmod{n}$. But $s - \mathrm{ord}_n(x) < \mathrm{ord}_n(x)$, which, by definition of $\mathrm{ord}_n(x)$, is a contradiction.   □

Lemma 7.3. *Let x and y be integers such that $0 \leq x, y < n$. Then*

(i) $x + y \pmod{n}$ can be computed in time $O(\log n)$;
(ii) $x \cdot y \pmod{n}$ can be computed in time $O(\log^2 n)$;
(iii) $x^y \pmod{n}$ can be computed in time $O(\log^3 n)$.

Proof. Remember that n and all other arithmetic values are written in binary and that $|n| = O(\log n)$. Thus, (i) and (ii) are obvious. The following algorithm computes $x^y \pmod{n}$ by the method of successive squares: Let $a_m \ldots a_1$ be the binary representation of $y \pmod{n}$.

$A := 1;$
$w := x;$
for $i := 1$ **to** m **do**
    begin
        if $a_i = 1$ **then** $A := A \cdot w \pmod{n}$
        $w := w^2 \pmod{n}$
    end
    $\{A = x^y \pmod{n}\}$

This algorithm executes $O(\log n)$ operations that can be computed in $O(\log^2 n)$ steps. Thus, $x^y \pmod{n}$ can be computed in time $O(\log^3 n)$.

Theorem 7.9. PRIMALITY *belongs to* NP.

Proof. Figure 7.2 contains a nondeterministic, recursive algorithm for testing whether an integer is prime. First we show that the algorithm is correct. Suppose the algorithm accepts n. After the first three steps, we know by Theorem 7.8 that $\mathrm{ord}_n(x)$ divides $n - 1$. After step 5 we know that $p_1 \cdots p_k = n - 1$ is a prime factorization of $n - 1$, and after step 6 we know that $\mathrm{ord}_n(x)$ does not divide any factor of $n - 1$.

Thus $\text{ord}_n(x) = n - 1$, so by Theorem 7.7 n is prime. Conversely, if n is prime, then there is an x such that $\text{ord}_n(x) = n - 1$, so there is a computation path that passes each test.

We need to show that the algorithm in Fig. 7.2 can be implemented by a nondeterministic Turing machine in polynomial time. By Lemma 7.3, step 3 can be done in $O(\log^3 n)$ steps. Since the maximum number of prime factors of $n - 1$ occurs in the case where $n - 1$ is a power of 2, the number of prime factors of $n - 1$ is at most $O(\log n)$. Hence, the value of k in step 4 is at most $\log n$, and by Lemma 7.3 step 4 requires at most $O(\log^3 n)$ steps. Each calculation of the form $x^{(n-1)/p_i} \pmod{n}$ can be done in $O(\log^3 n)$ steps. Step 6 contains at most $O(\log n)$ such calculations, so step 6 can be done in $O(\log^4 n)$ steps. To complete the analysis, we need to add the time taken for step 5. We calculate this by induction. More exactly, we prove by induction that the number of steps to recognize that n is prime is bounded by $O(\log^5 n)$. We assume as induction hypothesis that each recursive call can be executed in $O(\log^5 n)$ steps. So step 5 takes at most

$$\sum_{i=1}^{k} O(\log^5 p_i) \le O(\log^5 n)$$

steps. (To verify the inequality, observe that $\log^5 a + \log^5 b \le \log^5 ab$, and $\prod_{i=1}^{k} p_i$ is less than n.) Thus, the number of steps for an incarnation is

$$O(\log^3 n) + O(\log^3 n) + \sum_{i=1}^{k} O(\log^5 p_i) + O(\log^4 n) = O(\log^5 n),$$

and this completes the proof.   □

7.3.2 Reflection

Before continuing with our technical development, let's pause to reflect on the question of whether P = NP. As we have seen in our discussion of NP-complete and NP-hard problems, this question has great consequence for numerous areas of computer science and for computational problems in other sciences. The general belief among those who have thoughtfully considered the question is that P is not equal to NP. There is no compelling scientific basis for this belief, only the intuition developed over time by those working in this field.

Regardless of what might be proved in the future, technology needs to live with the current situation. That is, there is no known efficient method to solve NP-complete or NP-hard problems. For this reason many techniques for dealing with intractability have been developed. One of the triumphs of the theory of computing has been the creation of approximation algorithms for NP-complete problems. These are practical algorithms with provable performance guarantees that offer close to optimal solutions [Hoc97].

Intractability is by no means wholly a bad thing. Although we are not studying the relationship between complexity theory and cryptography in this text, let us mention that if P = NP, then modern cryptography would not exist and neither would much of the security of computer systems and digital transactions [Sel89]. As well, the beautiful and intricate theory that we have been studying, based on the underlying assumption that P differs from NP, would be nullified. This comment is true of the topic that we take up next.

7.4   The Polynomial Hierarchy

The polynomial hierarchy was defined by Stockmeyer [MS72, Sto76] and is a polynomial-time analog of the arithmetical hierarchy (Definition 3.11). In addition to Stockmeyer, several important properties were proved by Wrathall [Wra76]. The polynomial hierarchy adds a potential infinity of complexity classes between P and PSPACE and is another useful tool for the classification of combinatorial problems.

The oracle Turing machines we have considered so far are all deterministic, but now let us define a set A to be *nondeterministic Turing-reducible to B* in polynomial time $(A \leq_T^{NP} B)$ if there is a nondeterministic polynomial-time-bounded oracle Turing machine M such that $A = L(M, B)$. For any set A, let $P^A = \{B \mid B \leq_T^P A\}$ and let $NP^A = \{B \mid B \leq_T^{NP} A\}$. So P^A (NP^A) is the class of sets accepted deterministically (nondeterministically, respectively) in polynomial time relative to the set A. For a class of sets $\mathscr{C}$, let $P^{\mathscr{C}} = \bigcup \{P^A \mid A \in \mathscr{C}\}$ and $NP^{\mathscr{C}} = \bigcup \{NP^A \mid A \in \mathscr{C}\}$. Then the *polynomial hierarchy* is the collection of all classes $\{\Sigma_k^P, \Pi_k^P, \Delta_k^P\}_{k \geq 0}$, where these classes are defined inductively as follows:

$$\Sigma_0^P = \Pi_0^P = \Delta_0^P = P,$$

and, for $k \geq 0$,

$$\Sigma_{k+1}^P = NP^{\Sigma_k^P},$$

$$\Pi_{k+1}^P = \text{co-}\Sigma_{k+1}^P, \text{ and}$$

$$\Delta_{k+1}^P = P^{\Sigma_k^P}.$$

Example 7.1. 1. $\Sigma_1^P = NP^{\Sigma_0^P} = NP^P = NP$.
2. $\Pi_1^P = \text{co-NP}$.
3. $\Delta_1^P = P^P = P$.
4. $\Delta_2^P = P^{NP}$.
5. $\Sigma_2^P = NP^{NP}$.

We see from these examples that the polynomial hierarchy extends the classes P and NP. It is not known whether any of the classes are distinct or whether there are infinitely many classes. We will begin by establishing several basic properties.

Proposition 7.4. *For all $k \geq 0$, $\Sigma_k^P \cup \Pi_k^P \subseteq \Delta_{k+1}^P \subseteq \Sigma_{k+1}^P \cap \Pi_{k+1}^P$.*

For the proof, observe that $A \in \Sigma_k^P$ implies $\overline{A} \in P^{\Sigma_k^P} = \Delta_{k+1}^P$. Define $PH = \bigcup \{\Sigma_k^P \mid k \geq 0\}$.

Proposition 7.5. $PH \subseteq PSPACE$.

Proof. The proof is by induction, and cases $k = 0$ and $k = 1$ are already known. Assume $\Sigma_k^P \subseteq PSPACE$. Then $\Sigma_{k+1}^P = NP^{\Sigma_k^P} \subseteq NP^{PSPACE} = PSPACE$, by Corollary 5.7. □

It is not known whether $\Sigma_1^P \subset \Sigma_2^P$ or whether $\Sigma_k^P \subset \Sigma_{k+1}^P$ for any $k \geq 0$. After all,

$$P \subseteq NP = \Sigma_1^P \subseteq \Sigma_2^P \subseteq \cdots \subseteq PH \subseteq PSPACE,$$

and it is not known whether any of these classes separate.

Proposition 7.6. *The following are equivalent for all $k \geq 1$:*

(i) $\Sigma_k^P = \Sigma_{k+1}^P$;
(ii) $\Pi_k^P = \Pi_{k+1}^P$;
(iii) $\Sigma_k^P = \Pi_k^P$;
(iv) $\Sigma_k^P = \Pi_{k+1}^P$;
(v) $\Pi_k^P = \Sigma_{k+1}^P$.

Proof. Assertions (i) and (ii) are equivalent by definition. Only the proof that (iii) implies (i) is interesting. We leave all other directions as a homework exercise.

Assume $\Sigma_k^P = \Pi_k^P$ and let $L \in \Sigma_{k+1}^P$. There is a set $L' \in \Sigma_k^P$ such that $L \in NP^{L'}$. Then there are sets L_1 and L_2, both belonging to Σ_{k-1}^P, so that $L' \in NP^{L_1}$ and $\overline{L'} \in NP^{L_2}$. The latter is true because, by hypothesis, $\overline{L'} \in \Sigma_k^P$. Let M', M_1, and M_2 be machines that witness the oracle procedures $L \in NP^{L'}$, $L' \in NP^{L_1}$, and $\overline{L'} \in NP^{L_2}$, respectively. Observe that the set $L_1 \oplus L_2$ belongs to Σ_{k-1}^P. Design a nondeterministic oracle Turing machine M to accept L with oracle $L_1 \oplus L_2$ as follows, thereby demonstrating that $L \in \Sigma_k^P$: The machine M simulates M' except that M replaces queries q to L' by simultaneous simulations of M_1 and M_2 on input q to the oracle $L_1 \oplus L_2$. Specifically, M, when simulating M_1, replaces queries w to M_1's oracle with queries $0w$, and, when simulating M_2, replaces queries w with queries $1w$. Then M continues its simulation of M' in the "yes" state if M_1 accepts q, M continues its simulation of M' in the "no" state if M_2 accepts q, and M halts without accepting if neither M_1 nor M_2 accepts. It is easy to see that M behaves as we claimed. Thus, $\Sigma_{k+1}^P \subseteq \Sigma_k^P$ follows.   □

Homework 7.10 *Complete the proof of Proposition 7.6.*

In particular, $NP = co\text{-}NP \Leftrightarrow \Sigma_1^P = \Sigma_2^P$. The following result shows that if for some $k \geq 1$, $\Sigma_k^P = \Pi_k^P$, then for all $j \geq k$, $\Sigma_j^P = \Pi_j^P = \Sigma_k^P$. Thus, the polynomial hierarchy must be of one of the forms given in Fig. 7.3. No two "points" among Σ_k^P,

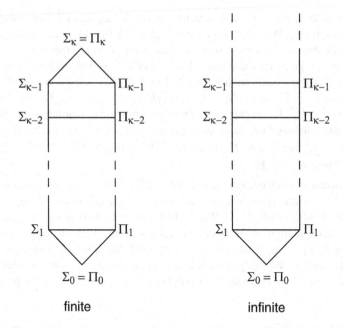

$\Sigma_\kappa = \Pi_\kappa$

$\Sigma_{\kappa-1}$ $\Pi_{\kappa-1}$

$\Sigma_{\kappa-2}$ $\Pi_{\kappa-2}$

Σ_1 Π_1

$\Sigma_0 = \Pi_0$

finite

$\Sigma_{\kappa-1}$ $\Pi_{\kappa-1}$

$\Sigma_{\kappa-2}$ $\Pi_{\kappa-2}$

Σ_1 Π_1

$\Sigma_0 = \Pi_0$

infinite

Fig. 7.3 The polynomial hierarchy

Π_k^P, $k \geq 1$, may be equal to any of the rest without the entire hierarchy collapsing from that point upward. Conversely, if any two points can be shown to be distinct, the entire "ladder" must exist at distinct points from that level down. In particular, NP = P if and only if PH = P.

Theorem 7.10. *If for some $k \geq 1$, $\Sigma_k^P = \Pi_k^P$, then for all $j \geq k$, $\Sigma_j^P = \Pi_j^P = \Sigma_k^P$.*

Proof. The proof is by induction on j. The base case $j = k$ is immediate. Assume as induction hypothesis that $\Sigma_{j-1}^P = \Pi_{j-1}^P \subseteq \Sigma_k^P$ for some $j > k$. Then, by Proposition 7.6, $\Sigma_j^P = \Sigma_{j-1}^P \subseteq \Sigma_k^P$ and $\Pi_j^P = \Sigma_{j-1}^P \subseteq \Sigma_k^P$. The conclusion immediately follows. $\qquad\square$

The following theorem generalizes Theorem 6.1.

Theorem 7.11. *For all $k \geq 1$, $L \in \Sigma_k^P$ if and only if there are a polynomial $q(n)$ and a relation $R(x, y_1, \ldots, y_k)$ in P such that*

$$x \in L \Leftrightarrow \exists y_1 \forall y_2 \ldots Q_k y_k R(x, y_1, \ldots, y_k), \tag{7.3}$$

where the quantifiers alternate ($Q_k = \forall$ if k is even, and $Q_k = \exists$ if k is odd) and $y_1, \ldots, y_k$ range over words of length $\leq q(|x|)$. Dually, $L \in \Pi_k^P$ if and only if

$$x \in L \Leftrightarrow \forall y_1 \exists y_2 \ldots Q_k' y_k R'(x, y_1, \ldots, y_k), \tag{7.4}$$

Proof. For each k, let $\mathscr{E}_k$ ($\mathscr{A}_k$) denote the set of all languages L that satisfy (7.3) ((7.4), respectively). We want to prove for all $k \geq 1$ that $\mathscr{E}_k = \Sigma_k^P$ and $\mathscr{A}_k = \Pi_k^P$. Note for all k that $\mathscr{A}_k = co - \mathscr{E}_k$, so if $\mathscr{E}_k = \Sigma_k^P$, then $\mathscr{A}_k = \Pi_k^P$ follows.

Theorem 6.1 gives the base case, $k = 1$. Let $k \geq 1$, and assume as induction hypothesis that the assertions hold for k. Let $L \in \mathscr{E}_{k+1}$ satisfy the conditions of (7.3). Define $L' = \{\langle x, y_1 \rangle \mid \forall y_2 \ldots Q_{k+1} y_{k+1} R(x, y_1, \ldots, y_{k+1})\}$. By the induction hypothesis, $L' \in \Pi_k^P$. L is accepted by a nondeterministic polynomial-time-bounded oracle Turing machine that, on input x, guesses $y_1 \leq q(|x|)$ and accepts if and only if the pair $\langle x, y_1 \rangle$ belongs to L'. Thus, $L \in NP^{\Pi_k^P}$. But $NP^{\Pi_k^P} = NP^{\Sigma_k^P} = \Sigma_{k+1}^P$, so $L \in \Sigma_{k+1}^P$. Thus, $\mathscr{E}_{k+1} \subseteq \Sigma_{k+1}^P$.

The converse is more complicated. Let $L \in \Sigma_{k+1}^P$. Let $L' \in \Sigma_k^P$ such that $L \in NP^{L'}$ and let M be a nondeterministic polynomial-time-bounded oracle Turing machine that accepts L with oracle L'. Define L_1 to be the set of all tuples $\langle x, y, u, v \rangle$ such that y is a computation of M on x that causes M to query its oracle about the strings in $u = \langle u_1, \ldots, u_m \rangle$ and $v = \langle v_1, \ldots, v_n \rangle$ and that causes M to accept x if the answers are "yes" to the strings in u and "no" to the strings in v. Observe that $L_1 \in P$ and $|y|$, $|u|$, and $|v|$ are bounded by a polynomial in $|x|$. The following property is satisfied:

$$x \in L \Leftrightarrow \exists y \exists u \exists v [\langle x, y, u, v \rangle \in L_1 \wedge u = \langle u_1, \ldots, u_m \rangle \wedge v = \langle v_1, \ldots, v_n \rangle$$
$$\wedge u_1 \in L' \wedge \cdots \wedge u_m \in L' \wedge v_1 \in \overline{L'} \wedge \cdots \wedge v_n \in \overline{L'}]. \tag{7.5}$$

By induction hypothesis, $L' \in \mathscr{E}_k$ and $\overline{L'} \in \mathscr{A}_k$. For each assertion $u_i \in L'$ and $v_j \in \overline{L'}$ that occurs in (7.5), substitute the corresponding alternating quantifier expression. Then move all quantifiers forward into prenex normal form in the usual way. The result is an expression with $k + 1$ blocks of alternating quantifiers such that the first quantifier is existential, all are bounded by a polynomial in the length of x, and the matrix is a relation in P. To complete the proof, we observe that a block of quantifiers of the same kind can be replaced by a single quantifier with the help of pairing functions: Recall that if $z = \langle x, y \rangle$, then $\tau_1(z) = x$, $\tau_2(z) = y$, and these functions are computable in polynomial time. The extension to arbitrary n-tuples appears in Sect. 3.3. Any formula $\exists z_1 \exists z_2 S(x, z_1, z_2)$ can be replaced by the equivalent formula $\exists z[S(x, \tau_1(z), \tau_2(z))]$, and $\forall z_1 \forall z_2 S(x, z_1, z_2)$ can be replaced by $\forall z[S(x, \tau_1(z), \tau_2(z))]$. Thus, the expression in (7.5) can be converted into an expression with $k + 1$ alternating quantifiers, thereby demonstrating that $L \in \mathscr{E}_{k+1}$. Therefore, $\mathscr{E}_{k+1} = \Sigma_{k+1}^P$ and $\mathscr{A}_{k+1} = \Pi_{k+1}^P$. □

The following example elucidates the proof techniques that we just described.

Example 7.2. Let $L \in \Sigma_3^P$ be given by $L \in NP^{L'}$, where $L' \in \Pi_2^P$. Assume

$$x \in L' \Leftrightarrow \forall z_1 \exists z_2 R(x, z_1, z_2). \tag{7.6}$$

Suppose L_1 is defined as in the proof of Theorem 7.11 and suppose that

$$x \in L \Leftrightarrow \exists y \exists u \exists v [\langle x,y,u,v \rangle \in L_1 \wedge u = \langle u_1,u_2 \rangle \wedge v = \langle v_1 \rangle \wedge u_1 \in L' \wedge u_2 \in L' \wedge v_1 \in \overline{L'}]. \tag{7.7}$$

We use (7.6) to substitute into (7.7) in order to get the following equivalence:

$$x \in L \Leftrightarrow \exists y \exists u \exists v [\langle x,y,u,v \rangle \in L_1 \wedge u = \langle u_1,u_2 \rangle \wedge v = \langle v_1 \rangle \wedge$$

$$\forall z_1 \exists z_2 R(u_1,z_1,z_2) \wedge \forall s_1 \exists s_2 R(u_2,s_1,s_2) \wedge \exists t_1 \forall t_2 \neg R(v_1,t_1,t_2)] \tag{7.8}$$

$$\Leftrightarrow \exists y \exists u \exists v \exists t_1 \forall z_1 \forall s_1 \forall t_2 \exists z_2 \exists s_2 [\langle x,y,u,v \rangle \in L_1 \wedge u = \langle u_1,u_2 \rangle$$

$$\wedge v = \langle v_1 \rangle \wedge R(u_1,z_1,z_2) \wedge R(u_2,s_1,s_2) \wedge \neg R(v_1,t_1,t_2)]. \tag{7.9}$$

Let $M(x,y,u,v,t_1,z_1,s_1,t_2,z_2,s_2)$ denote the matrix of the expression in line 7.9. Observe that the relation M belongs to P. Finally, writing $y_1 = \langle y,u,v,t_1 \rangle$, $y_2 = \langle z_1,s_1,t_2 \rangle$, and $y_3 = \langle z_2,s_2 \rangle$, we collapse like quantifiers to get the following:

$$x \in L \Leftrightarrow \exists y_1 \forall y_2 \exists y_3 M(x,\tau_{41}(y_1),\tau_{42}(y_1),\tau_{43}(y_1),\tau_{44}(y_1),\tau_{31}(y_2),\tau_{32}(y_2),$$

$$\tau_{33}(y_2),\tau_1(y_3),\tau_2(y_3)).$$

This is the three-alternating-quantifier expression that defines L.

Corollary 7.8. $A \leq_m^P B$ and $B \in \Sigma_n^P$ implies $A \in \Sigma_n^P$.

Corollary 7.9. Let $L \in \Sigma_k^P$, $k \geq 1$. There are a binary relation $R \in \Pi_{k-1}^P$ and a polynomial q such that

$$x \in L \Leftrightarrow \exists y [|y| \leq q(|x|) \text{ and } R(x,y)].$$

Given an oracle Turing machine M, we sometimes let $M^{(\ )}$ denote M and let M^A denote M operating with A as the oracle. Much of the theory about NP that we developed in Chap. 6 carries over with only minimal alteration of proofs to NP^A, for any oracle set A, and we may apply this fact with dispatch to obtain results about the polynomial hierarchy. For example, we attach polynomial-time clocks to nondeterministic polynomial-time-bounded oracle Turing machines to construct an effective enumeration $\{NP_i^{(\ )}\}_{i \geq 1}$ of nondeterministic polynomial-time-bounded oracle Turing machines such that for every oracle A, $\{NP_i^A\}_{i \geq 1}$ is an effective presentation of NP^A. We define $\mathcal{U}^A$ and K^A as follows:

$$\mathcal{U}^A = \{\langle i,x,0^n \rangle \mid \text{some computation of } NP_i^A \text{ accepts } x \text{ in fewer than } n \text{ steps}\},$$

and

$$K^A = \{i \mid NP_i^A \text{ accepts } i \text{ within } |i| \text{ steps}\}.$$

Theorem 7.12. *For any oracle A, $\mathscr{U}^A$ and K^A are $\leq_m^P$-complete for NP^A.*

The proofs are given in the proofs of Theorems 6.6 and 6.9. The only change is that i is the index of NP_i^A rather than NP_i. Now we will use this result to obtain complete sets for each level of the polynomial hierarchy. The discussion can be carried out with $\mathscr{U}^A$ as the starting point, but it is somewhat more traditional to use K^A. First, let us single out the following two consequences of Theorem 7.12.

Corollary 7.10. $NP^A \neq P^A$ *implies* $K^A \not\leq_T^P A$.

Corollary 7.11. $B \in NP^A$ *if and only if* $B \leq_m^P K^A$.

Define $K^{(1)} = K$, and for $n \geq 1$, $K^{(n+1)} = K^{K^{(n)}}$. Thus, $K^{(2)} = K^K$.

Theorem 7.13. *For all $n \geq 1$, $K^{(n)}$ is $\leq_m^P$-complete for Σ_n^P.*

Proof. The proof is by induction on n. The base $n = 1$ is given by Theorem 6.9. As induction hypothesis, suppose the assertion is true for some $n \geq 1$. By definition $K^{(n+1)} = K^{K^{(n)}}$, and by induction hypothesis $K^{(n)} \in \Sigma_n^P$. So $K^{(n+1)} \in NP^{\Sigma_n^P} = \Sigma_{n+1}^P$.

Let $B \in \Sigma_{n+1}^P$. For some $A \in \Sigma_n^P$, $B \in NP^A$, and by the induction hypothesis, $A \leq_m^P K^{(n)}$. It is easy to see that $B \in NP^{K^{(n)}}$: Let M be a nondeterministic polynomial-time-bounded Turing machine such that $B = L(M, A)$ and let f be a many-one polynomial-time reduction from A to $K^{(n)}$. Define M_1 to be an oracle Turing machine that simulates M except that whenever M enters a query state with a word w on its query tape, M_1 should write $f(w)$ on its query tape and then M_1 should query the oracle $K^{(n)}$. Obviously $B = L(M_1, K^{(n)})$, so $B \in NP^{K^{(n)}}$.

Using Corollary 7.11, we have $B \leq_m^P K^{K^{(n)}} = K^{(n+1)}$. Thus, $K^{(n+1)}$ is $\leq_m^P$-complete for Σ_{n+1}^P.   □

Definition 7.7. For each $k \geq 0$, define

$$A_k = \{\langle k, i, x, 0^m, 0^n \rangle \mid (\exists y_1, |y_1| \leq m) \cdots (Q_k y_k, |y_k| \leq m)$$

$$[P_i \text{ accepts } \langle x, y_1, \cdots, y_k \rangle \text{ in } \leq n \text{ steps}]\}.$$

Homework 7.11 *Use Theorem 7.11 to show for each $k \geq 0$ that A_k is $\leq_m^P$-complete for Σ_k^P.*

The first and most well-known collection of problems shown to be $\leq_m^P$-complete for Σ_k^P, $k \geq 1$, are extensions of the satisfiability problem that are formed by quantifying Boolean formulas with k alternating quantifiers. We define these now.

For $i = 1, \ldots, k$, let X^i be a sequence of Boolean variables $\{x[i, j] \mid 1 \leq j \leq n_i\}$, where $n_i \geq 1$. Consider a Boolean formula $F(X^1, \ldots, X^k)$ in which the occurrence of X^i denotes occurrences of $x[i, 1], \ldots, x[i, n_i]$, the variables in $X^1, \ldots, X^k$ occur in F, and no other variables occur in F. Let $\exists X^i$ denote $\exists x[i, 1] \ldots \exists x[i, n_i]$, and let $\forall X^i$ denote $\forall x[i, 1] \ldots \forall x[i, n_i]$.

Definition 7.8. For each $k \geq 1$, B_k is the set of all Boolean formulas $F(X^1, \ldots, X^k)$ such that

$$\exists X^1 \forall X^2 \cdots QX^k [F(X^1, \ldots, X^k) \text{ is true}].$$

Observe that B_1 is the set of all satisfiable formulas.

Example 7.3. Let $F = (x[1,1] \wedge x[1,2]) \vee x[2,1]$. Then $F \in B_2$.

We will prove, for all $k \geq 1$, that B_k is $\leq_m^P$-complete for Σ_k^P. By Theorem 7.11, for each $k \geq 1$, $B_k \in \Sigma_k^P$. Clearly, case $k = 1$ is a restatement of the important corollary to the Cook–Levin theorem, Corollary 6.2, so it is natural to give a proof by induction that uses the characterization given in Theorem 7.11. First we need to develop some technical apparatus. Consider functions ρ that map positive integers into Boolean formulas and have the following property: There exist $k \geq 1$, $v \geq 2$, and polynomials $p_1, \ldots, p_k$ such that for all $n \geq 1$, the variables in $\rho(n)$ are

$$X^m = \{x[m,j] \mid 1 \leq j \leq p_m(n)\}, 1 \leq m \leq k,$$

$$I = \{x[k+i,j] \mid 1 \leq i \leq n, 0 \leq j \leq v\}.$$

For a word $w = s_{k_1} \ldots s_{k_n}$ of length n over the finite alphabet $\{s_0, s_1, \ldots, s_v\}$, $\rho(n,w)$ denotes the formula resulting from $\rho(n)$ by the following assignment to the variables in the set I: $x[k+i,j] = 1$ if and only if the ith symbol of w is s_j. The only variables in $\rho(n,w)$ are the variables in $X^1, \ldots, X^k$.

Theorem 7.14. *For $k \geq 1$, for each language L in Σ_k^P or Π_k^P, there is a function ρ_L (as described in the previous paragraph) such that the function $(\lambda w)\rho_L(|w|, w)$ is computable in polynomial time and the following properties hold: If $L \in \Sigma_k^P$, then*

$$w \in L \Leftrightarrow \exists X^1 \forall X^2 \cdots QX^k [\rho_L(|w|, w) \text{ is true}]$$

$$\Leftrightarrow \rho_L(|w|, w) \in B_k;$$

and, if $L \in \Pi_k^P$, then

$$w \in L \Leftrightarrow \forall X^1 \exists X^2 \cdots Q'X^k [\rho_L(|w|, w) \text{ is true}].$$

Proof. The proof is by induction, and we consider the base case $k = 1$. Assume L belongs to NP and let M be a single-tape nondeterministic polynomial time-bounded Turing machine that accepts L in the manner described in Sect. 5.3. Recall the construction in the proof of Theorem 6.8 and recall that the formula constructed there may contain Boolean variables $S[i,j,m]$, for each $0 \leq i \leq p(n)$, $1 \leq j \leq p(n) + 1$, and $0 \leq m \leq v$, with the intended meaning that $S[i,j,m]$ should evaluate to true if at time i the jth tape square contains the symbol s_m. In particular, given an input word $w = s_{k_1} \ldots s_{k_n}$, group 4 contains the conjunction

$$S[0,1,k_1] \wedge S[0,2,k_2] \wedge \cdots \wedge S[0,n,k_n] \tag{7.10}$$

that binds the input to the first n squares of the tape before computation begins. Define $\rho_L(n)$ to be the formula constructed in Theorem 6.8 with the following exception: Replace the conjunction listed in 7.10 that binds the input word to the tape with the CNF-formula

$$\left(\bigvee_{1 \leq m \leq v} S[0,1,m] \right) \wedge \left(\bigvee_{1 \leq m \leq v} S[0,2,m] \right) \wedge \cdots \wedge \left(\bigvee_{1 \leq m \leq v} S[0,n,m] \right),$$

which stipulates that each of the first n tape squares contains a nonblank symbol but otherwise leaves the input word unspecified. Let X^1 be the set of all other variables. For each word $w = s_{k_1} \ldots s_{k_n}$ of length n, define $\rho_L(|w|,w)$ to be the formula that results by assigning

$$S[0,1,k_1] = \cdots = S[0,n,k_n] = 1$$

and all other variables in I to 0. Then, it follows from Theorem 6.8 that $(\lambda w)\rho_L$ $(|w|,w)$ is polynomial-time computable and that

$$w \in L \Leftrightarrow \rho_L(|w|,w) \text{ is satisfiable}$$

$$\Leftrightarrow \exists X_1 [\rho_L(|w|,w) \text{ is true}]$$

$$\Leftrightarrow \rho_L(|w|,w) \in B_1.$$

The assertion for $L \in \Pi_1^P$ follows immediately.

Let $k \geq 1$ and assume as induction hypothesis that the theorem holds for k. Let $L \in \Sigma_{k+1}^P$. By Corollary 7.9, there are a relation $R \in \Pi_k^P$ and a polynomial q such that

$$x \in L \Leftrightarrow \exists y[|y| \leq q(|x|) \text{ and } R(x,y)].$$

Let # be a symbol not in the alphabet of L, and let $L_1 = \{x\#y \mid R(x,y)\}$. $L_1 \in \Pi_k^P$, so by induction hypothesis there is a function ρ_{L_1} such that

$$x\#y \in L_1 \Leftrightarrow \forall X^1 \exists X^2 \cdots Q'X^k[\rho_{L_1}(|x\#y|,x\#y) \text{ is true}].$$

The input variables in $\rho_{L_1}(n+1+q(n))$ are

$$I_1 = \{x[k+i,j] \mid 1 \leq i \leq n, 0 \leq j \leq v\}$$

for an initial substring of length n of the input, all variables $x[k+n+1,j], 0 \leq j \leq v$, and

$$I_2 = \{x[k+i,j] \mid n+2 \leq i \leq q(n), 0 \leq j \leq v\}$$

for the remainder of the string.

We construct $\rho_L(n)$ from $\rho_{L_1}(n+1+q(n))$ as follows: Retain I_1 as the input variables I and set the variable $x[k+n+1,0] = 1$, assuming that $s_0 = \#$, and set $x[k+n+1,j] = 0$ for $j \geq 1$. Change X^k to X^{k+1}, X^{k-1} to X^k, ..., and X^1 to X^2. Then convert the variables that remain in I_2 to $X^1 = \{x[1, j] \mid 1 \leq j \leq (q(n) - (n+1))v\}$. $(\lambda w)\rho(|w|, w)$ is computable in polynomial time by the induction hypothesis. For any string w of length n, $w \in L$ if and only if there is an assignment I_2 in $\rho_{L_1}(n + 1 + q(n))$ such that if the variables in I_1 are assigned to describe w, then

$$\forall X^2 \exists X^3 \cdots Q' X^{k+1} [\rho_{L_1}(n+1+q(n)) \text{ with these assignments is true}].$$

Thus,

$$w \in L \Leftrightarrow \exists X_1 \forall X_2 \cdots Q X_k [\rho_L(|w|, w) = T].$$

This is what we needed to prove. The case for $L \in \Pi_{k+1}^P$ follows immediately. $\square$

Corollary 7.12. *For all $k \geq 1$, B_k is $\leq_m^P$-complete for Σ_k^P.*

Proof. Clearly, each B_k is in Σ_k^P. For each $k \geq 1$, and $L \in \Sigma_k^P$, $(\lambda w)\rho_L(|w|, w)$ is an $\leq_m^P$-reduction from L to B_k. $\square$

    Although the polynomial hierarchy was first defined and studied by Stockmeyer [Sto76], it was anticipated by Karp [Kar72]. Our proof that K^n is $\leq_m^P$-complete for Σ_n^P is a straightforward application of techniques that are standard in computability theory and that we hinted at in Sect. 3.9; their first use in complexity theory may be due to Heller [Hel81]. Theorem 7.11 is due to Wrathall [Wra76]. Stockmeyer [Sto76] discovered that B^n is $\leq_m^P$-complete for Σ_n^P. Our proof is adapted from Wrathall's [Wra76]. Natural complete problems are known for Δ_2^P [Kre88, Pap84] and for Σ_2^P [Sto76]. Natural complete problems are not known for higher levels of the polynomial hierarchy. Then again, in what sense would a problem that required at least three alternating quantifiers to describe be natural?

7.5 Complete Problems for Other Complexity Classes

Complete problems are not known for POLYLOGSPACE, but for all other complexity classes in our list of standard classes (Sect. 4.1), it is possible to define appropriate reducibilities and to find complete problems in the class with respect to those reducibilities. We will examine the more interesting cases here.

7.5.1 PSPACE

We give several approaches to showing the existence of $\leq_m^P$-complete problems for PSPACE.

Proposition 7.7. PSPACE *is effectively presentable.*

Letting DM_i be the ith deterministic Turing machine (Sect. 6.3) and M_j be a deterministic Turing machine that fully space-constructs $p_j(n) = n^j + j$, define PS_k, where $k = \langle i, j \rangle$, to be a single-tape deterministic Turing machine that behaves as follows: On an input word x of length n, PS_k first simulates M_j in order to mark $p_j(n)$ cells on the work-tape. Then, PS_k begins a multi-track one-tape simulation of DM_i. If DM_i ever attempts to leave the marked region, then PS_k halts and rejects its input. If DM_i reaches an accepting state without leaving the marked region, then PS_k halts and accepts.

Homework 7.12 *Prove Proposition 7.7 by showing that $\{PS_i\}_{i \geq 1}$ effectively presents PSPACE.*

Also, PSPACE is obviously closed under $\leq_m^P$-reductions.

Proposition 7.8. *$A \leq_m^P B$ and $B \in$ PSPACE implies $A \in$ PSPACE.*

In analogy with the set $\mathscr{U}$, which we easily showed to be NP-complete (Theorem 6.6), let us define

$$\mathscr{U}_{PS} = \{\langle i, x, 0^l \rangle \mid PS_i \text{ accepts } x \text{ in space } \leq l\}.$$

Homework 7.13 *Show that $\mathscr{U}_{PS}$ is $\leq_m^P$-complete for PSPACE.*

Theorem 7.15. *If for all $k \geq 0$, $\Sigma_k^P \subset \Sigma_{k+1}^P$, then PH $\subset$ PSPACE.*

Proof. We prove the contrapositive. If PSPACE $\subseteq$ PH, then for some $k \geq 0$, $\mathscr{U}_{PS} \in \Sigma_k^P$. Let $A \in$ PSPACE. Since $\mathscr{U}_{PS}$ is $\leq_m^P$-complete for PSPACE, $A \leq_m^P \mathscr{U}_{PS}$. However, by Corollary 7.8, $A \in \Sigma_k^P$. Thus, PSPACE $\subseteq \Sigma_k^P$, from which $\Sigma_{k+1}^P \subseteq \Sigma_k^P$ follows. □

Homework 7.14 *Show that the set of all $\leq_T^P$-complete sets for PSPACE is effectively presentable. (Hint: Study the proof of Lemma 7.2.)*

Theorem 7.16. *If PH $\subset$ PSPACE, then there exist sets in PSPACE that are not $\leq_T^P$-complete for PSPACE and that are not in the polynomial hierarchy.*

Proof. We use Theorem 7.6. If PH $\subset$ PSPACE, then $\mathscr{U}_{PS}$ is not in PH, as we have just shown. Thus, $A = \emptyset$, $B = \mathscr{U}_{PS}$, $\mathscr{C}_1 = \{\leq_T^P\text{-complete sets for PSPACE}\}$, and $\mathscr{C}_2 =$ PH satisfy the hypotheses of Theorem 7.6. □

If PH $\subset$ PSPACE, then the collection of problems that lie between PSPACE and PH turns out to be rich and have a complex structure [AS89]. Our next goal is to show that $A_\omega = \bigcup_{k \geq 1} A_k$ is $\leq_m^P$-complete for PSPACE, where A_k is defined in Definition 7.7.

Homework 7.15 *Show that $A_\omega \in$ DLBA.*

Theorem 7.17. *A_ω is $\leq_m^P$-complete for PSPACE.*

Proof. We need to show for all $L \in$ PSPACE that $L \leq_m^P A_\omega$. Let M be a single-tape, deterministic, polynomial-space-bounded Turing machine that accepts L. For some

$c > 0$ and polynomial p, M makes no more than $c^{p(n)}$ moves on any input of length n. Also, we assume that $p(n)$ is the length of every configuration of M on an input of length n. We let I_0^x denote the initial configuration of M on input x, and we define relations $INITIAL_M$ and $ACCEPT_M$ such that $INITIAL_M(I)$ if and only if I is an initial configuration and $ACCEPT_M(I)$ if and only if I is an accepting configuration of M. Observe that $INITIAL_M$ and $ACCEPT_M$ belong to P; i.e.; whether $INITIAL_M(I)$ or $ACCEPT_M(I)$ is true can be decided deterministically in polynomial time.

Next, for every $j \geq 1$, we effectively define a formula $F_j(I_1, I_2)$ such that $F_j(I_1, I_2)$ is true if and only if $I_1 \vdash_M^* I_2$ by a sequence of at most 2^j moves. With this accomplished, for every input word x, $x \in L$ if and only if

$$Q_x = \exists I_f [F_{p(n)\log c}(I_0^x, I_f) \wedge INITIAL_M(I_0^x) \wedge ACCEPT_M(I_f)]$$

is true.

The basis step, $j = 0$, is given by

$$F_0(I_1, I_2) = (I_1 = I_2) \vee (I_1 \vdash_M I_2).$$

The obvious approach to the induction step would be to write

$$F_j(I_1, I_2) = \exists I [F_{j-1}(I_1, I) \wedge F_{j-1}(I, I_2)].$$

However, were we to do this, F_j would have double the length of F_{j-1}, so the length of $F_{p(n)\log c}(I_0^x, I_f)$ would be at least $c^{p(n)}$ and therefore could not be written in polynomial time.

Instead, let us define

$$F_j(I_1, I_2) = \exists I \forall J \forall K [[(J = I_1 \wedge K = I) \vee (J = I \wedge K = I_2)]$$
$$\rightarrow F_{j-1}(J, K)].$$

The advantage is that here F_j contains only one copy of F_{j-1}.

Since $p(n)$ is the length of each configuration, the length of F_j is a polynomial in the length of n plus the length of F_{j-1}. Thus, the length of F_j is $O(jp(n))$, and the length of $F_{p(n)\log c}$ is $O(p(n)^2)$. In particular, $F_{p(n)\log c}$ can be constructed in polynomial time in the length of the input word. Let Q_x' be the result of transforming Q_x into prenex normal form and collapsing blocks of like quantifiers. The prefix of Q_x' is a block of at most a polynomial number of alternating quantifiers such that the first quantifier is existential, say $\exists y_1 \ldots Q y_k$, where $k = q(|x|)$ and q is a polynomial such that $q(|x|) = O(p(n)^2)$. The matrix of Q_x' is a Boolean combination of expressions of the form $INITIAL_M(I)$, $ACCEPT_M(I)$, and $I = J$. These relations are decidable in polynomial time. Thus, there is a deterministic, polynomial-time-boundedTuring machine P_i that decides the matrix of Q_x'. Furthermore, for each

$j \leq k$, $|y_j| \leq p(|x|)$. Thus, there is a polynomial r such that P_i decides membership of $\langle x, y_1, \ldots, y_k \rangle$ within $r(|x|)$ steps. To summarize, the following equivalences hold:

$x \in L \Leftrightarrow Q_x$ is true

$ \Leftrightarrow Q'_x$ is true

$ \Leftrightarrow (\exists y_1, |y_1| \leq p(|x|)) \cdots (Q_k y_k, |y_k| \leq p(|x|)) [\, P_i \text{ accepts } \langle x, y_1, \cdots, y_k \rangle$

$ \text{in } \leq r(|x|) \text{ steps} \,].$

$ \Leftrightarrow \langle k, i, x, 0^{p(|x|)}, 0^{r(|x|)} \rangle \in A_\omega.$

Let $f(x) = \langle k, i, x, 0^{p(|x|)}, 0^{r(|x|)} \rangle$, for all x. It is clear that f is a polynomial-time many-one reduction from L to A_ω. □

Homework 7.16 *Show that $B_\omega = \bigcup_{k \geq 1} B_k$, is $\leq_m^P$-complete for PSPACE. Hint: The proof is an analog of the Cook–Levin theorem, Theorem 6.8, in which a polynomial-space-bounded computation is simulated instead of a polynomial-time-bounded computation. The fact that the number of steps in the computation is $c^{p(n)}$ is handled exactly as in the proof of the previous theorem.*

PSPACE seems to capture the computational complexity of various games. Even and Tarjan [ET76], for example, have shown that a version of HEX is $\leq_m^P$-complete for PSPACE. We note in passing that complete languages for PSPACE are frequently complete for smaller space-bounded classes as well. For example, we have seen that A_ω belongs to DLBA. Thus, A_ω is $\leq_m^P$-complete for DLBA and LBA as well.

The results in this section should not suggest that forming the infinite union of complete sets for each Σ_n^P always produces a complete set for PSPACE. For example, it is not known whether $\bigcup_{n \geq 1} K^{(n)}$ is complete for PSPACE.

7.5.1.1   Oracles for the P =?NP Question

The next result demonstrates that the hypothesis of Corollary 7.10 does not always hold.

Theorem 7.18. *If A is a $\leq_m^P$-complete language for PSPACE, then $NP^A = P^A$.*

Proof. $NP^A \subseteq NP^{PSPACE} \subseteq PSPACE$, and, since A is complete for PSPACE, $PSPACE \subseteq P^A$. Thus, $NP^A \subseteq P^A$. □

In contrast, there exists an oracle A such that $NP^A \neq P^A$ [BGS75].

Theorem 7.19. *There exists a decidable set A such that $NP^A \neq P^A$.*

Proof. Following our discussion that led to Theorem 7.12, let $\{P_i^{(\,)}\}_{i \geq 1}$ be an effective enumeration of deterministic polynomial-time-bounded oracle Turing machines such that for every oracle A, $\{P_i^{(A)}\}_{i \geq 1}$ is an effective presentation of P^A. For each $i \geq 1$, p_i is an upper-bound on the running time of P_i.

Define
$$L(A) = \{x \mid \exists y[|y| = |x| \text{ and } y \in A]\}.$$
For any set A, $L(A) \in NP^A$. Our task is to define A such that for every $i \geq 1$,

$$L(A) \neq L(P_i^A).$$

We define A in stages. At each stage $i > 0$, A is already defined for all words of length less than some length n_i, and we call this set $A(n_i)$. At stage 0, $i_0 = 0$, and $A(0) = \emptyset$.

We do the following at stage i: Select the smallest positive integer n such that $n_i \leq n$ and $p_i(n) < 2^n$. Simulate $P_i^{A(n_i)}$ on input 0^n. This computation can query at most $p_i(n)$ strings, and the length of every query can be at most $p_i(n)$. By the first of these assertions, there must be some string of length n that this computation does not query. Let z be the lexicographically smallest such string.

If $P_i^{A(n_i)}$ rejects 0^n, then we put z into A as follows: Define $n_{i+1} = 2^n$ and define $A(n_{i+1}) = A(n_i) \cup \{z\}$. In this case, the construction guarantees the following claims:

1. $P_i^{A(n_{i+1})}$ rejects 0^n, and, since A will be an extension of $A(n_{i+1})$, P_i^A rejects 0^n;
2. $0^n \in L(A)$.

If $P_i^{A(n_i)}$ accepts 0^n, then we ensure that A contains no strings of length n as follows: Define $n_{i+1} = 2^n$ and define $A(n_{i+1}) = A(n_i)$. Then, $P_i^{A(n_{i+1})}$ accepts 0^n as well. Therefore, P_i^A accepts 0^n. However, $0^n \notin L(A)$.

This completes the construction of A. It should be clear that A is decidable and that, for each $i \geq 1$, $L(A) \neq L(P_i^A)$. $\square$

We are informed by these results that regardless of whether $P = NP$ or $P \neq NP$, an eventual proof will have to use techniques that do not generalize to all oracles. Many oracle results of this kind are known for other open questions about complexity classes. The deepest of these, due to Yao [Yao85] and Håstad [Hås89], asserts the existence of an oracle relative to which all classes of the polynomial hierarchy are distinct.

7.5.2 Exponential Time

As before, let $\{DM_i\}_{i \geq 1}$ be a standard enumeration of all deterministic Turing machines and $\{M_i\}_{i \geq 1}$ a standard enumeration of all Turing machines. Define

$$U_{EXP} = \{\langle i, x, l \rangle \mid DM_i \text{ accepts } x \text{ in } \leq l \text{ steps}\}$$

and

$$U_{NEXP} = \{\langle i, x, l \rangle \mid M_i \text{ accepts } x \text{ in } \leq l \text{ steps}\},$$

where in both cases l is written in binary.

Homework 7.17 *Show that $U_{\text{EXP}} \in$ E and $U_{\text{NEXP}} \in$ NE.*

Theorem 7.20. *U_{EXP} is $\leq_m^P$-complete for* EXP *and U_{NEXP} is $\leq_m^P$-complete for* NEXP.

Proof. Homework 7.17 provides part of the proof, and the other part is straightforward. Namely, if $L \in$ EXP, then there exists i such that DM_i is 2^{n^c} time-bounded and DM_i accepts L. Thus, $x \in L \Leftrightarrow \langle i, x, 2^{n^c} \rangle \in U_{\text{EXP}}$. Since 2^{n^c} is written in binary, the function f defined by $f(x) = \langle i, x, 2^{n^c} \rangle$ is computable in polynomial time. Thus, U_{EXP} is $\leq_m^P$-complete for EXP. The proof for U_{NEXP} is similar. $\square$

Since U_{EXP} belongs to E and is $\leq_m^P$-complete for EXP, it follows that U_{EXP} is $\leq_m^P$-complete for E also. Similarly, U_{NEXP} is $\leq_m^P$-complete for NE.

7.5.3   *Polynomial Time and Logarithmic Space*

We know that L $\subseteq$ NL $\subseteq$ P, but we do not know whether these classes are equal; computational experience suggests that they differ. We will see examples of complete languages L_1 for P such that L_1 belongs to L (NL) if and only if P $\subseteq$ L (P $\subseteq$ NL, respectively). Furthermore, remember that even though POLYLOGSPACE is not equal to P, there is no proof that P is not a subset of POLYLOGSPACE. Complete languages L_1 for P will have the property that $L_1 \in$ POLYLOGSPACE if and only if P $\subseteq$ POLYLOGSPACE. We will see complete languages L_2 for NL; they will have the property that $L_2 \in$ L if and only if NL $\subseteq$ L.

Completeness results for these classes do not suggest intractability as is the case for NP-complete problems or problems that are complete for PSPACE. But they help to show that completeness is a general phenomenon and they reinforce that differing resources are required even among problems that are relatively easy to compute.

We need a new kind of reducibility in order to define completeness for P in a meaningful way, because every set in P other than the emptyset and Σ^* is $\leq_m^P$-complete for P. We consider the logspace transducer. A *logspace transducer* is a $\log n$ space-bounded transducer, as defined in Sect. 4.1.1. A function f is *logspace computable* if there is a logspace transducer T that computes f.

Definition 7.9. A set A is *logspace-reducible* to a set B ($A \leq_m^{\log} B$) if there is a logspace-computable function f so that $x \in A \Leftrightarrow f(x) \in B$.

Proposition 7.9. *$A \leq_m^{\log} B$ implies $A \leq_m^P B$.*

Proof. Since a logspace transducer halts on every input, no configuration can appear in a computation more than once. By Lemma 5.1, there are at most n^c configurations for some constant $c > 0$. Thus, every logspace computation is polynomial-time-bounded. $\square$

In particular, if f is logspace-computable, then, for all x, $|f(x)| \leq |x|^c$ and $\log|f(x)| \leq c \cdot \log|x|$ for some constant $c > 0$.

Theorem 7.21. *The relation $\leq_m^{\log}$ is transitive.*

Next we prove transitivity of logspace reducibility. The proof is not at all obvious. Suppose that T_1 and T_2 are logspace transducers, that T_1 and T_2 compute f_1 and f_2, and that f_1 and f_2 reduce A to B and B to C, respectively. To prove $A \leq_m^{\log} C$, we want to show that the composition $f_2 \circ f_1$ is logspace-computable. The obvious approach would be to simulate T_1 on input x, store the output value $f_1(x)$ on a tape, and simulate T_2 on $f_1(x)$. However, the length of $f_1(x)$ may be larger than $\log|x|$ so it cannot be stored without exceeding the bound of a logspace transducer. Instead, we use a different technique to compute the composition of two functions. The idea is to simulate the entire computation of T_1 on input x each time the simulation of T_2 needs a new input symbol.

Proof. Let T_1 and T_2 be logspace transducers such that T_1 computes f_1 and T_2 computes f_2. Assume that f_1 logspace-reduces A to B, and f_2 logspace-reduces B to C. Clearly, $x \in A \Leftrightarrow f_2(f_1(x)) \in C$. We need to show that $f_2 \circ f_1$ is logspace-computable. Let c be a constant such that on any input x of length n, the length of the output word of T_1 on x cannot exceed n^c. We construct T_3 to logspace-compute $f_2 \circ f_1$ as follows: One storage tape of T_3 holds the input position of T_2 in base 2^c. Since the input position cannot exceed n^c, this number can be stored in $\log n$ space. The other storage tapes of T_3 simulate the storage tapes of T_1 and T_2. If at some time T_2's input head is at position i and T_2 makes a move left or right, T_3 adjusts the state and storage tapes of T_2 accordingly. Then T_3 restarts a simulation of T_1 on x from the beginning and waits until T_1 outputs $i-1$ or $i+1$ symbols, depending on whether T_2 moves left or right, respectively. The last symbol scanned is the new symbol scanned by T_2's input head (T_3 does not store the earlier symbols that are output), so T_3 continues its simulation of T_2. There are two special cases: If $i = 1$ and T_2 moves left, we assume that T_2 next scans its left endmarker, and if T_1 halts before producing $i+1$ output symbols on a right move of T_2, we assume that T_2 next scans its right endmarker. T_3 accepts its input when T_2 accepts its simulated input, and $f_2(f_1(x))$ is the final output value. $\square$

The identity function is logspace-computable, so logspace reducibility is reflexive as well.

Theorem 7.22. *If $A \leq_m^{\log} B$, then*

(i) $B \in P$ implies $A \in P$,
(ii) $B \in \text{DSPACE}(\log^k n)$ implies $A \in \text{DSPACE}(\log^k n)$, and
(iii) $B \in \text{NSPACE}(\log^k n)$ implies $A \in \text{NSPACE}(\log^k n)$.

Proof. Assertion (i) follows from Proposition 7.9. The second assertion is proved by an adaptation of the previous argument, where T_1 logspace-reduces A to B and T_2 is a $\log^k n$ space bounded Turing machine that accepts B. Assertion 3 is proved similarly. $\square$

Theorem 7.23. *1. If $A \in$ DSPACE($\log^k n$) is logspace-complete for* P, *then* P $\subseteq$ DSPACE($\log^k n$).
2. *If $A \in$ NSPACE($\log^k n$) is logspace-complete for* P, *then* P $\subseteq$ NSPACE($\log^k n$).
3. *If $A \in$ L is logspace-complete for* NL, *then* NL $\subseteq$ L.

Proof. Let $A \in$ DSPACE($\log^k n$) be logspace-complete for P. Let $B \in$ P. Then $B \leq_m^{\log} A$, so by Theorem 7.22, $B \in$ DSPACE($\log^k n$). Thus, P $\subseteq$ DSPACE($\log^k n$). The other assertions are proved similarly.   □

As has been our customary practice, the quickest way to show existence of a complete set for a complexity class is to show that the class has a universal language and that the universal language is complete. We do this now for P.

Theorem 7.24. *Define*

$$\mathscr{U}_\mathrm{P} = \{i\#x\#0^l \mid P_i \text{ accepts } x \text{ within } l \text{ steps}\},$$

where $\# \notin \Sigma = \{0,1\}$. $\mathscr{U}_\mathrm{P}$ *is logspace-complete for* P.

Proof. It should be clear that $\mathscr{U}_\mathrm{P}$ belongs to P. Let $A \in$ P, where $A = L(P_i)$ and $p_i(n) = n^c$. It is obvious that the function f, defined by $f(x) = i\#x\#0^{|x|^c}$, many-one reduces A to $\mathscr{U}_\mathrm{P}$. Thus, it suffices to show that f is logspace-computable. Design a transducer T so that, on input x, T writes $i\#x\#$ on the output tape. After this, T marks $\log|x|$ cells on a tape and uses these cells to count to $|x|^c$ in base 2^c, writing the symbol 0 every time it increments its counter. Clearly, T is a logspace transducer and T computes f.   □

Theorems 7.21–7.23 are proved by Jones [Jon75]. Jones [Jon75] and independently Stockmeyer and Meyer [SM73] realized that the reductions in [Coo71b] and [Kar72] are all logspace reductions. Indeed, all of the complete problems in this text are logspace-complete. (In certain instances we must replace use of a polynomial-time-computable pairing function with a simpler encoding scheme as in the definition of $\mathscr{U}_\mathrm{P}$.) The reason is that the need for memory in most of these reductions is to count up to $p(n)$ for some polynomial p, and this can be done in log space as we have amply demonstrated. A number of researchers have identified natural logspace-complete problems for P. The first natural problem we mention is due to Cook [Coo74] and the second is due to Jones and Laaser [JL76]. In both cases the proofs involve generic logspace transformations that result from encoding deterministic polynomial-time-bounded Turing machines into the appropriate structures.[1]

PATH SYSTEM ACCESSIBILITY
    instance A finite set X of "nodes," a relation $R \subseteq X \times X \times X$, and two
    sets $S, T \subseteq X$ of "source" and "terminal" nodes.

---

[1]In the UNIT RESOLUTION problem, we represent a clause $c = x_1 \vee \cdots \vee x_k$ as the set $c = \{x_1, \ldots, x_k\}$.

question Is there an "accessible" terminal node, where a node $x \in X$ is accessible if $x \in S$ or if there exist accessible nodes y and z such that $\langle x, y, z \rangle \in R$?

UNIT RESOLUTION

instance A set C of clauses on a set $X = \{x_1, \ldots, x_n\}$ of Boolean variables.
question Can the empty clause (indicating a contradiction) be derived from C by unit resolution, that is, does there exist a sequence $c_1, c_2, \ldots, c_m$ of clauses, with c_m being the empty clause, such that each c_i is either a clause from C or
there exist two previously derived clauses c_k and c_l, $k, l < i$, of the forms $c_k = \{x_j\}$, $c_l = \{\overline{x_j}\} \cup c_i$, or $c_k = \{\overline{x_j}\}$, $c_l = \{x_j\} \cup c_i$, for some $x_j \in X$?

The Graph Accessibility problem that we studied in Sect. 6.2 was shown to be logspace-complete for NL by Jones [Jon75]. Recall that we know that GAP belongs to P (Homework 6.2). (Briefly, A nondeterministic $\log n$ space-bounded Turing machine M accepts GAP by guessing a path vertex by vertex. M does not store the path, it only stores the vertex currently reached.)

Theorem 7.25. GAP *is logspace-complete for* NL.

Proof. Given a language L in NL, we sketch a logspace reduction from L to GAP. First, note that a directed graph with n vertices can be represented by its adjacency matrix of size n^2 and that this matrix can be represented as a string $w = row_1\ row_2\ \ldots\ row_n$ of length n^2 over the binary alphabet. Assume L is accepted by a nondeterministic $\log n$ space-bounded Turing machine M. Let x be an input string to M. Our reduction produces a directed graph G_x, as represented by the string encoding of its adjacency matrix. The vertices of G_x are the configurations of M on x, except that in each configuration I, the input head position is given while the input word itself is not. Thus, the length of each configuration is $\log |x|$ if we assume that our logspace transducer T has a sufficient number of tape symbols. The first vertex of G_x is the initial configuration of M on x. We assume that M has a unique accepting configuration and that it is the last vertex of G_x. T uses its work space to cycle through each configuration of M. For each configuration I, T puts its input head at the position given by I, then T generates an arc for each configuration J such that $I \vdash_M J$. (In this manner T outputs the row of the adjacency matrix that corresponds to configuration I.) Such a configuration J is easily constructed from I and requires no more than $\log n$ space.

There is a path in G_x from the initial configuration on x to the unique accepting configuration if and only if M accepts x. Thus, each language in NL is logspace-reducible to GAP, so GAP is logspace-complete for NL. □

7.5.4   A Note on Provably Intractable Problems

A few interesting problems have been proved to be intractable. The general approach
has been to prove that a problem is complete for a complexity class that is known
to contain intractable problems. Using the results of Sect. 5.5, we know several
complexity classes that contain intractable sets. If a set L is complete (using any of
the reducibilities we have studied) for a complexity class C that contains intractable
sets, then it is easy to see that L is intractable.

Using this approach, Meyer and Stockmeyer [MS72] proved that the problem
of inequivalence for regular expressions with "squaring" is intractable. That is,
they proved that this problem is $\leq_m^P$-complete for $\bigcup_{c>0} \text{DSPACE}(2^{n^c})$. Because
$\bigcup_{c>0} \text{DSPACE}(2^{n^c})$ includes EXP, and because, by the time hierarchy theorem,
Theorem 5.16, EXP contains sets that are intractable, their result follows.

Fischer and Rabin [FR74] proved that the theory of Presberger arithmetic is $\leq_m^P$-
hard for NEXP. Thus, the theory of Presberger arithmetic is intractable. Proofs of
both of these results can be found in the text by Hopcroft and Ullman [HU79].

7.6   Additional Homework Problems

Homework 7.18 *An approximation algorithm for the* VERTEX COVER *problem
is an algorithm that runs in polynomial time and that, given a graph G as input,
finds a vertex cover of G. For any graph G, let Opt-VC(G) be the size of a smallest
vertex cover of G. We would like an approximation algorithm that finds a vertex
cover whose size is as close to Opt-VC(G) as possible.*

1. *Prove that if there is an approximation algorithm for the* VERTEX COVER
   problem that always finds a vertex cover of size Opt-VC(G), then P = NP.
2. *Find an approximation algorithm for the* VERTEX COVER *problem with the
   property that, for any graph G, the algorithm finds a vertex cover of G whose size
   is no more than* $2(Opt\text{-}VC(G))$. *(Hint: A straightforward "greedy" algorithm for*
   VERTEX COVER *has this property.)*

Homework 7.19 *Consider the following generalization of decision problems. A
promise problem [ESY84] (P, Q) has the form*

> **instance** *x.*
> **promise** *P(x).*
> **question** *Q(x)?*

*We assume that P and Q are decidable predicates. A deterministic Turing
machine M that halts on every input solves (P, Q) if*

$$\forall x[P(x) \Rightarrow [Q(x) \Leftrightarrow M(x) = \text{``yes''}]].$$

We do not care how M behaves on input x if $P(x)$ is false. If M solves (P,Q), then we call $L(M)$ a solution of (P,Q). In general, a promise problem will have many solutions, and we are usually interested in finding a solution with low complexity.

1. Show that $P \cap Q$ is a solution.
2. Show that Q is a solution.

Homework 7.20 *1. Let $\oplus$ denote "exclusive or." Consider the following promise problem PP-SAT:*

> **instance** $\langle \phi, \psi \rangle$, *where ϕ and ψ and formulas of propositional logic.*
> **promise** $(\phi \in \text{SAT}) \oplus (\psi \in \text{SAT})$.
> **question** $\phi \in \text{SAT}$?

Show that PP-SAT has a solution in NP.
2. Show that PP-SAT has a solution in co-NP.
3. Show that every solution of PP-SAT is NP-hard.

Homework 7.21 *Show that if an $\leq_m^P$-complete set for PSPACE belongs to NP, then PSPACE $=$ NP.*

Homework 7.22 *Define a set A to be P-immune if A is infinite and no infinite subset of A belongs to P.*

1. Show that neither SAT nor its complement is P-immune.
2. Prove that there exists a P-immune set and explain whether the set you construct is decidable. (Hint: Construct one by a diagonalization argument.)

Homework 7.23 *Define a set A to be P-bi-immune if L is infinite, no infinite subset of L belongs to P, and no infinite subset of $\overline{L}$ belongs to P. Define a language A to be almost-everywhere complex if for every Turing machine M that accepts A and every polynomial p, M runs in time greater than $p(|x|)$ for all but finitely many words x [Ber76, Rab60].*

1. Prove that a set is P-bi-immune if and only if it is almost-everywhere complex [BS85].
2. Prove that almost-everywhere complex sets exist.

Homework 7.24 *A function f is computable in* linear time *if, for all x, $f(x)$ is computable in $O(|x|)$ steps. Prove that no set exists that is complete for P under linear-time reductions.*

Homework 7.25 *Define a set L to be* sparse *if there is a polynomial p such that for all n, $\|L \cap \Sigma^n\| \leq p(n)$. Prove that NE $=$ E if and only if every sparse set in NP belongs to P [HIS85]. Observe that this result subsumes Theorem 5.18.*

Chapter 8
Nonuniform Complexity

In this chapter we introduce and study Boolean circuits. Since real computers are built from electronic devices, digital circuits, this is reason enough to consider their complexity. The circuits that we consider here are idealizations of digital circuits just as the Turing machine is an idealization of real digital computers. A Boolean circuit consists of gates that compute the Boolean connectives, inputs, and wires that connect them. The formal definition follows:

Definition 8.1. A Boolean circuit is a labeled, acyclic, directed graph. Nodes with in-degree $= 0$ are called *input nodes*, and are labeled with a Boolean variable x_i or a constant 0 or 1. Nodes with out-degree $= 0$ are called *output nodes*. *Interior nodes* (i.e., nodes other than the input and output nodes) represent logical gates: they are labeled with AND, inclusive OR, or NOT. Arbitrary fan-out is allowed.

The constants 1 and 0 are the allowed inputs, where 1 denotes "true" and 0 denotes "false." If C is a circuit with exactly one output node and n input nodes, then C *realizes* a Boolean function $f : \{0,1\}^n \mapsto \{0,1\}$. When the input nodes receive their values, every interior value receives the value 0 or 1 in accordance with the logical gate that the interior node represents. If $x = x_1 x_2 \ldots x_n$ is a string in $\{0,1\}^n$ and C is a circuit with n input nodes, we say C *accepts* x if C outputs 1 when x is the input.

Example 8.1. The circuit in Fig. 8.1 realizes the exclusive or of two Boolean variables x and y.

Let $A \subseteq \{0,1\}^*$. Then, $A^n = \{x \mid |x| = n \text{ and } x \in A\}$ denotes the subset of A consisting of all strings in A of length n. We say A^n is *realized by* a circuit C if for all strings x of length n, C accepts x if and only if x belongs to A.

Similarly, if a circuit C has n input nodes and m output nodes, where $n, m \geq 1$, then C realizes a finite function $f : \{0,1\}^n \mapsto \{0,1\}^m$.

As we have described complexity theory thus far, one machine is expected to serve for inputs of all lengths. This machine (namely, a Turing machine) is "uniform;" it is finitely describable, but might accept an infinite number of strings.

S. Homer and A.L. Selman, *Computability and Complexity Theory*,
Texts in Computer Science, DOI 10.1007/978-1-4614-0682-2_8,
© Springer Science+Business Media, LLC 2011

Fig. 8.1 A Boolean circuit
that realizes the exclusive or
of two Boolean variables

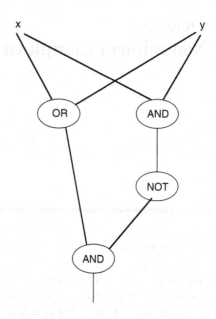

A circuit however serves only for inputs of one length. Therefore, it is not a single circuit that corresponds to a machine, or that can accept a language, but a family of circuits, one for each length. A family of circuits is "nonuniform;" it may require an infinite description.

Definition 8.2. A family of circuits $\{C_n\}_n$ *recognizes* a set A, $A \subseteq \{0,1\}^*$, if for each n, the circuit C_n realizes A^n.

Let $f : \{0,1\}^* \to \{0,1\}^*$. For each n, let f_n denote the restriction of f to the domain $\{0,1\}^n$. A family of circuits $\{C_n\}_n$ *computes* f if for each n, the circuit C_n realizes f_n.

Every circuit is equivalent to one without constant input nodes, but for convenience we will continue to use them.

Homework 8.1 *Let L be any tally language. Show that there is a family of circuits that recognizes L.*

As a consequence of Homework 8.1, since there are undecidable tally languages, there are families of circuits that recognize undecidable languages. Moreover, *every* set of strings is recognized by some family of circuits. To see this, let $f : \{0,1\}^n \to \{0,1\}$ be an arbitrary Boolean function. Any f is expressible in disjunctive normal form: $f(x_1,...,x_n) = \bigvee_i (z_{i,1} \wedge ... \wedge z_{i,n})$, where $i \leq 2^n$ and $z_{i,j} \in \{x_j, \overline{x_j}, 1\}$. This expression can be directly translated into a Boolean circuit C_f that realizes f. The circuit C_f will have at most $n2^n$ AND gates and 2^n OR gates. These observations make it clear that we could not use families of circuits to distinguish decidable from undecidable languages. Nevertheless, families of circuits provide useful complexity measures.

We will be concerned with the following two complexity measures on circuits: The *size* $s(C)$ of a circuit C is the number of nodes, and the *depth* $d(C)$ of C is the length (number of edges) of the longest path in C. For functions S and T, define

$$\text{SIZE}(S(n)) = \{A \mid \text{there is a family of circuits } \{C_n\}_n \text{ that recognizes } A \text{ and}$$
$$\text{there is a constant } k \text{ such that for each } n \geq 0, s(C_n) \leq kS(n)\}$$

and

$$\text{DEPTH}(T(n)) = \{A \mid \text{there is a family of circuits } \{C_n\}_n \text{ that recognizes } A \text{ and}$$
$$\text{there is a constant } k \text{ such that for each } n \geq 0, d(C_n) \leq kT(n)\}.$$

For every Boolean function $f : \{0,1\}^n \to \{0,1\}$, the circuit C_f has size $O(n2^n)$. Therefore, every set A is in the class $\text{SIZE}(n2^n)$. More is known: For every $\varepsilon > 0$, there exists $N > 1$ such that every Boolean function f of $n \geq N$ variables can be realized by a circuit of size $\frac{2^n}{n}(1+\varepsilon)$ [Lup58]. On the other hand, most Boolean functions cannot be realized by any circuit having fewer than $\frac{2^n}{kn}$ gates, for some positive integer k. This is due to a result of Muller [Mul56] that extends techniques of Shannon [Sha49]. The essential idea behind this claim is that while there exist 2^{2^n} Boolean functions of n variables, there are far fewer small circuits. To understand this claim, consider first the following proposition.

Proposition 8.1. *The number of distinct circuits with s nodes that compute a Boolean function of n variables is at most $3^s(s+n+1)^{2s}$.*

Proof. There are s nodes. An input to a node is either the output of one of the previous nodes (of which there are $s-1$ choices), one of the n input variables (n choices), or a constant (two choices). Since each node has at most two input nodes, there are at most $(s+n+1)^2$ ways to connect inputs to a given gate. Thus, there are at most $(s+n+1)^{2s}$ ways to connect s many nodes. In addition, each node may be labeled as an AND, OR, or NOT gate, so there are at most 3^s ways to label the nodes. Hence, there are at most $3^s(s+n+1)^{2s}$ circuits with s nodes. $\qquad\square$

Many of the choices in this proof will not be legal circuits, but the upper bound is good enough for our purposes. Suppose that $s = \frac{2^n}{kn}$, and compare

$$3^{\frac{2^n}{kn}}\left(\frac{2^n}{kn} + n + 1\right)^{2\frac{2^n}{kn}}$$

with 2^{2^n}. First, notice that $\frac{2^n}{kn} + n + 1 < 2^n$, so we have the following estimates:

$$3^{\frac{2^n}{kn}}\left(\frac{2^n}{kn} + n + 1\right)^{2\frac{2^n}{kn}} < 2^{\frac{\log 3}{k}\frac{2^n}{n}}2^{\frac{2}{k}2^n} = 2^{\lceil\frac{\log 3}{k}\frac{2^n}{n}+\frac{2}{k}2^n\rceil}.$$

The last expression grows more slowly than every i-th root of 2^{2^n}, for $\frac{1}{i} > \frac{\log 3}{kn} + \frac{2}{k}$. Therefore, most Boolean functions of n variables cannot be realized by circuits with $s = \frac{2^n}{kn}$ nodes.

Even though most sets can be recognized only by families of circuits having exponential size, we have no information about which sets these are. One of the great challenges of complexity theory is to find lower bounds to the circuit size of families of circuits that recognize explicit, interesting, combinatorial problems.

Definition 8.3. A set A has a *polynomial size (polynomial-depth)* family of circuits if for some polynomial p, $A \in \text{SIZE}(p(n))$ ($A \in \text{DEPTH}(p(n))$), respectively.

The size of a circuit is a measure of the quantity of the circuit's hardware. We will concentrate our focus in this section on polynomial size families of circuits. These are the only families that can feasibly be constructed. If, for every polynomial p, $A \notin \text{SIZE}(p(n))$, then A cannot be feasible.

Circuit depth corresponds to parallel processing time. We are not ready to fully justify this claim, which requires understanding the relationship between uniform and nonuniform computation. Basically, every parallel computation (on some parallel processor) can be unraveled to form a family of circuits with constant delay at each gate. For this reason circuit depth is a lower bound on parallel time. To wit, if $A \notin \text{DEPTH}(T(n))$, then no parallel computer can compute A in time $T(n)$.

Homework 8.2 *This exercise expands on Homework 8.1. Show that there is an undecidable language that is recognized by a family of circuits with depth 1. (Hint: Let L be an undecidable tally language and define $A = \{w \mid 1^{|w|} \in L\}$.)*

8.1 Polynomial Size Families of Circuits

We just have seen that every set is recognized by some exponential size family of circuits, that most sets require exponential size circuits, and that even some undecidable languages are recognizable by families of circuits with very simple depth. Nevertheless, as we remarked above, a language that does not have a polynomial-size family of circuits cannot be feasible.

Our first goal in this section is to prove that every language that is accepted by a Turing machine in time $T(n)$ has a family of circuits whose size is not much larger than $T(n)$: We will prove that

$$\text{DTIME}(T(n)) \subseteq \text{SIZE}(O(T(n)\log T(n))). \tag{8.1}$$

The first result along these lines was by Savage [Sav72], who proved that

$$\text{DTIME}(T(n)) \subseteq \text{SIZE}(O(T(n)^2)).$$

The improvement to $\text{SIZE}(O(T(n)\log T(n)))$ is due to Pippenger and Fischer [PF79] and is based on Theorem 5.6.

Given $L \in \text{DTIME}(T(n))$, for some $k > 0$, there is a k-tape, deterministic, $T(n)$ time-bounded Turing machine that accepts L. The proof that L belongs to $\text{SIZE}(O(T(n)\log T(n)))$ consists of the following steps:

1. By Theorem 5.6, L is accepted by an oblivious two-tape deterministic Turing machine N in time $O(T(n)\log T(n))$.
2. We will prove that every language that is accepted by an oblivious, deterministic Turing machine N in time $T(n)$ has a family of circuits of size $O(T(n))$.

Combining these steps, it follows that L is recognizable by a family of circuits of size $O(T(n)\log T(n))$; that is, there is a family of circuits $\{C_n\}_n$ such that $s(C_n) \in O(T(n)\log T(n))$, which is what we wish to prove.

Theorem 8.1. *If L is accepted by an oblivious, deterministic Turing machine N in time $T(n)$, then there is a family of circuits that recognizes L such that $s(C_n) \in O(T(n))$.*

Proof. We assume that N is an oblivious, deterministic, multitape Turing machine that accepts L. Following the logic above, it might make sense to assume that N is a two-tape Turing machine. In fact, merely to keep the details of our proof at a minimum, we will assume that N is a single-tape Turing machine, for the generalization to an arbitrary number of tapes is simple. We assume that N's tape is two-way infinite in order to maintain consistency with the construction in the proof of Theorem 5.6. Let Q and Γ be N's set of states and tape alphabet, respectively.

Let some $n \geq 1$ be given. Since N is $T(n)$ time-bounded, cells $-T(n), \ldots, T(n)$ are the only tape cells to be used in a computation on an input of length n. Initially, the input word $x = x_1 \ldots x_n$ is written in cells $0, \ldots, n-1$, and all other cells contain the blank symbol. Since N is oblivious, there is a fixed sequence of cells that N visits on any input of length n. Let this sequence be $S_0, \ldots, S_{T(n)}$. At time 0, N is in the initial configuration, so $S_0 = 0$. As is always the case, the computation proceeds from one step to the next by applying the transition function δ. Suppose that at some time $0 \leq i < T(n)$, the current state is q, cell S_i contains the symbol a, and $\delta(q,a) = (q',a',\Delta)$, where $\Delta \in \{L,R\}$. Then, N writes a' in cell S_i, shifts to scan cell S_{i+1}, and changes to state q'. Observe that because N is oblivious, we do not need to know the value of the direction Δ. Therefore, let us ignore the direction, and assume instead that δ maps $Q \times \Gamma$ into $Q \times \Gamma$.

We can encode Q and Γ as binary strings of length $\lceil \log \|Q\| \rceil$ and $\lceil \log \|\Gamma\| \rceil$, respectively. Letting $v = \lceil \log \|Q\| \rceil + \lceil \log \|\Gamma\| \rceil$, we can say that $\delta : \{0,1\}^v \to \{0,1\}^v$. Let $\hat{\delta}$ be the circuit with v input nodes and v output nodes that realizes the finite function δ. Despite this formality, it will be more convenient and more intuitive to think of the inputs and outputs to $\hat{\delta}$ as state-symbol pairs than as the v bits that encode these pairs.

The circuit C_n consists of $T(n) + 1$ levels, one level for each step of the computation. We make an assumption about N that will make this construction easier.

When N enters a halting configuration, either accepting or rejecting, then it remains in the same configuration for all time steps that follow. The first level consists of $\lceil \log \|Q\| \rceil + \lceil \log \|\Gamma\| \rceil (2T(n) + 1)$ nodes. These represent the input state and the input symbols to each of the cells $-T(n), \ldots, T(n)$, respectively. $\lceil \log \|\Gamma\| \rceil n$ of these nodes are input nodes that receive the initial contents of cells $0, \ldots, n - 1$. The remaining nodes have constant values that encode the information that q_0 is the initial state and that all other cells contain the blank symbol.

The first interior level of C_n consists of a copy of $\hat{\delta}$, with input wires from the nodes that encode the current state and the input symbol x_1 in cell $S_0 = 0$, and output wires that give the new state and the new symbol in cell S_0. Each interior level is a copy of $\hat{\delta}$. The copy at level $1 < i \leq T(n)$ has input wires from nodes that give the current state and the symbol at time i in cell S_i, and output wires that contain encodings of the new state and new symbol in cell S_i. Finally, there is a circuit E that connects some of the nodes at level $T(n)$ to a unique output node. The circuit E produces the output value 1 if the value of the state at level $T(n)$ is the accept state, and 0 otherwise.

Clearly C_n accepts a string x if and only if $x \in A^n$. $\hat{\delta}$ and E have constant size (depending on N only). C_n consists of $T(n)$ copies of $\hat{\delta}$, one instance of E, $O(n)$ input nodes, and $O(T(n))$ constant nodes. Thus, $s(C_n) \in O(T(n))$.   □

The theorem has important corollaries.

Corollary 8.1. DTIME$(T(n)) \subseteq$ SIZE$(O(T(n) \log T(n)))$.

Corollary 8.2. *Every language in* P *has a polynomial size family of circuits.*

Homework 8.3 *Consider the well-known oblivious Turing machine M that computes parity. M moves right only, and in the notation of the proof:*

$$Q = \{q_0, q_1, q_{accept}, q_{reject}\},$$
$$\Gamma = \{0, 1, B\},$$

and δ is defined by

$$\delta(q_0, 0) = (q_0, 0)$$
$$\delta(q_0, 1) = (q_1, 1)$$
$$\delta(q_0, B) = (q_{reject}, B)$$
$$\delta(q_1, 0) = (q_1, 0)$$
$$\delta(q_1, 1) = (q_0, 1)$$
$$\delta(q_1, B) = (q_{accept}, B)$$

Draw $\hat{\delta}$, E, and the circuit for inputs of length 4.

8.1.1 An Encoding of Circuits

Let C be a circuit. Number each node of the circuit $g_1, g_2, \ldots$. In particular, let 0 be the number of the output node and, where n is the number of variable input nodes, let $1, \ldots, n$ number the input nodes $x_1, \ldots x_n$, respectively. There are no other restrictions on the order in which nodes are numbered. We assume the numbering is such that the largest node number is $s(C)^{O(1)}$, so the gate numbers coded in binary have length $O(\log s(C))$. Encode the circuit as a collection of tuples $\langle g, b, g_l, g_r \rangle$, where

1. g is the number of a node;
2. If $g = 0$, then b is the empty word; if g is the number of an interior node, then b is the Boolean operation performed at node g; if $g \in \{1, \ldots, n\}$ is the number of a variable input node, then b is the empty word; if g is the number of an input node with constant value, then b is the constant value that labels the node;
3. If b is a binary Boolean operation, then g_l and g_r are the numbers of the nodes that provide the input values to g; if b is NOT, then g_r is the empty word; if g is an input node, then g_l and g_r are both the empty word.

Let $\overline{C}$ denote the encoding of a circuit C.

Homework 8.4 *Show that if L has a polynomial size family of circuits $\{C_n\}_{n>0}$, then there exists a polynomial p such that for all $n > 0$, $\overline{C_n}$ has length less than or equal to $p(n)$.*

The CIRCUIT VALUE PROBLEM (CVP) is the set of pairs $\langle x, y \rangle$ such that $x \in \{0,1\}^*$, y encodes a circuit with $|x|$ input gates, and y outputs 1 on input x.

Homework 8.5 *Show that* CVP *belongs to* P.

Now we can state the third corollary to Theorem 8.1.

Corollary 8.3. CVP is logspace-complete for P.

Proof. Let $L \in$ P and let M be a polynomial-time-bounded Turing machine that accepts L. Let M' be the oblivious polynomial-time-bounded Turing machine that accepts L that results from applying Theorem 5.6, and let y be the encoding of the circuit that we construct in the proof of Theorem 8.1 from M'. It is only necessary to show that a logspace transducer can compute the sequence of moves $S_0, \ldots, S_{T(n)}$ whose existence is asserted in the proof of Theorem 8.1. We leave it to the reader to once again carefully analyze the oblivious moves that M' makes in order to see that this can be done. $\square$

Homework 8.6 *Show that the reduction is implementable by a logspace transducer.*

The CIRCUIT SAT PROBLEM (CSP) is the set of encodings of circuits y such that for some input string x, y outputs 1.

Homework 8.7 *Show that* CSP *is NP-complete.*

8.1.2 Advice Classes

Definition 8.4. An *advice* function is a function $f : N \rightarrow \Sigma^*$. Given a language L and advice function f, define

$$L/f = \{x \mid \langle x, f(|x|) \rangle \in L\}.$$

Let $\mathscr{C}$ be a complexity class and $\mathscr{F}$ be a family of advice functions. Then

$$\mathscr{C}/\mathscr{F} = \{L/f \mid L \in \mathscr{C} \text{ and } f \in \mathscr{F}\}.$$

Let $poly = \{f : N \rightarrow \Sigma^* \mid \text{ for some polynomial } p, \text{ for every } n, |f(n)| \leq p(n)\}$. The most important advice class is $P/poly$.

Theorem 8.2. *Let A be a set. The following are equivalent:*

1. *A has a polynomial size family of circuits.*
2. *$A \in P/poly$.*
3. *For some sparse set S, $A \leq_T^P S$.*

Proof. Let $\{C_n\}_{n>0}$ be a polynomial size family of circuits that recognizes A. It is easy to show that $A \in P/poly$: For each $n > 0$, let $f(n) = \overline{C_n}$, the encoding of C_n. Then, for each string x,

$$C_n \text{ accepts } x \Leftrightarrow \langle x, f(|x|) \rangle \in \text{CVP}.$$

Since CVP belongs to P, this proves that item 1 implies item 2. (Also, let us note that the advice is the encoding of the circuit.)

Item 2 implies item 3: Let $A \in P/poly$; let f be the advice function and let B belong to P so that $A = B/f$. Define

$$S = \{x\#0^n \mid x \text{ is a prefix of } f(n)\}.$$

S is a sparse set because for each length l, the number of strings of length $\leq l$ is no more than l^2.

Homework 8.8 *Verify this fact.*

First, the straightforward prefix-search procedure given in Fig. 8.2 computes the advice function f using S as an oracle. Then, to determine membership in A, on an input word x, compute the pair $\langle x, f(|x|) \rangle$ and accept if and only if $\langle x, f(|x|) \rangle \in B$.

Now we show that item 3 implies item 1. Assume that $A \leq_T^P S$, where S is a sparse set. We need to prove that A is recognized by a polynomial size family of circuits. Let p and q be polynomials so that for each n, S contains no more than $p(n)$ strings of length $\leq n$, and q bounds the polynomial-time reduction from A to S. So $q(n)$ is also a bound on the size of strings in S that the reduction can query on inputs of length n. Note that the number of strings in S of length $\leq q(n)$ is $p(q(n))$ and their total length is bounded by $p(q(n)) * q(n)$.

Fig. 8.2 A polynomial-time-bounded reduction procedure computes the advice function f using oracle S

```
begin
  input x in {0,1}*;
  y := λ; {the empty string}
  while y0#0ⁿ ∈ S or y1#0ⁿ ∈ S {y ≠ f(n)} do
  if y0#0ⁿ ∈ S
      then y := y0
      else if y1#0ⁿ ∈ S then y := y1;
  output y
end.
```

Given an integer m, define the circuit C_m to accept A^m as follows: Consider the Turing machine M that, in addition to inputs of length n, also has auxiliary inputs of length $p(q(n)) * q(n)$. (Of course, the intent is that the auxiliary inputs will consist of all strings of S of length $\leq q(n)$.) On an input string x, M simulates the polynomial-time-bounded Turing reduction from A to S, except that whenever the reduction enters a query state with a query w to the oracle, instead M uses its auxiliary input to determine the next state. Obviously, in the case that the auxiliary input y is $S^{\leq q(n)}$, then M accepts $\langle x, y \rangle$ if and only if $x \in A$. Now we use Corollary 8.1. Let $\{D_n\}_{n>0}$ be the family of circuits that accepts $L(M)$. Let $n = m + p(q(m)) * q(m)$. Then C_m is the circuit, with m variable input nodes, obtained from D_n by replacing the $p(q(m)) * q(m)$ input nodes that correspond to M's auxiliary input with constant values that describe $S^{\leq q(m)}$. Since $\{D_n\}_{n>0}$ is a polynomial size family of circuits, as a function of the length of it's input strings, it follows that $\{C_n\}_{n>0}$ is a polynomial size family of circuits as a function of n. □

Homework 8.9 *Construct a language in* P/*poly that is decidable but not in* P.

Homework 8.10 *Construct a decidable language that is not in* P/*poly.*

Now we raise and address the question of whether NP $\subseteq$ P/*poly*, or, as we just learned, whether every set in NP has a polynomial size family of circuits.

Homework 8.11 *If* $B \in$ P/*poly and* $A \leq_m^P B$, *then* $A \in$ P/*poly.*

By Homework 8.11, NP $\subseteq$ P/*poly* if and only if SAT $\in$ P/*poly*. The question of whether NP $\subseteq$ P/*poly* is interesting, because, on the one hand, if we could prove that SAT does not belong to P/*poly*, then, by Corollary 8.2, we would conclude immediately that P $\neq$ NP. On the other hand, if we could prove that SAT belongs to P/*poly*, then that would suggest a possible approach to solving problems in NP: Given some reasonable length n and the polynomial-length advice string a_n for strings of length n, we could decide in polynomial time whether arbitrary formulas x of length n are satisfiable.

Our next result provides evidence that NP $\not\subseteq$ P/*poly*. We will prove the following theorem due to Karp and Lipton [KL80], which shows that the polynomial hierarchy collapses if SAT $\in$ P/*poly*. Our proof below is much less complicated that the original.

Theorem 8.3. *If* NP $\subseteq$ P/*poly, then the polynomial hierarchy collapses to* $\Sigma_2^P \cap \Pi_2^P$.

Homework 8.12 *If* SAT *has a polynomial size family of circuits, then there is a polynomial size family of circuits* $\{C_n\}_{n>0}$ *such that for each input x of length n, if x is satisfiable, then* C_n *outputs a satisfying assignment. Hint: Recall that there is an oracle Turing machine that in polynomial time computes the search problem for Satisfiability using* SAT *as the oracle.*

The following short proof of Theorem 8.3 is due to Samik Sengupta.

Proof. Assume that SAT has a polynomial size family of circuits, and let $\{C_n\}_{n>0}$ be the family of circuits that satisfies the conditions of Homework 8.12. Let $p(n)$ be a polynomial that bounds the size of each circuit C_n.

Our goal is to prove that $\mathrm{NP}^{\mathrm{NP}}$ belongs to Π_2^{P}. Let $L \in \mathrm{NP}^{\mathrm{SAT}}$ and let M be a polynomial-time-bounded oracle Turing machine that accepts L with oracle SAT. Let q be a polynomial that bounds the running time of M.

We begin by defining a polynomial-time decidable relation $V(x,y_1,y_2)$ as follows (While reading the definition of V, it might help to think of y_1 and y_2 as competing provers. Think of y_1 as trying to prove that $x \in L$, while y_2 is trying to demonstrate that y_1 is wrong. Then V is a verifier whose job is to determine which claim is correct.):

1. $V(x,y_1,y_2)$ holds only if y_1 is a string that encodes an accepting computation of M on input x together with a witness for each query to SAT for which the oracle returns "yes." Observe that this condition on y_1 is verifiable in polynomial time. Also, it is possible that a given string y_1 fulfills these conditions, but that x does not belong to L, because the computation might return "no" for a query to SAT that is satisfiable.
2. If y_1 is of the form specified in item 1, then $V(x,y_1,y_2)$ holds unless y_2 encodes a circuit C of size no greater that $p(q(n))$ and there is some query w in y_1's computation for which the oracle returns "no," but C on input w outputs a satisfying assignment of w. In this case, $V(x,y_1,y_2)$ does not hold.

We claim that $x \in L$ if and only if for every y_2 there exists y_1 such that $V(x,y_1,y_2)$. Since $L \in \mathrm{NP}^{\mathrm{SAT}}$, this will prove the theorem.

If $x \in L$, then let y_1 be the accepting computation of M on input x with oracle SAT. No y_2 can provide a counter-example, so for every string y_2, $V(x,y_1,y_2)$ holds.

If $x \notin L$, then let y_2 be the encoding of $C_{q(|x|)}$. V will not hold for any y_1 that does not satisfy item 1. Any y_1 that does satisfy item 1 must be incorrect about some query w for which the oracle returns "no,". Then, $C_{q(|x|)}$ on input w outputs a satisfying assignment of w, so $V(x,y_1,y_2)$ does not hold. This completes our proof.   □

There has been great interest in various extensions and improvements of the Karp–Lipton Theorem. Of these, we mention only the following, which has an easy proof even though the original proof, due to Abadi et al. [AFK89], was quite involved. The proof we present here is due to L. Hemaspaandra et al. [HHN+95]. It relies on the observation that the proof of Theorem 8.3 relativizes to arbitrary oracles. That is, for all oracles L, if $\mathrm{NP}^L \subseteq \mathrm{P}^L/poly$, then $\mathrm{PH}^L \subseteq \Sigma_2^{\mathrm{P}^L} \cap \Pi_2^{\mathrm{P}^L}$.

This is true as well of the development in this chapter on which the proof of Theorem 8.3 depends. In particular, for any oracle L, $A \in \mathrm{P}^L/poly$ if and only if there is a sparse set S such that $A \leq_{\mathrm{T}}^{\mathrm{P}} L \oplus S$ if and only if A has a family of polynomial-size circuits, where the circuits contain nodes that are oracle calls to L. We leave the straightforward verification of the claims in this paragraph to our readers. Also, recall, by Theorem 7.12, that K^L is the canonical NP^L-complete set and, by Theorem 6.9, that $K = K^{\emptyset}$ is the canonical complete set for NP.

Corollary 8.4. *If* $\mathrm{NP} \subseteq (\mathrm{NP} \cap \mathrm{co}\text{-}\mathrm{NP})/poly$, *then the polynomial hierarchy collapses to* $\Sigma_2^{\mathrm{P}} \cap \Pi_2^{\mathrm{P}}$.

Proof. Suppose that $\mathrm{NP} \subseteq (\mathrm{NP} \cap \mathrm{co}\text{-}\mathrm{NP})/poly$. Then $K \in (\mathrm{NP} \cap \mathrm{co}\text{-}\mathrm{NP})/poly$. Observing that $\mathrm{NP} \cap \mathrm{co}\text{-}\mathrm{NP} = \mathrm{P}^{(\mathrm{NP} \cap \mathrm{co}\text{-}\mathrm{NP})}$, we have $K \in \mathrm{P}^{(\mathrm{NP} \cap \mathrm{co}\text{-}\mathrm{NP})}/poly$. Thus, there exists a set $L \in \mathrm{NP} \cap \mathrm{co}\text{-}\mathrm{NP}$ such that $K \in \mathrm{P}^L/poly$. Thus, $\mathrm{NP}^L \subseteq \mathrm{P}^L/poly$, because $\mathrm{P}^L/poly$ is closed under $\leq_m^{\mathrm{P}}$-reductions. By the relativization of Theorem 8.3, $\mathrm{PH}^L \subseteq \Sigma_2^{\mathrm{P}^L} \cap \Pi_2^{\mathrm{P}^L}$. However, for $L \in \mathrm{NP} \cap \mathrm{co}\text{-}\mathrm{NP}$, $\mathrm{PH}^L = \mathrm{PH}$, $\Sigma_2^{\mathrm{P}^L} = \Sigma_2^{\mathrm{P}}$, and $\Pi_2^{\mathrm{P}^L} = \Pi_2^{\mathrm{P}}$. The theorem follows. □

Define $log = \{f : N \to \Sigma^* \mid$ for every n, $|f(n)| \leq O(\log(n))\}$.

Homework 8.13 *Use the self-reducibility of* SAT *to prove that* $\mathrm{NP} \subseteq \mathrm{P}/log$ *implies* $\mathrm{P} = \mathrm{NP}$.

The smallest class unconditionally proved not to be included in $\mathrm{P}/poly$ is $\mathrm{MA_{EXP}}$, [BFT98] which we have not yet defined. Kannan [Kan82] proved that $\mathrm{NEXP^{NP}}$ is not included in $\mathrm{P}/poly$, and also obtained the weaker result that there exist sets in EXPSPACE that do not have polynomial-size families of circuits. Since EXP has intractable sets, we also might expect an unconditional proof that EXP is not included in $\mathrm{P}/poly$. Unfortunately, no such result is currently known. Karp and Lipton [KL80] credit Meyer for proving that $\mathrm{EXP} \subseteq \mathrm{P}/poly$ if and only if $\mathrm{EXP} = \Sigma_2^{\mathrm{P}}$. Burhman and Homer [BH92] showed that if $\mathrm{EXP^{NP}} \subseteq \mathrm{P}/poly$, then $\mathrm{EXP^{NP}} = \mathrm{EXP}$. Recently Impagliazzo et al. [IKW01] showed that if $\mathrm{NEXP} \subseteq \mathrm{P}/poly$, then $\mathrm{NEXP} = \mathrm{MA}$. ($\mathrm{MA} \subseteq \Sigma_2^{\mathrm{P}}$.)

8.2 The Low and High Hierarchies

At this point we will digress from the main theme of nonuniform complexity in order to develop the low and high hierarchies of Schöning [Sch84, Sch83]. These developments will add further insight into the results that we just studied, and they will be helpful again later in the course.

Definition 8.5. A set A is generalized low$_n$ if $\Sigma_n^{\mathrm{P},A} \subseteq \Sigma_n^{\mathrm{P}}$. A set A is low$_n$ if $A \in \mathrm{NP}$ and A is *generalized low$_n$*. A set A is generalized high$_n$ if $\Sigma_{n+1}^{\mathrm{P}} \subseteq \Sigma_n^{\mathrm{P},A}$. A set A is high$_n$ if $A \in \mathrm{NP}$ and A is *generalized high$_n$*.

If A is an NP-complete set, then $NP^A = NP^{NP}$, so A is $high_1$. However, if $A \in P$, then $NP^A \subseteq NP$, so A is low_1.

It is useful to understand these classes in terms of reducibilities. For each $n \geq 0$, define the reducibility R_n^P by

$$A \; R_n^P \; B \text{ if and only if } \Sigma_n^{P,A} \subseteq \Sigma_n^{P,B}.$$

Homework 8.14

1. $R_0^P = \leq_T^P$.
2. For each $n \geq 0$, R_n^P is a reflexive and transitive relation.

Since R_n^P is reflexive and transitive, $R_n^P \cap (R_n^P)^{-1}$ is an equivalence relation. By definition, A set A is R_n^P-equivalent to $\emptyset$ if and only if

1. $\Sigma_n^{P,A} \subseteq \Sigma_n^{P,\emptyset} = \Sigma_n^P$, and
2. $\Sigma_n^P = \Sigma_n^{P,\emptyset} \subseteq \Sigma_n^{P,A}$.

The second condition is true for all sets A. Thus, A is R_n^P-equivalent to $\emptyset$ if and only if $\Sigma_n^{P,A} \subseteq \Sigma_n^P$. Thus, a set belongs to the zero degree of the R_n^P reducibility if and only if it is *generalized low$_n$*.

Proposition 8.2. *A set A is R_n^P-hard for NP if and only if A is generalized high$_n$.*

Proof.

$$A \text{ is } R_n^P\text{-hard for NP} \Leftrightarrow \text{SAT } R_n^P \; A$$
$$\Leftrightarrow \Sigma_n^{P,\text{SAT}} \subseteq \Sigma_n^{P,A}$$
$$\Leftrightarrow \Sigma_{n+1}^P \subseteq \Sigma_n^{P,A}$$
$$\Leftrightarrow A \text{ is } generalized \; high_n.$$

$\square$

As a consequence of Homework 8.14 and Proposition 8.2, A set A is *generalized high$_0$* if and only if it is $\leq_T^P$-hard, and A is *high$_0$* if and only if it is $\leq_T^P$-complete.

Proposition 8.3.

1. *For all $n \geq 0$, $A \; R_n^P \; B \Rightarrow A \; R_{n+1}^P \; B$.*
2. *For all $n \geq 0$, if A is generalized low$_n$, then A is generalized low$_{n+1}$.*
3. *For all $n \geq 0$, if A is generalized high$_n$, then A is generalized high$_{n+1}$.*

Proof. To prove item 1, suppose that $\Sigma_n^{P,A} \subseteq \Sigma_n^{P,B}$. We need to show that $\Sigma_{n+1}^{P,A} \subseteq \Sigma_{n+1}^{P,B}$. Let $L \in \Sigma_{n+1}^{P,A}$. By definition, there exists a set $S \in \Sigma_n^{P,A}$ such that $L \in NP^S$. By our supposition, $S \in \Sigma_n^{P,B}$, from which it follows that $L \in \Sigma_{n+1}^{P,B}$. This what we needed to prove.

If A is *generalized low$_n$*, then A R_n^P $\emptyset$. Thus, by item 1, A R_{n+1}^P $\emptyset$, so A is *generalized low$_{n+1}$*. If A is *generalized high$_n$*, then SAT R_n^P A. Thus, SAT R_{n+1}^P A. So, A is *generalized high$_{n+1}$*. □

We learn from these propositions and the remarks preceding them that *generalized high$_n$* is a generalization to R_n^P of NP-hardness and *high$_n$* is a generalization to R_n^P of NP-completeness. So *generalized high$_n$* is a hardness notion and *generalized low$_n$* is an easiness notion.

Homework 8.15

1. *For each $n \geq 0$, every generalized low$_n$ set belongs to Σ_n^P. (Thus, generalized low$_1$ and low$_1$ are identical.)*
2. *A set A is generalized low$_1$ if and only if $A \in$ NP $\cap$ co-NP.*

Theorem 8.4. *If there exists a set that is both generalized low$_n$ and generalized high$_n$, then $\Sigma_{n+1}^P = \Sigma_n^P$, so the polynomial hierarchy collapses to Σ_n^P.*

Proof. Suppose that A is both *generalized low$_n$* and *generalized high$_n$*. Then, by definition, $\Sigma_{n+1}^P \subseteq \Sigma_n^{P,A} \subseteq \Sigma_n^P$. □

Define

$$L_n = \{A \mid A \text{ is } low_n\},$$

$$H_n = \{A \mid A \text{ is } high_n\},$$

$$LH = \bigcup_{n \geq 0} L_n, \text{ and}$$

$$HH = \bigcup_{n \geq 0} H_n.$$

Observe that $L_0 = $ P, $L_1 = $ NP $\cap$ co-NP, and $L_0 \subseteq L_1 \subseteq L_2 \subseteq \ldots$ NP. Also, H_0 is the class of $\leq_T^P$-complete sets for NP and $H_0 \subseteq H_1 \subseteq H_2 \subseteq \ldots$ NP

Theorem 8.5. *If $\Sigma_{n+1}^P = \Sigma_n^P$, then for all $m \geq n$, $L_n = L_m = H_m = H_n = $ NP.*

Proof. Assume that $\Sigma_{n+1}^P \subseteq \Sigma_n^P$. For all sets $A \in$ NP, $\Sigma_n^P \subseteq \Sigma_n^{P,A} \subseteq \Sigma_{n+1}^P$. Then, by definition, every set in NP is both *low$_n$* and *high$_n$*. Thus, for $m \geq n$, NP $\subseteq L_n \subseteq L_m \subseteq$ NP and NP $\subseteq H_n \subseteq H_m \subseteq$ NP, which implies that $L_n = L_m = H_m = H_n = $ NP. □

Corollary 8.5.

1. *For all $n \geq 0$, either L_n and H_n are disjoint or $L_n = H_n = $ NP.*
2. *The polynomial hierarchy is infinite if and only if LH and HH are disjoint.*

Let's explain our interest in the low and high hierarchies. One of the results we will prove is that NP $\cap$ (P/*poly*) $\subseteq L_3$. Thus, assuming that the polynomial hierarchy is infinite, no hard set in NP has a polynomial size family of circuits and every set in NP that does is somewhat easy (i.e., with respect to R_n^P). Also, we will prove that

$SAT \in P/poly$ implies that $SAT \in L_2$. However, we know that $SAT \in H_0 \subseteq H_2$. Thus, by Theorem 8.4, we have an alternative proof of Theorem 8.3: If $SAT \in P/poly$, then $PH \subseteq \Sigma_2^P$. Before turning to these theorems, we need to complete our classification of NP into the low and high hierarchies. Thus far, we know that if the polynomial hierarchy is infinite, then LH and HH are disjoint. We need to show that the low and high hierarchies do not partition NP. That is, assuming that the polynomial hierarchy is infinite, there exist sets in NP that are neither in LH nor in HH. Our immediate goal is to prove the following results.

1. For each $n \geq 0$, $\Sigma_{n+1}^P \neq \Sigma_n^P$ if and only if there exist sets in NP that are neither in L_n nor in H_n.
2. If the polynomial hierarchy is infinite, then there are sets in NP that are neither in LH nor in HH.

The proofs are applications of Theorem 7.6. That necessitates tending to some technical details first. Define $K^{(1)}(A) = K^A$ and for $n \geq 1$, $K^{(n+1)}(A) = K^{K^{(n)}(A)}$. Theorem 7.13 relativizes to obtain that for $n \geq 1$, $K^{(n)}(A)$ is $\leq_m^P$-complete for $\Sigma_n^{P,A}$.

Lemma 8.1. *For all $n \geq 1$,*

1. *A is generalized low_n if and only if $K^{(n)}(A) \leq_m^P K^{(n)}$.*
2. *A is generalized $high_n$ if and only if $K^{(n+1)} \leq_m^P K^{(n)}(A)$.*

Proof. We prove the first assertion. Suppose that A is generalized low_n. Then $\Sigma_n^{P,A} \subseteq \Sigma_n^P$. Since $K^{(n)}(A) \in \Sigma_n^{P,A}$, $K^{(n)}(A) \in \Sigma_n^P$ follows. Then the conclusion, $K^{(n)}(A) \leq_m^P K^{(n)}$, holds because $K^{(n)}$ is $\leq_m^P$-complete for Σ_n^P.

Now we prove the other direction. Assume $K^{(n)}(A) \leq_m^P K^{(n)}$. Let $L \in \Sigma_n^{P,A}$. Then $L \leq_m^P K^{(n)}(A)$, so it follows that $L \leq_m^P K^{(n)}$. Hence $L \in \Sigma_n^P$. Thus, $\Sigma_n^{P,A} \subseteq \Sigma_n^P$, which completes the proof. $\square$

Homework 8.16 *Prove the second assertion.*

Theorem 8.6. *For each $n \geq 0$, L_n is effectively presentable.*

Proof. The class $L_0 = P$, which we know is effectively presentable. We have to prove the assertion for $n \geq 1$. Let $\{NP_i\}_i$ be an effective presentation of NP. Let $\{T_i\}_i$ be an effective enumeration of Turing machine transducers such that machine T_i runs in time $p_i(n) = n^i + i$. To construct an effective presentation $\{Q_k\}_k$ of the low_n sets, define Q_k, $k = \langle i, j \rangle$, as follows: On input x, for each string y such that $|y| < |x|$, Q_k tests whether

$$y \in K^{(n)}(L(NP_i)) \Leftrightarrow T_j(y) \in K^{(n)}.$$

If this test is true for all such y, then Q_k is to accept x if and only if $x \in L(NP_i)$. Otherwise, Q_k rejects x.

We need to prove that $L(Q_k)$ is low_n and we need to prove that if A is low_n, then for some k, $A = L(Q_k)$. We prove the latter assertion first. Suppose that A is low_n. Then $A \in NP$, so for some i, $A = L(NP_i)$. Also, for some j, by Lemma 8.1,

T_j computes a $\leq^P_m$-reduction from $K^{(n)}(L(NP_i))$ to $K^{(n)}$. Thus, letting $k = \langle i, j \rangle$, the test will always be true, from which it follows that $L(Q_k) = L(NP_i) = A$.

Now we prove that $L(Q_k)$ is low_n. If the test is true for all inputs x, then $A = L(NP_i)$ and for all y, $y \in K^{(n)}(A) \Leftrightarrow T_i(y) \in K^{(n)}$. Thus, by Lemma 8.1, $L(Q_k)$ is low_n. However, if for some input x the test fails, then it fails for all inputs z such that $|x| \leq |z|$. In this case $L(Q_k)$ is a finite set. Every finite set belongs to P, so clearly is low_n. $\quad\square$

Homework 8.17

1. *Suppose that* $\{\mathscr{C}_i\}_i$ *is a collection of classes of sets each of which is effectively presentable. Show that the union* $\bigcup_i \mathscr{C}_i$ *is effectively presentable. NOTE: This problem cannot be solved as stated. You need to add a uniformity condition, but we leave the formulation of this condition to you.*
2. *Show for each* $n \geq 1$, *that* H_n *has an effective presentation.*
3. *Show that LH, and HH are effectively presentable.*

Theorem 8.7. *For each* $n \geq 0$, $\Sigma^P_n \neq \Sigma^P_{n+1}$ *if and only if* NP *contains sets that are neither in* L_n *nor in* H_n.

Proof. Let $n \geq 0$ and assume that $\Sigma^P_n \neq \Sigma^P_{n+1}$. Then, by Theorem 8.4, SAT $\notin L_n$ and $\emptyset \notin H_n$. Observe that the hypotheses of Theorem 7.6 hold with $\mathscr{C}_1 = H_n$, $\mathscr{C}_2 = L_n$, $A = \emptyset$, and $B =$ SAT. (You can verify easily that L_n and H_n are closed under finite variation.) Thus, there exists a decidable set C such that $C \notin L_n$, $C \notin H_n$, $C \leq^P_m$SAT. The last condition lets us know that $C \in$ NP. $\quad\square$

Theorem 8.8. *If the polynomial hierarchy is infinite, then* NP *contains sets that are neither in LH nor in HH.*

Proof. Given the hypothesis, by Corollary 8.5, *LH* and *HH* are disjoint. We apply Theorem 7.6 with $A = \emptyset$, $B =$ SAT, $\mathscr{C}_1 = HH$, and $\mathscr{C}_2 = LH$ to get our conclusion. $\quad\square$

WARNING: Under the reasonable assumption that the polynomial hierarchy is infinite, we have the following picture:

$$P = L_0 \subseteq NP \cap co\text{-}NP = L_1 \subseteq L_2 \ldots \subseteq NP,$$

$$\left\{ \leq^P_T - \text{complete sets for NP} \right\} = H_0 \subseteq H_1 \subseteq \ldots \subseteq NP,$$

and

$$LH \cap HH = \emptyset.$$

However, our assumption provides no evidence as to whether L_i is a proper subset of L_{i+1}, or whether H_i is a proper subset of H_{i+1}, for any $i \geq 0$. Indeed, we have no reason to believe that the question of whether $P = NP \cap co\text{-}NP$ is related to the question of whether the polynomial hierarchy is infinite. For this reason, we do not use the low and high hierarchies in order to classify problems according to which level within these hierarchies a problem lies. Rather, our primary interest is to show that sets in NP with certain properties are in the low hierarchy, from which we conclude that they cannot be in the high hierarchy, and, therefore, in particular, are not complete sets. Now we will study some results of this kind.

Recall (Sect. 7.2) that for a set $A \in$ NP, the *search problem for A is reducible to A* if for some polynomial p_A and polynomial-time decidable relation $R_A(x,y)$ such that for all strings x,

$$x \in A \Leftrightarrow \exists y[|y| \le p_A(|x|) \text{ and } R_A(x,y)], \tag{8.2}$$

the problem of computing, for each input word $x \in A$, a witness y satisfying the right side of (8.2) is reducible in polynomial time to A. Also recall that the search problem for A reduces to A for all $\le_T^P$-complete sets for NP.

We begin with the following lemma. Observe that this lemma is a straightforward generalization to Homework 8.12.

Lemma 8.2. *If $A \in$ NP $\cap$ (P/poly) and the search problem for A reduces to A, then there exists a polynomial-time-bounded transducer T and advice function g such that, for some polynomial p_A and polynomial-time decidable relation R_A satisfying (8.2), for every input pair $\langle x, g(|x|) \rangle$ such that $x \in A$, T computes a witness y such that $|y| \le p_A(|x|)$ and $R_A(x,y)$.*

Proof. Let $B \in$ P and let f be an advice function such that $A = B/f$. Let q be a polynomial such that for all natural numbers n, $|f(n)| \le q(n)$. Suppose that p_A is a polynomial and $R_A(x,y)$ is a polynomial-time decidable relation satisfying (8.2). Let T' be a polynomial-time-bounded oracle transducer that on an input word $x \in A$, outputs a witness y when A is the oracle. Let p'_T be a polynomial that bounds the running time of T'. In particular, on words of length n, T' can only query words of length $\le p'_T(n)$.

Define the function g by $g(n) = f(0)\#f(1)\#\cdots\#f(p'_T(n))$. Then g is an advice function. Consider the transducer T that on an input word $\langle x, g(n) \rangle$, where $|x| = n$, simulates T' on input x, except that whenever T' enters its query state with a query w on the query tape, T, using the input word $g(n)$, begins a simulation of the Turing machine that decides B on input $\langle w, f(|w|) \rangle$. If this simulation accepts (in which case, $w \in A$), then T continues its simulation of T in the YES state, and, otherwise, T continues its simulation of T in the NO state. Finally, T halts and outputs a word y if and only if its simulation of T' does.

It should be clear that $g(n)$ provides the necessary advice strings for all queries to A that T' can generate on an input of length n. Thus, for all $x \in A$, T on input $\langle x, g(|x|) \rangle$ computes a witness y such that $|y| \le p_A(|x|)$ and $R_A(x,y)$. Also, it should be clear that T is a polynomial-time-bounded Turing machine transducer. $\square$

Theorem 8.9. *If $A \in$ NP $\cap$ (P/poly) and the search problem for A reduces to A, then $A \in L_2$.*

Proof. We need to show that $\Sigma_2^{P,A} \subseteq \Sigma_2^P$. Let $L \in \Sigma_2^{P,A}$. There is a polynomial p_L and polynomial-time decidable in A relation R_L^A such that for all strings x,

$$x \in L \Leftrightarrow \exists y_{|y| \leq p_L(|x|)} \forall z_{|z| \leq p_L(|x|)} R_L^A(x,y,z).$$

Let M be a polynomial-time oracle Turing machine such that

$$L^A(M) = \{\langle x,y,z \rangle \mid R_L^A(x,y,z)\}.$$

Let p_M be a polynomial that bounds the running time of M. Let q be a polynomial such that every query that M generates on input $\langle x,y,z \rangle$, where $|y| \leq p_L(|x|)$ and $|z| \leq p_L(|x|)$, has length $\leq q(|x|)$.

Now apply Lemma 8.2: Let T be a polynomial-time-bounded transducer, g be an advice function, and p_A and R_A be a polynomial and polynomial-time decidable relation, respectively, satisfying (8.2) such that for every $x \in A$, T, on an input pair $\langle x,g(|x|) \rangle$, computes a witness y such that $|y| \leq p_A(|x|)$ and $R_A(x,y)$.

Define the advice function h by $h(|x|) = g(0)\#g(1)\#\cdots\#g(q(|x|))$. Let l be a polynomial that bounds the length of h.

Let T' be a transducer that on input $\langle w,h(|x|) \rangle$, where $|w| \leq q(|x|)$, simulates T on input $\langle w,g(|w|) \rangle$. Therefore, if $w \in A$, then T' outputs a witness y verifying that $w \in A$.

Now we describe a polynomial-time-bounded Turing machine M' that on an input tuple $\langle x,y,z,a \rangle$, where $|y| \leq p_L(|x|)$, $|z| \leq p_L(|x|)$, and $|a| \leq l(|x|)$, simulates M on input $\langle x,y,z \rangle$, except that whenever M enters the query state with a query w to A, instead, the simulation answers "yes" if and only if $T'(w,a)$ outputs a witness verifying that $w \in A$.

To show that $L \in \Sigma_2^P$, the idea is to guess an advice string a, verify that it is correct, i.e., that $a = h(|x|)$, and verify for some y and all z that M'' accepts $\langle x,y,z,a \rangle$. This is formally expressed as follows: (To avoid the notation from becoming too cumbersome, we will leave off the polynomial bounds on the quantifiers.)

$$x \in L \Leftrightarrow \exists a[(a \text{ is correct}) \text{ and } \exists y \forall z[M' \text{ accepts } \langle x,y,z,a \rangle]]. \tag{8.3}$$

The second part of the "and" is a Σ_2^P predicate. It remains to show that "a is correct" is also. However, we cannot show that "$a = h(|x|)$" is a Σ_2^P predicate. This is alright, because for our purpose, it suffices to stipulate that a is correct if and only if

$$\forall w[|w| \leq q(|x|) \Rightarrow [w \in A \Leftrightarrow T'(w,a) \text{ outputs a witness verifying that } w \in A]].$$

This test simplifies to

$$\forall w[|w| \leq q(|x|) \Rightarrow [w \in A \Rightarrow T'(w,a) \text{ outputs a witness verifying that } w \in A]],$$

because the other direction must be true. Recalling that $A \in NP$, it is easy to see that this is a Π_1^P predicate. Now we can easily see that the right side of (8.3) is a Σ_2^P predicate. Hence, $L \in \Sigma_2^P$, which proves that A is low_2. $\qquad\square$

This theorem explains the Karp–Lipton phenomenon. SAT cannot belong to P/*poly*, because if it did, then SAT would be *low*$_2$. However, since SAT is NP-complete, SAT cannot be *low*$_2$ unless the polynomial hierarchy collapses to Σ_2^P. The next theorem shows that all sets in $A \in \mathrm{NP} \cap (\mathrm{P}/poly)$ are in the low hierarchy, not just those for which search reduces to decision.

Theorem 8.10. *If $A \in \mathrm{NP} \cap (\mathrm{P}/poly)$, then $A \in L_3$.*

Homework 8.18 *Show that if $A \in \mathrm{P}/poly$, then there is a set B in P and an advice function f so that for all n and all words x, $|x| \leq n$, $x \in A \Leftrightarrow \langle x, f(n) \rangle \in B$.*

Proof. Now we need to prove that $\Sigma_3^{\mathrm{P},A} \subseteq \Sigma_3^{\mathrm{P}}$. Let $L \in \Sigma_3^{\mathrm{P},A}$. There is a polynomial p_L and polynomial-time decidable in A relation R_L^A such that for all strings x,

$$x \in L \Leftrightarrow \exists y_1 \forall y_2 \exists y_3 R_L^A(x, y_1, y_2, y_3),$$

where the quantifiers are bounded by $p_L(|x|)$.

Let M be a polynomial-time oracle Turing machine such that

$$L^A(M) = \left\{ \langle x, y_1, y_2, y_3 \rangle \mid R_L^A(x, y_1, y_2, y_3) \right\}.$$

Let p_M be a polynomial that bounds the running time of M. Let q be a polynomial such that every query that M generates on input $\langle x, y_1, y_2, y_3 \rangle$, where $|y_1| \leq p_L(|x|)$, $|y_2| \leq p_L(|x|)$, and $|y_3| \leq p_L(|x|)$, has length $\leq q(|x|)$.

Using Homework 8.18, let f be an advice function and B belong to P such that for all n and all words w, $|w| \leq n$, $w \in A \Leftrightarrow \langle w, f(n) \rangle \in B$. Let l be a polynomial such that for all n, $|f(n)| \leq l(n)$.

Let p_A be a polynomial and R_A be a polynomial-time decidable relation such that

$$w \in A \Leftrightarrow \exists y_{|y| \leq p_A(|x|)} R_A(w, y).$$

Consider the polynomial-time-bounded Turing machine M' that on an input tuple $\langle x, y_1, y_2, y_3, a \rangle$, where $|y_1| \leq p_L(|x|)$, $|y_2| \leq p_L(|x|)$, $|y_3| \leq p_L(|x|)$, and $|a| \leq l(q(|x|))$, simulates M on input $\langle x, y_1, y_2, y_3 \rangle$, except that whenever M enters the query state with a query w to A, instead the simulation answers "yes" if and only if $\langle w, a \rangle \in B$. Observe that for all x,

$$x \in L \Leftrightarrow \exists y_1 \forall y_2 \exists y_3 [M' \text{ accepts } \langle x, y_1, y_2, y_3, f(q(|x|)) \rangle].$$

(Once again we leave off the polynomial bounds on the quantifiers.)

Now, as in the previous proof, we arrive at a point much like (8.3), but with three quantifier alternations:

$$x \in L \Leftrightarrow \exists a[(a \text{ is correct }) \text{ and } \exists y_1 \forall y_2 \exists y_3 [M' \text{ accepts } \langle x, y_1, y_2, y_3, a \rangle]]. \qquad (8.4)$$

The part of the expression to the right of the "and" is a Σ_3^P-predicate. We will show that "a is correct" is a Π_2^P-predicate. Our proof follows from that. By Homework 8.18, the string a is correct advice (for strings of length $\leq q(|x|)$) if and only if

$$\forall w[|w| \leq q(|x|) \Rightarrow [w \in A \Leftrightarrow \langle w, a \rangle \in B]].$$

This test is equivalent to the following expression:

$$\forall w_{\leq q(|x|)} [[\neg \exists y R_A(w, y) \vee \langle w, a \rangle \in B] \text{ and } [\neg \langle w, a \rangle \in B \vee \exists y R_A(w, y)]],$$

and it is easy to see that this is a Π_2^P-predicate. That completes our argument. □

Chapter 9
Parallelism

We consider the theory of synchronous highly parallel computations. VLSI chip technology is making it possible to connect together large numbers of processors to operate together synchronously. The question, of course, is what can be done with the result.

Several models of parallel computation have been proposed, and even though each model can simulate the other without much loss, the issue of "correct" model is not quite as settled as it is with sequential computation. The vector machine, which is considered by Pratt and Stockmeyer [PS78], is like a random access machine, but it can operate on vectors in one step. Other variations of random access machines have been considered by Hartmanis and Simon [HS74], Goldschlager [Gol78] (who considers the SIMDAG, a single instruction stream, multiple data stream, machine, which is based on a RAM that allows concurrent reads and writes in shared random access memory), and others. Fortunately, all of these devices can simulate one another with no more than a cubic increase in computation time. There is a well-developed theory of parallel random access machines (PRAMS). These models, while considered by many to be not entirely practical, nevertheless have been important for the development of practical parallel algorithms. Here we will examine two models of parallelism, "alternating Turing machines" and "uniform families of circuits," that are more important to studies in computational complexity.

9.1 Alternating Turing Machines

In the proof of Theorem 7.17, with the help of a sophisticated recursion, we proved that every language $L \in$ PSPACE is expressible in the following manner: There is a set $B \in$ P and polynomials p and q such that for all words $x \in \Sigma^*$,

$$x \in L \Leftrightarrow \exists y_1 \cdots Q y_{q(|x|)} \langle x, y_1, \ldots y_{q(|x|)} \rangle \in B, \tag{9.1}$$

S. Homer and A.L. Selman, *Computability and Complexity Theory*,
Texts in Computer Science, DOI 10.1007/978-1-4614-0682-2_9,
© Springer Science+Business Media, LLC 2011

where the quantifiers alternate (Q is an existential quantifier if and only if the number of quantifiers is odd), and for each quantified variable y_i, $|y_i| \leq p(|x|)$, $1 \leq i \leq q(|x|)$. This is a remarkable result, for naive intuition does not suggest that every language in PSPACE can be decomposed in this manner. In brief, an alternating Turing machine is a machine that implements the expression on the right hand side of (9.1). Informally, the initial process on input x immediately enters an "existential configuration" that causes $2^{p(n)}$ processes to operate in parallel, one process for each possible $y_1 \in \Sigma^{p(n)}$. If one of these processes accepts, then it reports acceptance back to its parent, and then the entire computation accepts. A process that became active by this action, in turn enters a "universal configuration" that causes another $2^{p(n)}$ processes to become active. This time, the universal configuration eventually reports acceptance to its parent if and only if all of the processes it spawns accept. Since there are only $q(n)$ quantifiers on an input of length n, the alternating Turing machine either accepts or rejects its input in a polynomial number of parallel steps. Studies of various models of parallel computation have led to the formulation of a "parallel computation thesis." This thesis asserts that

> parallel time is within a polynomial factor of deterministic space.

Our observation that the alternating Turing machine accepts every language in PSPACE in parallel polynomial time is an instance of the parallel computation thesis. Also, this observation demonstrates that presumably intractable languages, i.e., those in PSPACE, are capable of enormous speedup by using parallelism. This, however, is an impractical observation. Although it is true that the alternating Turing machine accepts languages in PSPACE in polynomial time, the total number of processes is exponential. No one will ever build parallel computers with an exponential number of processes. Parallelism will not make intractable problems tractable. One important result of the observation we just made is that researchers consider not just size (number of processes) and parallel time, but rather the combination of these two resources. We will return to that point later in this chapter.

Alternating Turing machines are due to Chandra, Kozen, and Stockmeyer [CKS81].

Definition 9.1. An *alternating Turing machine* is a tuple

$$M = \langle k, Q, \Sigma, \Gamma, B, \cent, \delta, q_0, q_{\text{accept}}, g \rangle,$$

where
k is the number of work tapes,
Q is the finite set of states,
Σ is the input alphabet,
Γ is the finite tape alphabet,
$B, \cent \in \Gamma - \Sigma$, B is the blank and $\cent$ is an endmarker,
δ is the transition function,
$q_0 \in Q$ is the initial state,
q_{accept} is the accepting state, and
$g : (Q - \{q_{\text{accept}}\}) \to \{\wedge, \vee\}$.

The transition function δ is a partial function

$$\delta : (Q - \{q_{\text{accept}}\}) \times \Gamma^k \times (\Sigma \cup \{\varsigma\}) \to \mathscr{P}(Q \times (\Gamma - \{\ell\})^k \times \{L, R\}^{k+1}).$$

If $g(q) = \wedge$, then q is a *universal* state, and if $g(q) = \vee$, then q is an *existential* state. The machine has a read-only input tape with endmarkers and k work tapes that are initially blank. The input word $w \in \Sigma^*$ is written on the input tape as $\varsigma w \varsigma$, the reading head is initialized to the first symbol in w, and the machine is not permitted to move left of the left endmarker or right of the right endmarker.

A configuration is a tuple containing the current state, the input, the nonblank contents of the k work tapes, and the $k + 1$ head positions. A configuration is *universal* (*existential, accepting*), if the current state of the configuration is universal (existential, accepting, respectively). A *computation* of an alternating Turing machine M on an input word w is a possibly infinite tree whose definition is the same as that for a nondeterministic Turing machine: The root of the tree is the initial configuration of M on w. The children of a node are the configurations that follow in one move. We define acceptance recursively as follows: A leaf is *eventually accepting* if it is an accepting configuration. An existential configuration is *eventually accepting* if at least one of its children is eventually accepting. (An existential configuration is the root of a subtree of the computation tree. Some of its computation paths might be infinite, some might be accepting, and others might halt in nonaccepting states.) A universal configuration is *eventually accepting* if all of its children are eventually accepting. (Thus, a universal configuration is accepting only if it is the root of a finite tree.) The machine M *accepts* the input word w if the root is eventually accepting.

A deterministic Turing machine is equivalent to an alternating Turing machine with a single-valued transition function, and a nondeterministic Turing machine is equivalent to an alternating Turing machine with no universal states.

We define time-bounded and space-bounded alternating Turing machines in the natural way: M accepts w in time $T(n)$ if M accepts w and the depth of the computation tree is at most $T(n)$. M accepts w in space $S(n)$ if M accepts w and the nonempty portion of every work tape in every configuration in the computation tree contains no more than $S(|w|)$ cells. We are interested in constructible time bounds and space bounds only, for which, all reasonable variations of these definitions are equivalent.

Define $\text{ATIME}(T(n))$ to be the set of all languages accepted by an alternating Turing machine in time $T(n)$. Similarly, define $\text{ASPACE}(S(n))$ to be the set of all languages accepted by an alternating Turing machine in space $S(n)$. In particular,

$$\text{AL} = \text{ASPACE}(\log(n)),$$

$$\text{AP} = \bigcup \{\text{ATIME}(n^k) \mid k \geq 1\},$$

$$\text{APSPACE} = \bigcup \{\text{ASPACE}(n^k) \mid k \geq 1\},$$

$$\text{AEXP} = \bigcup \{\text{ATIME}(2^{p(n)}) \mid p \text{ is a polynomial}\}.$$

Fig. 9.1 The recursive
procedure TEST2

```
FUNCTION TEST2(I₁,I₂,i): Boolean;
var I': configuration;
begin
  if (i = 0) and (I₁ = I₂)
      then return true;
  if (i = 1) and (I₁ ⊢_M I₂)
      then return true;
  if i > 1
      then for each I' of length at most S(n) do
              if TEST2(I₁,I',i/2) and TEST2(I',I₂,i/2)
                  then return true;
  return false;
end;
```

The following four theorems relate alternating time and space to deterministic
time and space. The main results about alternating Turing machines are corollaries
to these theorems.

Theorem 9.1. *If $S(n) \geq n$, then $\mathrm{NSPACE}(S(n)) \subseteq \mathrm{ATIME}(O(S^2(n)))$.*

Proof. We begin with the assumption that $S(n)$ is space-constructible in deterministic time $O(S^2(n))$, and we remove this restriction later. The proof is identical to the
technique used to prove Savitch's Theorem, Theorem 5.13. The recursive algorithm
is the same, but this time the implementation of the algorithm is by an alternating
Turing machine.

Let M be a nondeterministic Turing machine that accepts a language L in
$\mathrm{NSPACE}(S(n))$. Then there is a constant c so that $c^{S(n)}$ is greater than or equal
to the number of configurations for an input of length n. If M accepts a word w of
length n, then there is an accepting computation of length $\leq c^{S(n)}$. Each intermediate
configuration must have length at most $S(n)$. (We encode configurations in an
alphabet containing c symbols.)

Now we recall the algorithm that determines whether an initial configuration I_0
leads to an accepting configuration I_f. We determine this by the following procedure
that makes calls to a subroutine TEST2:

> **for** each accepting configuration I_f of length at most $S(n)$ **do**
>   **if** TEST2$(I_0,I_f,c^{S(n)})$
>   **then** accept;
> reject;

Figure 9.1 gives the definition of the computable function TEST2 that the
procedure calls. TEST2(I_1,I_2,i) returns true if and only if there is a sequence of
at most i moves, where i is a number in c-ary notation, $0 \leq i \leq c^{S(n)}$, from I_1 to I_2
such that each intermediate move has length at most $S(n)$.

The alternating Turing machine M' on input w, $|w| = n$, first marks off $S(n)$ tape
in time $O(S^2(n))$. Then it writes the initial configuration of M. It implements the for-
loop of the main procedure by guessing, using existential branching, an accepting

configuration of M of length at most $S(n)$. M' implements the recursive calls to the subroutine as follows: It guesses a middle configuration I' by existential branching. Then it verifies the two recursive calls in parallel, by universal branching.

The entire computation requires $\log c^{S(n)} = O(S(n))$ recursive calls, and each call takes $O(S(n))$ steps. Thus, there are $O(S^2(n))$ steps altogether.

Now let's remove the assumption that $S(n)$ is space-constructible in deterministic time $O(S^2(n))$. One possibility if for M' to iterate possible values of $S(n)$, $S(n) = 1, 2, \ldots$, and perform the above computation for each such value. If M accepts x, then the correct value of $S(n)$ will be discovered; if M does not accept x, then M' will not accept for any value. However, there is a problem with this iteration. Namely, for each i, $1 \leq i \leq S(n)$, the above computation takes $O(i^2)$ steps. So the total number of steps of this iterated process is too large. We can solve this problem by iterating on powers of two only. Then, the total number of steps is still $O(S^2(n))$. $\quad\square$

Homework 9.1 *Prove the claim made by the last sentence of the proof.*

The only reason that Theorem 9.1 requires the hypothesis $S(n) \geq n$ is because time must be at least n: An alternating Turing machine takes n steps to read its input. We will have occasion to be interested in alternating Turing machines with smaller time bounds, for which purpose we introduce a variation of the alternating Turing machine that has random access to its input. The input word x is not written on a tape, instead, the length of the input is written. The machine has a distinguished tape called the *index* tape. Whenever the machine needs to know the ith symbol of the input word, $i \leq |x|$, it writes i in binary on the index tape. This causes the machine to enter a state that provides the machine with this information. Whenever we use time-bounds less than n, we have this variation of the model in mind. In particular, we may now weaken the hypothesis of Theorem 9.1 to $S(n) \geq \log n$.

Theorem 9.2. *If $S(n) \geq \log n$, then $\text{NSPACE}(S(n)) \subseteq \text{ATIME}(O(S^2(n)))$.*

The following example illustrates the power of this model, the possibility of processing the input string x in parallel, and thereby using less than $|x|$ time to perform a useful computation. Define $\text{ALOGTIME} = \text{ATIME}(O(\log n))$.

Example 9.1. We show that the set of palindromes $\{ww^R \mid w \in \{0,1\}^*\}$ belongs to ALOGTIME. The length n of the input word is written on a tape. The alternating Turing machine uses universal branching to verify for all i, $1 \leq i \leq n$, that the ith and $(n - i + 1)$th positions contain the same symbol.

The running time is the time to write n and i, to calculate $(n - i + 1)$, and to branch. The latter appears to be a tree of height 2, but that would assume that the alternating Turing machine permits unbounded branching, or, at least, branching that depends on the length of the input word. Assuming our machine permits fan-out 2, the height of the tree increases to $\log n$. Thus the total running time is $O(\log n)$.

Let

$$\text{A-SPACE-TIME}(S(n), T(n))$$

be the set of languages that are accepted by an alternating Turing machine with simultaneous bounds of space $S(n)$ and time $T(n)$.

Corollary 9.1. *If $S(n) \geq \log n$, then* NSPACE$(S(n)) \subseteq$ A-SPACE-TIME$(O(S(n)),$ $O(S^2(n)))$.

Theorem 9.3. *If $T(n) \geq \log n$, then* ATIME$(T(n)) \subseteq$ DSPACE(T(n)).

Proof. Assume that $T(n)$ is tape constructible, and let M be an alternating Turing machine that accepts $L = L(M)$ in time $T(n)$. (Recall the proof of Theorem 5.10 that NTIME$(T(n)) \subseteq$ DSPACE(T(n)), for we use a similar technique here.) A deterministic Turing machine, on an input word w, constructs $T(n)$, writes the initial configuration of M on a tape, and then builds and traverses in depth-first order the computation tree of M on w. At the same time, it is necessary to determine, by a postorder search, whether the computation is eventually accepting. We leave out the details, except to note, that when visiting a node, the deterministic machine has to store only the current configuration and the address of the current configuration.

If $T(n)$ is not tape constructible, then iterate possible values of $T(n)$, $T(n) = 1, 2, \ldots$, and for each possible value, repeat the above computation. Since M accepts L in time $T(n)$, the computations cannot use more than $T(n)$ space. $\square$

The following corollary illustrates the parallel computation thesis for alternating Turing machines, demonstrating that the alternating Turing machine is a strong model of parallel computing:

Alternating time is within a polynomial factor of deterministic space.

Corollary 9.2. *For $S(n) \geq \log n$,* DSPACE$(S(n)^{O(1)}) =$ ATIME$(S(n)^{O(1)})$.

Proof.

$$\text{ATIME}(S(n)^{O(1)}) \subseteq \text{DSPACE}(S(n)^{O(1)}), \text{ by Theorem 9.3}$$

$$\subseteq \text{NSPACE}(S(n)^{O(1)})$$

$$\subseteq \text{ATIME}(O(S^{O(1)}(n))), \text{ by Theorem 9.1.}$$ $\square$

Corollary 9.3. AP $=$ PSPACE.

The introductory paragraph of this section gives an alternate proof of the corollary: For each language $L \in$ PSPACE, an alternating Turing machine determines in polynomial time whether (9.1) holds. Therefore, PSPACE $\subseteq$ AP follows. Equation (9.1) even suggests an alternate proof of the other direction: Suppose that $L \in$ AP. Let M be an alternating Turing machine that accepts L and that runs in time $q(n)$. We can assume that the initial state of M is existential and we can assume that M can enter a universal state if and only if its current state is existential. Define B in P to be the set of all sequences $\langle x, y_1, y_2, \ldots, y_{p(n)} \rangle$, where y_1 is the initial configuration of M on x, for each i, $1 \leq i < p(n)$, y_{i+1} is a successor configuration of y_i, and $y_{p(n)}$ is an accepting configuration. Then, $x \in L$ if and only if

$$\exists y_1 \cdots Q y_{q(|x|)} \langle x, y_1, \ldots y_{q(|x|)} \rangle \in B,$$

from which, it follows that $L \in$ PSPACE.

Corollary 9.4. AEXP = EXPSPACE.

The next results relate alternating space with deterministic time.

Theorem 9.4. *If S is fully time-constructible and* $S(n) \geq \log n$, *then*

$$\text{ASPACE}(S(n)) \subseteq \text{DTIME}(2^{O(S(n))}).$$

Proof. The proof is essentially the same as the proof of Corollary 5.8 that

$$\text{NSPACE}(S(n)) \subseteq \text{DTIME}(2^{O(S(n))}).$$

Given an alternating Turing machine M that accepts L in $S(n)$ space, we want to construct a deterministic Turing machine N so that N can find all configurations that are reachable from an initial configuration of M. For some constant c, there are at most $c^{S(n)}$ configurations of size $S(n)$. Assume that $S(n)$ is space-constructible in time exponential in $S(n)$. N on input x first constructs $S(n)$, $|x| = n$. Then N writes a list of all configurations of size $\leq S(n)$. The length of this list is at most $c^{S(n)}$. So the list sits on a tape of size at most $S(n) \cdot c^{S(n)}$. N needs to determine whether the initial configuration is eventually accepting. Configurations that do not have successor configurations are labeled either accepting or nonaccepting already. So N scans the tape containing the list, and labels as eventually accepting all existential configurations for which at least one successor is already labeled as eventually accepting, and labels as eventually accepting all universal configurations for which all successors are already labeled as eventually accepting. N repeats this process iteratively until the initial configuration is labeled. Then, N accepts if and only if the initial configuration is eventually accepting. For some constant d, each iteration takes $d^{S(n)}$ steps. The maximum number of iterations is at most $c^{S(n)}$. Thus, the entire process takes time exponential in $S(n)$.

If S is not space-constructible in time exponential in $S(n)$, then we iterate on possible values of $S(n)$ as we did in the proof of Theorem 9.3. In this case, for some constant k, the running time of N is at most

$$\sum_{m=1}^{S(n)} k^m,$$

which is still at most exponential in $S(n)$. $\qquad\square$

Discussion question: Why is $S(n)$ fully time-constructible?

Theorem 9.5. *If* $T(n) \geq n$, *then* $\text{DTIME}(T(n)) \subseteq \text{ASPACE}(O(\log T(n)))$.

Proof. Let $L \in \text{DTIME}(T(n))$ and let M be a one-tape Turing machine that accepts L in time $cT^2(n)$, for some constant $c > 0$. Recall that we can write configurations of M on an input word x as a string $\alpha q \beta$, where $\alpha\beta$ is the nonblank portion of the tape, and q is the current state. For each input word x, we assume that M does not halt on x prior to $cT^2(n)$ steps. Also, we assume that M accepts x by entering the

Fig. 9.2 The recursive procedure TABLE

```
FUNCTION TABLE(i, j, b): Boolean;
begin
if (j = 0) and (i = 1)
    then
            if b = q₀ then return true else return false;
if (j = 0) and (1 < i ≤ n + 1)
    then
            if b = x_{i-1} then return true else return false;
if (j = 0) and (n + 1 < i ≤ T²(n) + 1)
    then
            if b = B then return true else return false;
if j ≥ 1
    then existentially guess symbols b₁, b₂, b₃, b₄ such that
        TABLE(i − 1, j − 1, b₁), TABLE(i, j − 1, b₂),
        TABLE(i + 1, j − 1, b₃), TABLE(i + 2, j − 1, b₄), and
        the previous four conditions yield TABLE(i, j, b)
end;
```

accept state q_{accept} in square 1 on the completely blank tape, and we assume that once this occurs, then all configurations thereafter are identical. We can make these assumptions without loss of generality.

As always, a computation of M is a sequence of configurations. This suggests that we can represent the computation of M on x as a table, of length and width $O(T^2(n))$. The length of the table is the number of configurations in the sequence, and the width of the table is the length of the configurations. For each time $0 \le j \le cT^2(n)$, location $1 \le i \le T^2(n) + 1$, we will be interested in determining the symbol in the i-th position of the j-th configuration. The most important observation to make is that the symbol b that occurs at location i of configuration j depends entirely on the four symbols that occur at locations $i - 1, i, i + 1$, and $i + 2$ at time $j - 1$.

Let us assume for now that $T^2(n)$ is computable in space $(O(\log T(n)))$; we will remove this assumption later. Figure 9.2 gives the definition of a procedure TABLE(i, j, b) that returns true if and only if the i-th location of configuration j is b. Then, the algorithm to determine whether M accepts $x = x_1 x_2 \cdots x_n$ is simply

$$\text{TABLE}(1, cT^2(n), q_{\text{accept}}).$$

We design an alternating Turing machine M' to implement this algorithm.

The alternating Turing machine verifies the recursive calls by universal branching. M' only needs to store i and j. These values are between 0 and $O(T^2(n))$, so they require $O(\log T(n))$ space.

Now let's remove the assumption that $T^2(n)$ is computable in space $(O(\log T(n)))$: Perform the above computation for all possible values $(1, 2, \ldots)$ of $T^2(n)$. If M accepts x, then it will accept within $O(T^2(n))$ time, so none of these computations use more than $(O(\log T(n)))$ space. $\qquad\square$

Theorem 9.5 is a very nice result. It is not an extension of a result that we knew already for nondeterministic space. Nondeterminism provides a limited amount of parallelism (existential branching only), but we know no theorem that gives an efficient decomposition of deterministic time in nondeterministic space.

Corollary 9.5. *If S is fully time-constructible and $S(n) \geq \log n$, then*

$$\text{ASPACE}(O(S(n))) = \text{DTIME}(2^{O(S(n))}).$$

Corollary 9.6. $\text{AL} = \text{P}$.

Corollary 9.7. $\text{APSPACE} = \text{EXP}$.

We learned that alternation shifts one level to the right the hierarchy

$$\text{L} \subseteq \text{P} \subseteq \text{PSPACE} \subseteq \text{EXP} \subseteq \text{EXPSPACE}.$$

Namely,

$$
\begin{array}{ccccccccc}
\text{L} & \subseteq & \text{P} & \subseteq & \text{PSPACE} & \subseteq & \text{EXP} & & \subseteq \text{EXPSPACE} \\
& & = & & = & & = & & = \\
\text{AL} & \subseteq & \text{AP} & & \subseteq \text{APSPACE} & \subseteq & \text{AEXP} & & \subseteq \text{AEXPSPACE}
\end{array}
$$

9.2 Uniform Families of Circuits

Families of Circuits would provide a simple and effective model of parallel computation were it not for the fact that small families of circuits can recognize undecidable languages. We repair this flaw by introducing uniformity. The definition is due to Borodin and Cook [Coo79] and several of the results to follow are due to Borodin [Bor77].

Definition 9.2. A family of circuits $\{C_n\}_n$ is *logspace uniform* if there exists a deterministic Turing machine M such that, for each $n \geq 1$, on input 1^n, M computes $\overline{C_n}$, the encoding of C_n, in space $O(\log(s(C_n)))$.

The idea behind this definition is that it should be fairly easy to construct these circuits.

For functions S and T, define

$$\text{USIZE}(S(n)) = \{A \mid \text{ there is a logspace uniform family of circuits } \{C_n\}_n$$
$$\text{that recognizes } A \text{ and for each } n \geq 0, s(C_n) \in O(S(n))\}$$

and

$$\text{UDEPTH}(T(n)) = \{A \mid \text{ there is a logspace uniform family of circuits } \{C_n\}_n$$
$$\text{that recognizes } A \text{ and for each } n \geq 0, d(C_n) \in O(T(n))\}.$$

If $S(n)$ is a size bound for a family of circuits $\{C_n\}_n$, then we may assume that $S(n) \geq n$, for all n, because circuit C_n contains n input gates. We want to show that these classes contain decidable languages only, but, more than that, we have the following results.

Theorem 9.6. $\text{USIZE}(S(n)) \subseteq \text{DTIME}(S(n)^{O(1)})$.

Proof. Let $A \in \text{USIZE}(S(n))$, and let M construct $\{C_n\}_n$ in space $O(\log(s(C_n)))$ so that $\{C_n\}_n$ recognizes A and for each $n \geq 0$, $s(C_n) \in O(S(n))$. Let N be a Turing machine that decides CVP in polynomial time. We define a Turing machine M' to accept A as follows: On input w, $|w| = n$, M' simulates M on 1^n in order to compute $\overline{C_n}$. Since M uses space $O(\log(s(C_n)))$, by Corollary 5.6, this step uses time $S(n)^{O(1)}$. Next M' simulates N on input $\langle w, \overline{C_n} \rangle$, and accepts its input if and only if $\langle w, \overline{C_n} \rangle$ is a positive instance of CVP. Since $|\overline{C_n}| = O(S(n))$, this step uses time $S(n)^{O(1)}$ also. Thus, $A \in \text{DTIME}(S(n)^{O(1)})$. $\square$

Corollary 9.8. $\text{USIZE}(S(n)^{O(1)}) = \text{DTIME}(S(n)^{O(1)})$.

Proof.

$$\text{USIZE}(S(n)^{O(1)}) \subseteq \text{DTIME}(S(n)^{O(1)}), \text{ by Theorem 9.6,}$$

$$\subseteq \text{USIZE}(S(n)^{O(1)}), \text{ by Corollary 8.1 and Homework 8.6.}$$

$\square$

Corollary 9.9. $\text{P} = \text{USIZE}(n^{O(1)})$

Proof. By Theorem 9.6, $\text{USIZE}(n^{O(1)}) \subseteq \text{P}$, and by Corollary 8.2 and Homework 8.6, $\text{P} \subseteq \text{USIZE}(n^{O(1)})$. $\square$

Now we need a lemma that refines the result of Homework 8.5.

Lemma 9.1. *There is a deterministic Turing machine M that accepts the set of positive instances of CVP such that on input $\langle w, \overline{C} \rangle$, M uses space bounded by $d(C) + \log(s(C))$.*

Proof. On input w and $\overline{C}$, we need to evaluate the circuit C on input w. We do this with a depth-first search from the output node that always examines left descendants before examining right descendants. A recursive implementation of this algorithm uses a stack. The top of the stack is the node currently examined and the contents of the stack are the nodes on the path from the root (i.e., the output node) to this node. Thus, the depth of the stack is bounded by $d(C)$. The entries of the stack have size $O(\log(s(C)))$. So a straightforward implementation of the stack uses $d(C) \cdot \log(s(C))$ space. Fortunately, we can do better: Only store the full address of the node currently being evaluated. For all other nodes, the stack stores only one symbol for each entry (i.e., for each node on the path from the root to the current node). If the type of a node v is a binary Boolean operation and the search proceeds left from v, then store the symbol l on the stack. If the search proceeds right from v, then store the value of the left input (T or F) on the stack. Thus, for all nodes on the stack other than the current node, only constant space is required. Thus, we can implement the stack using $d(C) + \log(s(C))$ space. We can recompute the address of any node on the stack by working up from the bottom of the stack (i.e., the output node) via the status entries. $\square$

Theorem 9.7. *For $T(n) \geq \log n$, UDEPTH$(T(n)) \subseteq$ DSPACE$(T(n))$.*

Proof. Let $A \in$ UDEPTH$(T(n))$, and let M construct $\{C_n\}_n$ in space $O(\log(s(C_n)))$ so that $\{C_n\}_n$ recognizes A and for each $n \geq 0$, $d(C_n) \in O(T(n))$. Let N satisfy the conditions of Lemma 9.1. The straightforward idea would be to define a Turing machine M' that on input w, $|w| = n$, first simulates M on 1^n in order to compute $\overline{C_n}$. Think of this as a preprocessing step. This step only uses space $O(\log(s(C_n)))$. Then N would run on the input tuple $\langle w, \overline{C_n} \rangle$. This step only uses space $T(n) + \log(s(C_n))$. Since $d(C_n) = T(n)$, $s(C_n)$ is bounded by $O(1)^{T(n)}$. Therefore, $\log(s(C_n)) \in O(T(n))$. The only problem with this approach is that the size of C_n may be too large to write $\overline{C_n}$ within the $T(n)$ space-bound. For this reason, we cannot use the preprocessing step. Instead, whenever the simulation of N requires the i-th bit of $\overline{C_n}$, N restarts a simulation of M on 1^n to provide this information within the allowed space-bound. (This "trick" is similar to the technique used to prove that logspace reducibility is transitive, Theorem 7.21).   □

Theorem 5.12 and Corollary 5.8 gives an upper bound of $2^{O(n)}$ for the sequential time required to deterministically simulate nondeterministic space $S(n)$. Recalling that circuit depth of a uniform family of circuits is a measure of parallel time, the next result gives an upper bound for the parallel time required to perform this task. Also, the proof of the following result is similar to its predecessor result, Theorem 5.12.

Theorem 9.8. *For $S(n) \geq \log n$ and space-constructible,*

$$\text{NSPACE}(S(n)) \subseteq \text{UDEPTH}(S(n)^{O(1)}).$$

Proof. Let M be a nondeterministic, $S(n)$ space-bounded, off-line Turing machine, where $S(n) \geq \log n$ and $S(n)$ is space-constructible. Given an input word of length n, define a *partial configuration* to consist of the current state, the input-tape head position, the work-tape head position, and the contents of the work tape. Note that the notion of partial configuration depends on n but not on the input word. Let V_n be the set of all $S(n)$ space-bounded partial configurations of M on input words of length n, and let $N = \|V_n\|$. For some constant k, for all $n \geq 0$, N is at most $k^{S(n)}$ (Lemma 5.1). Order the members of V_n so that 1 is the number of the initial partial configuration of M, and the remaining partial configurations are ordered lexicographically. Let $X = (x_{ij})$ be the $N \times N$ Boolean matrix that represents the next-move relation $\vdash_M$ restricted to partial configurations in V_n. In other words, for $1 \leq i, j \leq N$, $x_{ij} = 1$ if and only if $I_i \vdash I_j$. (What do we mean by this? I_i is a partial configuration, hence I_i specifies some input-tape head position, but I_i does not specify the value of the input tape at position i. Thus, I_i cannot specify a next move of M, i.e., it cannot be known whether $I_i \vdash I_j$ for arbitrary i and j until an input word is given. Nevertheless, we can define $X = (x_{ij})$ now. Later we will describe how X obtains values.) Let $X^* = (x_{ij}^*)$ be the transitive closure of X. Then $x_{ij}^* = 1$ if and only if there is a computation path from I_i to I_j.

We need to describe a circuit C_n of depth at most $S(n)^{O(1)}$ that contains n input nodes $w_1, \ldots, w_n$ and that outputs 1 if and only if M accepts input word $w = w_1 \ldots w_n$. The construction assumes you know how to construct a transitive-closure circuit of depth $\log^2 N$. This is a circuit with N^2 input nodes $x_{11}, x_{12}, \ldots, x_{1N},$ $\ldots, x_{NN}$ that computes the transitive closure of the $N \times N$ Boolean matrix $X = (x_{ij})$. The circuit C_n consists of connections from the n input nodes of C_n to the input nodes of the transitive-closure circuit, and of connections from the output nodes of the transitive-closure circuit to the output node of C_n.

For $i \leq N$, let k be the input-tape head position of partial configuration I_i. Then for each $j \leq N$, the connection from input node w_k to x_{ij}, if there is one, depends on whether there is a move from partial configuration I_i to partial configuration I_j, and, most importantly, on whether these moves depend on the symbol written in square k of the input tape. Details follow:

1. Connect w_k directly to x_{ij} if there is a move from I_i to I_j only if the kth input bit is 1.
2. Connect the negation of w_k to x_{ij} if there is a move from I_i to I_j only if the kth input bit is 0.
3. Do not connect w_k to x_{ij} if there is a move, or there is no move, from I_i to I_j that is independent of the value of the kth input bit. Instead, set x_{ij} to 1 if there is a move from I_i to I_j independent of the value of the kth input bit, and set x_{ij} to 0 in the other case.

It is easy to connect the output nodes of the transitive-closure circuit to the output node of C_n. The idea is to connect each node x_{1j}^* such that I_j is an accepting configuration to an OR-gate. The number of such j is at most N. We can realize an OR-gate having N input nodes with a circuit of depth $O(\log N)$. Since $N \leq k^{S(n)}$ this circuit has depth at most $O(S(n))$.

To complete the proof of the theorem, we leave it as a homework exercise to prove that a Turing machine can on input 1^n, compute $\overline{C_n}$ in space $O(\log(s(C_n)))$. $\square$

The following homework exercise formalizes your need to examine certain details in the proof of Theorem 9.8.

Homework 9.2 *1. Show that an OR-gate with N input nodes can be realized by a Boolean circuit of depth $O(\log N)$.*
2. Show how to construct a transitive-closure circuit for $N \times N$ Boolean matrices with depth $\log^2 N$.
3. Show that there is a deterministic Turing machine that on input 1^n computes $\overline{C_n}$ in space $O(\log(s(C_n)))$.

Corollary 9.10. *For $T(n) \geq \log n$ and space-constructible,*

$$\text{UDEPTH}(T(n)^{O(1)}) = \text{DSPACE}(T(n)^{O(1)}).$$

This important corollary is our second expression of the parallel computation thesis: Parallel time, *à la* circuit depth, is within a polynomial factor of deterministic space. In particular, Theorem 9.8 parallelizes arbitrary space-bounded computations.

Proof.

$$\text{UDEPTH}(T(n)^{O(1)}) \subseteq \text{DSPACE}(T(n)^{O(1)}), \text{ by Theorem 9.7,}$$

$$\subseteq \text{NSPACE}(T(n)^{O(1)})$$

$$\subseteq \text{UDEPTH}(T(n)^{O(1)}), \text{ by Theorem 9.8.}$$

$\square$

Homework 9.3 *Prove that* $\text{EXP} \subseteq \text{USIZE}(o(2^n/n))$ *implies* $\text{P} \neq \text{NP}$.

9.3 Highly Parallelizable Problems

We begin this section with a discussion of Greenlaw et al. [GHR95]: We have seen already that parallelism will not make intractable problems tractable. Therefore, if we are to dramatically improve performance it must be by reducing polynomial sequential time to subpolynomial parallel time. We achieve this by trading numbers of processors for speed. The goal of practical parallel computation is to develop algorithms that use a reasonable number of processors and are exceedingly fast. What do we mean by that? We assume that a polynomial number of processors is reasonable, and more than a polynomial number of processors in unreasonable. Can fewer than a polynomial number of processors suffice? To answer this question, observe that

(sequential time)/(number of processors) ≤ (parallel time).

Taking sequential time to be polynomial time, obviously, if parallel time is to be subpolynomial, then a polynomial number of processors must be used. We will focus on the class of problems that have uniform families of circuits with polynomial size $n^{O(1)}$ and "poly-log", i.e., $(\log n)^{O(1)}$, depth. So *highly parallel* problems are those for which we can develop algorithms that use a polynomial number of processors to obtain poly-log parallel time bounds.

Let us define

$$\text{U-SIZE-DEPTH}(S(n), T(n))$$

to be the set of languages L that are recognized by a logspace uniform family of circuits of size $S(n)$ and depth $T(n)$.

Definition 9.3. For all $i \geq 0$, define

$$\text{NC}^i = \text{U-SIZE-DEPTH}(n^{O(1)}, O(\log^i n))$$

and define

$$NC = \bigcup_{i \geq 0} NC^i.$$

Researchers identify the class NC with the collection of highly parallel problems, much as we identify P with the collection of feasibly computable problems. This identification follows naturally from the discussion above. NC stands for "Nick's class." Steve Cook named the class NC in honor of Nick Pippenger, who obtained an important characterization of it [Pip79].

Not all researchers agree with the identification of NC with the notion of highly parallel. In sequential computing the difference between polynomial and exponential time-bounds is dramatic, and appears with inputs of reasonable size. In parallel computing, circuit depth $\log^3 n$ is asymptotically faster than depth $\sqrt{n}$, but the difference appears only with inputs about $n = 10^{12}$. For inputs of this size, a polynomial number of processors makes no sense. (Some believe that NC^2 is the class of highly parallel problems.) Nevertheless, we will proceed with the identification of highly parallel with NC for two important reasons. The first reason is that the class NC has proved to be useful. Many practical parallel algorithms for problems have been found only after the problems were shown first to belong to NC. The second reason is that one of our interests is to identify problems that are not highly parallel. Clearly, NC encompasses all those that are highly parallel. So this gives us a way of distinguishing those that are not.

There is another issue that we should mention about the definition of NC. Primarily complexity classes are defined to be collections of languages even though real computational problems require substantial output. We are fairly well justified in allowing this simplification, because, for the problems in which we are most interested, for example, search problems for NP-complete languages, the complexity of the search problem is equivalent to the complexity of the corresponding decision problem. However, this justification no longer holds in the world of parallel computing. For this reason, some researchers define NC and the classes NC^i to be classes of functions. We will not do that, but it is convenient for us to define FNC to be the class of functions that are computable by logspace-uniform families of circuits of polynomial size and polylog depth. Since every function f in FNC is computable by a family of polynomial-size circuits, it follows immediately that every function in FNC is polynomial-length-bounded.

Theorem 9.9. $NC \subseteq P$.

The proof follows immediately from Corollary 9.9.

Theorem 9.10.
$$NC^1 \subseteq L \subseteq NL \subseteq NC^2.$$

Proof. The proof of the first inclusion requires examining the proofs of Theorem 9.7 and Lemma 9.1. Let $L \in NC^1 = \text{U-SIZE-DEPTH}(n^{O(1)}, O(\log n))$. A deterministic Turing machine M in logspace constructs a family of circuits $\{C_n\}_n$ that recognizes

L and that satisfies the NC^1 conditions. By Lemma 9.1, let N be the deterministic Turing machine that decides instances of CVP using space bounded by $d(C) + \log(s(C))$. Then, N on input $\langle x, \overline{C_n} \rangle$, where $|x| = n$ operates in space $O(\log n)$.

As in the proof of Theorem 9.7, to decide L in logspace, begin a simulation of N on input x. Noting that N is a Turing machine that takes two input strings, whenever N requires the ith bit of C_n, N simulates M to provide this information.

To prove the third inclusion, we need to examine the proof of Theorem 9.8. Let $L \in NL$. The depth of the transitive-closure circuit is $\log^2 N$, where for some $k > 0$, $N = k^{\log n}$. Thus, the depth of the transitive-closure circuit is $O(\log^2 n)$; this circuit dominates the depth of the circuit C_n that recognizes L^n. So the depth of C_n is $O(\log^2 n)$. Similarly, the size of C_n is dominated by the size of the transitive-closure circuit, which is a polynomial in N. Since $N = k^{\log n}$, the size of the transitive-closure circuit is $n^{O(1)}$. This completes the proof. □

The following proposition follows immediately from the definition of FNC.

Proposition 9.1. *A polynomial length-bounded function* $f : \{0,1\}^* \to \{0,1\}^*$ *belongs to the class* FNC *if and only if the set*

$$\text{bit-}f = \{\langle x, i \rangle \mid 1 \le i \le |f(x)| \text{ and the } i\text{th bit of } f(x) \text{ is } 1\}$$

belongs to NC.

The following corollary to Theorem 9.10 follows immediately from the proposition.

Corollary 9.11. *Every logspace computable function belongs to* FNC.

We define a set A to be FNC-reducible to a set B (in symbols, $A \le_m^{FNC} B$) if there is a function $f \in FNC$ so that $x \in A \Leftrightarrow f(x) \in B$.

Theorem 9.11. *If* $A \le_m^{FNC} B$ *and* $B \in NC$, *then* $A \in NC$.

Proof. Let $B \in NC$ and let $f \in FNC$ be a many-one reduction from A to B. Let p be a polynomial such that for all x, $|f(x)| = p(|x|)$. Let $\{C_n\}_n$ be a logspace uniform family of circuits of size $n^{O(1)}$ and depth $\log^k n$ that recognizes B, and let $\{D_n\}_n$ be a logspace uniform family of circuits of size $n^{O(1)}$ and depth $\log^{k'} n$ that computes f. Then, for any $n \ge 0$, an appropriate wiring of the circuits D_n and $C_{p(n)}$ recognizes A^n. The resulting family of circuits is still logspace uniform, and has polynomial size and polylog depth. □

Corollary 9.12. *If* $A \le_m^{\log} B$ *and* $B \in NC$, *then* $A \in NC$.

The major open question about NC is whether P is equal to NC. Most researchers believe that NC is a proper subset of P. (The situation is completely analogous to the question of whether P and NP are the same.)

Corollary 9.13. $P = NC$ *if and only if some* P-*complete problem belongs to* NC.

We believe that P-complete problems are *inherently sequential*. The book "Limits to Parallel Computation" of Greenlaw et al. [GHR95] contains a large list of P-complete problems.

9.4   Uniformity Conditions

Our purpose in this and the next section is to demonstrate robustness of NC. In the next section, we compare finally the two models of parallel processing that we have considered. We will show that uniform circuit size $S(n)$ and depth $T(n)$ is the same as alternating Turing machine space $\log S(n)$ and time $T(n)$.

Let us recall the proof of Theorem 9.7. We let A be a set that has a logspace uniform family of circuits $\{C_n\}_n$. Logspace uniformity specifies that a deterministic Turing machine, for each $n \geq 1$, computes the mapping $1^n \to \overline{C_n}$ in space $O(\log s(C_n))$. However, in that proof, the simulation did not have the space to store $\overline{C_n}$, so we had to work around this difficulty. In order to obtain the results we want to prove in the next section, we will again require simulations that cannot store $\overline{C_n}$.

We defined the class NC in terms of logspace uniformity. Here we will introduce other uniformity notions. The new uniformity conditions will be more convenient for the simulations in the next section. Second, we learn from the results in this and the next section that the exact form of uniformity does not matter: the definition of NC is fairly robust. The results in both of these sections are due to Ruzzo [Ruz81].

Let $C = \{C_n\}_n$ be a family of circuits. Given a gate g in C_n and path $p \in \{L,R\}^*$, let $g(p)$ denote the gate reached by following the path p of inputs to g. For example, $g(\lambda) = g$, $g(L)$ is g's left input node, $g(LR)$ is $g(L)$'s right input node, etc. Now we will define two languages: The *direct connection language* of C encodes the type of each gate and the names of its immediate predecessors. The *extended connection language* of C encodes this information for all predecessors within distance $\log s(C_n)$.

Definition 9.4. The *direct connection language* L_{DC} of the family of circuits $C = \{C_n\}_n$ is the set of strings of the form $\langle n, g, p, y \rangle$ such that $n \in \{0,1\}^*$, $g \in \{0,1\}^*$, $p \in \{\lambda, L, R\}$, $y \in \{x, \wedge, \vee, \neg\} \cup \{0,1\}^*$, g is the number of a node in C_n, and either

1. $p = \lambda$ and g is a node of type y (In particular, if g is an input node, then $y = x$, and if g is an output node, then $y = \lambda$.), or
2. $p \neq \lambda$ and y is the number of node $g(p)$.

The *extended connection language* L_{EC} of C is defined exactly the same way, except that $p \in \{L,R\}^*$ and $|p| \leq \log s(C_n)$.

Definition 9.5. Let $C = \{C_n\}_n$ be a family of circuits of size $S(n)$ and depth $T(n)$.

1. C is U_D-*uniform* if there is a deterministic Turing machine that accepts L_{DC} in time $O(\log S(n))$.

2. C is U_E-*uniform* if there is a deterministic Turing machine that accepts L_{EC} in
   time $O(\log S(n))$.
3. C is U_{E^*}-*uniform* if there is an alternating Turing machine that accepts L_{EC} in
   time $O(T(n))$ and space $O(\log S(n))$.

In order to have a common notation for comparing these uniformity conditions,
we will let U_{BC}-uniform (named after Borodin and Cook [Coo79]) denote logspace
uniformity. There is a fundamental difference between U_{BC}-uniformity and the new
uniformity conditions. The former requires a Turing machine to write the entire
encoding $\overline{C_n}$, and the length of this string is a polynomial in the size of the circuit.
The latter are languages, and each tuple that belongs to the language contains only
local information about a given node.

Lemma 9.2. *The following conditions are equivalent:*

1. *The mapping* $1^n \to \overline{C_n}$ *is computable in space* $O(\log S(n))$.
2. $L_{EC} \in \mathrm{DSPACE}(O(\log S(n)))$.
3. $L_{DC} \in \mathrm{DSPACE}(O(\log S(n)))$.

Proof. We prove that item 1 implies item 2: Let M be a deterministic Turing
machine that computes the mapping $1^n \to \overline{C_n}$ in space $O(\log S(n))$. We design
a Turing machine N to accept L_{EC}. Given an input tuple $\langle n, g, p, y \rangle$, first N tests
whether $|p| \leq \log S(n)$ by comparing the length of p with the size of M's workspace
on input 1^n. If p passes this test, then N implements the procedure in Fig. 9.3 and
accepts $\langle n, g, p, y \rangle$ if and only if the procedure returns the value true. The procedure
is self explanatory and obviously correct. However, both steps of the algorithm that
ask for simulating M on input 1^n require explanation. Since N can use at most
$O(\log S(n))$ space, it cannot write 1^n on one of its work tapes, so how can it simulate
M on input 1^n? (This is similar to the difficulty we had in proving Theorem 9.7.)
The answer is to maintain a buffer of size $\log n$ on a work tape. The buffer will hold
the value i, where $1 \leq i \leq n$, if and only if N is currently scanning the ith bit of its
input tape. Either N will increment or decrement the value in the buffer according to
the direction that N moves the input head. So N can test whether $|p| \leq \log S(n)$ and,
in the procedure, N can perform this simulation to find a tuple $\langle g, b, g_l, g_r \rangle$ in space
$O(\log S(n))$. The procedure calls itself a maximum of $|p| \leq \log S(n)$ times, but each
time, we reuse the same space. Therefore, $L_{EC} \in \mathrm{DSPACE}(O(\log S(n)))$.

It is trivial that item 2 implies item 3. Now we prove that item 3 implies
item 1. Assume that $L_{DC} \in \mathrm{DSPACE}(O(\log S(n)))$. We describe a procedure,
implementable in space $O(\log S(n))$, that outputs $\overline{C_n}$. There are two major steps
to the procedure. The first step is to compute the value *maxgateno*, the largest gate
number of any gate in C_n. To do this, set g to 0; while for some $y \in \{\lambda, x, \wedge, \vee, \neg\}$,
$\langle n, g, \lambda, y \rangle \in L_{DC}$, increment the value of g. Then set *maxgateno* to be the final value
of g. The next step is to start with gate $g = 0$, the unique sink of C_n, find its type
y, its left input g_l, its right input g_r, output the tuple $\langle g, y, g_l, g_r \rangle$, and repeat this
process for all $g \leq$ *maxgateno*. We accomplish this for each g by finding y such that
$\langle n, g, \lambda, y \rangle \in L_{DC}$, searching for each $g_l \leq$ *maxgateno*, whether $\langle n, g, L, g_l \rangle \in L_{DC}$,

```
FUNCTION ECTEST(⟨n,g,p,y⟩): Boolean;
var p': path;
simulate M on input 1ⁿ until it outputs the tuple ⟨g,b,gₗ,gᵣ⟩, for some b, gₗ, and gᵣ;
if p = λ
      then if b = y {so y is the type of g }
              then return true else return false;
      while p ≠ λ do
           begin
              let p = Dp', where D ∈ {L,R};
              if p' = λ
                  then if (D = L  and  y = gₗ) or (D = R  and  y = gᵣ) {so g(D) = y}
                          then return true else return false
                  else if ECTEST(⟨n,g(D),p',y⟩)
                          then return true else return false;
           end;
```

Fig. 9.3 The recursive procedure ECTEST

and searching for each $g_r \leq maxgateno$, whether $\langle n,g,R,g_r \rangle \in L_{DC}$. Since each test takes at most $O(\log S(n))$ space, it is clear that the procedure computes $\overline{C_n}$ on input 1^n in space $O(\log S(n))$. $\qquad\Box$

Homework 9.4 *For any Boolean circuit C of depth t and size s, show that $t \geq \log s$.*

Theorem 9.12. *The following hold for any family of circuits $C = \{C_n\}_n$.*

1. *U_E-uniform $\Rightarrow$ U_D-uniform $\Rightarrow$ U_{BC}-uniform.*
2. *U_E-uniform $\Rightarrow$ U_{E^*}-uniform.*
3. *If $T(n) \geq \log^2 S(n)$, then U_{BC}-uniform $\Rightarrow$ U_{E^*}-uniform.*

Proof.

1. The first implication of Item 1 follows immediately by definition. We let C be U_D-uniform, so $L_{DC} \in \text{DTIME}(O(\log S(n)))$. Therefore, $L_{DC} \in \text{DSPACE}(O(\log S(n)))$. By Lemma 9.2, the function mapping $1^n \to \overline{C_n}$ is computable in space $O(\log S(n))$, so C is U_{BC}-uniform.
2. Letting C be U_E-uniform, there is a deterministic Turing machine M that accepts L_{EC} in time $O(\log S(n))$. Clearly, M uses space $\leq O(\log S(n))$ also. Therefore, an alternating Turing machine accepts L_{EC} in simultaneous time $O(\log S(n))$ and space $O(\log S(n))$. By Homework 9.4, $T(n) \geq \log S(n)$, so an alternating Turing machine accepts L_{EC} in simultaneous time $T(n)$ and space $O(\log S(n))$. Thus, C is U_{E^*}-uniform.
3. Assume that $T(n) \geq \log^2 S(n)$ and that the circuit family C is logspace uniform. By Lemma 9.2, $L_{EC} \in \text{DSPACE}(O(\log S(n)))$. By Corollary 9.1,

$$L_{EC} \in \text{A-SPACE-TIME}(O(\log S(n)), O(\log^2 S(n)),$$

because $S(n) \geq n$. Then, by the hypothesis,

$$L_{EC} \in \text{A-SPACE-TIME}(O(\log S(n)), O(T(n)),$$

which completes the proof. □

We learn from Theorem 9.12 that U_E is the strongest of the uniformity conditions. However, this theorem deals with a fixed family of circuits. Of greater interest is the question, given a set A, of what we can say about its circuit complexity with respect to different uniformity conditions. We will return to this question. For now, given a uniformity condition U_X, let us define

$$U_X\text{-SIZE-DEPTH}(S(n), T(n))$$

to be the set of languages L that are recognized by a U_X family of circuits of size $S(n)$ and depth $T(n)$.

9.5 Alternating Turing Machines and Uniform Families of Circuits

Theorem 9.13. *Let* $S(n) \geq \log n$ *and let* $T(n)$ *and* $S(n)$ *be computable by deterministic Turing machines from input* n *(in binary) in time* $O(S(n))$. *Then*

$$\text{A-SPACE-TIME}(S(n), T(n)) \subseteq U_E\text{-SIZE-DEPTH}(2^{O(S(n))}, O(T(n))).$$

Proof. Let $S(n)$ and $T(n)$ satisfy the hypotheses and let

$$A \in \text{A-SPACE-TIME}(O(S(n)), O(T(n))).$$

Let M be an alternating Turing machine that accepts A with space bound $S(n)$ and time bound $T(n)$. We will define a U_E-uniform family of circuits $C = \{C_n\}_n$ of size $2^{O(S(n))}$ and depth $T(n)$ that recognizes A. We need to analyze the behavior of M on all input words of length n. Since we are assuming random access to input words via the index tape, configurations are independent of the input word, so we use these to formalize our analysis of M. Recall once again that there exists a constant k such that the total number of possible configurations of M on an input of length n, is bounded by $k^{S(n)}$. We assume without loss of generality that M at each step either branches into exactly 2 successor configurations, reads (by random access) a cell on the index tape, or accepts or rejects. Now consider the *full computation tree* of M on input words of length n. This tree is similar to the computation tree of M on an input word x of length n, except that if in configuration I, M reads an input value x_i of the input word, then the full computation tree contains an existential branch depending on whether x_i is 1 or 0. Note that the depth of the full computation tree is $T(n)$, and note that M accepts a word x of length n if and only if the subtree of the full computation determined by x (in the natural way) is accepting.

We construct the circuit C_n from the full computation tree. The gates of C_n will consist primarily of AND and OR gates. However, we define two types of these gates. Type N gates are ordinary AND and OR gates. Type L gates are AND and OR gates that have labels (t,I), where $0 \leq t \leq T(n)$ and I is a configuration of M. The following rules give the construction of C_n:

1. The output gate is $(0,I_0)$, where I_0 is the initial configuration.
2. If I is a configuration at level t of the full computation tree that branches universally into I' and I'', then C_n contains an AND gate labeled (t,I) whose inputs are $(t+1,I')$ and $(t+1,I'')$.
3. If I is a configuration at level t of the full computation tree that branches existentially into I' and I'', then C_n contains an OR gate labeled (t,I) whose inputs are $(t+1,I')$ and $(t+1,I'')$.
4. Suppose I is a configuration at level t that accesses the input symbol x_i and that existentially branches to I' or I'' depending on whether x_i is 1 or 0. Then C_n contains an OR gate (t,I) whose inputs are two ordinary AND gates (of type N). The inputs to the left AND gate are $(t+1,x_i)$ and $(t+1,I')$; the inputs to the right AND gate are $(t+1,\overline{x_i})$ and $(t+1,I'')$. The input to every gate of the form $(t+1,x_i)$ is x_i and to every gate of the form $(t+1,\overline{x_i})$ is the negation of x_i.
5. If I is an accepting configuration at level t, then C_n contains the gate (t,I) with constant input 1. If I is a rejecting configuration at level t, then C_n contains the gate (t,I) with constant input 0.

It should be clear that C_n accepts an input word x if and only if M accepts x. That is, C_n recognizes $A^{=n}$.

Homework 9.5 *Show by induction that a node labeled I at depth t in the full computation tree is the root of an accepting subtree if and only if gate (t,I) has value 1 in the circuit. The assertion that C_n recognizes $A^{=n}$ follows immediately.*

By hypothesis, there exists a Turing machine N that computes $T(n)$ in time $O(S(n))$. N uses no more than $O(S(n))$ space to write $T(n)$. Thus, $T(n) \leq 2^{O(S(n))}$. There are $2T(n) + T(n) \cdot 2^{O(S(n))} \in O(2^{O(S(n))})$ type L gates. The number of type L gates dominates the number of N gates. Therefore, the total number of gates in C_n is $O(2^{O(S(n))})$. The depth of C_n is $T(n) + T(n) \in O(T(n))$.

We have to show that $L_{EC} \in \mathrm{DTIME}(O(S(n)))$. A deterministic Turing machine, given $\langle n,g,p,y \rangle$, decodes g as (t,I). Then it simulates the moves of M starting at I following path p. By hypothesis, $S(n)$ and $T(n)$ are computable from n in time $O(S(n))$, so this machine can recognize whether the path reaches past depth $T(n)$ or space $S(n)$, and respond accordingly. □

Corollary 9.14. *For all $i \geq 0$,*

$$\text{A-SPACE-TIME}(\log n, \log^i n) \subseteq NC^i.$$

Proof.

$$\text{A-SPACE-TIME}(\log n, \log^i n) \subseteq U_E\text{-SIZE-DEPTH}(n^{O(1)}, O(\log^i n))$$

$$\subseteq U_{BC}\text{-SIZE-DEPTH}(n^{O(1)}, O(\log^i n))$$

$$= \text{NC}^i,$$

by Theorems 9.13 and 9.12, respectively.   □

Now we show how to simulate uniform families of circuits with an alternating Turing machine. Recall for arbitrary functions f and g that $f \in \Omega(g)$ if there exist n_0 and $k > 0$ such that for all $n \geq n_0$, $f(n) \geq k \cdot g(n)$.

Theorem 9.14. *For $T(n) \in \Omega(\log n)$,*

$$U_{E^*}\text{-SIZE-DEPTH}(n^{O(1)}, T(n)) \subseteq \text{A-SPACE-TIME}(O(\log n), O(T(n))).$$

Proof. Let $A \in U_{E^*}\text{-SIZE-DEPTH}(n^{O(1)}, T(n))$ and let $C = \{C_n\}_n$ be a U_{E^*}-uniform family of circuits that recognizes A. Let M be an alternating Turing machine that accepts L_{EC} in space $O(\log n)$ and time $O(T(n))$. We want to design an alternating Turing machine N that accepts A in space $O(\log n)$ and time $O(T(n))$. The general idea is that the alternating Turing machine on an input word w of length n should simulate the gates of the circuit C_n, but of course, this is a difficulty, because, as in previous simulations, C_n is too large. To get around this, we have our alternating Turing machine query membership in L_{EC}. Even this is a difficulty, because L_{EC} contains information about only short paths in the circuits. We define a recursive "circuit value" Boolean function $\text{CV}(w, g, p)$, where g is a gate and p is a path, so that $\text{CV}(w, g, p)$ if and only if $g(p)$ evaluates to 1 on input w. CV is a recursive procedure that contains a clever strategy for subdividing paths in C_n into subpaths of length $\leq \log n$. The alternating Turing machine N implements CV and, on input w, $|w| = n$, calls $\text{CV}(w, 0, \lambda)$. Then N accepts w if and only if $\text{CV}(w, 0, \lambda)$ returns true, which holds if and only if C_n on input w evaluates to 1. Figure 9.4 gives the definition of CV.

It is clear that CV is correct – that's the beauty of recursive procedures. Thus, N accepts w if and only if C_n on input w evaluates to 1. It is easy to see that the space complexity is $O(\log n)$. We need to examine the time complexity. Since the depth of C_n is $T(n)$, the recursion contributes depth $O(T(n))$ to N's computation tree on an input of length n. Simulations of M to verify that a tuple belongs to L_{EC} take time $O(T(n))$. However, it is important to note that no verification of membership in L_{EC} is part of the recursion, and each verification of membership in L_{EC} occurs, using universal branching, simultaneous with the recursion. Therefore, the total depth of N's computation tree is $O(T(n))$.   □

The following important corollary shows that both uniform families of circuits and alternating Turing machines describe the class of highly parallelizable

```
FUNCTION CV(w, g, p): Boolean;
{|w| = n}
if |p| < log n then
       begin
              {compute the address h and type t of gate g(p) }
              use existential branching to guess h ∈ {0,1}^{log n} and t ∈ {x, ∧, ∨, ¬};
              use universal branching to do the following:
                     begin
                     verify that ⟨n, g, p, h⟩ ∈ L_{EC};
                     verify that ⟨n, h, λ, t⟩ ∈ L_{EC};
                     { evaluate g(p) }
                     case t of
                            x: return the hth symbol of the input;
                            ∧: use universal branching to return CV(w, g, pL) ∧ CV(w, g, pR);
                            ∨: use existential branching to return CV(w, g, pL) ∨ CV(w, g, pR);
                            ¬: return ¬CV(w, g, pL)
                     end {of case}
                     end {of universal branch}
       end
else
       if |p| = log n then
              begin
              {compute h = g(p) }
              use existential branching to guess h ∈ {0,1}^{log n};
              use universal branching to do the following:
                     begin
                     verify that ⟨n, g, p, h⟩ ∈ L_{EC};
                     CV(w, h, λ)
                     end {of universal branching}
              end
```

Fig. 9.4 The recursive procedure CV

problems. One might interpret the proofs of the two theorems that we just proved as informing us that computation trees of alternating Turing machines *are* uniform circuits.

Corollary 9.15. *For all $i \geq 2$,*

$$\mathrm{NC}^i = \text{A-SPACE-TIME}(O(\log n), O(\log^i n)).$$

Proof. Corollary 9.14 gives the proof in one direction. For the other direction, letting $i \geq 2$,

$$\mathrm{NC}^i = U_{BC}\text{-SIZE-DEPTH}(n^{O(1)}, O(\log^i n))$$

$$\subseteq U_{E^*}\text{-SIZE-DEPTH}(n^{O(1)}, O(\log^i n)), \text{ by Theorem 9.12}$$

$$\subseteq \text{A-SPACE-TIME}(O(\log n), O(\log^i n)), \text{ by Theorem 9.14.}$$

$\square$

The next corollary completes the task that we began in the last section of showing that the exact uniformity condition we use to define NC does not matter.

Corollary 9.16. NC *is the same class under definitions* U_E, U_D, U_{BC}, *and* U_{E^*}. *Furthermore, for* $i \geq 2$, NC^i *is identical under these four definitions.*

Proof. Let $i \geq 2$. Then

$$U_E\text{-SIZE-DEPTH}(n^{O(1)}, O(\log^i n)) \subseteq U_D\text{-SIZE-DEPTH}(n^{O(1)}, O(\log^i n))$$

$$\subseteq U_{BC}\text{-SIZE-DEPTH}(n^{O(1)}, O(\log^i n))$$

$$\subseteq U_{E^*}\text{-SIZE-DEPTH}(n^{O(1)}, O(\log^i n))$$

$$\subseteq \text{A-SPACE-TIME}(O(\log n), O(\log^i n))$$

$$\subseteq U_E\text{-SIZE-DEPTH}(n^{O(1)}, O(\log^i n)),$$

where the last three inclusions follow from Theorems 9.12, 9.14, and 9.13, respectively. □

We defined NC in terms of logspace uniformity because it is a straightforward assertion that captures the notion of easily constructing a circuit. Recall that $\text{NC}^1 \subseteq L \subseteq \text{NC}^2$. That should suggest to us that logspace uniformity might not be appropriate for defining NC^i for $i < 2$, because in this case the complexity of the circuit constructor is more than the complexity of the circuits constructed. Furthermore, if we focus on U_E-uniformity instead, then we obtain the following stronger version of Corollary 9.15. For these reasons, some researchers who study NC prefer to use the extended connection language to describe circuits and to use U_E-uniformity to define NC.

Corollary 9.17. *For all* $i > 0$,

$$U_E\text{-SIZE-DEPTH}(n^{O(1)}, O(\log^i n)) = \text{A-SPACE-TIME}(O(\log n), O(\log^i n)).$$

Proof.

$$U_E\text{-SIZE-DEPTH}(n^{O(1)}, O(\log^i n)) \subseteq U_{E^*}\text{-SIZE-DEPTH}(n^{O(1)}, O(\log^i n))$$

$$\subseteq \text{A-SPACE-TIME}(O(\log n), O(\log^i n))$$

$$\subseteq U_E\text{-SIZE-DEPTH}(n^{O(1)}, O(\log^i n)),$$

by Theorem 9.12, Theorem 9.14, and Theorem 9.13, respectively. □

Homework 9.6 *Show that if* $\text{NC}^i = \text{NC}^{i+1}$, *then* $\text{NC} = \text{NC}^i$.

Homework 9.7 *For each* $i \geq 0$, *define* AC^i *to be the class of languages defined by logspace uniform families of circuits of polynomial size and depth* $\log^i n$ *with unbounded fan-in. Define* $\text{AC} = \bigcup\{\text{AC}^i \mid i \geq 0\}$. *Prove that* $\text{NC}^i \subseteq \text{AC}^i \subseteq \text{NC}^{i+1}$. *Conclude that* $\text{AC} = \text{NC}$.

Chapter 10
Probabilistic Complexity Classes

In this chapter we study the benefits of adding randomness to computations. We treat randomness as a resource. Probabilistic algorithms allow computations to depend on the outcomes of an ideal random generator (i.e., on unbiased coin tosses). They can be classified by classifying the languages they are defined to accept. Important computational problems that seem to be infeasible by ordinary deterministic computations have efficient solutions using probabilistic algorithms. Such algorithms can be easily implemented, and fast and reliable solutions to otherwise difficult problems are then possible. There is a cost to this added efficiency, however, in that probabilistic algorithms do sometimes make errors.

In order to precisely define probabilistic complexity classes, we need to define the concept of a probabilistic Turing machine. A *probabilistic* Turing machine is just a nondeterministic Turing machine, but acceptance is defined differently. Each nondeterministic choice is considered as a random experiment in which each outcome has equal probability. We may assume that each nondeterministic branch has exactly two possible outcomes, so that each has probability 1/2. A probabilistic Turing machine has three kinds of final states, *accepting* or 1-states, *rejecting* or 0-states, and *undetermined* or ?-states. The outcome of the machine on an input is now a random variable whose range is $\{1, 0, ?\}$. We let $\Pr[M(x) = a]$ denote the probability that machine M on input x halts in an a-state. The probability of a given path is obtained by raising 1/2 to a power equal to the number of nondeterministic choices along it. The probability that M accepts an input x, $\Pr[M(x) = 1]$, is the sum of the probabilities of all accepting paths.

10.1 The Class PP

We can define several different probabilistic complexity classes. These classes were defined originally by Gill [Gil77] and by Adleman and Manders [AM77]. Each consists of languages accepted by restricting the machines to polynomial time.

S. Homer and A.L. Selman, *Computability and Complexity Theory*,
Texts in Computer Science, DOI 10.1007/978-1-4614-0682-2_10,
© Springer Science+Business Media, LLC 2011

The first class, PP, for polynomial probabilistic time, is the easiest to define, but is the least useful. Let χ_A denote the characteristic function of A.

Definition 10.1. PP is the class of languages A for which there is a probabilistic, polynomial time-bounded Turing machine M such that for all x,

$$\Pr[M(x) = \chi_A(x)] > 1/2.$$

That is,

$$x \in A \Rightarrow \Pr[M(x) = 1] > 1/2$$

and

$$x \notin A \Rightarrow \Pr[M(x) = 0] > 1/2.$$

These Turing machines are of the "Monte Carlo" type. They are allowed to lie (i.e., terminate in a 0-state when $x \in A$, or terminate in a 1-state when $x \notin A$) with small probability. On the other hand, "Las Vegas" algorithms may terminate with "?" with small probability, but they are not allowed to lie.

One would like to increase the reliability of a probabilistic Turing machine by repeating its computation a large number of times (a large number of independent trials) and giving as output the majority result. This is not possible with PP, and this is why there is no practical interest in this class.

Lets consider another view of probabilistic Turing machines. Recall that a set A belongs to NP if and only if there exist a polynomial p and a deterministic, polynomial time-bounded Turing machine M such that for all words x,

$$x \in A \Leftrightarrow \exists y[|y| = p(|x|) \wedge M(x,y)].$$

Let us take a similar approach, but interpret the string y to be the outcomes of fair coin tosses instead of a witness: We let $\Pr_{r \in \{0,1\}^{p(n)}}[M(x,r) = a]$ denote the probability that deterministic machine M on input x halts in an a-state, where r is chosen uniformly at random from $\{0,1\}^{p(n)}$. That is, we assume the uniform distribution on binary sequences of length $p(n)$; hence r is a random string of length $p(n)$. Frequently we simplify this notation to $\Pr_r[M(x,r) = a]$.

Proposition 10.1. PP *is the class of languages A for which there is a polynomial p and a deterministic polynomial time-bounded Turing machine M such that for all x,*

$$\Pr_r[M(x,r) = \chi_A(x)] > 1/2.$$

Proof. If A satisfies the conditions of the Proposition, then clearly A belongs to PP. Assume that A belongs to PP and let M be a probabilistic Turing machine that satisfies Definition 10.1. The difficulty is if not all computation paths of the probabilistic Turing machine M have the same length (that is, the same number of nondeterministic choices), but this is easy to circumvent. Let p be the polynomial time-bound of M. Define deterministic Turing machine $M'(x,r)$, where $|r| = p(|x|)$, to halt in an a-state if and only there is a prefix s of r such that s is a computation path of M on x that terminates in an a-state. The conclusion follows readily.   □

It would not make sense to define PP by the condition that $\Pr_r[M(x,r) = \chi_A(x)] \geq 1/2$, but the following is possible.

Theorem 10.1. *If there exist a polynomial p and a probabilistic polynomial time-bounded Turing machine M such that*

$$x \in A \Rightarrow \Pr[M(x) = 1] > 1/2$$

and

$$x \notin A \Rightarrow \Pr[M(x) = 0] \geq 1/2,$$

then $A \in$ PP.

Proof. We design a new deterministic Turing machine M' whose inputs are strings x and random strings sr, where $|s| = p(|x|) + 1$ and $|r| = p(|x|)$. We define M' so that $M'(x, s_1 \ldots s_{p(|x|)+1} r_1 \ldots r_{p(x)})$ enters the 0-state if $s_1 = \cdots = s_{p(|x|)+1} = 0$. Otherwise, $M'(x, s_1 \ldots s_{p(|x|)+1} r_1 \ldots r_{p(x)})$ simulates $M(x, r_1 \ldots r_{p(x)})$.

On input (x, sr), M' begins its computation with one of two moves: M' enters the 0-state with probability $2^{-(p(|x|)+1)}$ or it simulates $M(x,r)$. Thus,

$$\Pr_{sr}[M'(x,sr) = 1] = \left(1 - 2^{-(p(|x|)+1)}\right) \Pr_r[M(x,r) = 1],$$

and

$$\Pr_{sr}[M'(x,sr) = 0] = \left(1 - 2^{-(p(|x|)+1)}\right) \Pr_r[M(x,r) = 0] + 2^{-(p(|x|)+1)}.$$

If $x \in A$, then $\Pr_r[M(x) = 1] > 1/2$. So this value must be greater than 1/2 by at least $2^{-p(|x|)}$, for that is the amount that one computation path contributes to the probability. That is, $\Pr_r[M(x) = 1] \geq 1/2 + 2^{-p(|x|)}$. (This is the key observation of our argument. The idea of the proof, the manner in which M' is defined, is to bias the probabilities toward 0 by an amount less than $2^{-p(|x|)}$. Then, if $x \in A$, the probability of acceptance remains greater than 1/2, while if $x \notin A$, then the probability of rejection becomes greater than 1/2.) We have the following calculations:
If $x \in A$, then

$$\Pr_{sr}[M'(x,sr) = 1] \geq \left(1 - 2^{-(p(|x|)+1)}\right)\left(1/2 + 2^{-p(|x|)}\right)$$

$$= 1/2 + 2^{-p(|x|)} - 2^{-(p(|x|)+2)} - 2^{-(2p(|x|)+1)}$$

$$> 1/2,$$

and if $x \notin A$, then

$$\Pr_{sr}[M'(x,sr) = 0] \geq 1/2 \left(1 - 2^{-(p(|x|)+1)}\right) + 2^{-(p(|x|)+1)}$$

$$> 1/2.$$

This completes the proof.   □

The next theorem strongly suggests that PP does not correspond to probabilistic algorithms that provide fast, reliable solutions, for it would be remarkable if that could be accomplished for all of NP.

Theorem 10.2. NP∪co-NP ⊆ PP ⊆ PSPACE.

Proof. The second inclusion is straightforward, for we know already that we can simulate all computations of any nondeterministic polynomial time-bounded Turing machine in polynomial space. All that is necessary is to count the number of accepting and rejecting computations.

Let $A \in$ NP. Let p be a polynomial and M be a deterministic, polynomial time-bounded Turing machine such that for all words x,

$$x \in A \Leftrightarrow \exists y[|y| = p(|x|) \wedge M(x,y)].$$

We design a new deterministic Turing machine M' whose inputs are strings x and random strings ar, where $|a| = 1$ and $|r| = p(|x|)$. We define M' so that $M'(x, ar_1 \ldots r_{p(|x|)})$ enters the 1-state, if $a = 0$, and simulates $M(x, r_1 \ldots r_{p(|x|)})$, otherwise.

On input (x, ar), M' begins its computation with one of two moves: M' enters the 1-state with probability 1/2 or it simulates $M(x, r)$. Then

$$\Pr_{ar}[M'(x, ar) = 1] = 1/2 + 1/2 \cdot \Pr_{r}[M(x, r) = 1]$$

and

$$\Pr_{ar}[M'(x, ar) = 0] = 1/2 \cdot \Pr_{r}[M(x, r) = 0].$$

If $x \in A$, then $\Pr_{ar}[M'(x, ar) = 1] > 1/2$, because there exists at least one witness r such that $M(x, r)$ accepts. However, if $x \notin A$, then $\Pr_{ar}[M'(x, ar) = 0] = 1/2$, for, in this case, $M(x, r)$ rejects, for all strings r.

Thus, M' satisfies the conditions of Theorem 10.1. So, $A \in$ PP. By definition, PP is closed under complements. So, co-NP ⊆ PP as well.   □

10.2 The Class RP

We define the class RP, for randomized polynomial time, somewhat in analogy with the class NP.

Definition 10.2. RP is the class of languages A for which there is a probabilistic, polynomial time-bounded Turing machine M such that for all x,

$$x \in A \Rightarrow \Pr[M(x) = 1] \geq 1/2$$

and

$$x \notin A \Rightarrow \Pr[M(x) = 1] = 0.$$

RP-algorithms are known as *yes-biased* Monte Carlo algorithms, because a "yes" answer is always correct, but a "no" answer might be incorrect. That is, if the algorithm enters the 1-state, then $x \in A$; conversely, if $x \in A$, then the algorithm enters the 1-state with probability at least 1/2.

It is obvious from the definition that $P \subseteq RP \subseteq NP$. We will show that the value 1/2 in the definition is somewhat arbitrary. The class does not change even if we demand arbitrarily large reliability for acceptance when $x \in A$, that is, even if we demand that the error probability is arbitrarily small. This result states that probabilities can be *amplified*. Also, the class does not change even if the probability of acceptance is small (but not too small).

Let RP_{small} denote the class of languages A for which there is a polynomial p and a probabilistic, polynomial time-bounded Turing machine M such that for all x,

$$x \in A \Rightarrow \Pr[M(x) = 1] \geq 1/p(|x|)$$

and

$$x \notin A \Rightarrow \Pr[M(x) = 1] = 0.$$

Let RP_{large} denote the class of languages A for which there is a polynomial p and a probabilistic, polynomial time-bounded Turing machine M_p such that for all x,

$$x \in A \Rightarrow \Pr[M_p(x) = 1] \geq 1 - 2^{-p(|x|)}$$

and

$$x \notin A \Rightarrow \Pr[M_p(x) = 1] = 0.$$

Theorem 10.3. $RP = RP_{small} = RP_{large}$.

Proof. It is obvious that $RP \subseteq RP_{small}$ and $RP_{large} \subseteq RP$. We will show that $RP_{small} \subseteq RP_{large}$.

Let $A \in RP_{small}$, let p be a polynomial and M be a probabilistic, polynomial time-bounded Turing machine that satisfy the definition of RP_{small}. Define M_p so that on an input x it iterates $M(x)$ with $p(|x|)^2$ independent trials; it enters the 1-state if $M(x) = 1$ occurs in at least one trial, and otherwise, enters the 0-state.

Let $x \in A$. Then

$$\Pr[M_p(x) \neq 1] = \Pr[M(x) \neq 1]^{p(|x|)^2}$$
$$< (1 - 1/p(|x|))^{p(|x|)^2}$$
$$= [(1 - 1/p(|x|))^{p(|x|)}]^{p(|x|)}$$
$$\leq (1/e)^{p(|x|)}$$
$$< (1/2)^{p(|x|)},$$

where e is the base of the natural logarithm, and the last inequality holds because $e > 2$. Thus, $\Pr[M_p(x) = 1] \geq 1 - 2^{-p(|x|)}$.

It is obvious that if $x \notin A$, then $\Pr[M_p(x) = 1] = 0$. $\square$

10.2.1   The Class ZPP

Next we consider the class ZPP, for zero-error probabilistic polynomial time.

Definition 10.3. ZPP is the class of languages A for which there is a probabilistic, polynomial time-bounded Turing machine M such that for all x,

$$\Pr[M(x) =?] \leq 1/2$$

and

$$\Pr[M(x) = \chi_A(x) \text{ or } M(x) =?] = 1$$

Theorem 10.4. ZPP $=$ RP $\cap$ co-RP.

Proof. First we show that ZPP $\subseteq$ RP. Let M witness that $A \in$ ZPP. If $x \notin A$, then it is immediate that $\Pr[M(x) = 1] = 0$. If $x \in A$, then either $M(x) = 1$ or $M(x) =?$. Then, since $\Pr[M(x) =?] \leq 1/2$, it follows that $\Pr[M(x) = 1] \geq 1/2$.

Similarly, ZPP $\subseteq$ co-RP. So, ZPP $\subseteq$ RP $\cap$ co-RP.

Let $A \in$ RP $\cap$ co-RP; let M_1 witness $A \in$ RP and let M_2 witness $A \in$ co-RP. Define M' by

$$M'(x) = [\text{ if } M_1(x) = 1 \text{ then } 1 \text{ else if } M_2(x) = 1 \text{ then } 0 \text{ else } ?].$$

If $M_1(x) = 1$, then $x \in A$, and if $M_2(x) = 1$, then $x \in \overline{A}$. So M' never gives a wrong answer. Thus, $\Pr[M'(x) = \chi_A(x) \text{ or } M'(x) =?] = 1$. If $x \in A$, then $\Pr[M_1(x) = 1] \geq 1/2$, and if $x \notin A$, then $\Pr[M_2(x) = 1] \geq 1/2$. So, $\Pr[M'(x) \neq ?] \geq 1/2$, from which it follows that $\Pr[M'(x) =?] \leq 1/2$. Therefore, $A \in$ ZPP. $\square$

Observe that ZPP is closed under complements and that P $\subseteq$ ZPP $\subseteq$ NP $\cap$ co-NP.

Solovay and Strassen [SS77] and Miller and Rabin [Mil76, Rab80] developed efficient probabilistic algorithms that place the COMPOSITE NUMBER decision problem in the class RP. The text by Stinson [Sti95] contains an exposition. In 1987, Adleman and Huang [AH87] proved that testing for PRIMALITY belongs to RP. Therefore, since COMPOSITE NUMBER belongs to RP, it follows from Theorem 10.4 that PRIMALITY belongs to ZPP. This line of research culminated with the brilliant recent result of Agrawal et al. [AKS04] that PRIMALITY belongs to P. Nevertheless, to this date, the probabilistic algorithms remain the most useful.

10.3   The Class BPP

The error probability is the probability that a probabilistic machine gives the wrong answer on a given input. The next class we define bounds the error probability away from 1/2, and that restriction, in contrast to PP, makes it possible to increase reliability (by decreasing the error probability). We define the class BPP, for bounded-error probabilistic polynomial time, as follows.

Definition 10.4. BPP is the class of languages A for which there is a probabilistic, polynomial time-bounded Turing machine M and a number ε, $0 < \varepsilon < 1/2$, such that

$$\Pr[M(x) = \chi_A(x)] > 1/2 + \varepsilon.$$

This class is again of the Monte-Carlo type. Obviously, $P \subseteq RP \subseteq BPP \subseteq PP$ and BPP is closed under complements. We will show that $BPP \subseteq \Sigma_2^P \cap \Pi_2^P$. [Lau83, Sip83] Our first task, however, is to show that BPP is nearly as feasible a class as is P. We will show, as we did for the class RP, that, by iterating a large number of times, we can make the error probability arbitrarily small. For this reason, BPP-algorithms can be used in practice with great reliability. Our proof uses a technique due to Schöning [Sch86].

Lemma 10.1. *Let E be an event that occurs with probability $\geq 1/2 + \varepsilon$, where $0 < \varepsilon < 1/2$. Then, E occurs within t independent trials, where t is odd, more than $t/2$ times with probability at least*

$$1 - \frac{1}{2}(1 - 4\varepsilon^2)^{t/2}.$$

Note that for fixed ε, this probability goes to 1 as $t \to \infty$.

Proof. Let E be an event that occurs with probability q. The probability q_i that E occurs exactly i times in t independent trials is

$$\binom{t}{i} q^i (1 - q)^{t-i}.$$

Given that $q = 1/2 + \varepsilon$, we have

$$q_i = \binom{t}{i}(1/2+\varepsilon)^i(1/2-\varepsilon)^{t-i}.$$

Taking $t/2 \geq i$, we have

$$q_i \leq \binom{t}{i}(1/2+\varepsilon)^i(1/2-\varepsilon)^{t-i}\left(\frac{1/2+\varepsilon}{1/2-\varepsilon}\right)^{t/2-i}$$

$$= \binom{t}{i}(1/2+\varepsilon)^{t/2}(1/2-\varepsilon)^{t/2}$$

$$= \binom{t}{i}(1/4-\varepsilon^2)^{t/2}.$$

Then, the probability that E occurs more than $t/2$ times is

$$1 - \sum_{i=0}^{\lfloor t/2 \rfloor} q_i \geq 1 - \sum_{i=0}^{\lfloor t/2 \rfloor} \binom{t}{i}(1/4-\varepsilon^2)^{t/2}$$

$$= 1 - (1/4-\varepsilon^2)^{t/2}\sum_{i=0}^{\lfloor t/2 \rfloor} \binom{t}{i}$$

$$= 1 - (1/4-\varepsilon^2)^{t/2}2^{t-1}$$

$$= 1 - 2^{-t}(1-4\varepsilon^2)^{t/2}2^{t-1}$$

$$= 1 - \frac{1}{2}(1-4\varepsilon^2)^{t/2}.$$

$$\square$$

Now we give the amplification result for BPP.

Theorem 10.5. *Let $A \in$ BPP. For each polynomial q, there is a probabilistic, polynomial time-bounded Turing machine M such that*

$$\Pr[M(x) = \chi_A(x)] > 1 - 2^{-q(|x|)}.$$

Proof. Let M and ε witness that $A \in$ BPP. Let q be a polynomial. Given a positive, odd value t, define M_t so that on an input x it iterates $M(x)$ with t independent trials and enters the 1-state if and only if the majority of the trials enters the 1-state. To be more precise, it enters the 1-state, if $M(x) = 1$ occurs for more than $t/2$ trials, and it enters the 0-state, if $M(x) = 0$ occurs for more than $t/2$ trials.

By Lemma 10.1, we want to choose t such that

$$1 - \frac{1}{2}(1 - 4\varepsilon^2)^{t/2} \geq 1 - 2^{-q(|x|)}.$$

Equivalently, we want

$$2^{q(|x|)} \leq 2 \left(\frac{1}{1 - 4\varepsilon^2} \right)^{t/2},$$

which, taking the logarithm on both sides, is equivalent to

$$q(|x|) \leq 1 + (t/2)\log(1/(1 - 4\varepsilon^2)).$$

Now we solve this inequality for t, to obtain $c(q(|x|) - 1) \leq t$, where $c = \frac{2}{\log(1/(1-4\varepsilon^2))}$. Therefore, it suffices to take $t = t(|x|) = cq(|x|)$. Finally, observe that the Turing machine M_t is $O(q(n)p(n))$ time-bounded, where p is the time-bound for M.   □

Suppose that M is a probabilistic Turing machine that witnesses membership of A in the class BPP. The *error probability* of M on an input x is defined by $\Pr[M(x) \neq \chi_A(x)]$. The following corollary states that what distinguishes BPP is that (by amplification) the error probability can be made arbitrarily small. The proof follows immediately from Theorem 10.5.

Corollary 10.1. *Let $A \in$ BPP. For every ε, $0 < \varepsilon < 1/2$, there is a probabilistic, polynomial time-bounded Turing machine M_ε such that for every input x, the error probability of M_ε on x is less than ε.*

Now we show that BPP is included in the polynomial hierarchy.

Theorem 10.6. BPP $\subseteq \Sigma_2^P \cap \Pi_2^P$.

Proof. Since BPP is closed under complements, it suffices to prove that BPP $\subseteq \Sigma_2^P$. Let $A \in$ BPP. There is a polynomial p and a deterministic, polynomial time-bounded Turing machine M such that

$$\Pr_{r \in \{0,1\}^{p(|x|)}} [M(x,r) = \chi_A(x)] \geq 1 - 2^{-|x|}.$$

Therefore,

$$\|\{r \in \{0,1\}^{p(|x|)} \mid M(x,r) = \chi_A(x)\}\| \geq 2^{p(|x|)} - 2^{p(|x|)-|x|}.$$

We introduce the following notation: $n = |x|$, $k = \lceil p(n)/n \rceil$,

$$Y = \{r \in \{0,1\}^{p(|x|)} \mid M(x,r) = 1\},$$

and

$$N = \{r \in \{0,1\}^{p(|x|)} \mid M(x,r) = 0\}.$$

Choose m such that for all $i \geq m$, $k < 2^i$. Define the polynomial relation $R(x,y,z)$ as follows:

$$R(x,y,z) \Leftrightarrow [|x| < m \wedge x \in A] \vee [|x| \geq m \wedge |y| = kp(n) \wedge |z| = p(n) \wedge y \oplus z^k \notin N^k].$$

We claim for each $x \in \Sigma^*$, that

$$x \in A \Leftrightarrow \exists y \in \{0,1\}^{kp(n)} \forall z \in \{0,1\}^{p(n)} R(x,y,z).$$

Let $x \in \Sigma^*$. Consider first the case that $|x| < m$. Then, by definition, $x \in A \Leftrightarrow R(x,y,z)$. So the claim follows immediately.

Now we consider the case that $|x| \geq m$. Suppose that $x \in A$. In this case, we wish to show that the set

$$B = \{y \in \{0,1\}^{kp(n)} \mid \exists z \in \{0,1\}^{p(n)}[y \oplus z^k \in N^k]\}$$

is not identical to $\Sigma^{kp(n)}$. To show this, we begin by establishing an estimate of the size of N: Since $\chi_A(x) = 1$, it follows that

$$\|\{r \in \{0,1\}^{p(|x|)} \mid M(x,r) = 1\}\| \geq 2^{p(n)} - 2^{p(n)-n}.$$

Thus,

$$\|\{r \in \{0,1\}^{p(|x|)} \mid M(x,r) \neq 1\}\| < 2^{p(n)-n}.$$

So,

$$\|\{r \in \{0,1\}^{p(|x|)} \mid M(x,r) = 0\}\| < 2^{p(n)-n}.$$

Hence, $\|N\| < 2^{p(n)-n}$. Now note that $B = \{w \ominus z^k \mid w \in N^k \text{ and } z \in \{0,1\}^{p(n)}\}$. So,

$$\|B\| = \|N\|^k 2^{p(n)} < 2^{kp(n)-nk+p(n)} \quad (\text{since } \|N\| < 2^{p(n)-n})$$

$$\leq 2^{kp(n)} \quad (\text{since } nk \geq p(n)).$$

Therefore, $\{0,1\}^{kp(n)} - B \neq \emptyset$. There exists a string $y \in \{0,1\}^{kp(n)}$ such that $y \notin B$. Thus,

$$\exists y \in \{0,1\}^{kp(n)} \forall z \in \{0,1\}^{p(n)}[y \oplus z^k \notin N^k].$$

Hence,

$$\exists y \in \{0,1\}^{kp(n)} \forall z \in \{0,1\}^{p(n)} R(x,y,z).$$

We still need to prove the equivalence in the other direction. Assume that $|x| \geq m$ and $x \notin A$. Since $\chi_A(x) = 0$,

$$\|\{r \in \{0,1\}^{p(n)} \mid M(x,r) = 0\}\| \geq 2^{p(n)} - 2^{p(n)-n}.$$

So,

$$\|N\| \geq 2^{p(n)} - 2^{p(n)-n}.$$

Let $y \in \{0,1\}^{kp(n)}$. We define the set $B_y = \{z \in \{0,1\}^{p(n)} \mid y \oplus z^k \in N^k\}$, and will show that $B_y \neq \emptyset$. It follows from this claim that

$$\exists z \in \{0,1\}^{p(n)}[y \oplus z^k \in N^k].$$

That is,

$$\forall y \in \{0,1\}^{kp(n)} \exists z \in \{0,1\}^{p(n)} \neg R(x,y,z),$$

which is what we want to prove.

Write $y = y_1 \ldots y_k$, where for each $i = 1, \ldots, k$, $|y_i| = p(n)$. Then,

$$B_y = \{z \in \{0,1\}^{p(n)} \mid y \oplus z^k \in N^k\}$$

$$= \bigcap_{i=1}^{k} \{z \in \{0,1\}^{p(n)} \mid y_i \oplus z \in N\}$$

$$= \bigcap_{i=1}^{k} \{w \oplus y_i \mid w \in N\}.$$

Next, in order to show that $B_y \neq \emptyset$, we estimate the cardinality of $\{0,1\}^{p(n)} - B_y$:

$$\|\{0,1\}^{p(n)} - B_y\| = \left\| \{0,1\}^{p(n)} - \bigcap_{i=1}^{k} \{w \oplus y_i \mid w \in N\} \right\|$$

$$= \left\| \bigcup_{i=1}^{k} (\{0,1\}^{p(n)} - \{w \oplus y_i \mid w \in N\}) \right\|$$

$$\leq \sum_{i=1}^{k} \|\{0,1\}^{p(n)} - \{w \oplus y_i \mid w \in N\}\|$$

$$= k(2^{p(n)} - \|N\|)$$

$$< k(2^{p(n)} - (2^{p(n)} - 2^{p(n)-n}))$$

$$= k2^{p(n)-n}$$

$$< 2^n 2^{p(n)-n} \quad \text{(since } k < 2^n)$$

$$= 2^{p(n)}.$$

Therefore, $B_y \neq \emptyset$, which, as we established, completes the proof. $\qquad\square$

We learned in Chap. 8 that membership in $P/poly$ is an attribute of feasible languages. For this reason, we interpret the following remarkable theorem as giving further evidence to the feasibility of languages in BPP.

Theorem 10.7. BPP $\subseteq P/poly$.

Proof. Let p be a polynomial and let M be a deterministic, polynomial time-bounded Turing machine such that

$$\Pr_{r \in \{0,1\}^{p(|x|)}} [M(x,r) = \chi_A(x)] \geq 1 - 2^{-|x|}. \tag{10.1}$$

Equation 10.1 tells us that *for every* x and *for most* r, $M(x,r)$ computes the correct answer. We will show that a kind of *quantifier switch* is possible. We show that *there exists* a string r such that *for every* x, $M(x,r)$ is correct. This is an important proof technique.

Equivalent to (10.1), the error probability is small:

$$\Pr_{r \in \{0,1\}^{p(|x|)}} [M(x,r) \neq \chi_A(x)] < 2^{-|x|}.$$

Then,

$$\Pr_{r \in \{0,1\}^{p(|x|)}} [\exists x \in \{0,1\}^n M(x,r) \neq \chi_A(x)] \leq \sum_{x \in \{0,1\}^n} \Pr_{r \in \{0,1\}^{p(|x|)}} [M(x,r) \neq \chi_A(x)]$$

$$< 2^n \cdot 2^{-n}$$

$$= 1.$$

The first inequality follows from the *union bound* of probability theory, which states that for every series of sets $\{L_i\}_i$ and random variable X,

$$\Pr\left[X \in \bigcup_i^n L_i\right] \leq \sum_i^n \Pr[X \in L_i].$$

Thus, there exists a string $r \in \{0,1\}^{p(|x|)}$ such that

$$\forall x \in \{0,1\}^n [M(x,r) = \chi_A(x)].$$

This string r is good advice for $A^{=n}$. That is, define the advice string $a_n = r$. Then, for each string $x \in \{0,1\}^n$,

$$x \in A \Leftrightarrow M(x,a_n) = 1.$$

Hence, $A \in P/poly$.   □

In this proof, we showed existence of a string r such that

$$\forall x \in \{0,1\}^n [M(x,r) = \chi_A(x)]$$

by showing that the probability that the opposite occurs is less than one. This method of proof is called the *probabilistic method*.

Corollary 10.2. *If* $NP \subseteq BPP$, *then the polynomial hierarchy collapses to* $\Sigma_2^P \cap \Pi_2^P$.

It is not known whether any of the probabilistic classes we have been considering have complete problems. There is an oracle relative to which BPP does not have complete problems [Sip82]. None of the inclusions we have stated in this chapter are known to be proper. Also, although randomness seems to provide more power than determinism, there is not much combinatorial evidence to suggest that P is a proper subset of BPP.

10.4   Randomly Chosen Hash Functions

We introduce an important tool for the study of probabilistic complexity classes. Let $\Sigma = \{0,1\}$.

Definition 10.5. We define a *random hash function*

$$h : \Sigma^t \to \Sigma^m$$

to be given by a Boolean (m,t)-matrix $h = (m_{ij})$, where each entry $m_{ij} \in \{0,1\}$ is chosen uniformly at random and independently. Then, for $a = a_1 \ldots a_t \in \Sigma^t$, and $1 \le j \le m$, the j-th bit of $h(a) = (m_{j1} \wedge a_1) \oplus \cdots \oplus (m_{jt} \wedge a_t)$. That is, $h(a)$ is obtained by multiplying the m rows of h with a.

Proposition 10.2. *Given a random hash function* $h : \Sigma^t \to \Sigma^m$ *and string* $a \in \Sigma^t$ *that is not identically 0,*
$$\Pr[h(a) = 0] = 2^{-m}.$$

Proof. Since each $0/1$ entry of h is chosen independently, the rows are independent too. So it suffices to show that each inner product is 0 with probability $1/2$.

Let $a = a_1 \ldots a_t$ such that $a \ne 0$ and fix i, $1 \le i \le t$, such that $a_i \ne 0$. For each bit $b \in \{0,1\}$, consider the vectors $I_b = \{v \in \Sigma^t \mid v \cdot a = b\}$ that have inner product b with a. Let $v \in I_0$ and define v' to be identical to v except that the ith bit is flipped. That is, $v' = v_1 \ldots v_{i-1}(1-v_i)v_{i+1} \ldots v_t$. Then, $v' \in I_1$. Furthermore, and this is the important observation, the mapping $v \mapsto v'$ is a bijection between I_0 and I_1. Therefore,

$$\|I_0\| = \|I_1\| = 2^{t-1}.$$

So,

$$\Pr_{v \in \Sigma^t} [v \cdot a = 0] = 1/2,$$

which is what we wanted to prove. $\square$

Proposition 10.3. *Let $h : \Sigma^t \to \Sigma^m$ be a random hash function. Let $x \neq y$, where $x, y \in \Sigma^t$. Then,*

$$\Pr[h(x) = h(y)] = 2^{-m}.$$

Proof. Since h is a linear function,

$$h(x) = h(y) \Leftrightarrow h(x) \oplus h(y) = 0$$
$$\Leftrightarrow h(x \oplus y) = 0.$$

Since $x \neq y$, $x \oplus y \neq 0$. So we can apply Proposition 10.2, which proves the claim.

$\square$

Let $\mathscr{H} = \{h_1, \ldots, h_{m+1}\}$ be a collection of random hash functions and let $X \subseteq \Sigma^t$. We say $\mathscr{H}$ has a *collision* on X if there exists a string $x \in X$ such that for every h_i, $i = 1, \ldots, m+1$, there exists $y \in X$, $y \neq x$ so that $h_i(x) = h_i(y)$. Otherwise, $\mathscr{H}$ on X is *collision-free*. The important "Coding Lemma," which we prove next, states that $\mathscr{H}$ is likely to be collision-free on "small" sets, but guaranteed to have a collision on sufficiently "large" sets. This lemma is due to Sipser [Sip83] and the notion of random hash functions is due to Carter and Wegman [CW79].

We introduce the following predicate to denote collision-free: Define

$$\mathrm{SEP}_X(\mathscr{H}) \Leftrightarrow \forall x \in X \exists h \in \mathscr{H} \forall y \in X - \{x\}[h(x) \neq h(y)].$$

Notice that

$$\mathrm{SEP}_X(\{h_1, \ldots, h_{m+1}\}) \Leftrightarrow$$
$$\forall x \in X[\forall y \in X - \{x\}[h_1(x) \neq h_1(y)] \vee \ldots \vee \forall y \in X - \{x\}[h_{m+1}(x) \neq h_{m+1}(y)]].$$

$$(10.2)$$

Lemma 10.2 (Coding Lemma). *Let $\mathscr{H} = \{h_1, \ldots, h_{m+1}\}$ be a collection of random hash functions from Σ^t to Σ^m and let $X \subseteq \Sigma^t$.*

1. If $\|X\| \leq 2^{m-1}$, then

$$\Pr[\mathrm{SEP}_X(\{h_1, \ldots, h_{m+1}\})] \geq 3/4.$$

2. If $\|X\| > (m+1)2^m$, then

$$\Pr[\mathrm{SEP}_X(\{h_1, \ldots, h_{m+1}\})] = 0.$$

Proof. By Proposition 10.3, for $x, y \in \Sigma^t$, $x \neq y$, and given h_i, $\Pr[h_i(x) = h_i(y)] = 2^{-m}$. Hence, for given $x \in X$, $\Pr[\exists y \in X - \{x\}, h_i(x) = h_i(y)] \leq \|X\| \cdot 2^{-m} \leq 1/2$. The random hash functions $h_1, \ldots, h_{m+1}$ are chosen independently. So, for given $x \in X$,

$$\Pr[\forall i \leq m+1 \exists y \in X - \{x\}, h_i(x) = h_i(y)] \leq (1/2)^{m+1}.$$

Finally, the probability of a collision is at most

$$\|X\| \cdot 2^{-(m+1)} \leq 2^{m-1-m-1} = 2^{-2} = 1/4.$$

This proves the first assertion.

To prove the second assertion, first note that every function h_i can be one-to-one only on domains of size at most 2^m. Suppose $\mathrm{SEP}_X(\{h_1, \ldots, h_{m+1}\})$. Then,

$$\forall x \in X \exists i \leq m+1 \forall y \in X - \{x\}[h_i(x) \neq h_i(y)].$$

So we can identify each $x \in X$ with a unique pair $(i, h_i(x))$ so that for $x \neq y$, the pair identified with x is not the same as the pair identified with y. Thus, $\|X\|$ is bounded by the number of distinct pairs of the form $(i, h_i(x))$, which is $(m+1)2^m$. Hence, $\mathrm{SEP}_X(\{h_1, \ldots, h_{m+1}\})$ cannot hold.   □

10.4.1   Operators

We can generalize the definitions of probabilistic classes such as BPP and RP by defining operators that apply to arbitrary complexity classes. Let $\mathscr{C}$ be a class of languages.

Definition 10.6. $\mathrm{R} \cdot \mathscr{C}$ is the class of languages A for which there is a set $L \in \mathscr{C}$ and polynomial p such that for all x,

$$x \in A \Rightarrow \Pr_{y \in \{0,1\}^{p(|x|)}} [(x,y) \in L] \geq 1/2$$

and

$$x \notin A \Rightarrow \Pr_{y \in \{0,1\}^{p(|x|)}} [(x,y) \in L] = 0.$$

Definition 10.7. $\mathrm{BP} \cdot \mathscr{C}$ is the class of languages A for which there is a set $L \in \mathscr{C}$, a polynomial p, and a number ε, $0 < \varepsilon < 1/2$, such that for all x,

$$\Pr_{y \in \{0,1\}^{p(|x|)}} [(x,y) \in L \Leftrightarrow x \in A] > 1/2 + \varepsilon.$$

Note that $\mathrm{RP} = \mathrm{R} \cdot \mathrm{P}$ and $\mathrm{BPP} = \mathrm{BP} \cdot \mathrm{P}$. Analogous to these definitions, it should be clear how to define other operators, for example co-R·. The amplification results that we proved already apply to these operator classes as well.

Homework 10.1 *Show that*
co-$(\mathrm{R} \cdot \text{co-NP}) = \text{co-R} \cdot \mathrm{NP}$.

Homework 10.2 *Let $A \in \mathrm{BP} \cdot \mathrm{NP}$. Show that there is a set $L \in \mathrm{NP}$ and a polynomial p such that*

$$\Pr_{r \in \Sigma^{p(n)}} [A^{\leq n} = \{x \mid (x,r) \in L\}^{\leq n}] \geq 1 - 2^{-n}.$$

Using operator classes, we will illustrate application of the Coding Lemma, Lemma 10.2, to obtain a refinement of Theorem 10.6.

Theorem 10.8. $\text{BPP} \subseteq \text{R} \cdot \text{co-NP}$.

This theorem is interesting because of the following corollary.

Corollary 10.3. $\text{BPP} \subseteq \text{ZPP}^{\text{NP}} \subseteq \Sigma_2^P \cap \Pi_2^P$.

We give the proof of the corollary first.

Proof. Since BPP is closed under complement, by Homework 10.1, we have $\text{BPP} \subseteq \text{R} \cdot \text{co-NP} \cap \text{co-R} \cdot \text{NP}$. Therefore, $\text{BPP} \subseteq \text{RP}^{\text{NP}} \cap \text{co-RP}^{\text{NP}}$. The proof of Theorem 10.4 relativizes. So we conclude that $\text{BPP} \subseteq \text{ZPP}^{\text{NP}}$. The second inclusion holds because $\text{ZPP} \subseteq \text{NP}$ and because ZPP is closed under complement. □

Proof. For the proof of Theorem 10.8, let $L \in \text{BPP}$, let M be a deterministic, polynomial time-bounded Turing machine, and let p be a polynomial such that for all $x \in \Sigma^n$,

$$\Pr_{r \in \Sigma^{p(n)}} [M(x,r) = \chi_L(x)] > 1 - 2^{-n}.$$

Let $N = \{r \in \Sigma^{p(n)} \mid M(x,r) = 0\}$ be the set of reject paths of M on some input x. Let $t = p(n)$ and let $m = t - n + 1$. It follows immediately, for $x \in \Sigma^n$, that

$$x \in L \Rightarrow \|N\| \leq 2^{p(n)-n} = 2^{m-1}.$$

We will show that

$$x \notin L \Rightarrow \|N\| > (m+1)2^m.$$

For the moment, let assume that this inequality holds.

Note that $N \subseteq \Sigma^t$. By the Coding Lemma, for any collection $\mathcal{H} = \{h_1, \ldots, h_{m+1}\}$ of random hash functions,

$$x \in L \Rightarrow \Pr[\text{SEP}_N(\{h_1, \ldots, h_{m+1}\})] \geq 3/4,$$

and

$$x \notin L \Rightarrow \Pr[\text{SEP}_N(\{h_1, \ldots, h_{m+1}\})] = 0.$$

Since N belongs to P, it follows from (10.2) that $\text{SEP}_N(\{h_1, \ldots, h_{m+1}\} \in \text{co-NP}$. Therefore, $L \in \text{R} \cdot \text{co-NP}$ follows immediately.

Now we have to prove that the inequality holds: By definition, if $x \notin L$, then

$$\|N\| > 2^{p(n)} - 2^{p(n)-n} = 2^t - 2^{m-1} = 2^t - 2^{t-n}.$$

We claim that $2^t - 2^{t-n} \geq (m+1)2^m$.

$$2^t - 2^{m-1} \geq (m+1)2^m \Leftrightarrow 2^n 2^t - 2^t \geq (m+1)2^m 2^n = (m+1)2^{t+1}$$
$$\Leftrightarrow 2^t[2^n - 1] \geq (m+1)2^{t+1}$$
$$\Leftrightarrow 2^n - 1 \geq 2(m+1),$$

which holds for sufficiently large n. This completes the proof. $\qquad\square$

As we observed in the proof of Corollary 10.3, since BPP is closed under complements, by Theorem 10.8 and Homework 10.1, it follows that $BPP \subseteq co\text{-}R \cdot NP$. The following theorem is a generalization of this observation.

Theorem 10.9. $BP \cdot NP = co\text{-}R \cdot NP$.

Proof. Clearly, $co\text{-}R \cdot NP \subseteq BP \cdot NP$. We need to prove that $BP \cdot NP \subseteq co\text{-}R \cdot NP$. We will use the Coding Lemma in its obvious dual form. Let $A \in BP \cdot NP$. By definition, there is a set $L \in NP$ and polynomial p such that

$$\Pr_{y \in \{0,1\}^{p(n)}} [(x,y) \in L \Leftrightarrow x \in A] > 1 - 2^{-n}.$$

Let $Y = \{y \in \Sigma^{p(n)} \mid (x,y) \in L\}$. Then, using the estimates we calculated in the proof of Theorem 10.8,

$$x \in A \Rightarrow \|Y\| > 2^{p(n)} - 2^{p(n)-n} \geq (m+1)2^m$$

and

$$x \notin A \Rightarrow \|Y\| \leq 2^{p(n)-n} = 2^{m-1}.$$

Hence, by the Coding Lemma,

$$x \in A \Rightarrow \Pr[\neg SEP_Y(\{h_1, \ldots, h_{m+1}\})] = 1$$

and

$$x \notin A \Rightarrow \Pr[\neg SEP_Y(\{h_1, \ldots, h_{m+1}\})] \leq 1/4.$$

Recall that $\neg SEP_Y(\{h_1, \ldots, h_{m+1}\})$ asserts existence of a collision, which we may write as follows:

$$\exists y \forall i \leq m+1 \exists z[(x,y) \in L \text{ and } (x,z) \in L \text{ and } y \neq z \text{ and } h_i(y) = h_i(z)].$$

Since $L \in NP$, $\neg SEP_Y(\{h_1, \ldots, h_{m+1}\}) \in NP$ follows. Therefore, $A \in co\text{-}R \cdot NP$. $\qquad\square$

By Theorem 10.9, $BP \cdot NP \subseteq co\text{-}RP^{NP} \subseteq \Pi_2^P$. Also, since $BPP \subseteq BP \cdot NP$ and BPP is closed under complements, $BPP \subseteq R \cdot co\text{-}NP$. Therefore, Theorem 10.9 subsumes Theorem 10.8.

10.5   The Graph Isomorphism Problem

In Sect. 7.3.1, we stated that Schöning [Sch88] has shown that GRAPH ISO-MORPHISM is "nearly" in $NP \cap co\text{-}NP$, and that the technical result provides strong evidence that GRAPH ISOMORPHISM is not NP-complete. Now we are able to state and prove the technical result. Schöning's result is that GRAPH ISOMORPHISM belongs to the class L_2, the second level of the low hierarchy. It follows immediately that GI cannot be complete for NP unless the polynomial hierarchy collapses to Σ_2^P.

Let $G_1 \simeq G_2$ denote that G_1 and G_2 are isomorphic graphs. Let GI denote the set

$$GI = \{(G_1, G_2) \mid G_1 \simeq G_2\},$$

and let GNI denote the complement of GI, so that

$$GNI = \{(G_1, G_2) \mid G_1 \not\simeq G_2\}.$$

Given a graph $G = (V, E)$, where $V = \{1, \ldots, n\}$, and given a permutation p on $\{1, \ldots, n\}$, let $p(G) = (V, E')$, where $(p(u), p(v)) \in E' \Leftrightarrow (u, v) \in E$. Then p is an *automorphism* of G if $p(G) = G$. Let $Aut(G)$ be the set of automorphisms of G. (It is easy to see that $Aut(G)$ is a group under the composition operator.) $G_1 \simeq G_2$ if and only if $G_2 = p(G_1)$, for some permutation p. The number of different isomorphic graphs to G is

$$n! / \|Aut(G)\|.$$

Given two graphs G_1 and G_2 with n vertices, define

$$H(G_1, G_2) = \ \{(H, p, i) \mid H \text{ is isomorphic to either } G_1 \text{ or } G_2,$$

$$\text{and } p \text{ is an automorphism of } G_i, \text{ where } i \in \{1, 2\}\}.$$

We can easily see that $H(G_1, G_2) \in NP$: Given an input tuple (H, p, i), guess a permutation q and $j \in \{1, 2\}$. Verify whether $p(G_i) = G_i$ and $H = q(G_j)$.

Define $num(G_1, G_2) = \|H(G_1, G_2)\|$.

Lemma 10.3. *If $G_1 \simeq G_2$, then $num(G_1, G_2) = 2n!$. If $G_1 \not\simeq G_2$, then $num(G_1, G_2) \geq 4n!$.*

Proof. Suppose $G_1 \simeq G_2$. Then $\|Aut(G_1)\| = \|Aut(G_2)\|$, and the set of graphs isomorphic to G_1 is identical to the set of graphs isomorphic to G_2. So,

$$num(G_1, G_2) = \frac{n!}{\|Aut(G_1)\|} (\|Aut(G_1)\| + \|Aut(G_2)\|) = 2n!.$$

Suppose $G_1 \not\simeq G_2$. Then, the $n! / \|Aut(G_1)\|$ isomorphic versions of G_1 are different from the $n! / \|Aut(G_2)\|$ versions of G_2. So,

$$num(G_1, G_2) = \left(\frac{n!}{\|Aut(G_1)\|} + \frac{n!}{\|Aut(G_2)\|} \right) (\|Aut(G_1)\| + \|Aut(G_2)\|)$$

$$= n! \left(\frac{1}{\|Aut(G_1)\|} + \frac{1}{\|Aut(G_2)\|} \right) (\|Aut(G_1)\| + \|Aut(G_2)\|).$$

Let us write the expression on the right hand side as

$$\left(\frac{1}{A} + \frac{1}{B} \right) (A + B)$$

to see that its value is ≥ 4:

$$\left(\frac{1}{A} + \frac{1}{B} \right) (A + B) = \frac{B(A+B) + A(A+B)}{AB}$$

$$= 2 + \frac{BB}{AB} + \frac{AA}{AB}$$

So we have to see that $\frac{BB}{AB} + \frac{AA}{AB} \geq 2$. This is easy:

$$\frac{B}{A} + \frac{A}{B} - 2 \geq 0 \Leftrightarrow \frac{AB^2}{A} + \frac{A^2 B}{B} - 2AB \geq 0$$

$$\Leftrightarrow B^2 + A^2 - 2AB \geq 0$$

$$\Leftrightarrow (A - B)^2 \geq 0,$$

which, of course, is correct.   □

We are going to prove that GNI $\in$ BP $\cdot$ NP. To do so, we would like to apply the Coding Lemma to the set $H(G_1, G_2)$. However, the estimates we obtained in Lemma 10.3 for the size of $H(G_1, G_2)$ are not adequate. For this reason, we introduce the following set instead. Let $Y = H(G_1, G_2)^n$, where G_1 and G_2 are graphs with n vertices, Let $m = 1 + \lceil n \cdot \log(2n!) \rceil$.

Homework 10.3 Show the following: If $G_1 \simeq G_2$, then $\|Y\| \leq 2^{m-1}$. If $G_1 \not\simeq G_2$, then $\|Y\| > (m+1)2^m$.

Theorem 10.10. GNI $\in$ BP $\cdot$ NP.

Proof. Applying the Coding Lemma to Homework 10.3,

$$(G_1, G_2) \in \text{GNI} \Rightarrow \Pr[\neg SEP_Y(\{h_1, \ldots, h_{m+1}\})] = 1$$

and

$$(G_1, G_2) \notin \text{GNI} \Rightarrow \Pr[\neg SEP_Y(\{h_1, \ldots, h_{m+1}\})] \leq 1/4$$

follows immediately. Then, as in the proof of Theorem 10.9, since $Y \in$ NP, we can easily see that $\neg SEP_Y(\{h_1, \ldots, h_{m+1}\}) \in$ NP. Therefore, GNI $\in$ co-R $\cdot$ NP, which implies our result. $\square$

The next theorem completes our exposition showing that GI is low_2:

Theorem 10.11. NP$\cap$co-(BP$\cdot$NP)$\subseteq L_2$.

Corollary 10.4. GI $\in L_2$.

The Corollary follows immediately from Theorems 10.10 and 10.11. The proof of Theorem 10.11 will require the following lemma, the proof of which uses the same technique as that which we used to prove Theorem 10.6.

Lemma 10.4. If $E \subseteq \Sigma^{p(n)}$ such that $\|E\| \geq (1 - 2^{-n})2^{p(n)}$, then the following conditions hold, where $\oplus$ denotes bitwise addition modulo 2:

$$\exists u = (u_1, \ldots, u_{p(n)}), |u_i| = p(n), \forall v, |v| = p(n), [\exists i \leq p(n), u_i \oplus v \in E] \qquad (10.3)$$

and

$$\forall u = (u_1, \ldots, u_n), |u_i| = p(n), \exists v, |v| = p(n)[\forall i \leq p(n), u_i \oplus v \in E]. \qquad (10.4)$$

Proof. Suppose that Condition 10.3 is false. Then,

$$\forall u = (u_1, \ldots, u_{p(n)}), |u_i| = p(n), \exists v, |v| = p(n)[u_1 \oplus v \notin E \wedge \ldots \wedge u_{p(n)} \oplus v \notin E].$$

Let $U = \{u = (u_1, \ldots, u_{p(n)}) \mid |u_i| = p(n)\}$ be the set of all $p(n)$-tuples. Let v_j denote the j-th string of length $p(n)$ in lexicographical order. Define

$$U_j = \{u \mid u_1 \oplus v_j \notin E \wedge \ldots \wedge u_{p(n)} \oplus v_j \notin E\}.$$

Then, $\bigcup_{j=1}^{2^{p(n)}} U_j \supseteq U$. Hence, there exists j, $1 \leq j \leq 2^{p(n)}$, such that $\|U_j\| \geq \|U\|/2^{p(n)} = 2^{p^2(n)-p(n)}$. Let

$$B = \{(u_1 \oplus v_j, u_2 \oplus v_j, \ldots, u_{p(n)} \oplus v_j) \mid (u_1, \ldots, u_{p(n)}) \in U_j\},$$

and observe that $B \subseteq \overline{E}^{p(n)}$ and $\|B\| = \|U_j\| \leq \|\overline{E}^{p(n)}\|$. Therefore, $\|\overline{E}\|^{p(n)} \geq 2^{p^2(n)-p(n)}$. Thus, $\|\overline{E}\| \geq 2^{p(n)-1}$, which contradicts our assumption about the size of E.

Now suppose that Condition 10.4 is false. Fix $u = (u_1, \ldots, u_{p(n)})$, $|u_i| = p(n)$, such that

$$\forall v, |v| = p(n)[\exists i \leq p(n), u_i \oplus v \notin E].$$

Let $V = \{v \mid v \in \Sigma^{p(n)}\}$ and, for each $j = 1, \ldots, p(n)$, let

$$V_j = \{v \in V \mid u_j \oplus v \notin E\}.$$

Then, $V \subseteq \bigcup_{j=1}^{p(n)} V_j$. Hence, there exists j, $1 \leq j \leq p(n)$, such that $\|V_j\| \geq \|V\|/p(n)$. Let

$$B = \{u_j \oplus v \mid v \in V_j\}.$$

Observe that $B \subseteq \overline{E}$ and $\|V_j\| = \|B\|$. So,

$$\|\overline{E}\| \geq \|B\| = \|V_j\| \geq \|V\|/p(n) = 2^{p(n)}/p(n).$$

This estimate contradicts our assumption about the size of E.   □

Now we prove Theorem 10.11.

Proof. Let $L \in \Sigma_2^{P,A}$, where $A \in \text{NP} \cap \text{co-}(\text{BP} \cdot \text{NP})$. We need to show that $L \in \Sigma_2^P$. Let M be a deterministic, polynomial-time-bounded oracle Turing machine and q be a polynomial such that

$$L = \{x \mid \exists y \forall z (x,y,z) \in L(M,A)\},$$

where the quantifiers are bounded by $q(|x|)$. Let M' be a nondeterministic, polynomial-time-bounded Turing machine such that $A = L(M')$. By Homework 10.2, let $B \in \text{NP}$ and let p be a polynomial such that

$$\Pr_{r \in \Sigma^{p(n)}} \left[\overline{A}^{\leq n} = \{x \mid (x,r) \in B\}^{\leq n} \right] \geq 1 - 2^{-n}. \tag{10.5}$$

Let M'' be a nondeterministic, polynomial-time-bounded Turing machine that accepts B.

Define

$$E = \{r \in \Sigma^{p(n)} \mid \overline{A}^{\leq n} = \{x \mid (x,r) \in B\}^{\leq n}\}$$

to be the set of all strings r that satisfy Condition 10.5. Then, $\|E\| \geq 2^{p(n)} - 2^{p(n)-n} = 2^{p(n)}(1 - 2^{-n})$. So E satisfies the hypothesis of Lemma 10.4. We will use the conditions of Lemma 10.4 to prove the following characterization of L:

$$L = \{x \mid \exists u \exists y \forall v \forall z [\exists i \leq p(n), (u_i \oplus v, x, y, z) \notin K]\},$$

where $K \in \text{NP}$. Once we have proved this characterization, we are done, for then $\overline{K}$ belongs to co-NP, and it follows immediately that $L \in \Sigma_2^P$.

The following nondeterministic, polynomial-time-bounded Turing machine M_K defines K: On input (r,x,y,z), M_K simulates M on (x,y,z), except that oracle calls are to be simulated in the manner we will describe, and M_K accepts its input if and only if M rejects. To simulate oracle calls, suppose that s is the query string. M_K nondeterministically guesses whether $s \in A$ or $s \in \overline{A}$. In the first case, M_K simulates M' on s and continues with answer "yes" if M' accepts. Otherwise, M_K halts without accepting. In the second case, M_K simulates M'' on (s,r) and continues with answer "no" if M'' accepts. Again, M_K halts without accepting, if M'' does not accept.

The reader can easily verify, for all $r \in E$, where n is chosen large enough so that all queries of M_K on input (r,x,y,z) have length $\leq n$, that

$$(r,x,y,z) \in K \Leftrightarrow (x,y,z) \notin L(M,A).$$

The essential point, given a query s, is that M'' accepts (s,r) if and only if $s \in \overline{A}$.

Now we can see that the characterization of L is correct. Suppose $x \in L$. Then, $\exists y \forall z (x,y,z) \in L(M,A)$. By Condition 10.3, $\exists u \forall v [\exists i \leq p(n), u_i \oplus v \in E]$. Therefore, by the observation in the previous paragraph,

$$\exists u \exists y \forall v \forall z [\exists i \leq p(n), (u_i \oplus v, x, y, z) \notin K].$$

Now suppose that $x \notin L$. Then, $\forall y \exists z (x,y,z) \notin L(M,A)$. By Condition 10.4,

$$\forall u \exists v [\forall i \leq p(n), u_i \oplus v \in E].$$

Therefore, again by the previous paragraph,

$$\forall u \forall y \exists v \exists z [\forall i \leq p(n), (u_i \oplus v, x, y, z) \in K].$$

This completes the proof.   □

Corollary 10.5. $NP \cap BPP \subseteq L_2$.

Proof. $BPP \subseteq BP \cdot NP$. Therefore, $BPP \subseteq co\text{-}(BP \cdot NP)$.   □

Thus, we see again that NP cannot be included in BPP unless the polynomial hierarchy collapses.

Corollary 10.6. $RP \subseteq L_2$.

As a consequence of the results we learned in this section, GRAPH ISOMOR-PHISM cannot be complete for NP, using any of the polynomial-time reducibilities we studied, unless the polynomial hierarchy collapses.

10.6 Additional Homework Problems

Homework 10.4 *Prove that the GRAPH ISOMORPHISM problem is self-reducible: Specifically, let Q be an oracle that encodes (solves) the answer to GI for any pair of graphs of size $n-1$. Prove that there is a polynomial-time algorithm that uses Q as an oracle and that decides GI for any pair of graphs G and H of size n.*

Homework 10.5 *Prove that $BP \cdot NP \subseteq NP/poly$.*

Homework 10.6 *Show that if $NP \subseteq BPP$, then $NP = RP$.*

Chapter 11
Introduction to Counting Classes

Our interest in nondeterministic polynomial time-bounded Turing machines has been concerned primarily with the question of whether, given an input x, there exists at least one accepting computation. However, this is not entirely so, for the definition of PP is that the majority of computations are accepting. Now we will be interested in the following classes, which use counting explicitly in their definitions.

Definition 11.1. $\oplus$P (pronounced "parity P") is the class of all languages L for which there exists a nondeterministic polynomial time-bounded Turing machine M such that

$$L = \{x \mid M \text{ has an odd number of accepting computations on input } x\}.$$

For any nondeterministic polynomial time-bounded Turing machine M, let $\#acc_M(x)$ denote the number of distinct accepting computations of M on input x.

Definition 11.2. #P (pronounced "sharp P") is the class of functions $f : \Sigma^* \to N$ such that there exists a nondeterministic polynomial time-bounded Turing machine M such that for each x,

$$f(x) = \#acc_M(x).$$

We stress that #P is a class of functions and let $P^{\#P} = \{L \mid L$ is accepted relative to a function in #P by a deterministic functional oracle Turing machine in polynomial time$\}$.

Define the function #SAT by

$$\#SAT(F) = \text{ the number of satisfying assignments of } F,$$

where F is a formula of propositional logic. Let L be an arbitrary set in NP and let M be a nondeterministic polynomial-time bounded Turing machine that accepts L. Recall the comment after the proof of the Cook–Levin Theorem, Theorem 6.8, which tells us that the reduction f_L that maps accepting computations of M on x to satisfying assignments of $f_L(x)$ is *parsimonious*. This term means that the reduction

S. Homer and A.L. Selman, *Computability and Complexity Theory*,
Texts in Computer Science, DOI 10.1007/978-1-4614-0682-2_11,
© Springer Science+Business Media, LLC 2011

preserves the number of solutions (i.e., of accepting computations). Thus, we have $\#acc_M(x) = \#\text{SAT}(f_L(x))$, for all input words x. For this reason, we say that #SAT is *complete* for #P.[1] Similarly, one can define, for example #HAM, that counts the number of Hamiltonian circuits of a graph, and show that it is #P-complete, for reductions between the standard NP-complete problems are parsimonious. Valiant [Val79] proved that the permanent is #P-complete.

Define the set

$$\oplus \text{SAT} = \{F \mid \text{formula } F \text{ has an odd number of satisfying assignments}\}.$$

The following proposition follows for the same reason.

Proposition 11.1. $\oplus\text{SAT}$ *is* $\leq_m^P$*-complete for* $\oplus$P.

Now we define the following language version of #SAT and prove that it is $\leq_m^P$-complete for the class PP. This result, Theorem 11.1 below, was proved by Simon in his dissertation [Sim75]; we follow the exposition of Balcázar et al. [BBS86].

Definition 11.3. $L_{\#\text{SAT}} = \{\langle F, i \rangle \mid i \geq 0$ and F is a propositional formula that has more than i distinct satisfying assignments$\}$.

The following Homework exercise is used in the proof of Theorem 11.1.

Homework 11.1 *Given an integer i and string 0^n, with $0 \leq i \leq 2^n$, deterministically in polynomial time compute a formula $G(x_1, \ldots, x_n)$ that has exactly $2^n - i$ satisfying assignments.*

Theorem 11.1. $L_{\#\text{SAT}}$ *is* $\leq_m^P$*-complete for the class* PP.

Proof. First we show that $L_{\#\text{SAT}}$ belongs to PP. We describe a Turing machine that on input a Boolean formula F with variables $x_1, \ldots, x_n$ and integer i between 0 and 2^n accepts $\langle F, i \rangle$ with probability at least 1/2 if and only if F has more than i satisfying assignments. To begin, using the result of Homework 11.1, let G be the formula that has exactly $2^n - i$ satisfying assignments. Then construct the formula

$$H(x_1, \ldots, x_n, y) = (y \wedge F(x_1, \ldots, x_n)) \vee (\bar{y} \wedge G(x_1, \ldots, x_n)).$$

Nondeterministically guess a satisfying assignment of H.

Note that $\#\text{SAT}(F) > i$ if and only if H has more than $i + (2^n - i) = 2^n = 2^{n+1}/2$ satisfying assignments. So this machine accepts $\langle F, i \rangle$ with probability at least 1/2 if and only if F has more than i satisfying assignments if and only if $\langle F, i \rangle \in L_{\#\text{SAT}}$.

Now we show that every language $A \in$ PP is m-reducible to $L_{\#\text{SAT}}$. Let M witness the fact that $A \in$ PP. Again using the fact that the reduction f_M of the Cook-Levin Theorem is parsimonious, we observe that f_M maps $x \in \Sigma^*$ to a formula $F = f_M(x)$

---

[1] We can define an appropriate many-one reduction between functions in order to formalize this notion, but leave this to the reader.

such that $\#SAT(F) = \#acc_M(x)$. Let p bound M's running time and assume that M on x has $2^{p(|x|)}$ leaves. Then $A \leq_m^P L_{\#SAT}$ by the reduction that maps x to the pair $\langle f_M(x), 2^{p(|x|)-1} \rangle$.   □

The following theorem is due to Balcázar et al. [BBS86].

Theorem 11.2. $P^{PP} = P^{\#P}$

Proof. First we show that $P^{PP} \subseteq P^{\#P}$. To do this we show that oracle queries to a set A belonging to PP can be replaced by suitable queries to an oracle in #P. By Proposition 10.1, let M be a nondeterministic Turing machine with running time exactly $p(|x|)$ on every input x, where p is a polynomial, such that $x \in A \Leftrightarrow \#acc_M(x) > 2^{p(|x|)-1}$. In this way, we replace each query x to A with a query to #P to compute $\#acc_M(x)$.

To prove that $P^{\#P} \subseteq P^{PP}$, we let L be in $P^{\#P}$ and let M witness this fact. Assume that M's oracle is #SAT, a function that is complete for #P. From time to time, M may generate the encoding of a formula $F(x_1,\ldots,x_n)$ and query its oracle for the value of $\#SAT(F)$. We show how to replace each such query by appropriate queries to the language $L_{\#SAT}$ belonging to PP.

On query the encoding of a formula F, perform a binary search for values $i \in \{0,\ldots,2^n\}$ until finding the largest i such that $\langle F,i \rangle \in L_{\#SAT}$. For this value of i, F has exactly $i+1$ satisfying assignments. The oracle machine M continues its computation as if $i+1$ is the answer given by M's functional oracle.   □

In the rest of this chapter, we study two celebrated results, one by Valiant and Vazirani [VV86] and the other by Toda [Tod91].

Valiant and Vazirani observed that a characteristic of NP-complete problems is that instances of them may have zero, one, several, or exponentially many solutions. They ask whether the inherent difficulty in solving NP-complete problems is caused by the unpredictability of the number of solutions. In their paper they give a negative answer to this question in the following sense: We are given formulas of propositional logic that are either unsatisfiable or have exactly one satisfying assignment. We show that if we can determine in polynomial time whether such formulas are satisfiable, then $NP = RP$.

Toda's theorem, which builds on Valiant and Vazirani's result, shows that PP is hard for the polynomial hierarchy. Specifically, we will prove that $PH \subseteq P^{PP} = P^{\#P}$.

11.1 Unique Satisfiability

In this section we consider the unique satisfiability problem, which we formalize as a promise problem. Promise problems were introduced briefly in Chap. 7 in Homeworks 7.19 and 7.20. We repeat the definition here.

A *promise problem* [ESY84] (P,Q) has the form

instance x.
promise $P(x)$.
question $Q(x)$?

We assume that P and Q are decidable predicates. A deterministic Turing machine M that halts on every input *solves* (P,Q) if

$$\forall x[P(x) \Rightarrow [Q(x) \Leftrightarrow M(x) = \text{"yes"}]].$$

We do not care how M behaves on input x if $P(x)$ is false. If M solves (P,Q), then we call $L(M)$ a *solution* of (P,Q). In general, a promise problem will have many solutions, and we are usually interested in determining whether there is a solution with low complexity. We say that (P,Q) belongs to P if there is a solution L that belongs to P.

Note that a decision problem is a special case of a promise problem where the promise is universal, it holds for every problem instance. For example, SAT can be considered as the promise problem where the instance is a Boolean formula F, the promise $P(x)$ holds for every formula F, and the question is "Is F satisfiable?"

In this section we study the following promise problem Unique-SAT:

Unique-SAT
        instance a formula F of propositional logic
        promise F has either 0 or 1 satisfying assignments
        question Does F have a satisfying assignment?

To capture the complexity of Unique-SAT, we define the following randomized reduction $\leq_{rand}$ on promise problems:

Definition 11.4. Given two promise problems (P,Q) and (R,S), we say that $(P,Q) \leq_{rand} (R,S)$ if there is a probabilistic polynomial-time algorithm $\mathscr{A}$ and a polynomial p such that for all instances x, $|x| = n$,

$$P(x) \wedge Q(x) \Rightarrow R(\mathscr{A}(x)) \wedge S(\mathscr{A}(x)) \text{ with probability } \geq 1/p(n)$$

and
$$P(x) \wedge \neg Q(x) \Rightarrow S(\mathscr{A}(x)) \text{ with probability } 0.$$

Now we can state the theorem of Valiant and Vazirani.

Theorem 11.3. SAT $\leq_{rand}$ Unique-SAT

As is usual with promise problems, if $(P,Q) \leq_{rand} (R,S)$, and x is an instance for which the promise P(x) is false, then we don't care what properties $\mathscr{A}(x)$ might have. However, in the case of our Theorem, the promise is always true. If F is an instance of SAT that is satisfiable, then with probability at least $1/p(n)$, the reduction will output a formula G that has a unique satisfying assignment; if F is not satisfiable, then G is not satisfiable.

Before studying the proof of Theorem 11.3, we state the important corollaries.

Corollary 11.1. *If* Unique-SAT $\in$ P, *then* NP $=$ RP.

By Corollary 10.2, since RP $\subseteq$ BPP, if NP $=$ RP, then the polynomial hierarchy collapses. For the proof of Corollary 11.1, first observe that randomized reductions are defined so that if L is a solution of Unique-SAT, then SAT $\leq_{rand} L$. We are given that some solution L of Unique-SAT belongs to P. Then it follows from Theorem 10.3 that SAT is in the class RP. Since SAT is NP-complete, it follows that NP $=$ RP.

Corollary 11.2. NP $\subseteq$ RP$^{\oplus P}$ $\subseteq$ BPP$^{\oplus P}$.

Proof. First we observe that SAT $\leq_{rand}$ $\oplus$SAT: If $F \in$ SAT, then with probability $1/p(n)$ the formula G output by the $\leq_{rand}$ reduction has exactly one satisfying assignment and so is in $\oplus$SAT. If $F \notin$ SAT, then G is not satisfiable and hence is not in $\oplus$SAT.

By Theorem 10.3, SAT $\in$ RP$^{\oplus P}$, from which NP $\subseteq$ RP$^{\oplus P}$ follows immediately. The second inclusion is straightforward. $\Box$

The proof of Theorem 11.3 uses randomly chosen hash functions that are defined slightly differently from those in Sect. 10.4. Instead of the hash function h being given by a randomly chosen $m \times t$ Boolean matrix, the new hash function $l : \{0,1\}^t \rightarrow \{0,1\}^m$ is defined by the same size $m \times t$ Boolean matrix M and also a randomly chosen Boolean vector V of length m. For any $a \in \{0,1\}^t$, $l(a)$ is obtained by "multiplying" the m rows of l by a and then adding (mod 2) the resulting $m \times 1$ vector to the vector V.

Formally, for $1 \leq i \leq m$, the ith element of $l(a)$, $l(a)_i = \oplus_{1 \leq k \leq t}(M_{i,k} \wedge a_k) \oplus V_i$. We will sometimes abbreviate this equation as $Ma \oplus V = l(a)$.

The properties satisfied by l and h are similar and we list these now. Similar to Proposition 10.2, we have the following. (Note that we do not require that $a \neq 0$.)

Proposition 11.2. *Given a random hash function* $l : \Sigma^t \rightarrow \Sigma^m$ *(i.e., M and V are chosen uniformly at random) and string* $a \in \Sigma^t$,

$$\Pr[l(a) = 0] = 2^{-m}.$$

Homework 11.2 *Prove Proposition 11.2*

Random hash functions l shares the second property proved about h exactly.

Proposition 11.3. *Let* $l : \Sigma^t \rightarrow \Sigma^m$ *be a random hash function. Let* $x \neq y$, *where* $x, y \in \Sigma^t$. *Then,*

$$\Pr[l(x) = l(y)] = 2^{-m}.$$

Homework 11.3 *Prove Proposition 11.3 (as is done for Proposition 10.3.)*

Finally, l has one new property that is useful here. Families of random hash functions that satisfy this property are called *2-universal* [CW79].

Proposition 11.4. *For all t bit strings x and x' with $x \neq x'$ and any m bit strings y and y',*

$$\Pr[l(x) = y \wedge l(x') = y'] = 1/4^m.$$

Proof. First note that $\Pr[l(x) = y] = \Pr[Mx \oplus V = y] = \Pr[V = Mx \oplus y] = 1/2^m$, because the vector V is randomly chosen in Σ^m. Hence for any $x \neq x'$, y, and y',

$$\Pr[l(x) = y \wedge l(x') = y'] = \Pr_{M,V}[Mx \oplus V = y \text{ and } Mx' \oplus V = y']$$

$$= 1/2^m \cdot 1/2^m = 1/4^m.$$

$\square$

We require the following lemma.

Lemma 11.1. *Let $l : \{0,1\}^n \rightarrow \{0,1\}^m$ be a random hash function. Let S be a nonempty subset of $\{0,1\}^n$ and let m, where $2 \leq m \leq n+1$, be such that $2^{m-2} \leq \|S\| \leq 2^{m-1}$. Then $\Pr[\exists! x \in S \text{ with } l(x) = 0^m] \geq 1/8.$*[2]

Proof. By Proposition 11.2, For every $x \in S$,

$$\Pr[l(x) = 0^m] = 2^{-m}.$$

By Proposition 11.4, for $y \in S$ and $y \neq x$,

$$\Pr[l(x) = 0^m \wedge l(y) = 0^m] = 1/4^m.$$

Then, for $x \in S$,

$$\Pr[l(x) = 0^m \wedge \forall y \in (S - \{x\})l(y) \neq 0^m] \geq \Pr[l(x) = 0^m]$$

$$- \Sigma_{y \in S - \{x\}} \Pr[l(y) = l(x) = 0^m]$$

$$\geq 1/2^m - |S|/4^m$$

$$\geq 1/2^{m+1}. \tag{11.1}$$

The last inequality holds because $\|S\| \leq 2^{m-1}$. Finally,

$$\Pr[\exists! x \in S \text{ with } l(x) = 0^m] = \Sigma_{x \in S} \Pr[l(x) = 0^m \wedge \forall y \in (S - \{x\})l(y) \neq 0^m]$$

$$\geq \|S\|/2^{m+1} \text{(by line 11.1 above)}$$

$$\geq 1/8,$$

where the last inequality holds because $\|S\| \geq 2^{m-2}$.

$\square$

Now we are ready to present the proof of Theorem 11.3.

---

[2] $\exists! x$ is a quantifier denoting "there exists a unique x."

Proof. We have to describe the randomized algorithm $\mathscr{A}$. Let F be an instance of SAT with n variables. The algorithm randomly chooses $m \in \{2, \ldots, n+1\}$. Then $\mathscr{A}$ chooses a random hash function $l : \{0,1\}^n \to \{0,1\}^m$.

Now we observe the following, and this is the important step. Define the set

$$W_m = \{(F,l) \mid F \text{ and } l \text{ are chosen as above and for some } t \in \{0,1\}^n, F(t) \text{ and } l(t) = 0^m\}$$

The set W_m is in NP and so by the Cook–Levin Theorem, there is a formula G_m of propositional logic such that every assignment t satisfying $F(t)$ and $l(t) = 0^m$ corresponds to an assignment x that satisfies G_m. Furthermore, x is a unique assignment satisfying G_m if and only if t is unique.

Algorithm $\mathscr{A}$ outputs the formula G_m. Clearly, if F is not satisfiable, then neither is G_m.

Assume that F is satisfiable and let S be the set of satisfying assignments of F. With probability $1/n$, m has been chosen such that $2^{m-2} \leq \|S\| \leq 2^{m-1}$. By Lemma 11.1, there is a unique $t \in S$ such that $l(t) = 0^m$ with probability $1/8$. So with probability at least $1/8n$ the algorithm $\mathscr{A}$ outputs a formula with a unique satisfying assignment. This proves our theorem. □

11.2 Toda's Theorem

Here we prove that $\text{PH} \subseteq \text{P}^{\text{PP}} = \text{P}^{\#\text{P}}$. There are two substantial parts to the proof. The first part asserts that

$$\text{PH} \subseteq \text{BPP}^{\oplus \text{P}}$$

and the second part states that

$$\text{BPP}^{\oplus \text{P}} \subseteq \text{P}^{\#\text{P}}.$$

Observe that the first assertion strengthens Corollary 11.2 to apply not only to NP, but to the entire polynomial hierarchy. Thus, $\oplus \text{P}$ is as hard as the polynomial hierarchy albeit by randomized reductions. This assertion is proved by a not straightforward induction, whose basis step is given in Corollary 11.2, and which relies on results to be proved in the following section.

11.2.1 *Results on BPP and $\oplus$P*

Theorem 11.4. $\text{BPP}^{\text{BPP}^O} = \text{BPP}^O$, *for every oracle O.*

Theorem 11.4 tells us that BPP is self low, and is due to Ko [Ko82]. To keep the proof readable, we prove the unrelativized version and claim that the extension is straightforward.

Proof. We need to show that $\text{BPP}^{\text{BPP}} \subseteq \text{BPP}$. Let $L \in \text{BPP}^A$, where $A \in \text{BPP}$. We prove that $L \in \text{BPP}$.

Let q be an arbitrary strictly increasing polynomial. Observe that Theorem 10.5, the amplification theorem for BPP, relativizes to all oracles. So there is a probabilistic polynomial-time oracle Turing machine D such that

$$\Pr[D^A(x) = \chi_L(x)] > 1 - 2^{-q(|x|)}.$$

Let p be a polynomial such that, for any oracle, D on input x, queries at most $p(|x|)$ strings to the oracle.

We replace the oracle A by the set $A' = \Sigma^* \times A = \{(x,y) \mid y \in A\}$. Since A belongs to BPP, so does A'. Thus, by Theorem 10.5, there is a probabilistic polynomial-time Turing machine N such that for input words u, $\Pr[N(u) = \chi_{A'}(u)] > 1 - 2^{-q(|u|)}$. Also we replace the oracle Turing machine D by oracle Turing machine D', where D' on input x simulates D on input x, substituting for each query y to A, the query (x,y) to A'. (Notice that each query of D' on input x is at least as long as the input x.)

Finally, let M be a probabilistic polynomial-time Turing machine that on an input word x simulates D' on x, except that when D' makes a query u to the oracle, instead, M simulates N on u to decide the oracle answer.

Probabilistic Turing machine D' on input x makes at most $p(|x|)$ queries, and for every query u, N on input u makes an error with probability at most $2^{-q(|u|)} \leq 2^{-q(|x|)}$, because $|u| \geq |x|$ and q is strictly increasing. For every input x, the probability that the computation of M differs from that of $D'^{A'}$ is at most $p(|x|)2^{-q(|x|)}$. Since $2^{-q(|x|)}$ bounds the error probability of $D^A(x)$, the error probability of M is bounded by $p(|x|)2^{-q(|x|)} + 2^{-q(|x|)} = (p(|x|)+1)/2^{-q(|x|)}$, which for sufficiently large x is less than $1/4$. Hence, $L \in \text{BPP}$. $\qquad\square$

Corollary 11.3.

$$\text{BPP} = \text{P}^{\text{BPP}} = \text{BPP}^{\text{BPP}}.$$

Just observe that $\text{BPP} \subseteq \text{P}^{\text{BPP}} \subseteq \text{BPP}^{\text{BPP}} \subseteq \text{BPP}$. We turn to some facts about $\oplus \text{P}$.

Proposition 11.5.

1. A language $L \in \oplus\text{P}$ if and only if there exists a polynomial p and a language $A \in \text{P}$ such that for every $x \in \Sigma^*$,

$$x \in L \Leftrightarrow \|\{y \in \Sigma^{p(|x|)} \mid \langle x,y \rangle \in A\}\| \text{ is odd.} \qquad (11.2)$$

2. The class $\oplus\text{P}$ is closed under complement.

Proof. Let L be in $\oplus\text{P}$ and let M be a nondeterministic polynomial-time Turing machine such that for every $x \in \Sigma^*$, $x \in L \Leftrightarrow \#acc_M(x)$ is odd. Let R be the binary relation defined in (6.1) of Sect. 6.1:

$$R(x,y) \Leftrightarrow [y \text{ is an accepting computation of } M \text{ on input } x].$$

Then there is a polynomial p such that for every $x \in \Sigma^*$,

$$x \in L \Leftrightarrow \|\{y \mid |y| \leq p(|x|) \text{ and } R(x,y)\}\| \text{ is odd.}$$

By a simple padding technique (given in the proof of Theorem 6.8), we have $y \in \Sigma^{p(|x|)}$ for every pair such that $R(x,y)$. We simply define $A = \{\langle x,y \rangle \mid R(x,y)\}$ to obtain Proposition 11.2. This proves the first item from left to right. The proof from right to left is obvious.

To prove the second item, again we let L be in $\oplus P$ and let M be a nondeterministic polynomial-time Turing machine such that for every $x \in \Sigma^*$, $x \in L \Leftrightarrow \#acc_M(x)$ is odd. Construct M^c to be a nondeterministic Turing machine that on every input x has exactly one more accepting computation than $M(x)$. So the parity of $\#acc_M(x)$ is always opposite the parity of $\#acc_{M^c}(x)$. In particular, for every x $x \in \Sigma^*$, $x \in \overline{L} \Leftrightarrow \#acc_{M^c}(x)$ is odd. Thus, $\overline{L} \in \oplus P$. $\qquad \square$

Proposition 11.5 holds relative to all oracles, as do all the results in this section whether explicitly stated or not. The next theorem was shown by Papadimitriou and Zachos [PZ83].

Theorem 11.5. $\oplus P^{\oplus P^O} = \oplus P^O$, *for every oracle O.*

Proof. Let $L \in \oplus P^{\oplus P}$. There is a nondeterministic polynomial-time oracle Turing machine M and a set $A \in \oplus P$ such that for every x, $x \in L$ if and only if the number of accepting paths of M^A on input x is odd. Let N_0 witness the fact that $A \in \oplus P$ and, by Proposition 11.5, let N_1 witness the fact that $\overline{A} \in \oplus P$. We need to design a nondeterministic polynomial-time Turing machine M' to witness $L \in \oplus P$. Let M' on input x simulate M on x. However, whenever M enters the query state with a query q to the oracle A, instead, M' does the following. First, M' at this configuration nondeterministically selects one of two paths. One path intuitively guesses that $q \in A$ and the other that $q \in \overline{A}$. Formally, the first path enters a simulation of N_0 on input q and if this simulation accepts, then M' continues its simulation of M in the YES state. Similarly, the second path enters a simulation of N_1 on input q and if this simulation accepts, then M' continues its simulation of M in the NO state. The machine M' accepts along a path if and only if the simulation of M accepts and each simulation of N_0 and N_1 accepts.

Now we have to see that $x \in L \Leftrightarrow \#acc_{M'}(x)$ is odd. Suppose that $x \in L$ and that τ is an accepting computation path of M with oracle A. If q is a query in τ such that $q \in A$, then N_0 has an odd number of accepting simulations, all of which will return to M'. Observe that N_1 is contributing an even number of accepting simulations so that the total number of accepting simulation for this query is odd. Similarly, if $q \in \overline{A}$, then N_1 has an odd number of accepting simulations and N_0 has an even number of simulations. The correct simulations that correspond to τ contribute in total an odd number of simulations, because a product of odd numbers is an odd number. A product of numbers is odd if and only if each term in the product is odd. Hence we can observe that incorrect simulations corresponding to τ contribute even numbers of accepting computations, even if only one incorrect choice of N_b,

$b \in \{0,1\}$, is made. Thus, the total number of accepting computations of M' that correspond to τ is odd. Furthermore, since we are assuming that $x \in L$, there are an odd number of accepting computation paths of M with oracle A, and the sum of an odd number of odd numbers is again odd.

If $x \notin L$, then M^A on x has an even number of accepting computations, from which, it follows that M' on x has in total an even number of accepting computations. Therefore, $L \in \oplus P$. $\qquad\square$

Theorem 11.6. $\oplus P^{BPP} \subseteq BPP^{\oplus P}$.

Proof. Let $L \in \oplus P^{BPP}$. By part 1 of Proposition 11.5, there is a polynomial p and a language $A \in P^{BPP}$ such that for every $x \in \Sigma^*$,

$$x \in L \Leftrightarrow \|\{y \in \Sigma^{p(|x|)} \mid \langle x,y \rangle \in A\}\| \text{ is odd.}$$

By Corollary 11.3, $A \in BPP$. By the fact that $BPP = BP \cdot P$ and the amplification theorem for the BP operator, we have the following: Let $r(n) = p(n) + 2$, for all n. There exists a polynomial q and a language $B \in P$ such that for every u,

$$\Pr_{v \in \Sigma^{q(|u|)}} [u \in A \Leftrightarrow \langle u,v \rangle \in B] \geq 1 - 2^{-r(|u|)}. \tag{11.3}$$

Let s be the polynomial such that, for every $x \in \Sigma^*$ and $y \in \Sigma^{p(|x|)}$, $s(|x|) = q(|\langle x,y \rangle|)$. Define

$$C = \langle x,v \rangle \mid v \in \Sigma^{s(|x|)} \wedge \|\{y \in \Sigma^{(p(|x|))} \mid \langle \langle x,y \rangle, v \rangle \in B\}\| \text{ is odd}.$$

Clearly, $C \in \oplus P$. For each $x \in \Sigma^*$, let

$$a(x) = \|\{y \in \Sigma^{p(|x|)} \mid \langle x,y \rangle \in A\}\|.$$

For each $x \in \Sigma^*$ and $v \in \Sigma^{s(|x|)}$, let

$$c(\langle x,v \rangle) = \|\{y \in \Sigma^{p(|x|)} \mid \langle \langle x,y \rangle, v \rangle \in B\}\|.$$

By (11.3), for every $x \in \Sigma^*$,

$$\Pr_{v \in \Sigma^{s(|x|)}} [\forall y \in \Sigma^{p(|x|)} (\langle x,y \rangle \in A \Leftrightarrow \langle \langle x,y \rangle, v \rangle \in B)] \geq 1 - 2^{p(|x|)} 2^{-r(s(|x|))}$$

$$\geq 1 - 2^{p(|x|) - p(s(|x|)) - 2}$$

$$\geq 1 - 2^{-2} = 3/4.$$

It follows that

$$\Pr_{v \in \Sigma^{s(|x|)}} [a(x) = c(\langle x,v \rangle)] \geq 3/4.$$

Thus, for every $x \in \Sigma^*$, for at least 3/4 of $v \in \Sigma^{s(|x|)}$, $a(x)$ is odd if and only if $c(\langle x, v \rangle)$ is odd. Now $a(x)$ is odd if and only if $x \in L$ and $c(\langle x, v \rangle)$ is odd if and only if $\langle x, v \rangle \in C$. Therefore, for every $x \in \Sigma^*$,

$$\Pr_{v \in \Sigma^{s(|x|)}} [x \in L \Leftrightarrow \langle x, v \rangle \in C] \geq 3/4,$$

and so $L \in \mathrm{BPP}^{\oplus \mathrm{P}}$.   □

11.2.2 The First Part of Toda's Theorem

Now we prove the first part of Toda's Theorem, that $\mathrm{PH} \subseteq \mathrm{BPP}^{\oplus \mathrm{P}}$. We know already, by Corollary 11.2, that $\mathrm{NP} \subseteq \mathrm{BPP}^{\oplus \mathrm{P}}$, and this is the basis step of the following induction argument. It is important to observe here that the proof of Corollary 11.2 relativizes to all oracles – this observation is critical for application in the next proof.

Theorem 11.7. $\mathrm{PH} \subseteq \mathrm{BPP}^{\oplus \mathrm{P}}$.

Proof. We show for each $i \geq 1$, that $\Sigma_i^{\mathrm{P}} \subseteq \mathrm{BPP}^{\oplus \mathrm{P}}$. The basis step, $i = 1$, is given by Corollary 11.2. For the induction step, we assume as induction hypothesis that $\Sigma_i^{\mathrm{P}} \subseteq \mathrm{BPP}^{\oplus \mathrm{P}}$ and we prove that $\Sigma_{i+1}^{\mathrm{P}} \subseteq \mathrm{BPP}^{\oplus \mathrm{P}}$. The argument follows:

$$\Sigma_{i+1}^{\mathrm{P}} = \mathrm{NP}^{\Sigma_i^{\mathrm{P}}}, \text{ by definition,}$$

$$\subseteq \mathrm{NP}^{\mathrm{BPP}^{\oplus \mathrm{P}}}, \text{ by the induction hypothesis,}$$

$$\subseteq \mathrm{BPP}^{\oplus \mathrm{P}^{\mathrm{BPP}^{\oplus \mathrm{P}}}}, \text{ by Corollary 11.2, relativized,}$$

$$\subseteq \mathrm{BPP}^{\mathrm{BPP}^{\oplus \mathrm{P}^{\oplus \mathrm{P}}}}, \text{ by Theorem 11.6,}$$

$$\subseteq \mathrm{BPP}^{\oplus \mathrm{P}}, \text{ by Theorems 11.4 and 11.5.}$$ □

11.2.3 The Second Part of Toda's Theorem

We complete our exposition of Toda's Theorem by proving the following theorem.

Theorem 11.8. $\mathrm{BPP}^{\oplus \mathrm{P}} \subseteq \mathrm{P}^{\#\mathrm{P}}$.

Proof. Let $L \in \mathrm{BPP}^{\oplus \mathrm{P}}$. Then there is a set $A \in \oplus \mathrm{P}$ and a constant $k \geq 1$ such that for all x,

$$\Pr_{y \in \{0,1\}^{|x|^k}} [x \in L \Leftrightarrow \langle x, y \rangle \in A] \geq 3/4.^3$$

---

[3] The reader should verify this assertion.

Let M be a nondeterministic Turing machine such that for every string z, $z \in A$ if and only if $\#acc_M(z)$ is odd.

Now consider the particular polynomial $p(x) = 3x^4 + 4x^3$. Specifically we define inductively

$$\tau_0(z) = z,$$

and for $i \geq 1$,

$$\tau_i(z) = 3(\tau_{i-1}(z))^4 + 4(\tau_{i-1}(z))^3.$$

These polynomials have the following useful property.

Claim 11.1. For every $i \geq 0$ and every $z \in N$,

1. If z is odd, then $\tau_i(z) \equiv -1 \pmod{2^{2^i}}$.
2. If z is even, then $\tau_i(z) \equiv 0 \pmod{2^{2^i}}$.

Proof. For the base case $i = 0$, $2^{2^0} = 2$; if z is even, then z is a multiple of 2, and if z is odd, then $z + 1$ is a multiple of 2.

Let $i = i_0$, for some $i_0 \geq 1$, and assume that the claim is true for all i such that $0 \leq i < i_0$. First we suppose that z is even. By the induction hypothesis, $\tau_{i-1}(z)$ is divisible by $2^{2^{i-1}}$. Note that $\tau_i(z)$ is divisible by $(\tau_{i-1}(z))^2$ and $2^{2^i} = (2^{2^{i-1}})^2$. So $\tau_i(z)$ is divisible by 2^{2^i}.

Suppose that z is odd. By the induction hypothesis, for some integer m, $\tau_{i-1}(z) = m2^{2^{i-1}} - 1$. Then[4],

$$
\begin{aligned}
\tau_i(z) &= 3\left(m2^{2^{i-1}} - 1\right)^4 + 4\left(m2^{2^{i-1}} - 1\right)^3 \\
&= 3\left[m^4 2^{4(2^{i-1})} - 4m^3 2^{3(2^{i-1})} + 6m^2 2^{2(2^{i-1})} - 4m2^{2^{i-1}} + 1\right] \\
&\quad + 4\left[m^3 2^{3(2^{i-1})} - 3m^2 2^{2(2^{i-1})} + 3m2^{2^{i-1}} - 1\right] \\
&= 3m^4 2^{4(2^{i-1})} - 12m^3 2^{3(2^{i-1})} + 18m^2 2^{2(2^{i-1})} - 12m2^{2^{i-1}} + 3 \\
&\quad + 4m^3 2^{3(2^{i-1})} - 12m^2 2^{2(2^{i-1})} + 12m2^{2^{i-1}} - 4 \\
&= 3m^4 2^{4(2^{i-1})} - 8m^3 2^{3(2^{i-1})} + 6m^2 2^{2(2^{i-1})} - 1.
\end{aligned}
$$

Now observe that

$$
\begin{aligned}
2^{3(2^{i-1})} &= 2^{2(2^{i-1})} \cdot 2^{2^{i-1}} \\
&= 2^{2^i} \cdot 2^{2^{i-1}}
\end{aligned}
$$

----

[4]Recall that

$$(a+b)^3 = a^3 + 3a^2 b + 3ab^2 + b^3$$

and

$$(a+b)^4 = a^4 + 4a^3 b + 6a^2 b^2 + 4ab^3 + b^4.$$

and

$$2^{4(2^{i-1})} = 2^{3(2^{i-1})} \cdot 2^{2^{i-1}}$$
$$= 2^{2^i} \cdot 2^{2^{i-1}} \cdot 2^{2^{i-1}}$$
$$= 2^{2^i} \cdot 2^{2^i}.$$

So

$$\tau_i(z) = 2^{2^i}\left(3m^4 2^{2^i} - 8m^3 2^{2^{i-1}} + 6m^2\right) - 1$$

Thus the Claim holds for odd z □

For every $x \in \{0,1\}^*$, define $l_x = \lceil \log |x|^k + 1 \rceil$ (the number of bits to write $|x|^k$ in binary plus one). Define $r_x(z) = (\tau_{l_x}(z))^2$, and define $g(x) = r_x(\#acc_M(x))$. An easy induction argument shows that $r_x(z)$ is a polynomial of degree $2^{4l_x} = 2^{4\lceil \log |x|^k + 1\rceil}$, which is a polynomial in $|x|$. All of the coefficients of $r_x(z)$ are nonnegative, because they start out nonnegative and the rule that defines $\tau_i(z)$ from $\tau_{i-1}(z)$ preserves this property. Since the number of terms in $r_x(z)$ is bounded by the degree of $r_x(z)$, which is a polynomial in $|x|$, and we compute $r_x(z)$ inductively, starting with $\tau_0(z)$, we see that $r_x(z)$ is polynomial-time computable.

Claim 11.2. $g(x) \in \#P$

Proof. The following nondeterministic Turing machine G has the property that $\#acc_G(x) = g(x)$. Machine G on input x performs the following steps:

1. G computes

$$r_x(z) = a_0 z^0 + a_1 z^1 + \cdots + a_m z^m \left(m = 2^{4l_x}\right),$$

2. G computes the set $I = \{i \mid 0 \le i \le m \wedge a_i \ne 0\}$,
3. G nondeterministically selects $i \in I$,
4. G nondeterministically selects d such that $1 \le d \le a_i$,
5. G simulates M on input x i times. That is, after simulation number 1, each accepting path is used for simulation number 2, and so on.

G accepts if and only if M accepts for each of the simulations. □

By Claim 11.1, the following conditions hold:

1. If $x \in A$, then $\#acc_M(x)$ is odd, so $g(x)$ is of the form $m2^{|x|^k+1} + 1$, for some m.
2. If $x \notin A$, then $\#acc_M(x)$ is even, so $g(x)$ is of the form $m2^{|x|^k+1}$, for some m.

Define

$$h(x) = \sum_{|y|=|x|^k} g(\langle x, y \rangle).$$

Consider the nondeterministic polynomial-time Turing machine H that on input x guesses $y \in \{0,1\}^{|x|^k}$ and simulates G on input $\langle x, y \rangle$. Then, $\#acc_H(x) = h(x)$. So $h \in \#P$. To complete the proof of our theorem, we need to see that with one query to $h(x)$ we can determine membership of $x \in L$: The important observation, using Conditions 1 and 2, is that the lowest $|x|^k + 1$ bits of $h(x)$ contain the number I of $y \in \{0,1\}^{|x|^k}$ such that $\langle x, y \rangle \in A$.[5] If $x \in L$, then $I \geq 3/4 \cdot 2^{|x|^k}$, and if $x \notin L$, then $I \leq 1/4 \cdot 2^{|x|^k}$. Hence, $L \in P^{\#P}$. $\square$

Corollary 11.4. $PH \subseteq P^{PP} = P^{\#P}$.

11.3   Additional Homework Problems

Homework 11.4 *Let* PF *denote the family of all polynomial-time computable functions. Prove that* $\#P = PF$ *if and only if* $PP = P$.

Homework 11.5 *Prove that* $P^{\#P} \subseteq BPP^{NP}$ *implies that* $\Sigma_3^P = \Pi_3^P$.

Homework 11.6 *Prove the following analog of the Karp–Lipton Theorem, Theorem 8.3, for counting classes: We say that a circuit C computes #3SAT on n variables if for all 3CNF formulas F of n variables, $C(F)$ outputs the number of satisfying assignments of F. Show that if #3SAT has a polynomial size family of circuits computing it, then* $P^{\#P} = \Sigma_2^P$. *Hint: First show that*

$$L = \{(C, 1^n) \mid C \text{ computes #3SAT on } n \text{ variables}\}$$

is in co-NP. *Then use this fact to show that any set $S \in P^{\#P}$ is included in* Σ_2^P.

---

[5]To see this, note that a 1 is added to the low order bits of the sum whenever $g(\langle x, y \rangle)$ is odd, and in either case (odd or even), everything else added to the sum is at least $2^{|x|^k+1}$, so does not affect the low order bits.

Chapter 12
Interactive Proof Systems

Recall the characterization of NP as the class of languages A having a polynomial-time verifier (Corollary 6.1). The verifier is capable of checking that a string is a short (polynomial-length) proof that an element is in the NP set A. Furthermore the verifier works in polynomial time. We do not put any restriction on how the verifier obtains the proof itself, it is sufficient that the proof exists. For example, the proof might be provided by a powerful prover with unrestricted computational power.

Consider a generalization of these ideas where we allow a dialogue (or protocol) between the verifier and a prover to decide language membership. As before there is no restriction placed on the computational power of the prover, and the verifier is restricted to be only polynomially powerful. We add one more ingredient to this mix by allowing randomization. That is, we allow the verifier, whose time is polynomially limited, to use a random sequence of bits and require only that he be convinced with high likelihood, and not with complete certainty, of the membership claim being made. So the verifier is a probabilistic polynomial-time Turing machine with acceptance probability bounded away from 1/2, i.e. a Monte Carlo algorithm.

As this model generalizes that of the NP verifier, it is clear that as before NP problems are those for which membership can be proved by the prover by giving the verifier a polynomial length "proof" and the verifier validating that proof in deterministic polynomial time. The model also easily captures the class BPP as any BPP problem can be decided by the probabilistic polynomial time verifier without any information from the prover.

12.1 The Formal Model

An interactive proof system (P, V) is a protocol (i.e., two-party game) between a prover P and a verifier V. The goal of the protocol is to decide membership in a language L with small probability of error. For any input $x \in L$, an honest prover should be able to convince the verifier that x is in L with high probability. On the

S. Homer and A.L. Selman, *Computability and Complexity Theory*,
Texts in Computer Science, DOI 10.1007/978-1-4614-0682-2_12,
© Springer Science+Business Media, LLC 2011

other hand, if x is not in L, then no prover, including a dishonest prover, should be able to wrongly convince V that x is in L except with low probability.

Definition 12.1. An *interactive proof system* consists of a pair of interacting algorithms (i.e., Turing machines) (P, V). Here V is a probabilistic polynomial-time computable function and P is an arbitrary computable function. Thus, P is computationally unbounded.

The function P takes two inputs, the input string x and the *history* of messages that P and V send to each other as defined below. The function V takes three inputs, the input x, the message history, and a randomly chosen string, which is not known to P. The protocol proceeds through a number of *rounds* of communication between P and V. It ends when V either accepts x or rejects x. Each round consists of a pair of messages, one, y_i, passed from P to V, and the other, z_i, passed from V to P. All of the messages as well as the number of rounds of communication are bounded by some fixed polynomial in $|x|$. The first message, y_1, depends only on the input x to P. That is, $P(x) = y_1$. Similarly, P's subsequent messages y_j depend on the input and the previous messages passed between P and V. That is,

$$y_j = P(x, y_1, z_1, \ldots, y_{j-1}, z_{j-1}).$$

The verifier's messages, z_j, to the prover depend on the input x, the previous messages passed between P and V, and a polynomially long random string r_j that V uses in round j. That is,

$$z_j = V(x, y_1, z_1, \ldots, y_{j-1}, z_{j-1}, y_j, r_j).$$

The random string r_j is private and is not known by the prover.

The protocol halts when at the end of some round, the verifier outputs either "accept" or "reject" as its message. The *length* of a protocol is the number of rounds it takes before it halts.

Definition 12.2. A language L is in the class IP if there is a polynomial-round interactive proof system (P, V) such for each input string x, the following properties hold:

Completeness   If $x \in L$, then (P, V) on input x accepts with probability $\geq 2/3$.
Soundness   If $x \notin L$, then for every prover P', (P', V) accepts with probability $\leq 1/3$.

Completeness expresses that there is a prover that for any $x \in L$, causes the protocol to accept with high probability. Soundness expresses that for any $x \notin L$, no prover will cause the protocol to accept with high probability.

By the observations at the beginning of this chapter, we see that NP $\subseteq$ IP and that BPP $\subseteq$ IP. The full power of IP will become clear in remaining sections of this chapter.

The choice of parameters $2/3$ and $1/3$ in the definitions of completeness and soundness are convenient but somewhat arbitrary, as the following proposition states.

Proposition 12.1. *Let $L \in$ IP. For every polynomial q, there is an interactive proof system for L that achieves error probability at most $2^{-q(n)}$, where n is the length of the input x.*

The proof follows from Lemma 10.1 and is nearly identical to the proof of Theorem 10.5.

The following definition refines this notation by taking into account the number of rounds in a protocol.

Definition 12.3. Let m be an integer-valued function. Then IP$[m]$ is the class of languages that have an interactive proof system that for each input word x uses no more than $m(|x|)$ rounds.

Of course, m cannot be greater than some polynomial-bounded function.

Before continuing, we should note that interactive proof systems were introduced by Goldwasser et al. [GMR89], and an important variation, which we will discuss also, is due to Bábai [Bab85].

12.2   The Graph Non-Isomorphism Problem

We describe an interactive proof system for the graph non-isomorphism problem

$$\text{GNI} = \{(G_1, G_2) \mid G_1 \not\cong G_2\},$$

which we studied in Sect. 10.5. This interesting example is due to Goldreich, Micali, and Widgerson [GMW86]. This problem is in co-NP and unknown to be in NP, but we proved membership in BP $\cdot$ NP (Theorem 10.10). Consider the requirements for a protocol for GNI. We are given two graphs G_1 and G_2 as input and would like to determine whether the two graphs are non-isomorphic. We assume (without loss of generality) that the two graphs have the same number of vertices and edges, and that the vertex set of both graphs is just $\{1, 2, \dots, n\}$. Consider the following two-round protocol:

Round 1.   This stage starts with an empty first move by the prover. Then the verifier randomly chooses one of the two graphs, G_d, where $d \in \{1, 2\}$, and chooses also a random permutation $\rho \in S_n$ of the vertices of G_d. Here S_n is the symmetric group of degree n. (That is S_n is the set of all permutations on $\{1, 2, \dots, n\}$). The verifier keeps its choices private, but sends the prover the graph $H = \rho(G_d)$.

Round 2.   The prover sends a value $i \in \{1, 2\}$ to the verifier. The verifier accepts if and only if $i = d$.

If G_1 and G_2 are not isomorphic, then a prover will be able to distinguish isomorphic copies of G_1 from isomorphic copies of G_2. However, if G_1 and G_2 are isomorphic, then G_d is isomorphic to both of these graphs, and the prover's answer will be distributed identically to a random isomorphic copy of either graph.

Now we prove correctness and soundness of this protocol.

Theorem 12.1. GNI $\in$ IP[2].

Proof. We begin by noting that the verifier can be implemented in probabilistic polynomial time. (On the other hand, the honest prover has to decide isomorphism between two graphs, and it is an open question whether this can be done in polynomial time.)

We prove completeness: Assume that G_1 and G_2 are not isomorphic and that the prover acts correctly according to the protocol. Then exactly one of these graphs is isomorphic to G_d and the other graph is not. Thus, i found by the prover in Round 2 is unique. Hence d chosen in Round 1 is equal to i, and so the verifier accepts. (The verifier accepts with probability 1. This is called *perfect completeness*. An interesting result states that if a language has an interactive proof system, then it has one with perfect completeness [GMS87].)

Now we prove soundness: Assume that $G_1 \simeq G_2$. The graph H sent by the verifier to the prover is isomorphic to both G_1 and G_2. For each $d \in \{1,2\}$, let

$$T_d = \{\sigma \in S_n \mid \sigma G_d = H\}.$$

The permutation ρ that the verifier chose to select H belongs to T_d. Let τ be an isomorphism between G_1 and G_2, so that $G_1 = \tau G_2$. For every $\sigma \in T_1$, the permutation $\sigma\tau \in T_2$, because $\sigma\tau G_2 = \sigma G_1 = H$. So τ is a one-one mapping from T_1 to T_2 and, similarly, τ^{-1} is a one-one mapping from T_2 to T_1. Therefore, $\|T_1\| = \|T_2\|$.

Bayes rule says that

$$\Pr[d = 1 \mid \rho(G_d) = H] = Pr[\rho(G_d) = H \mid d = 1](\Pr[d = 1]/\Pr[\rho(G_d) = H]).$$

Now

$$\begin{aligned}
\Pr[\rho(G_d) = H \mid d = 1] &= Pr[\rho(G_1) = H] \\
&= \Pr[\rho \in T_1] \\
&= \Pr[\rho \in T_2] \\
&= \Pr[\rho(G_d) = H \mid d = 2].
\end{aligned}$$

Hence,

$$\begin{aligned}
\Pr[\rho(G_d) = H \mid d = 1]&(\Pr[d = 1]/\Pr[\rho(G_d) = H]) \\
&= \Pr[\rho(G_d) = H \mid d = 2](\Pr[d = 2]/\Pr[\rho(G_d) = H]).
\end{aligned}$$

Since $(\Pr[d = 1] = \Pr[d = 2])$, we obtain

$$Pr[d = 1 \mid \rho(G_d) = H] = \Pr[d = 2 \mid \rho(G_d) = H].$$

This last equality says that, given $\rho(G_d)(= H)$, d is equally likely to be 1 or 2. Hence even a cheating prover cannot convince the verifier he knows the value of d with any probability greater than 1/2.

By Proposition 12.1, it suffices to obtain this bound. $\square$

Observe that this protocol works precisely because the choices made by the verifier are private. That is, the verifier's random strings are not communicated to the prover.

12.3 Arthur-Merlin Games

Now we turn our attention to interactive protocols where the random strings are exactly what the verifier communicates to the prover. It is harder to design such protocols, but it permits us to define and study complexity classes just beyond NP. These are the interactive proof systems introduced by Bábai [Bab85] and Bábai and Moran [BM88].

Essentially, an *Arthur-Merlin* protocol is an interactive proof system that is played by Arthur (the verifier), a probabilistic polynomial-time machine, and by a powerful prover called Merlin, a computationally unbounded Turing machine. Arthur can use random bits, but these bits are public, i.e., Merlin can see them and move accordingly.

Given an input string x, Merlin tries to convince Arthur that x belongs to some language L. The game consists of a predetermined finite number of moves with Arthur and Merlin moving alternately. In each move one of the players communicates a message to the other player. Arthur's move depends on his random string, which itself is communicated to Merlin. After the last move, Arthur either accepts or does not accept x. It is important to realize that an Arthur-Merlin game is a special case of an interactive proof system. Thus, every language that has an Arthur-Merlin game has an interactive proof system, i.e., belongs to the class IP.

We distinguish the cases where Arthur moves first from the cases where Merlin makes the first move. The *length* of the game is the total number of moves. Let $m(n)$ be a polynomially-bounded function of n, where n is the length of the input string x. Languages accepted by Arthur-Merlin games of length $\leq m(n)$ where Arthur moves first form the classes $\mathrm{AM}[m]$ and games where Merlin moves first form the classes $\mathrm{MA}[m]$. In particular,

$$\mathrm{AM}[poly] = \mathrm{MA}[poly] = \bigcup \{\mathrm{AM}[n^k] \mid k > 0\}.$$

The next definition summarizes some of the important details.

Definition 12.4 ([Bab85,BM88]). A language L is in AM$[m]$ (respectively MA$[m]$) if for every string x of length n

- The game consists of m moves
- Arthur (resp., Merlin) moves first
- After the last move, Arthur behaves deterministically to either accept or not accept the input string
- If $x \in L$, then there exists a sequence of moves by Merlin that leads to the acceptance of x by Arthur with probability at least $2/3$
- If $x \notin L$ then for all possible moves of Merlin, the probability that Arthur accepts x is less than $1/3$.

For $m(n) = k$, where k is a constant, strings of length k denote the sequence of players. For example, AM$[3] = AMA$ and MA$[1] = M$. It should be clear that MA$[1] = $ NP and AM$[1] = $ BPP. Bábai [Bab85] proved that MA $\subseteq$ AM. The class AM is especially important, because Bábai and Moran [BM88] proved for all constants $k > 1$, that AM$[k]$ is the same as AM$[2] = $ AM. Fortunately, we have studied the class AM already, for the class BP $\cdot$ NP is merely an equivalent formulation of AM. We leave the proof of this important observation as a homework exercise.

Theorem 12.2.
$$AM = BP \cdot NP.$$

Homework 12.1 *Provide a proof of Theorem 12.2.*

In light of Theorem 12.2, the following Corollary summarizes what we know from Chap. 10 about the class AM.

Corollary 12.1.
$$NP \cup BPP \subseteq AM \subseteq \Pi_2^P$$

and
$$GNI \in AM.$$

As a consequence, it follows immediately that GNI $\in$ IP without using the protocol of Sect. 12.2. However, that protocol is elegant and helps our understanding of these protocols.

Let us consider the reverse situation: Goldwasser and Sipser [GS89] showed that any interactive proof system with a polynomial number m rounds can be simulated by a $2m + 4$-move Arthur-Merlin protocol. Therefore, we have the important result that
$$IP = IP[poly] = AM[poly].$$

Also, from the two-round protocol for GNI that we studied in Sect. 12.2, we conclude that GNI has an eight-move Arthur-Merlin protocol. Then, by the result of Bábai and Moran [BM88], it follows that GNI $\in$ AM. Since we are not studying the proofs of Goldwasser and Sipser and of Bábai and Moran, in this exposition we elected to prove directly that GNI belongs to AM.

12.4   IP Is Included in PSPACE

Our goal is to prove that IP = PSPACE, one of the central results of computational complexity. In this section we demonstrate that IP $\subseteq$ PSPACE. This is considered to be the easy direction.

Theorem 12.3. IP $\subseteq$ PSPACE.

Proof. Let A belong to IP. Then there is a verifier V, honest prover P, and appropriate protocol (P,V) for A. Without loss of generality we assume that each run of the protocol lasts exactly q rounds and ends with V either accepting or rejecting. Here q is the value of a polynomial that depends on the length of the input word x. We want to find a PSPACE-algorithm that decides A.

We define a *communication history* H_k of the protocol $(P,V)(x)$ for k ($1 \leq k \leq q$) rounds to be a sequence Y_k of messages $(y_1, z_1, \ldots y_{k-1}, z_{k-1}, y_k)$ or Z_k of the form $(y_1, z_1, \ldots y_{k-1}, z_{k-1}, y_k, z_k)$ which P and V generate and send to each other during the first k rounds of the IP protocol. We define $H_0 = Z_0 = ()$, the empty list. Recall that y_i, which is output by P, depends on earlier message strings and on x, while z_i, which is output by V, depends on earlier messages, on x and on the random string r used by V during its computation.

The last message z_q is the result of V's computation after receiving its last message y_q from P and equals either accept or reject. Furthermore, we assume here that V has one random string r, of length polynomial in $|x|$, and that in each round V uses the next part of that string (earlier denoted r_i) as part of its computation.

We prove that A is in PSPACE by exhibiting a PSPACE algorithm that on input x simulates V and calculates the maximum probability w that any prover P can convince V that $x \in A$. That is, $w = \max_P \Pr_r [(P,V)(x) \text{ accepts}]$.

This strategy suffices as the value w will be at least $2/3$ if in fact $x \in A$ and at most $1/3$ if not.

In order to calculate w in PSPACE, we define a function W, also in PSPACE, which takes as input a communication history H_k. W's output is the maximum probability over all provers P that $(P,V)(x)$ accepts when the initial messages are those in H_k.

We want to define W so that the following properties hold:

$$W(H_k) = \max_P \Pr_r [(P,V)(x) \text{ accepts starting with } H_k]$$

$$= (\text{by definition}) \Pr[V \text{ accepts } x \text{ starting with } H_k].$$

Note: In the case that no prover P and no string r results in $(P,V)(x)$ accepting starting with H_k, then we define $W(H_k) = 0$

Definition 12.5. We now inductively define $W(H_k)$ for any communication history H_k. The definition is given recursively in $2q + 1$ steps starting with $k = q$ and ending with $k = 0$.

Base case   For a communication history Z_q we define a function $W(Z_q) = 1$ if for some string r, Z_q is consistent with V's messages when computing with random string r, and $z_q = $ accept. Otherwise let $W(Z_q) = 0$.

Inductive case   There are two subcases.

The communication history is a Y_k sequence   In this case we define $W(Y_k) = E_k\{W(Z_k)\}$, where the expected value E_k is the weighted average of the previously defined values $W(Z_k)$ weighted by the probability that V sent the messages in the communication stream that produces the value z_k, and where $Z_k = $ the message list with z_k appended to the Y_k list. (We denote this message list as $Z_k = (Y_k|z_k)$.)

Formally,

$$W(Y_k) = \sum_{z_k} (\Pr_r[V(x, r, Y_k) = z_k] \cdot W(Y_k|z_k)).$$

The communication history is a Z_k sequence   We define

$$W(Z_k) = \max_{y_{k+1}} \{W(Z_k|y_{k+1})\},$$

where $Z_k|y_{k+1}$ denotes the Y_{k+1} message sequence starting with Z_k and then appending y_{k+1} as the $(k+1)^{st}$ message.

The following two lemmas suffice to complete the proof of our theorem. The first states that for a message history H_k, $0 \le k \le q$, the inductive definition of $W(H_k)$ correctly defines $\Pr[(P, V)(x)$ accepts starting with the message history $H_k]$.

We defined H_0 to be the empty list and so

$$W(H_0) = \Pr[(P, V) \text{ accepts } x \text{ starting with } H_0] = w,$$

which is our goal.

Lemma 12.1. *For every k with $0 \le k \le q$,*

$$W(Y_k) = \Pr[(P, V)(x) \text{ accepts starting with history } Y_k]$$

and

$$W(Z_k) = \Pr[(P, V)(x) \text{ accepts starting with history } Z_k].$$

Proof. The proof is by induction starting at $k = q$ as in the base case above, and ending at $k = 0$.

Base step   In this case $k = q$ and hence $W(Z_q) = z_k$ is either 1 or 0 (accept or reject), and clearly $W(Z_q) = \Pr[(P, V)(x)$ accepts starting at $Z_q]$.

Inductive step   Again there are two subcases.

1. We assume that the claim is true for Y_{k+1} for $k+1 \le q$ and prove it for Z_k. By definition, we have

$$W(Z_k) = \max_{y_{k+1}}\{W(Z_k|y_{k+1})\}$$

$$= \max_{y_{k+1}} \Pr[(P,V) \text{ accepts } x \text{ starting with } Y_{k+1}],$$

because by induction

$$W(Y_{k+1}) = \max_{y_{k+1}} \Pr[(P,V) \text{ accepts } x \text{ starting with } Y_{k+1}].$$

Then $W(Z_k) = \Pr[(P,V) \text{ accepts } x \text{ starting with } Z_k]$ because the prover that sends the string y_{k+1} that results in the maximum value for $W(Z_k|y_{k+1})$ could send that message to achieve the maximum value, and no prover P could do better.

2. Assume the claim true for Z_k for some $k \leq q$ and prove it for Y_k. By definition, we have

$$W(Y_k) = \sum_{z_k} \left(\Pr_r[V(x,r,Y_k) = z_k] \cdot W(Z_k) \right), \text{ where } Z_k = (Y_k|z_k)$$

$$= \sum_{z_k} \left(\Pr_r[(P,V) \text{ accepts } x \text{ starting with } Z_k] \right),$$

again by induction.

Then $W(Y_k) = \Pr[(P,V) \text{ accepts } x \text{ starting with } Y_k]$, as in this case Z_k is the message history Y_k extended by the message z_k, the output of $V(x,r,Y_k)$.

This proves the Lemma. □

The final lemma tells us that we can calculate W, and specifically our goal w, in PSPACE.

Lemma 12.2. *The value $w = W(H_0)$ can be calculated in polynomial space.*

Proof. The value $w = W(H_0)$ can be calculated using the inductive definition of $W(Y_k)$ and $W(Z_k)$ with $0 < k \leq q$, and considering every history sequence H_k.

If we are in the first subcase, then the communication history is a Y_k sequence. So we need to calculate the weighted average defined in W's definition. That is,

$$W(Y_k) = \sum_{z_k} \left(\Pr_r[V(x,r,Y_k) = z_k] \cdot W(Z_k) \right).$$

To do this calculation, we cycle through all strings r of length q. Since q is bounded by a polynomial in $|x|$, we can cycle through all such r in PSPACE. Any r which causes V to produce a string not in the history Z_k is ignored. For each history Z_k we keep track of the number of r's that result in outputs consistent with Z_k, and using this compute the weighted average.

If we are in the second subcase, then $W(Z_k) = \max_{y_{k+1}}\{W(Z_k|y_{k+1})\}$. Then computing this value directly from the $W(Z_k|y_{k+1})$ values is straightforward and in PSPACE.

Finally, once w is calculated in PSPACE, we accept x if and only if $w \geq 2/3$.   □

This completes the proof of the theorem.   □

Corollary 12.2. *Every language $L \in$ IP has an interactive proof system (P,V) for which the honest prover P is computable in polynomial space.*

The proof of the theorem gives the result.

12.5   PSPACE Is Included in IP

We have seen that NP, BPP, and even AM $=$ BP $\cdot$ NP are subsets of the class IP. We showed that GNI, a problem that belongs to co-NP, which is not known to belong to NP, still belongs to IP. In this section we present the strong result that PSPACE $\subseteq$ IP. This result is due to Shamir [Sha92], and is based on work of Lund et al. [LFKN92]. We will proceed slowly, because this direction introduces an important new proof technique.

12.5.1   The Language ESAT

We begin with the following definition of the language ESAT.

Definition 12.6.

ESAT $= \{(F,k) \mid F$ is a 3CNF formula with exactly k satisfying truth assignments$\}$.

As an aside, we mention that ESAT is the standard complete problem of a powerful counting class called $C_=P$. This class, which we do not define, captures the notion of "exact counting" [Wag86, Gre88]. (Recall that #SAT$(F) =$ the number of satisfying assignments of F. It is probably the case that ESAT is not as powerful as $P^{\#P}$, in the sense that it unlikely that ESAT can be used as an oracle for computing #SAT.)

Here we show that ESAT has an interactive proof system. While the protocol for ESAT is quite straightforward, there is one complication. We cannot work with ESAT directly, but rather introduce the important notion of *arithmetization*. The idea is to convert a Boolean formula F to a polynomial p_F, its arithmetization, from which the number of satisfying assignments of F can be computed. Then we develop an interactive protocol for computing the value of the polynomial.

The conversion from F to the polynomial p_F over the integers Z is as follows, where G and H are subformulas of F:

- Replace $G \wedge H$ with GH.
- Replace $G \vee H$ with $G + H - GH$.
- Replace $\neg G$ with $1 - G$.

Using these simple transformations, we can convert any Boolean formula to a polynomial.

Example 12.1. Letting

$$F = (\bar{x} \vee \bar{y} \vee z) \wedge (y \vee \bar{z}),$$

the polynomial

$$p_F = (1 - xy + xyz)(1 - z + yz) \tag{12.1}$$

$$= 1 - z - xy + yz + xyz \tag{12.2}$$

with coefficients in Z.

Homework 12.2 *For any Boolean formula F with variable $x_1, x_2, \ldots, x_n$ and derived polynomial p_F,*

$$\#SAT(F) = \sum_{x_1=0}^{1} \sum_{x_2=0}^{1} \cdots \sum_{x_n=0}^{1} p_F(x_1, x_2, \ldots, x_n). \tag{12.3}$$

In the following protocol we will have occasion to evaluate p_F on non-Boolean integral values that come from a large finite field. The integer values we obtain in this way have no direct relation with the value of the formula F, but we will see that they are useful in analyzing and verifying the number of satisfying assignments.

We now present, for a 3CNF-formula F with n variables and m clauses and an integer value k, an n round protocol that a prover can use to convince a verifier that k is the value of $\#SAT(F)$. Input to the protocol is a pair (F, k), which is known to both the prover and the verifier. The protocol attempts to prove whether or not the formula F has exactly k satisfying assignments. (The reader is advised to trace through this protocol using the example following the end of the proof.)

Two sequences of values, $r_1, r_2, \ldots, r_n$ and $v_0, v_1, v_2, \ldots, v_n$ will be defined. Initially, $v_0 = k$ and $i = 1$.

Round i. 1. The prover P sends the verifier a univariate polynomial p_i. (Note: The verifier will treat p_i as if it were the polynomial in (12.3) with the outer summation removed and the inner summations unchanged. Observe that p_i has one free variable, say x, corresponding to the variable of the outermost summation. Furthermore, if the prover is working honestly, then, letting p_i^h be the polynomial produced by the honest prover, $p_i(x)$ is in fact this polynomial. If not, then $p_i(x)$ may be any univariate polynomial with degree less than or equal to the number of clauses m in the formula F.)

2. The verifier computes $p_i(0) + p_i(1)$ and checks that it evaluates to the value v_{i-1}. If not, then V rejects. If $i = n$, then V accepts.
3. Otherwise, the verifier picks a random number r_i from a fixed field F_q of size q, computes $p_i(r_i)$, sets $v_i = p_i(r_i)$, and sends v_i to the prover. The protocol proceeds to round $i + 1$. (Note: We choose q to be a prime number $\geq 3^{n+m}$, and F_q is then simply Z_q. All arithmetic in the protocol is carried out in the field F_q.)

Note: Assuming the prover is honest then the equation 12.3 that is used in item 1 is the same as in the previous round except that the outermost (leftmost) summation is removed and $p_F(x_i, \dots, x_n)$ is replaced by $p_F(r_i, \dots, x_n)$. So Round $i + 1$ proceeds with equation 12.3 defined using a polynomial p_F with one fewer variable.

Now the verifier challenges the prover to prove that the value v_i sent to the prover is correct. This is just like the original problem but on a polynomial defined with one fewer summation. Eventually, after executing all n rounds of the protocol, the polynomial becomes a sum of constants whose value can be directly checked by the verifier. If all of the claims of the prover turn out to be correct (i.e., the verifier has never rejected), then the verifier accepts; otherwise, the verifier has rejected at some round.

Theorem 12.4. ESAT $\in$ IP.

Proof. Let $(F, k) \in$ ESAT and suppose that the prover P acts correctly according to the protocol. To prove completeness, we note in this case that the verifier V accepts with probability one.

Now we need to prove soundness: Suppose that F does not have exactly k satisfying assignments. Then we need to show that no prover can make V accept with high ($\geq 2/3$) probability. Let P^h denote that honest prover and let p_i^h be the polynomial produced by the honest prover at stage i of the protocol. The honest prover P^h must fail at the first step of the protocol when it sends p_1^h to the verifier, as the verifier will then evaluate $p_1^h(0) + p_1^h(1)$, find that it is not equal to k, and reject. So only a prover that is not honest in Round 1 has any chance of convincing the verifier to accept an input (F, k) that is not in ESAT.

So now consider any dishonest prover P'. First note that P' must send an incorrect value for p_1 in Round 1; otherwise, V would reject immediately. Then, in Item 2 of Round 2, V must compute an incorrect value for at least one of $p_1(0)$ or $p_1(1)$. So the coefficients of the polynomial in x that P' sent to V must not all be correct.

Claim. Assume that in Round i of the protocol the verifier determines that $p_i^h(0) + p_i^h(1) \neq v_{i-1}$ and that V does not reject. Then $\Pr[p_i^h(r_i) \neq v_i] > (q - m)/q$.

Proof. We have seen that if the dishonest prover sends p_i^h as his polynomial p_i, then V rejects immediately. Otherwise, the dishonest prover sends some $p_i \neq p_i^h$, and p_i passes the verifier's test. (Since otherwise V rejects.) Now, since p_i and p_i^h are both of degree at most m, $p_i(r_i) = p_i^h(r_i)$ for at most m many r_i in F_q, i.e.,

$$\|\{r_i \in F_q \mid p_i(r_i) = p_i^h(r_i)\}\| \leq m.$$

Since V chooses a random r_i from F_q, and recalling that $p_i(r_i) = v_i$, we have $\Pr[p_i^h(r_i) = v_i] \le m/q$, proving the claim. $\square$

Now, continuing with the proof of soundness, we will see that this follows directly from the Claim. We will prove that if the number of satisfying assignments of F is not k, then for any prover, the verifier rejects with probability greater than 2/3.

As noted above, in the first round of the protocol the verifier determines that $p_1^h(0) + p_1^h(1) \ne k = v_0$. Repeatedly applying the Claim, and the fact that for any $i > 1$, $p_i^h(r_i) = p_i^h(0) + p_i^h(1)$, we obtain that $p_n^h(r_n) \ne v_n$ with probability

$$> ((q - m)/q)^n > 1 - (nm/q) > 2/3.$$

Now $p_n^h(r_n) = p_F(r_1, \ldots, r_n)$ and so V rejects at the last step of the protocol; so V rejects with total probability greater than 2/3. $\square$

The following extended example is a continuation of Example 12.1.

Example 12.2. We consider again

$$F = (\bar{x} \vee \bar{y} \vee z) \wedge (y \vee \bar{z})$$

with

$$p_F = (1 - xy + xyz)(1 - z + yz) \tag{12.4}$$

$$= 1 - z - xy + yz + xyz. \tag{12.5}$$

First, it is straightforward to check that #SAT$(F) = 5$ and that

$$\sum_{x=0}^{1} \sum_{y=0}^{1} \sum_{z=0}^{1} (1 - z - xy + yz + xyz) = 5.$$

Let's consider the protocol with input $(F, 5)$, when the prover $P = P^h$ is the honest prover: The protocol begins with P sending

$$p_1(x) = \sum_{y=0}^{1} \sum_{z=0}^{1} (1 - z - xy + yz + xyz)$$

$$= 3 - x$$

to V. The prover sends the reduced polynomial $3 - x$ and not the longer version, which may be too long to send to V. (Remember that the only restriction on the prover is that the length of messages sent is bound by a polynomial in the length of the input.)

In step 2, the verifier checks that $p_1(0) + p_1(1) = 3 + 2 = 5$. (If not so, then the verifier rejects.) The verifier then, step 3 of Round 1, picks a random number r_1, say $r_1 = 6$, computes $v_1 = p_1(r_1) = 3 - 6 = -3$, and sends $v_1 = -3$ to the prover P.

Round 2 is now entered, with V awaiting the receipt of p_2 from P. The verifier wants the prover to prove that the value -3 is correct and is in fact $p_2(0) + p_2(1)$. The protocol continues, but with one fewer summation and the prover and verifier proceed in the same way, repeating the three steps of each round:

$$p_2(y) = \sum_{z=0}^{1}(1 - z - 6y + yz + 6yz)$$

$$= (1 - 6y) + (1 - 1 - 6y + y + 6y)$$

$$= 1 - 5y$$

So P sends $p_2(y) = 1 - 5y$ to V. Then V computes $p_2(0) + p_2(1) = 1 + 1 - 5 = -3$, the correct value for $p_2 = p_1(6)$.

Again the verifier chooses a random number r_2, say 4, computes $v_2 = p_2(r_2) = -19$, and sends -19 to P.

Now Round 3 begins: The honest prover computes

$$p_3(z) = (1 - z - 6(4) + 4z + 6(4)z)$$

$$= -23 + 27z$$

and sends $p_3(z) = -23 + 27z$ to V.

The verifier checks that $p_3(0) + p_3(1) = -23 + 4 = -19$, as claimed. This concludes the final check and as the prover has passed each test, the verifier is finally convinced and accepts $(F, 5)$.

12.5.2   True Quantified Boolean Formulas

In the next section we will prove the strong result that every language in PSPACE is contained in IP. We do so by proving that a complete language for PSPACE has an interactive proof system. Here we briefly introduce the canonical PSPACE complete language TQBF that we will use.

A quantified Boolean formula is a well-formed Boolean formula where every variable in the formula is bound by either an existential or universal quantifier. Every quantified Boolean formula evaluates to either true or false.

Example 12.3.

$$\phi = \forall x \exists y \forall z ((\bar{x} \lor \bar{y} \lor z) \land (y \lor \bar{z}))$$

is a quantified Boolean formula that is false: When we set $x = 1$, then the resulting formula is equivalent to

$$\phi' = \exists y \forall z((\bar{y} \vee z) \wedge (y \vee \bar{z})).$$

For either of the cases $y = 0$ or $y = 1$, it is not the case that the result is true.

The True Quantified Boolean Formulas (TQBF) is the set of quantified Boolean formulas that evaluate to true. It is obvious that TQBF is accepted by an alternating Turing machine in polynomial time. Therefore TQBF belongs to PSPACE, because, by Corollary 9.3, AP = PSPACE.

TQBF is essentially a variation of the PSPACE-complete language B_ω that we met in Sect. 7.5.1. In any case, we leave it to the reader to observe that

$$B_\omega \equiv_m^P \text{TQBF}.$$

Therefore, TQBF is PSPACE-complete.

12.5.3   The Proof

The proof that PSPACE $\subseteq$ IP follows generally the lines of the proof that ESAT $\in$ IP. We will prove that the PSPACE-complete language TQBF has as interactive proof system. Then the proof follows from the following homework exercise.

Homework 12.3 *If $B \in$ IP and $A \leq_m^P B$, then $A \in$ IP.*

To develop a protocol for TQBF we will use an arithmetization of quantified Boolean formulas that is similar to the one for unquantified Boolean formulas that we just used for proving ESAT $\in$ IP.

The method of arithmetization of the quantifiers $\forall$ and $\exists$ is similar to the way that we arithmetize $\vee$ and $\wedge$:

- Replace $\forall x\, p(\ldots,x)$ with $p(\ldots,0) \cdot p(\ldots,1)$
- Replace $\exists x\, p(\ldots,x)$ with $p(\ldots,0) + p(\ldots,1) - p(\ldots,0)p(\ldots,1)$.

It might seem that this is the only addition that is needed. However, the following example points up a difficulty requiring one more ingredient in our proof.

Example 12.4. We continue with

$$\phi = \forall x \exists y \forall z((\bar{x} \vee \bar{y} \vee z) \wedge (y \vee \bar{z})),$$

as in the previous example, and note that ϕ is an extension of formula F in Example 12.1. Recall that the arithmetization of F is $f_3(x,y,z) = 1 - z - xy + yz + xyz$. Then define

$$f_2(x,y) = \forall z f_3(x,y,z)$$
$$= f_3(x,y,0) \cdot f_3(x,y,1)$$
$$= (1-xy)(1-1-xy+y+xy)$$
$$= y - xy^2.$$

Replacing the existential quantifier in $\exists y f_2(x,y)$, we obtain

$$f_1(x) = \exists y f_2(x,y)$$
$$= f_2(x,0) + f_2(x,1) - f_2(x,0)f_2(x,1)$$
$$= 1-x$$

Finally, arithmetizing $\forall x$ yields $f_0 = f_1(0) \cdot f_1(1) = 1 \cdot 0 = 0$, just we reasoned above in Example 12.3.

So far so good, but there is an added complication due to having to arithmetize the string of quantifiers. Quantified Boolean formulas have n many quantifiers, where n is the number of variables. Each time that a quantifier is eliminated we multiply the previous two polynomials together. In doing this the degree of the polynomial might double. Hence, the degree of the resulting polynomial may be as large as 2^n. Then the verifier might have to run for exponential time just to read the exponentially many coefficients that the prover would send the verifier – and of course the prover cannot send this many coefficients either.

The answer to this problem is to repeatedly reduce the degree of the polynomial using an operator that makes the degree linear in each of its variables. This operator originated with Shen [She92] in his proof of IP = PSPACE. The operator Rx works simply by replacing every power of x by x itself. For example,

$$Rx(x^2z + yz - x^3y) = (xz + yz - xy).$$

It is equivalent to taking the original polynomial mod $(x - x^2)$. Since, for all $n \geq 1$, $0^n = 0$ and $1^n = 1$, this operator does not affect the value of the arithmetized formula on Boolean circuits. So the Boolean value of the polynomial, considered as a Boolean function, which is what we want to calculate, is not changed by the Rx operator.

Now we can perform degree reductions on the polynomials alternating with the arithmetization of the quantifiers in order to lessen the degrees of the polynomials that arise in the arithmetization. We do this by inserting R operators, operating on all previously bound variables, between the $\forall$ and $\exists$ quantifiers in the original formula.

Example 12.5. In the prefix of the formula

$$\phi = \forall x \exists y \forall z ((\bar{x} \vee \bar{y} \vee z) \wedge (y \vee \bar{z}))$$

we insert R's to obtain

$$\forall x R x \exists y R x R y \forall z R x R y R z \; f_3(x,y,z),$$

where $f_3(x,y,z)$ is the arithmetization of the formula $((\overline{x} \vee \overline{y} \vee z) \wedge (y \vee \overline{z}))$.

We can arithmetize this quantified formula by proceeding from right to left through the string of $\forall$, $\exists$, and R operators, each time obtaining a polynomial. This time though, the number of different polynomials we obtain is equal to the length of the quantifier string, including the R's. However, the final polynomial we obtain, after arithmetizing the leftmost $\forall x$ quantifier, is still $f_0 = 0$ just as derived in Example 12.4.

When an Rx operator is applied during this arithmetization, the degree of x is reduced to 1 in the polynomial. Hence, as the arithmetized quantifiers never more than double the degree of any variable, the degree of a variable in the process is never any greater than 2.

We can now present the interactive proof system for TQBF. Input to the protocol is a quantified Boolean formula ϕ, where

$$\phi = Q_1 x_1 Q_2 x_2 \ldots Q_n x_n F(x_1, x_2, \ldots, x_n)$$

and $F(x_1, x_2, \ldots, x_n)$ is an unquantified Boolean formula with variables $x_1, \ldots, x_n$.

The verifier moves first in this protocol. To begin, the verifier converts the Boolean formula $F(x_1, x_2, \ldots, x_n)$ to a polynomial $p_F(x_1, x_2, \ldots, x_n)$ preceded by a string of quantifiers and R operators as we have described in Example 12.5. This has the form

$$Q_1 x_1 R x_1 Q_2 x_2 R x_1 R x_2 \ldots Q_n R x_1 R x_2 \ldots R x_n p_F(x_1, x_2, \ldots, x_n).$$

(In our example, p_F is the polynomial $f_3(x,y,z)$ obtained by arithmetizing the original, unquantified propositional formula.)

Let t be the number of quantifiers and R operators in the above prefix. We define polynomials $p_0, p_1, \ldots, p_t$ in turn by proceeding from right to left through the above prefix string, eliminating each operator in turn, each time obtaining a new polynomial. (An example of this process follows the proof.) The process starts with the polynomial $p_0 = p_F$. The polynomial p_{i+1} is obtained from p_i by the rules described above for arithmetizing $\forall, \exists$ and R. Variables are eliminated each time that a $\forall$ or $\exists$ is reached as the arithmetization proceeds. Note that when an R operator is processed, the resulting polynomial does not have fewer variables than the previous polynomial, but may have the same number. The final polynomial p_t has no remaining variables and is simply a Boolean value 0 or 1.

We now continue with the protocol, which proceeds in $t + 2$ rounds.

Round 0. The verifier V sends the prover P a prime q. All arithmetic in the rest of the protocol is carried out in the field Z_q. The size of the prime q will be determined later.

The prover P sends the Boolean value p_t (either 1 or 0) to the verifier. Then V checks that $p_t = 1$ and if not, then rejects.

At each remaining round the prover transmits a polynomial to V and tries to convince V that the polynomial transmitted is correct.

Round 1.   The prover sends the polynomial $p_{t-1}(x_1)$, which is claimed to be the polynomial equivalent to the formula

$$Rx_1 Q_2 x_2 Rx_1 Rx_2 \ldots Q_n Rx_1 Rx_2 \ldots Rx_n p_0(x_1, x_2, \ldots, x_n),$$

which is ϕ with the first quantifier Q_1 eliminated.

The outermost quantifier Q_1 is either $\forall$ or $\exists$, so the verifier checks p_{t-1} in one of the following ways:

1. If Q_1 is $\forall$, then V checks that $p_{t-1}(0)p_{t-1}(1) = p_t = 1$.
2. If Q_1 is $\exists$, then V checks that $p_{t-1}(0) + p_{t-1}(1) - p_{t-1}(0)p_{t-1}(1) = p_t = 1$.

If the check fails, then V rejects.

Round i, where $2 \le i \le t$.   The prover P sends the coefficients of the polynomial

$$p_{t-i}(r_1, r_2, \ldots, v),$$

which is claimed to be the polynomial equivalent to the formula ϕ with only the $t - i$ rightmost quantifiers and instances of the R operator. The single variable v in p_{t-i} is the variable referred to by the ith quantifier or R operator, that is, the one currently considered at round i. The variables to the left of this ith variable in the formula ϕ are replaced by random values that the verifier has chosen in earlier rounds.

The verifier selects a random number r, where $r < q$, and sends it to the prover. The leftmost remaining operator is either R or a $\forall$ or $\exists$ quantifier, giving rise to three cases:

1. If the outer remaining operator is a $\forall$ quantifier, then V checks that

$$p_{t-i}(r_1, r_2, \ldots, v) = p_{t-(i-1)}(r_1, r_2, \ldots, 0) p_{t-(i-1)}(r_1, r_2, \ldots, 1)$$

where the value of r_i corresponding to the universal quantifier $\forall$ is set to r.
2. If the outer operator is an $\exists$ quantifier, then V checks that

$$p_{t-i}(r_1, r_2, \ldots, v)$$
$$= p_{t-(i-1)}(r_1, r_2, \ldots, 0) + p_{t-(i-1)}(r_1, r_2, \ldots, 1)$$
$$- p_{t-(i-1)}(r_1, r_2, \ldots, 0) p_{t-(i-1)}(r_1, r_2, \ldots, 1),$$

where the value of r_i corresponding to the existential quantifier $\exists$ is set to r.

3. If the outer operator is Rv, then V checks that

$$p_{t-i}(r_1, r_2, \ldots, v) \equiv p_{t-(i-1)}(r_1, r_2, \ldots, v) \pmod{v^2 - v}$$

evaluated at $v = r$.

If the check fails, then V rejects.

Note that after t rounds all quantifiers and R operators have been eliminated.

Round t + 1. At this point all that is left is the polynomial p_0 with all of its variables substituted by random values that have been chosen during the protocol. Now the verifier evaluates $p_0(r_1, r_2, \ldots, r_n)$ and also evaluates its original arithmetization of the unquantified Boolean formula F with the same substituted random values. The verifier V accepts if and only if the two values agree.

Theorem 12.5. TQBF $\in$ IP.

Proof. We show that if the prime q is chosen to be greater than n^4, then the protocol is complete and sound. Clearly, if $\phi \in$ TQBF, then an honest prover can convince the verifier that ϕ is true (with probability 1) simply by sending V the correct answers at each step.

Now we prove soundness. We show for any prover P and any quantified Boolean formula ϕ, that if ϕ is false, then P cannot convince the verifier that ϕ is true with probability $\geq 1/3$. So let ϕ be a false quantified Boolean formula with n variables (all of which are quantified) and let P be any prover. Recall that we work over the finite field $F = Z_q$ of q elements, where q is a prime greater than n^4. We use the following fact in the proof: If f and g are polynomials of degree $\leq n$ and $f \neq g$, then the number of elements $r \in F$ such that $f(r) = g(r)$ is at most n. At each round of the protocol the prover sends a polynomial f to the verifier. Each variable in each term of f has degree at most 2 (as noted previously), and so each term of f has degree bounded by $2n$, and the verifier uses only polynomial time in each round to carry out the protocol.

Consider an arbitrary round of the protocol. Since the prover is trying to convince the verifier of the truth of a false formula ϕ, it must be the case that the prover is dishonest. Then, f must not be equal to the correct polynomial, which should have been sent to V in this round. The verifier V chooses an element $r \in F$ at random and checks whether $f(r)$ gives the right value of v. Since r is chosen randomly, the probability that $f(r)$ is the correct value of v is at most $n/(n^4)$. This is because of the fact that only n of the $\geq n^4$ elements of F can be equal to the correct value of the polynomial.

Moreover, this must happen at each round of the protocol in order for the protocol to succeed and have V accept. There are at most n^2 rounds to the protocol. So the probability that V is fooled at every stage is less than

$$n^2(n/(n^4)) = n^3/n^4 = 1/n.$$

This probability is less that $1/3$ as long as $n > 3$. $\qquad\square$

The following extended example may help to understand the protocol.

Example 12.6. Let the quantified Boolean formula be

$$\phi = \exists x \exists y ((x \vee y) \wedge (\bar{y})).$$

Add appropriate R operators to obtain

$$\exists x R x \exists y R x R y ((x \vee y) \wedge (\bar{y})).$$

Next we compute the polynomials $p_0, p_1, p_2, p_3, p_4, p_5$ that arise from arithmetizing the various quantifiers. We will need these in the protocol when we are producing the values sent by the prover:

The polynomial p_0 is the arithmetization of $(x \vee y) \wedge (\bar{y})$, which we know from Sect. 12.5.1, is

$$p_0 = (x + y - xy)(1 - y)$$
$$= x + y - xy - xy - y^2 + xy^2.$$

We use the rules for quantifier arithmetization proceeding from right to left through the quantifiers, applying them to the preceding polynomials, to obtain polynomials $p_1, \ldots, p_5$ as follows:

$$p_1 = R y p_0$$
$$= x + y - xy - xy - y + xy$$
$$= x - xy;$$
$$p_2 = R y p_1$$
$$= x - xy;$$
$$p_3 = \exists y p_2$$
$$= x + x - x - x(x - x)$$
$$= x;$$
$$p_4 = R x p_3$$
$$= x;$$
$$p_5 = \exists x p_4$$
$$= 0 + 1 - 0(1)$$
$$= 1.$$

The polynomial p_5 is true, as it should be.

Now we can illustrate the protocol on the TQBF formula ϕ. The idea is that the prover is trying to convince the verifier that ϕ is true. This formula together with the interpolated R operators is now traversed from left to right. At each successive stage the verifier generates a random number r and sends it to the prover. The prover responds with the coefficients of the next polynomial p with r substituted for the next quantified variable. The verifier checks that the polynomial received from the prover is consistent with the polynomial q from the previous step of the protocol, when the value r is substituted as the value of the variable quantified in p:

Round 0.   The prover sends $p_5 = 1$ to V. (This is just to be sure that the prover is claiming the formula to be true.)

Round 1.   The prover sends the polynomial p_4 to V. Then V checks whether p_4 yields true, given that x is existentially quantified. That is, V verifies that

$$p_4(0) + p_4(1) - p_4(0)p_4(1) = 0 + 1 - 0 = 1.$$

Next, V generates a random number r in the finite field of the protocol. Say here that $r = 5$. V sends 5 to P and requests p_3 from P.

Round 2. P sends $p_3(x) = x$. Verifier V checks that $p_3(x) \bmod (x^2 - x)$ with 5 substituted for x is $p_4(5)$. The check is trivial, because $p_3(x) \bmod (x^2 - x) = p_4(x) = x$ and so $p_3(x) \bmod (x^2 - x)$ evaluated at $5 = 5 = p_4(5)$.

The random number r is retained by setting a variable $r_1 = r = 5$. While a series of random numbers are generated during the protocol, only two are saved, r_1's value is substituted for x and r_2's is substituted for y.

V generates a new random number r and send it to P, say $r = 3$.

Round 3.   (In this round the prover wants to convince V that p_3 is correct, assuming that p_2 is correct.) The prover P sends the polynomial p_2 with 3 substituted for x. So this polynomial is $p_2(y) = 3 - 3y$.

Verifier V checks that

$$\begin{aligned}
p_2(3) &= \text{the polynomial representing } \exists y(3 - 3y) \\
&= 3 + (3 - 3) - 3(3 - 3) \\
&= 3 \\
&= p_3(3).
\end{aligned}$$

The random number 3 is assigned to the variable r_1.

V randomly selects a new number r, say $r = 7$, sending 7 to P.

Round 4.   (Now P wants to convince V that p_2 is correct.) The prover P sends the polynomial p_1 with 7 substituted for y. So this polynomial is $p_1(x) = x - x7$.

V, knowing that p_2 should correspond to $Rxp_1 = x(x - x7)$, checks that these two polynomials are equal when $r_1 = 3$. That is, V checks that $p_2(7) = 3 - 4(7)$ $= -18$ and likewise that $p_1(x) \equiv -18 \pmod{x^2 - x}$, when 3 is substituted for x. The random number 7 is assigned to the variable r_2.

V randomly selects a new r, say $r = 2$.

Round 5.   The prover P sends to V polynomial $p_0(x,y) = x + y - 2xy - y^2 + xy^2 \bmod (y^2 - y)$, with $r_2 = 7$ substituted for y.

V checks that $Rp_0 = p_1$ by checking that these two polynomials are equal when $r = 2$ is substituted for x. In this case, $p_1(2,7) = 2 - 2(7) = -12$ and $p_0(2,y) \equiv -12 \pmod{y^2 - y}$ as well, when $y = 7$, because $2 + 7 - 28 - 7 + 14 = -12$. The random number 2 is assigned to r_1.

V selects a new random number, $r = 8$, which is assigned to r_2.

Round 6.   Finally, V evaluates $p_0(x,y)$ with $x = 2$ and $y = 8$, yielding $2 + 8 - 32 - 64 + 128 = 42$, and V checks that its arithmetization of the original unquantified Boolean formula $p_0(x,y) = (x + y - xy)(1 - y)$ with $x = 2$ and $y = 8$ equals $-6(-7) = 42$. So, V accepts ϕ.

12.6   Additional Homework Problems

Homework 12.4 *Consider the Boolean formula*

$$F(w,y,z) = (\overline{w} \wedge \overline{y}) \vee (w \wedge y \wedge z).$$

1. *Find a Boolean formula $G(w,y,z)$ in conjunctive normal form that is equivalent to F. (So in particular F and G have the same satisfying assignments.) How many satisfying truth assignments does G have?*
2. *Exhibit a run of the protocol in Sect. 12.5.1 showing that $(G,3)$ is in ESAT.*

Homework 12.5 *This is a continuation of the previous problem. Consider*

$$G' = \forall w \exists y \exists z G(w,y,z).$$

1. *Verify that G' is in TQBF. You need not give a strict proof; just explain the reasoning that G' is true.*
2. *Exhibit a run of the protocol in Sect. 12.5.3 showing that G' is in TQBF.*

Homework 12.6 *Prove that UNSAT, the set of unsatisfiable Boolean formulas, is in IP. Do this directly by giving an interactive proof system, and not by using the theorem that IP contains PSPACE.*

Homework 12.7 *Suppose we define a superstrong version of IP, SSIP, by changing the value $1/3$ in the Soundness property of Definition 12.2 of IP to 0. Show that SSIP = NP.*

Homework 12.8 *Prove that PSPACE $\subseteq$ P/poly implies that PSPACE = MA.*

References

[AFK89]   M. Abadi, J. Feigenbaum, J. Kilian. On hiding information from an oracle. J. Comput. Syst. Sci. **39**, 21–50 (1989)

[AH87]   L. Adleman, M-D. Huang. Recognizing primes in random polynomial time. In *Proceedings of the Nineteenth Annual ACM Symposium on Theory of Computing*, pp. 462–469, 1987

[AKS04]   M. Agrawal, N. Kayal, N. Saxena. Primes is in P. Ann. Math. **160**(2), 781–793 (2004)

[AM77]   L. Adleman, K. Manders. Reducibility, randomness, and intractability. In *Proceedings of the Nineth Annual ACM Symposium on Theory of Computing*, pp. 151–163, 1977

[AS89]   K. Ambos-Spies. On the relative complexity of hard problems for complexity classes without complete problems. Theor. Comput. Sci. **63**, 43–61 (1989)

[Bab85]   L. Babai. Trading group theory for randomness. In *Proc. 17th Annual ACM Symposium on Theory of Computing*, pp. 421–429, 1985

[BBS86]   J. Balcázar, R. Book, U. Schöning. The polynomial-time hierarchy and sparse oracles. J. Assoc. Comput. Mach. **33**(3), 603–617 (1986)

[Ber76]   L. Berman. On the structure of complete sets: Almost everywhere complexity and infinitely often speedup. *Proceedings of the 17th Annual Symposium on Foundations of Computer Science*, pages 76–80 (1976)

[Ber78]   P. Berman. Relationships between density and deterministic complexity of NP-complete languages. In *Proceedings of the Fifth Colloqium on Automata, Languages, and Programming, Lecture Notes in Computer Science*, volume 62, pages 63–71. Springer-Verlag, Berlin, 1978

[BFT98]   H. Buhrman, L. Fortnow, T. Thierauf. Nonrelativizing separations. In *Proceedings of 3rd Annual IEEE Conference on Computational Complexity*, pages 8–12, 1998.

[BG70]   R. Book, S. Greibach. Quasi-realtime languages. Math. Syst. Theor. **4**, 97–111 (1970)

[BGS75]   T. Baker, J. Gill, R. Solovay. Relativizations of the P =? NP question. SIAM J. Comput. **4**(4), 431–441 (1975)

[BGW70]   R. Book, S. Greibach, B. Wegbreit. Time- and tape-bounded Turing acceptors and AFL's. J. Comput. Syst. Sci. **4**, 606–621 (1970)

[BH92]   H. Buhrman, S. Homer. Superpolynomial circuits, almost sparse oracles and the exponential hierarchy. In *Proceedings of 12th Conference on Foundations of Software Technology and Theoretical Computer Science*. Lecture Notes in Computer Science, vol. 652 (Springer-Verlag, 1992), pp. 116–127

[BM88]   L. Babai, S. Moran. Arthur-merlin games: A randomized proof system, and a hierarchy of complexity classes. J. Comput. Syst. Sci. **36**, 254–276 (1988)

S. Homer and A.L. Selman, *Computability and Complexity Theory*,
Texts in Computer Science, DOI 10.1007/978-1-4614-0682-2,
© Springer Science+Business Media, LLC 2011

[Boo72]   R. Book. On languages accepted in polynomial time. SIAM J. Comput. **1**(4), 281–287 (1972)

[Boo74]   R. Book. Tally languages and complexity classes. Inform. Contr. **26**, 186–193 (1974)

[Boo76]   R. Book. Translational lemmas, polynomial time, and $(logn)^j$-space. Theor. Comput. Sci. **1**, 215–226 (1976)

[Bor77]   A. Borodin. On relating time and space to size and depth. SIAM J. Comput. **6**, 733–744 (1977)

[BS85]   J. Balcázar, U. Schöning. Bi-immune sets for complexity classes. Math. Syst. Theor. **18**(1), 1–10 (1985)

[Chu36]   A. Church. An unsolvable problem of elementary number theory. Am. J. Math. **58**, 345–363 (1936)

[CKS81]   A. Chandra, D. Kozen, L. Stockmeyer. Alternation. J. ACM **28**(1), 114–133 (1981)

[Coo71a]   S. Cook. Characterizations of pushdown machines in terms of time-bounded computers. J. ACM **19**, 175–183 (1971)

[Coo71b]   S. Cook. The complexity of theorem-proving procedures. In *Proceedings of the Third ACM Symposium on Theory of Computing*, pp. 151–158, 1971

[Coo73]   S. Cook. A hierarchy for nondeterministic time complexity. J. Comput. Syst. Sci. **7**(4), 343–353 (1973)

[Coo74]   S. Cook. An observation on time-storage tradeoff. J. Comput. Syst. Sci. **9**, 308–316 (1974)

[Coo79]   S. Cook. Deterministic CFL's are accepted simultaneously in polynomial time and log squared space. In *Proceedings of the 11th Annual ACM Symposium on Theory of of Computing*, pp. 338–345, 1979

[CR73]   S. Cook, R. Reckhow. Time bounded random access machines. J. Comput. Syst. Sci. **7**, 353–375 (1973)

[CW79]   J. Carter and M. Wegman. Universal classes of hash functions. J. Comput. Syst. Sci. **18**, 143–154 (1979)

[Dav65]   M. Davis. The Undecidable. Raven Press, 1965

[ESY84]   S. Even, A. Selman, and Y. Yacobi. The complexity of promise problems with applications to public-key cryptography. Inform. Contr. **61**(2), 159–173 (1984)

[ET76]   S. Even, R. Tarjan. A combinatorial problem which is complete in polynomial space. J. ACM **23**, 710–719 (1976)

[FR74]   M. Fischer, M. Rabin, in: *Super-exponential complexity of presberger arithmetic*, ed. by R. Karp. Complexity of Computation (American Mathematical Society, Providence, RI, 1974), pp. 43–73

[GHR95]   R. Greenlaw, H. Hoover, W. Ruzzo. Limits to Parallel Computation: P-completeness Theory. (Oxford University Press, New York, NY, 1995)

[Gil77]   J. Gill. Computational complexity of probabilistic Turing machines. SIAM J. Comput. **6**(4), 675–695 (1977)

[GJ79]   M. Garey, D. Johnson. Computers And Intractability: A Guide To The Theory of NP-Completeness. (W.H. Freeman, San Francisco, 1979)

[GMR89]   S. Goldwasser, S. Micali, C. Rackoff. The knowledge complexity of interactive proof systems. SIAM J. Comput. **18**(1), 186–208 (1989)

[GMS87]   O. Goldreich, Y. Mansour, M. Sipser. Interactive proof systems: Provers that never fail and random selection. In *Proc. 28th Annual IEEE Symposium on Foundations of Computer Science*, pp. 449–461, 1987

[GMW86]   O. Goldreich, S. Michali, A. Wigderson. Proofs that yield nothing but their validity and a methodology of cryptographic protocol design. In *Proc. 27th Annual IEEE Symposium on Foundations of Computer Science*, pp. 174–187, 1986

[Gol78]   L. Goldschlager. A unified approach to models of synchronous parallel machines. In *Proc. 11th Annual ACM Symp. on Theory of Comput.*, pp. 89–94, 1978

[Gre88]   F. Green. On the power of deterministic reductions to $C_=P$. SIAM J. Comput. **17**(2), 309–355 (1988)

[GS89]   S. Goldwasser, M. Sipser, in: *Private coins versus public coins in interactive proof systems*, ed. by S. Micali. Randomness and Computation, Advances in Computing Research. (Jai Press, 1989)

[Háj79]   P. Hájek. Arithmetical hierarchy and complexity of computation. Theor. Comput. Sci. **8**, 227–237 (1979)

[Hås89]   J. Håstad, in: *Almost optimal lower bounds for small depth circuits*, ed. by S. Micali. Randomness and Computation, Advances in Computing Research, (JAI Press, Greenwich, 1989) vol. 5, pp. 143–170

[Hel81]   H. Heller. Relativized Polynomial Hierarchies Extending Two Levels. PhD thesis, Universität München, 1981

[Her94]   R. Herken (ed.), The Universal Turing Machine: A Half-Century Survey. Springer, Wien, 1994

[HHN⁺95]   L. Hemaspaandra et al., Nondeterministically selective sets. Int. J. Found. Comput. Sci. **6**(4), 403–416 (1995)

[HIS85]   J. Hartmanis, N. Immerman, V. Sewelson. Sparse sets in NP-P: EXPTIME versus NEXPTIME. Inform. Contr. **65**, 158–181 (1985)

[HLS65]   J. Hartmanis, P. Lewis, R. Stearns. Hierarchies of memory limited computations. In *Proceedings of the Sixth Annual IEEE Symposium on Switching Circuit Theory and Logical Design*, pp. 179–190 (1965)

[Hoc97]   D. Hochbaum. Approximation Algorithms for NP-Hard Problems. PWS Publishing Company, 1997

[Hod83]   A. Hodges. Alan Turing: The Enigma. Simon and Schuster, New York, 1983

[HPV77]   J. Hopcroft, W. Paul, L. Valiant. On time versus space. J. ACM **24**, 332–337 (1977)

[HS65]   J. Hartmanis, R. Stearns. On the computational complexity of algorithms. Trans. Am. Math. Soc. **117**, 285–306 (1965)

[HS66]   F. Hennie, R. Stearns. Two-tape simulation of multitape Turing machines. J. ACM **13**, 533–546 (1966)

[HS74]   J. Hartmanis, J. Simon. On the power of multiplication in random access machines. In *Proc. 15th Annual IEEE Symp. on Switching and Automata Theory*, pp. 13–23, 1974

[HU69]   J. Hopcroft, J. Ullman. Some results on tape bounded Turing machines. J. ACM **16**, 168–188 (1969)

[HU79]   J. Hopcroft, J. Ullman. Introduction to Automata Theory, Languages, and Computation. Addison-Wesley, Reading, Massachusetts, 1979

[Iba72]   O. Ibarra. A note concerning nondeterministic tape complexities. J. Comput. Syst. Sci. **19**(4), 609–612 (1972)

[IKW01]   R. Impagliazzo, V. Kabanets, A. Widgderson. In search of an easy witness: exponential time vs. probabilistic polynomial time. In *Proceedings of the 16th Annual IEEE Conference on Computational Complexity*, pp. 2–12, 2001

[Imm88]   N. Immerman. Nondeterministic space is closed under complementation. SIAM J. Comput. **17**(5), 935–938 (1988)

[JK76]   D. Johnson, S. Kashdan. Lower bounds for selection in $x + y$ and other multisets. Technical Report 183, Pennsylvania State Univ., University Park, PA, 1976

[JL76]   N. Jones, W. Laaser. Complete problems for deterministic polynomial time. Theor. Comput. Sci. **3**, 105–117 (1976)

[Jon73]   N. Jones. Reducibility among combinatorial problems in log n space. In *Proceedings of the Seventh Annual Princeton Conference on Information Sciences and Systems*. (Department of Electrical Engineering, Princeton University, Princeton, NJ, 1973), pp. 547–551

[Jon75]   N. Jones. Space-bounded reducibility among combinatorial problems. J. Comput. Syst. Sci. **11**, 68–85 (1975)

[JS74]   N. Jones, A. Selman. Turing machines and the spectra of first-order formulas. J. Symbolic Logic **29**, 139–150 (1974)

[Kan82]   R. Kannan. Circuit-size lower bounds and nonreducibility to sparse sets. Inform. Contr. **55**, 40–56 (1982)

[Kar72]   R. Karp. Reducibility among combinatorial problems. In Complexity of Computer Computations, pp. 85–104. Plenum Press, New York, 1972

[KL80]   R. Karp, R. Lipton. Some connections between nonuniform and uniform complexity classes. In *Proceedings of the Twelfth Annual ACM Symposium on Theory of Computing*, pp. 302–309, 1980. An extended version has appeared in L'Enseignement Mathématique, 2nd series 28, 1982, pp. 191–209

[Ko82]   K. Ko. Some observations on the probabilistic algorithms and NP-hard problems. Inform. Process. Lett. **14**(1), 39–43 (1982)

[Ko83]   K. Ko. On self-reducibility and weak P-selectivity. J. Comput. Syst. Sci. **26**, 209–211 (1983)

[Kre88]   M. Krentel. The complexity of optimization problems. J. Comput. Syst. Sci. **36**, 490–509 (1988)

[Kur64]   S. Kuroda. Classes of languages and linear bounded automata. Inform. Contr. **7**(2), 207–223 (1964)

[Lad75]   R. Ladner. On the structure of polynomial time reducibility. J. ACM **22**, 155–171 (1975)

[Lau83]   C. Lautemann. BPP and the polynomial hierarchy. Inform. Process. Lett. **17**, 215–217 (1983)

[Lev73]   L. Levin. Universal sorting problems. Probl. Inform. Transm. **9**, 265–266 (1973) English translation of original in *Problemy Peredaci Informacii*

[LFKN92] C. Lund et al., in *Algebraic methods for interactive proof systems*. J. ACM **39**(4), 859–868 (1992)

[LLS75]   R. Ladner, N. Lynch, A. Selman. A comparison of polynomial time reducibilities. Theor. Comput. Sci. **1**, 103–123 (1975)

[Lup58]   O. Lupanov. A method for synthesizing circuits. Izv. vysshykh uchebnykh zavedenii, Radiofizika **1**, 120–140 (1958)

[Mag69]   G. Mager. Writing pushdown acceptors. J. Comput. Syst. Sci. **3**(3), 276–319 (1969)

[Mil76]   G. Miller. Reimann's hypothesis and tests for primality. J. Comput. Syst. Sci. **13**, 300–317 (1976)

[MP79]   A. Meyer and M. Paterson. With what frequency are apparently intractable problems difficult? Technical Report MIT/LCS/TM-126, M.I.T., 1979

[MS72]   A. Meyer and L. Stockmeyer. The equivalence problem for regular expressions with squaring requires exponential space. In *Proceedings of the Thirteenth IEEE Symposium on Switching and Automata Theory*, pp. 125–129, 1972

[Mul56]   D. Muller. Complexity in electronic switching circuits. IRE Transactions on Electronic Computers **5**, 15–19 (1956)

[MY78]   M. Machtey, P. Young. An Introduction to the General Theory of Algorithms. The Computer Science Library, Theory of Computation Series (Elsevier North Holland, Inc., 52 Vanderbilt Ave., New York NY 10017, 1978)

[Myh60]   J. Myhill. Linear bounded automata. WADD 60-165, Wright Patterson AFB, Ohio, 1960

[Pap84]   C. Papadimitriou. On the complexity of unique solutions. J. ACM **31**, 392–400 (1984)

[PF79]   N. Pippenger and M. Fischer. Relations among complexity measures. J. ACM **26**, 361–381 (1979)

[Pip79]   N. Pippenger. On simultaneous resource bounds. In *Proceedings of the 20th Annual IEEE Symposium on Foundations of Computer Science*, pp. 307–311, 1979

[Pos44]   E. Post. Recursively enumerable sets of integers and their decision problems. Bull. Am. Math. Soc. **50**, 284–316 (1944)

[Pos65]   E. Post, in: *Absolutely unsolvable problems and relatively undecidable propositions: Account of an anticipation*, ed. by M. Davis. The Undecidable: Basic Papers on Undecidable Propositions, Unsolvable Problems and Computable Functions (Raven Press, New York, 1965), pp. 340–433

[PPST83]   W. Paul, N. Pippenger, E. Szemerédi, and W. Trotter. On determinism and non-determinism and related problems. In *Proceedings of the Twenty-fourth ACM Symposium on Theory of Computing*, pp. 429-438, 1983

[Pra75]   V. Pratt. Every prime has a succinct certificate. SIAM J. Comput. **4**, 214–220 (1975)

[PS78]   V. Pratt, L. Stockmeyer. A characterization of the power of vector machines. J. Comput. Syst. Sci. **12**, 198–221 (1978)

[PZ83]   C. Papadimitriou, S. Zachos, in: *Two remarks on the power of counting*, ed. by A. Cremers, H. Kriegel. Proceedings of the 6th GI conference on Theoretical Computer Science (Springer-Verlag, Berlin, 1983), vol. 145, pp. 268–276

[Rab60]   M. Rabin. Degree of difficulty of computing a function and a partial ordering of recursive sets. Technical Report 2, The Hebrew University, Jerusalem, 1960

[Rab80]   M. Rabin. Probabilistic algorithms for testing primality. J. Number. Theor. **12**, 128–138 (1980)

[Reg]   K. Regan. Personal Communication

[Rog67]   H. Rogers, Jr. Theory of Recursive Functions and Effective Computability. McGraw-Hill, New York, 1967

[Ros67]   A. Rosenberg. Real-time definable languages. J. ACM **14**, 645–662 (1967)

[Ruz81]   W. Ruzzo. On uniform circuit complexity. J. Comput. Syst. Sci. **22**, 365–383 (1981)

[Sav70]   W. Savitch. Relationships between nondeterministic and deterministic time complexities. J. Comput. Syst. Sci. **4**(2), 177–192 (1970)

[Sav72]   J. Savage. Computational work and time on finite machines. J. ACM **19**, 660–674 (1972)

[Sch82]   U. Schöning. A uniform approach to obtain diagonal sets in complexity classes. Theor. Comput. Sci. **18**, 95–103 (1982)

[Sch83]   U. Schöning. A low and a high hierarchy within NP. J. Comput. Syst. Sci. **27**, 14–28 (1983)

[Sch84]   U. Schöning. Generalized polynomial reductions, degrees, and NP-completeness. Fundamenta Informaticae **7**, 77–81 (1984)

[Sch86]   U. Schöning. Complexity and Structure. Lecture Notes in Computer Science, vol. 211 (Springer-Verlag, 1986)

[Sch88]   U. Schöning. Graph isomorphism is in the low hierarchy. J. Comput. Syst. Sci. **37**(3), 312–323 (1988)

[Sch90]   U. Schöning, in: *The power of counting*, ed. by A. Selman. Complexity Theory Retrospective (Springer-Verlag, 1990), pp. 204–223

[Sel79]   A. Selman. P-selective sets, tally languages, and the behavior of polynomial time reducibilities on NP. Math. Syst. Theor. **13**, 55–65 (1979)

[Sel88]   A. Selman. Natural self-reducible sets. SIAM J. Comput. **17**, 989–996 (1988)

[Sel89]   A. Selman, in *Complexity issues in cryptography*, ed. by J. Hartmanis. Computational Complexity Theory, Proceedings of Symposia in Applied Mathematics (American Mathematical Society, 1989), vol. 38, pp. 92–107

[SFM78]   J. Seiferas, M. Fischer, A. Meyer. Separating nondeterministic time complexity classes. J. ACM **25**(1), 146–147 (1978)

[SG77]   I. Simon, J. Gill. Polynomial reducibilities and upward diagonalizations. In *Proceedings of the Ninth Annual ACM Symposium on Theory of Computing*, pp. 186–194, 1977

[Sha49]   C. Shannon. The synthesis of two–terminal switching circuits. Bell System Technical Journal **28**, 59–98 (1949)

[Sha92]   A. Shamir. IP=PSPACE. J. ACM **39**(4), 869–877 (1992)

[She92]   A. Shen. IP=PSPACE: Simplified proof. J. ACM **39**(4), 878–880 (1992)

[Sim75]   J. Simon. On some central problems in computational complexity. PhD thesis, Cornell University, 1975

[Sip78]   M. Sipser. Halting space-bounded computations. In *Proceedings of the 19th Annual IEEE Symposium on Foundations of Computer Scienc*, pp. 73–74, 1978

[Sip82]   M. Sipser. On relativization and the existence of complete sets. In *Automata, Languages, and Programming, Lecture Notes in Computer Science*, vol. 140 (Springer-Verlag, 1982)

[Sip83]   M. Sipser. A complexity theoretic approach to randomness. In *Proceedings of the Fifteenth ACM Symposium on Theory of Computing*, pp. 330–335, 1983

[SM73]   L. Stockmeyer, A. Meyer. Word problems requiring exponential time. In *Proceedings of the Fifth Annual ACM Symposium on Theory of Computing*, New York, pp. 1–9, 1973

[Soa80]   R. Soare. Recursively Enumerable Sets and Degrees. Springer-Verlag, 1980

[SS63]   J. Shepherdson, H. Sturgis. Computability of recursive functions. J. ACM **10**(2), 217–255 (1963)

[SS77]   R. Solovay, V. Strassen. A fast monte-carlo test for primality. SIAM J. Comput. **6**, 84–85 (1977)

[Sti95]   D. Stinson. Cryptography: Theory and Practice. Discrete Mathematics and its Applications. CRC Press, Inc., Boca Raton, Florida, 1995

[Sto76]   L. Stockmeyer. The polynomial-time hierarchy. Theor. Comput. Sci. **3**, 1–22 (1976)

[Sze88]   R. Szelepcsényi. The method of forced enumeration for nondeterministic automata. Acta Inform **26**, 279–284 (1988)

[Tod91]   S. Toda. PP is as hard as the polynomial-time hierarchy. SIAM J. Comput. **20**(5), 865–877 (1991)

[Tur36]   A. Turing. On computable numbers with an application to the entscheidungsproblem. *Proceedings of the London Mathematical Society* **42**, 230–365 (1936)

[Val79]   L. Valiant. The complexity of computing the permanent. SIAM J. Comput. **8**, 189–201 (1979)

[VV86]   L. Valiant, V. Vazirani. NP is as easy as detecting unique solutions. Theor. Comput. Sci. **47**, 85–93 (1986)

[Žák83]   S. Žák. A Turing machine time hierarchy. Theor. Comput. Sci. **26**, 327–333 (1983)

[Wag86]   K. Wagner. Compact descriptions and the counting polynomial time hierarchy. Acta Inform **23**, 325–356 (1986)

[War62]   S. Warshall. A theorem on boolean matrices. J. ACM **9**, 11–12 (1962)

[Wra76]   C. Wrathall. Complete sets and the polynomial hierarchy. Theor. Comput. Sci. **3**, 23–33 (1976)

[Yao85]   A. Yao. Separating the polynomial-time hierarchy by oracles. In *Proceedings of the 26th IEEE Symposium on Foundations of Computer Science*, pp. 1–10, 1985

Author Index

S. Homer and A.L. Selman, *Computability and Complexity Theory*,
Texts in Computer Science, DOI 10.1007/978-1-4614-0682-2,
© Springer Science+Business Media, LLC 2011

289

Subject Index

Symbols
$\langle , \rangle$, 46
$\subset$ denoting proper inclusion, 111
#$\mathrm{acc}_M(x)$, 247
#HAM, 248
#P, 247
#P-complete, 248
#SAT, 247
symbol, 94
$\oplus$, 157
$\oplus$P, 247, 253–257
$\oplus$SAT, 248
δ, 24
$\Delta^P k$, 161–162
λ, 1
$\leq m$, 60
$\leq$T, 60
$\leq_m^{\log}$, 174–176
$\leq_T^{NP}$, 161
$\leq^P$r-complete set, 149
$\leq^P$r-hard set, 149
$\leq^P m$, 129–130
$\leq^P m$, 149
$\leq^P T$, 146–147
$\equiv_T^P$, 152
ϕ, 28, 67
ϕ(d), 19
ϕ(m), 18
ϕ_e, 44
Π_k, 63
Π_2^P, 233
Π_k^P, 162–163
Π_0, 63
ψ^A, 61
ψ_{univ}, 54
Σ, 1, 3
Σ_2, 64

Σ_2^P, 233
$\Sigma^P k$, 162–163
$\Sigma*$, 2
Σ_0, 63
τ_k, 47
$|\omega|$, 1
ε_k, 164

A
A_k, 164, 166
A_ω, 170
Abadi, 190
ACCEPT$_M$, 171
Acceptable programming system, 54
Accepting, 203
Accepting configuration, 26
Accepts, 181
Adaptive group of integers, 15
Adjacent vertices, 4
Advice function, 188
AEXP, 203
AFK89, 190
AL, 203
Algebra, 10–21
ALOGTIME, 205
Alphabet, finite, 1
Alternating Turing machines, 201, 202
AM, 266
AM [m], 265
AM[poly], 265
Amplification, 232
Amplified, 229
Ancestor, 5
Antisymmetric binary relation, 10
AP, 203, 275
Approximation algorithm for vertex cover, 178

S. Homer and A.L. Selman, *Computability and Complexity Theory*,
Texts in Computer Science, DOI 10.1007/978-1-4614-0682-2,
© Springer Science+Business Media, LLC 2011